# Emerald Drifters

# Emerald Drifters

Cig Harvey

Afterword by
Ocean Vuong

M

## 5.2

## *EYE AND CAMERA*

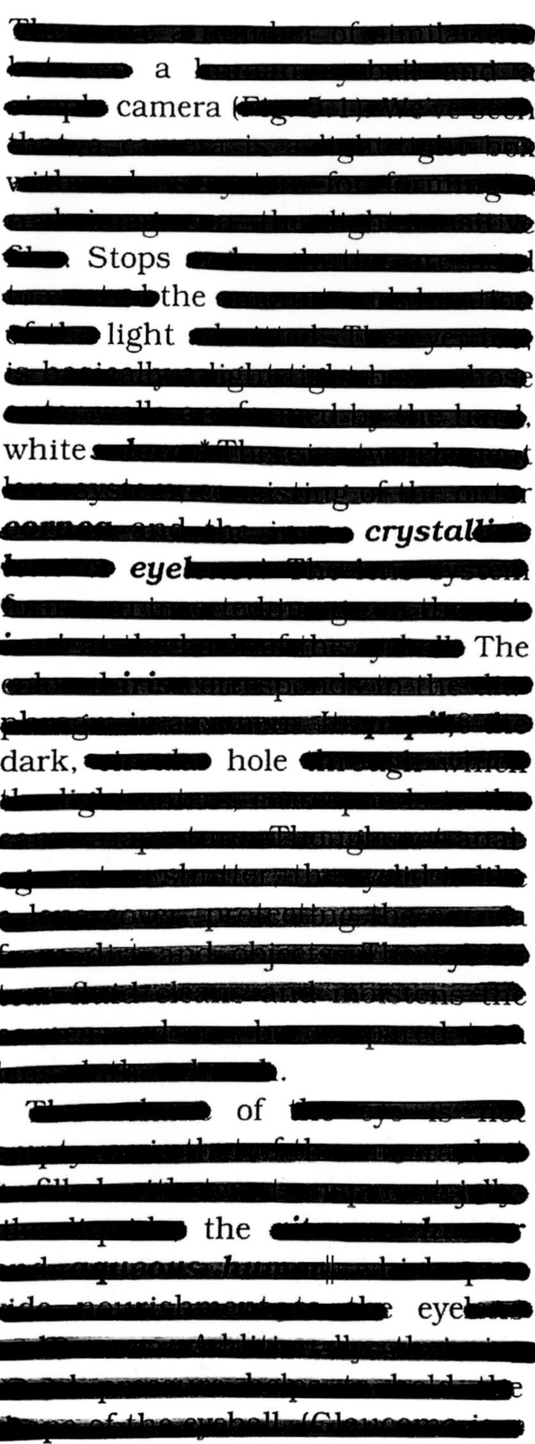

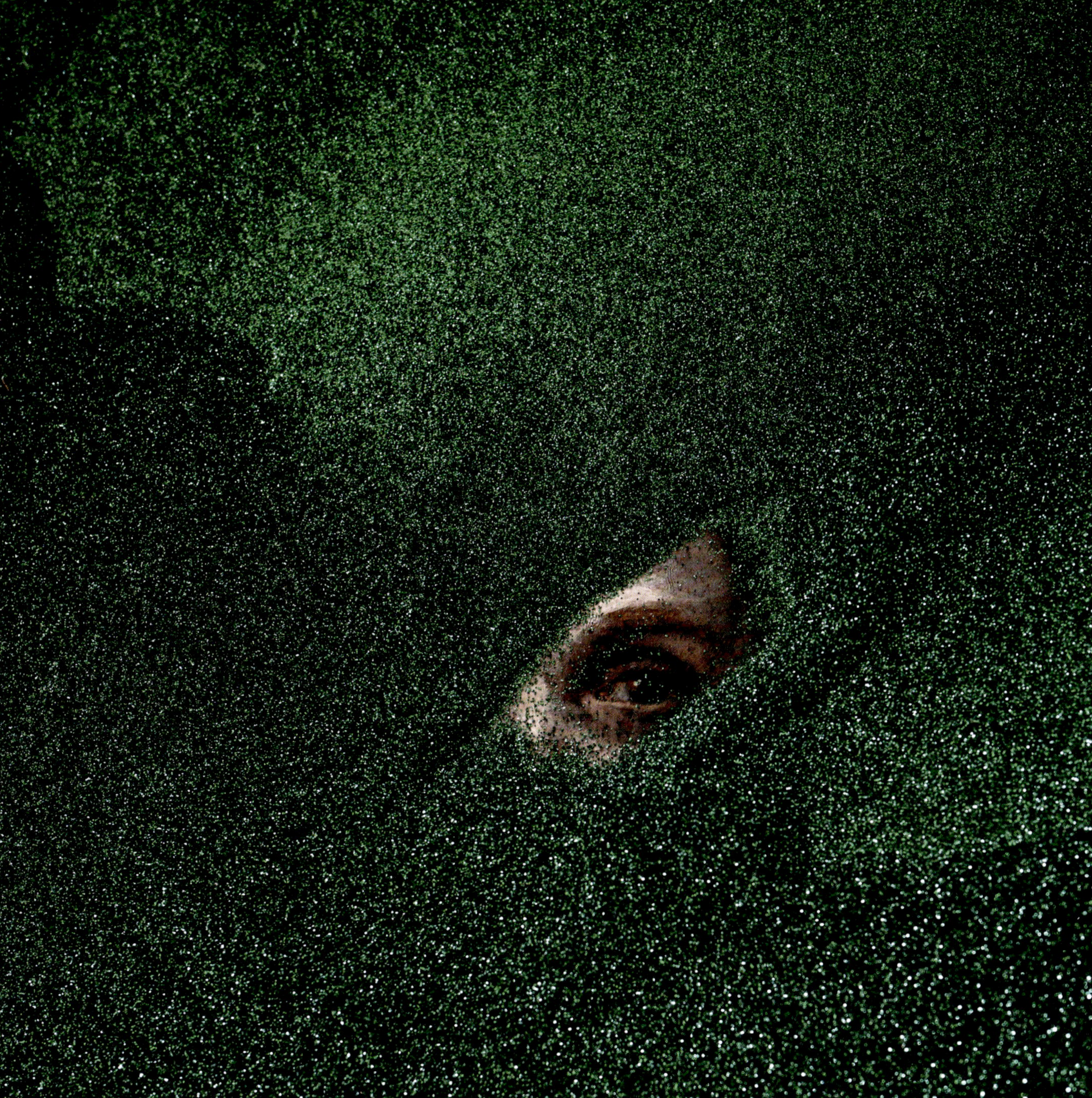

I can no longer see as I used to. Three years ago, my eyesight began to change. The precision of a royal blue pen, the decisive moment on the page, now just lines and shapes. Camera controls organized by touch, four twists left for a sixtieth of a second, five clicks to the right for F2.8.

At the optician in Augusta, I stare into a bunch of machines that hiss, spit, and flash. After thirty minutes, he tells me that I'm fine, just getting older, and I leave the office with a prescription for reading glasses.

I take the back roads home in the dappled-late-afternoon-anything-is-possible light—a flickering strobe of sunlight that, for a brief moment, gives me back my youth. Flashes of greens, orange, blues, blacks, yellow—a color continuum of time, light, and space. Driving through that emerald tunnel of summertime, with its smell of pines, past the black holes of lakes, into the infinite blue sky, I'm thirty-one again full throttle in a skiff across the harbor; twenty-five drinking a beer in the back of a pickup; seventeen, cruising the Chagford road across the moors in Devon. My right shoulder doesn't ache. I don't need readers. There's nowhere to be. No responsibility. I am free and limitless.

In that light, I feel my relationship with sight—especially with color—grow more desperate.

My work is an urgent call to live. A primal roar telling me not to waste a second, to be here now.

Look at this.
Experience this.
Feel this.

Time is the only currency. A birthday remembered by five red cherries wet on a pale pink tablecloth. A trip to Russia mapped in light coming through thin yellow scalloped curtains. A series of multicolored cakes memorializing a woman who loved to live. I want you to have the same experience with this collection of pictures as I had when I first found the images—the feeling in the body that comes with bearing witness to something rare.

In the time it took to write this sentence, somebody died, somebody was born, a language disappeared, a forest burn began, an insect was crushed, an idea inched forward. When I am dying, I want to think of the bounty of an orchard, a tree laden with one thousand apples, rosso corsa, and bees abounding.

Earlier this year in a discussion about my work, a friend told me I had dedicated my life to something that doesn't exist. He said, *Color isn't real; it's just our brains' interpretation of light wavelengths.*

I have been annoyed ever since. —CH

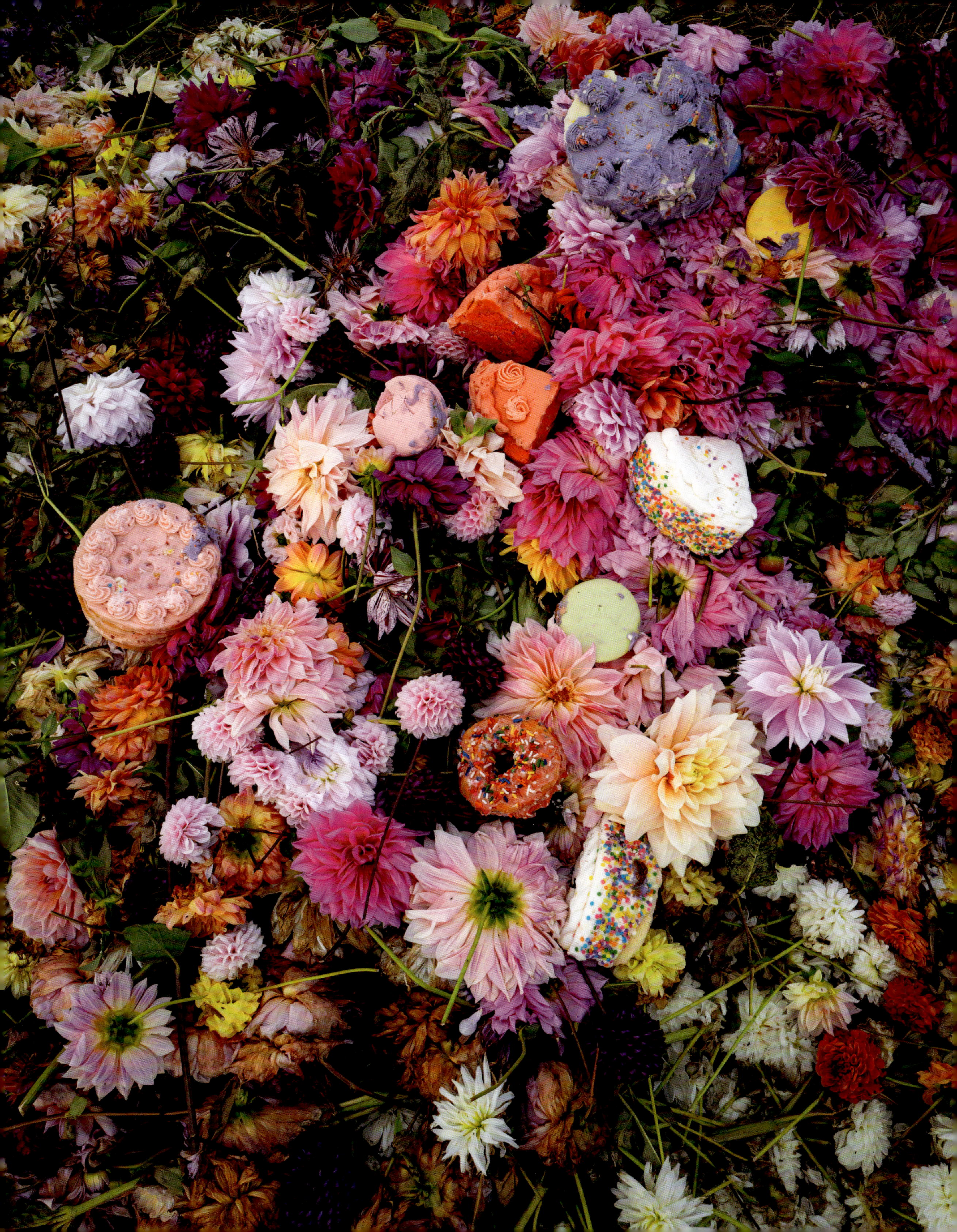

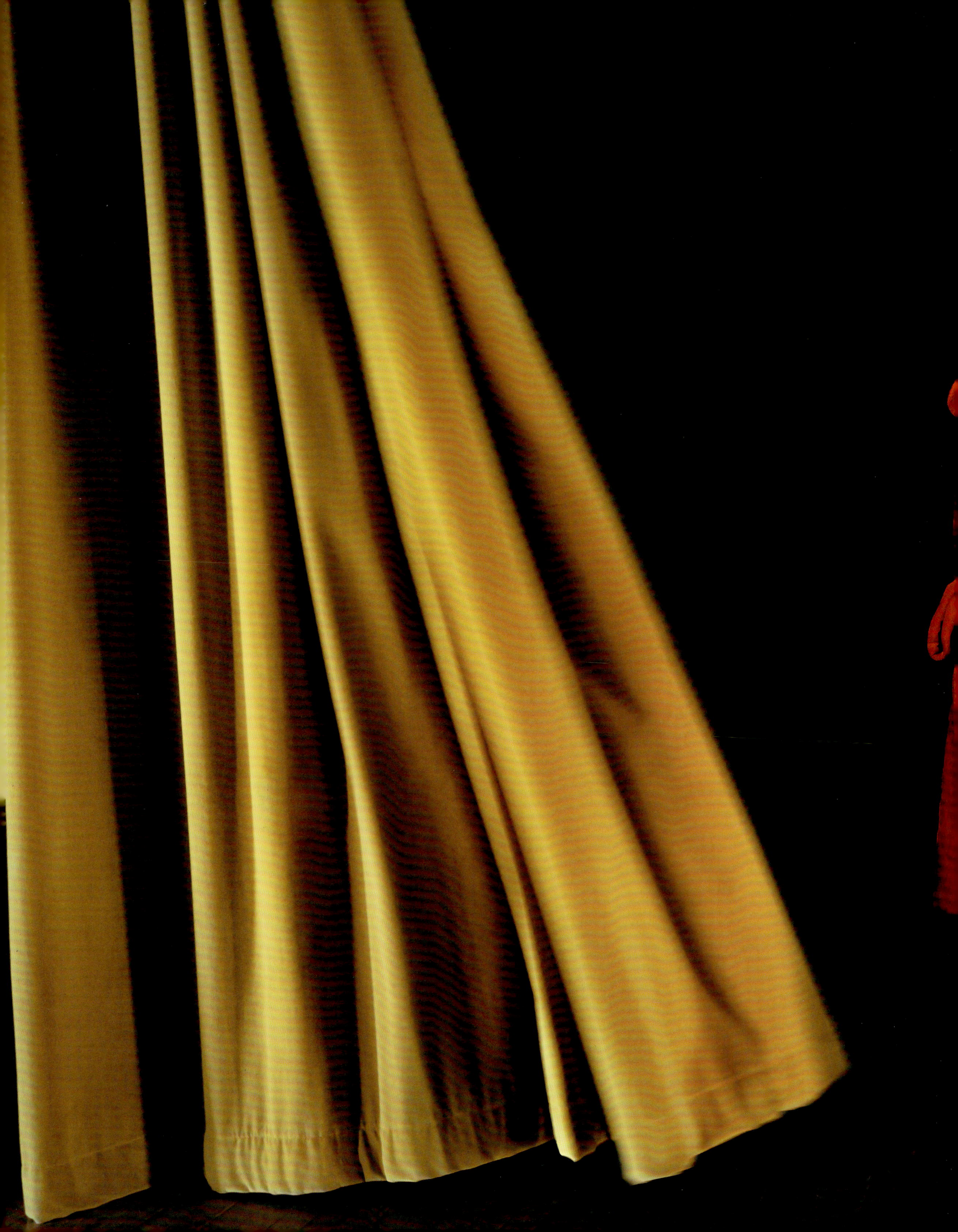

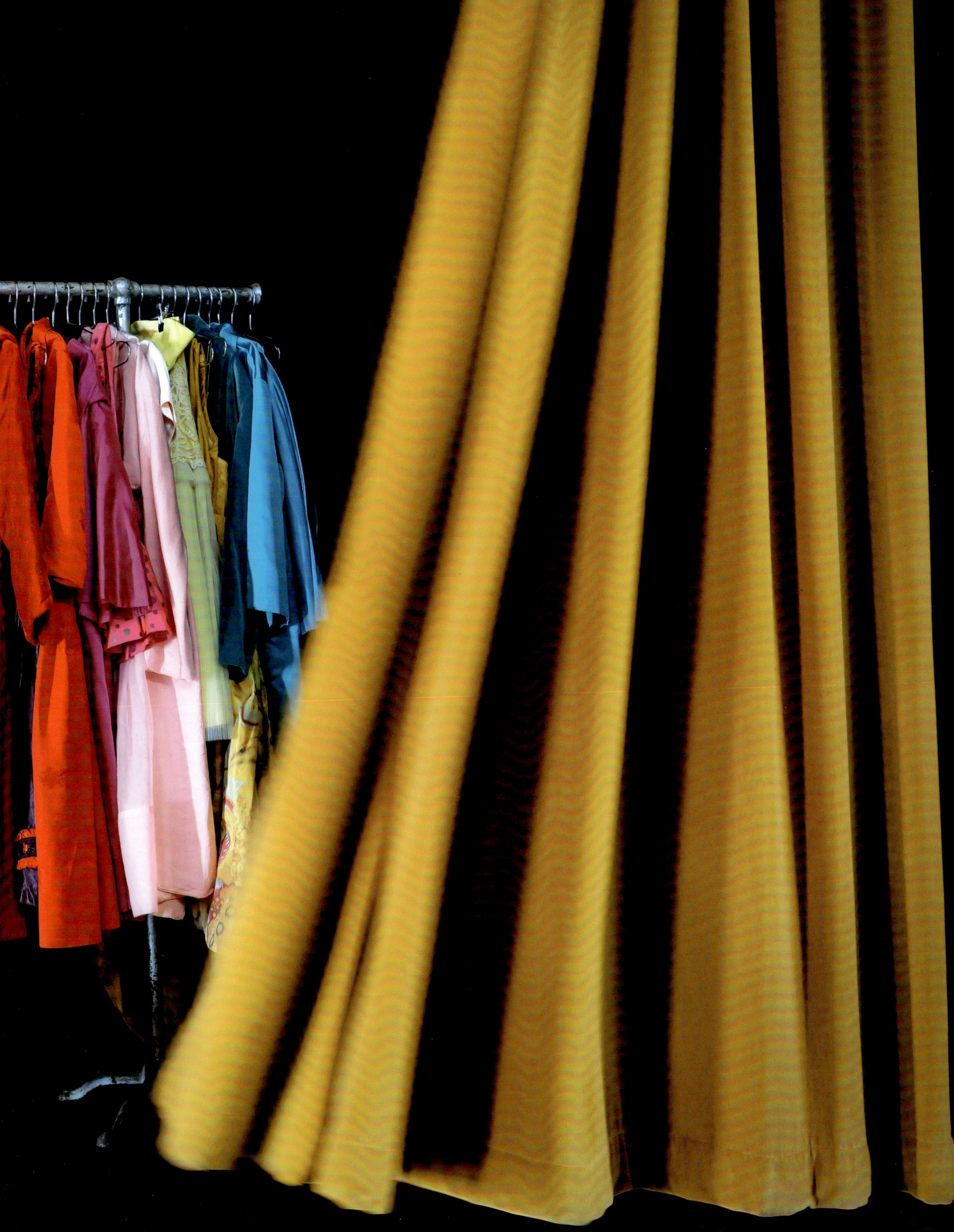

# The Sky Is Blue Only for You

Deep inside our eyes, next to the dark velvet lake of the aqua vitreous, are cones and rods. The rods allow us to see in the gloaming dusk, but only in gray scale. The cones are responsible for color, but they need light to work.

The camera sees things differently than our eyes do. This is the reason photographing at night is so addictive. The camera becomes the youthful eye. The camera is an owl. We are shown something outside of typical human perception.

We have three types of cone receptors in each eye: red, green, and blue sponges. If you stare at a slice of red velvet cake for one minute and then look at a white wall, you will see that cake projected in a verdant bluey-green. This is because your red cones have become utterly exhausted. Certain animals have more cone receptors than we do and can see well beyond our red-to-violet visual light spectrum. Butterflies have at least five kinds of cones. Mantis shrimp have as many as sixteen. This means that a mantis shrimp—an animal that lives in the shallows not the deep—sees millions more variants of colors than humans do. Mantis shrimp only speak color. A few people, primarily women, have four types of cones. These women are tetrachromats, so seeing color is one of their many superpowers. But some people, primarily men, only have two cone variations, making them color-blind in the color they are missing. If you are missing red, then a juicy strawberry appears beige. No wonder some men overcompensate.

We see color in two ways. Seeing the color in a rainbow or TV screen is the result of wavelengths of light coming straight and uninterrupted to the eye. But when we see something red, like a ruby, it is because all the other colors have been absorbed by its most basic structure. And red—its ruby-ness, its atoms—has been spat back out for us to see. It's counterintuitive, but a forest is only green because it refuses its greenness. Color resists logic. Color is magic. Matisse said, *With color one obtains an energy that seems to stem from witchcraft.* A peach is only peach because it will not soak up that orangey-yellow, pushing it back out into the world and keeping all the other colors absorbed safely inside. The overflow of that peach color is called scattering. This seeping out helps us discern the depth, texture, and shape of things, the roundness of the circle, the silkiness of the silk.

What makes some apples red and some green? It is not the appleness that defines the color; it is the molecular structure of the surface pigment, which differs from apple to apple. We tend to think of pigment as paint, but there is pigment in everything: a foxglove, a flamingo, a fig.

Pigment, when in the skin, is called melanin and lives in the epidermis, a paper-thin layer of skin a mere one millimeter thick. Humans have varying amounts of this same pigment which results in skin tone. My original skin color matched Pantone 97–7C*—a pale beige. As a teen, my sister and I regularly burned ourselves to a crisp, sunbathing while eating french fries on holiday. Then, at twenty, backpacking around Europe, I fell asleep on a beach in Athens, while waiting for the Magic Bus back to London, and shredded red the backs of my legs. I couldn't walk for a week. As I lived more life in the sun—years working in Spain then Bermuda—my skin darkened to protect against UV rays and regulate vitamin D synthesis. People need the right amount of vitamin D, not too much and not too little, for the orchestra of the body to function correctly. There are almost no genetic differences between humans in terms of what we call race. And yet, skin tone has been used as the pretext of oppression, seemingly stretching back as far as our consciousness goes.

Color is beauty. This is why people go to such extremes to replicate color in the forms of dyes and paints or to possess color in the form of gems and precious stones. To live without color is like watching the symphony on mute. But color can come at a deadly cost. The mining of stones and pigments for paints and dyes has always been, and still is, at the heart of colonialism, using a workforce of slave labor. There were trade wars for emeralds, sapphires, and the magnetic red dye from cochineal beetles. Indigo vats boiling blue, oozed a toxic, putrid smell on the outskirts of towns all over India and the slave-owning Caribbean and American South. In the sixteenth century, European aristocratic women slowly poisoned their bodies by painting their faces with Venetian ceruse, a white lead foundation that smoothed their blemishes while rotting their organs. In the early twentieth century, factory girls throughout the United States licked clean the silver radium tips of their brushes after painting yellow glow-in-the-dark ten-to-two clock hands on watches. The radium grew tumors in their jaws, and their facial bones crumbled like dirt.

Particles like water and dust in the air allow us to see the colors in the sky. Traumas in the world—earthquakes, forest fires, bombs—create excess particles in the atmosphere, resulting in more beautiful sunsets. We are oohing and aahing at spectacular grief. The sky is only blue because the shortest rays on the spectrum are blue, and like all small, fast things, these rays scatter the most, overwhelming the other colors. Blue has the softest but most insistent voice. But remember, the sky is blue only for you. Light is real; color is a perception. At sunset, when the sun is closest to the horizon, only the lazy, long, slutty colors—reds, oranges, and yellows—are left, giving it all away for free.

Imagine living under a colorless sky. The color blue was unnamed for thousands of years of human existence—that lonely blue. Achilles wept for two reasons: his feet hurt, and the sky and ocean were an endless gray. Isaac Newton was obsessed with blue and divided almost half the visible light spectrum into its three variants: blue, indigo, and violet. However, many scientists believe that indigo doesn't have enough wavelengths to warrant being its own color and so indigo, like the planet Pluto, is about to be pink-slipped.

Our history is made up of fictions.

It takes 8.3 seconds for light from the sun to reach earth—that first orange line on the horizon at dawn is a reason to wake up. The deep, rich blue of twilight is a gift to each of us. When the sun sets every day, we face our mortality—a little death each evening to remind us to pay attention and not to take living for granted.

*See the work of Angélica Dass

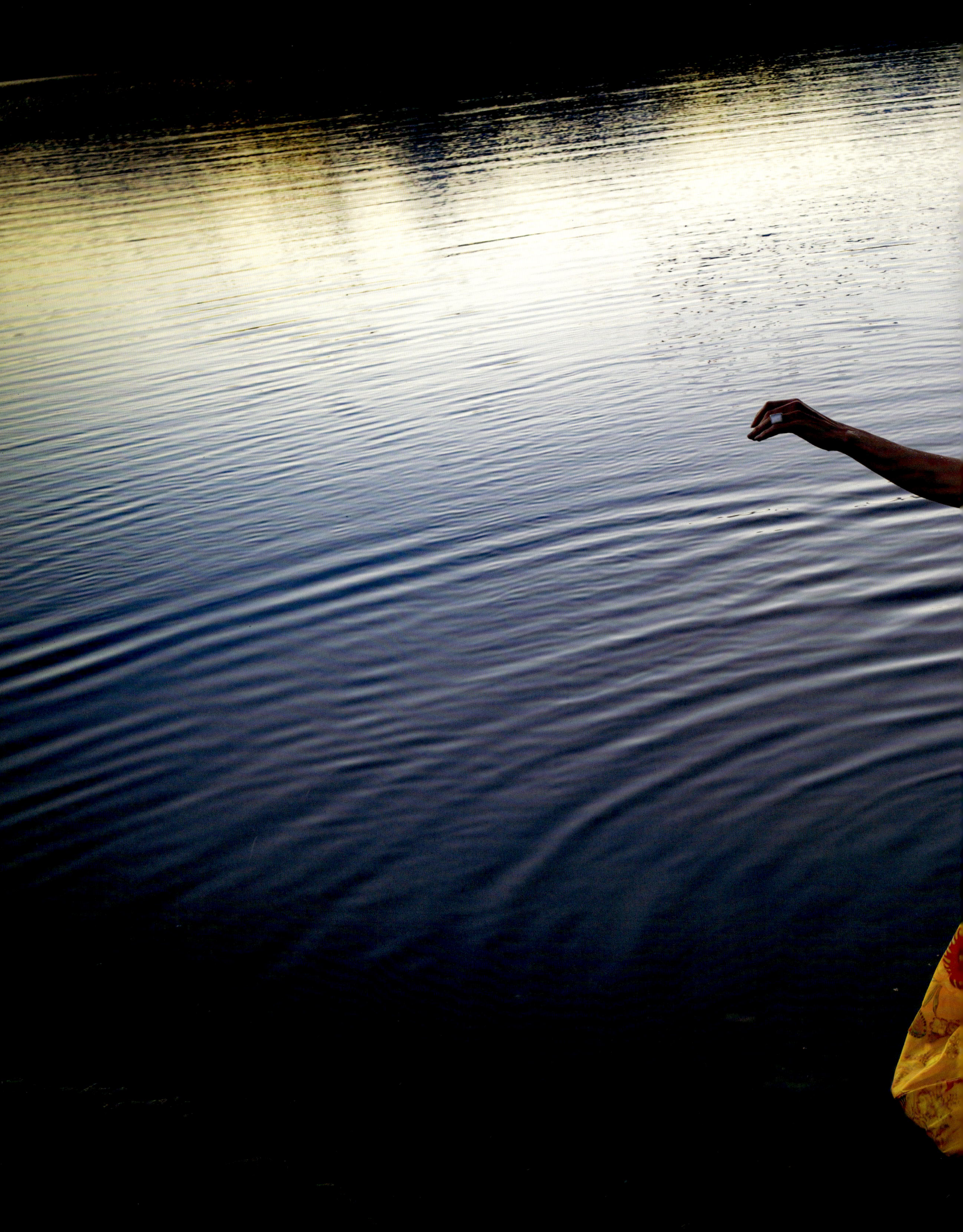

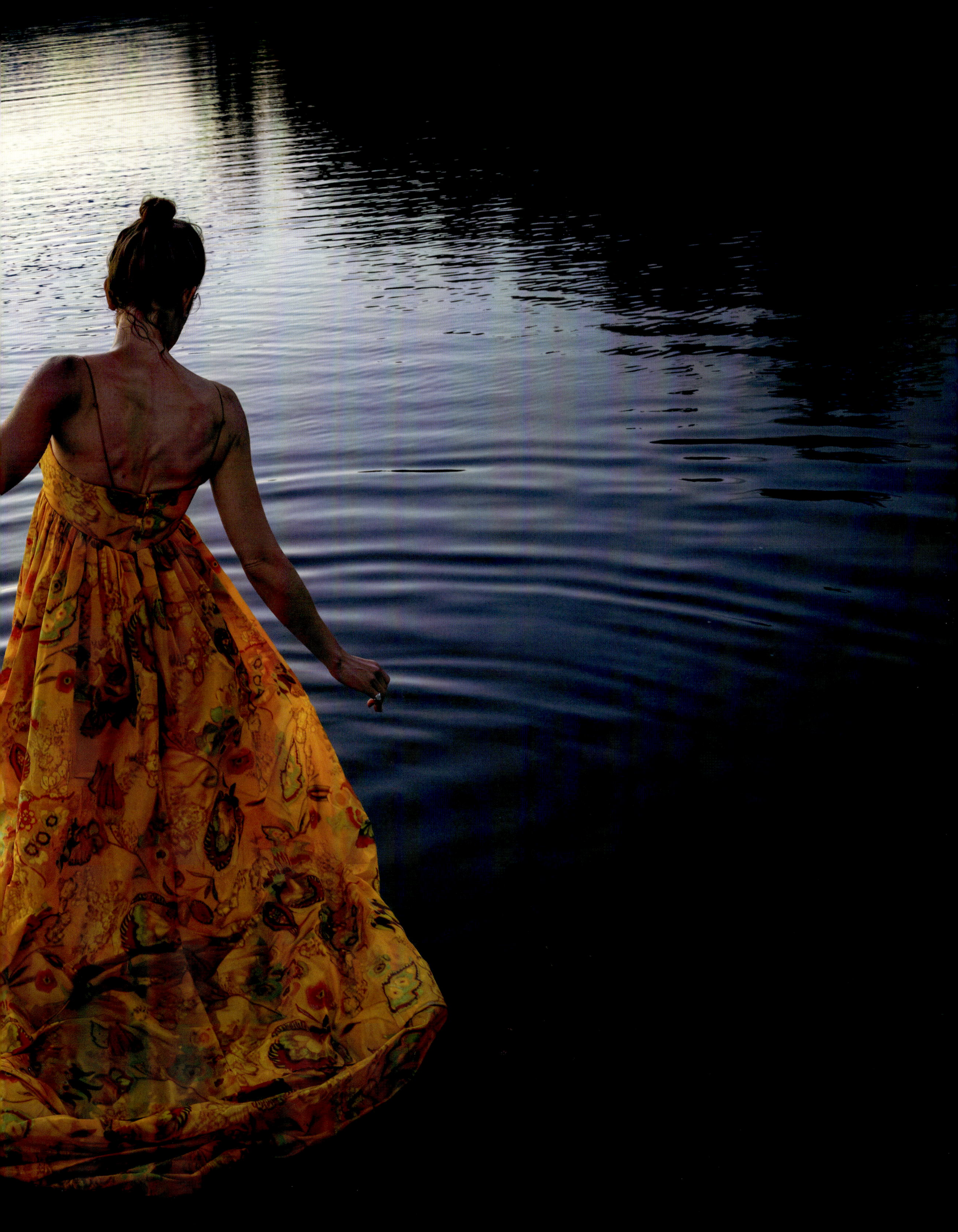

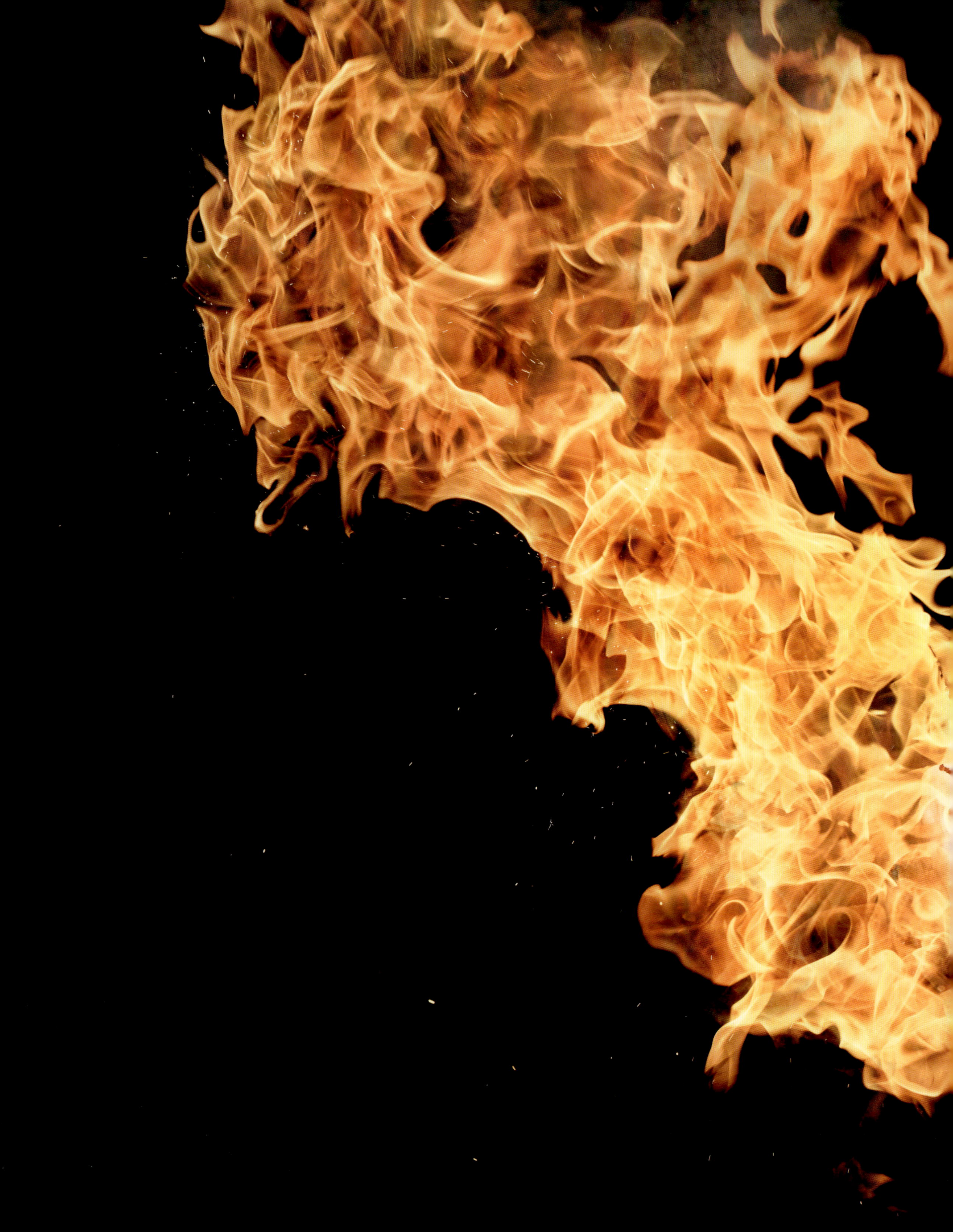

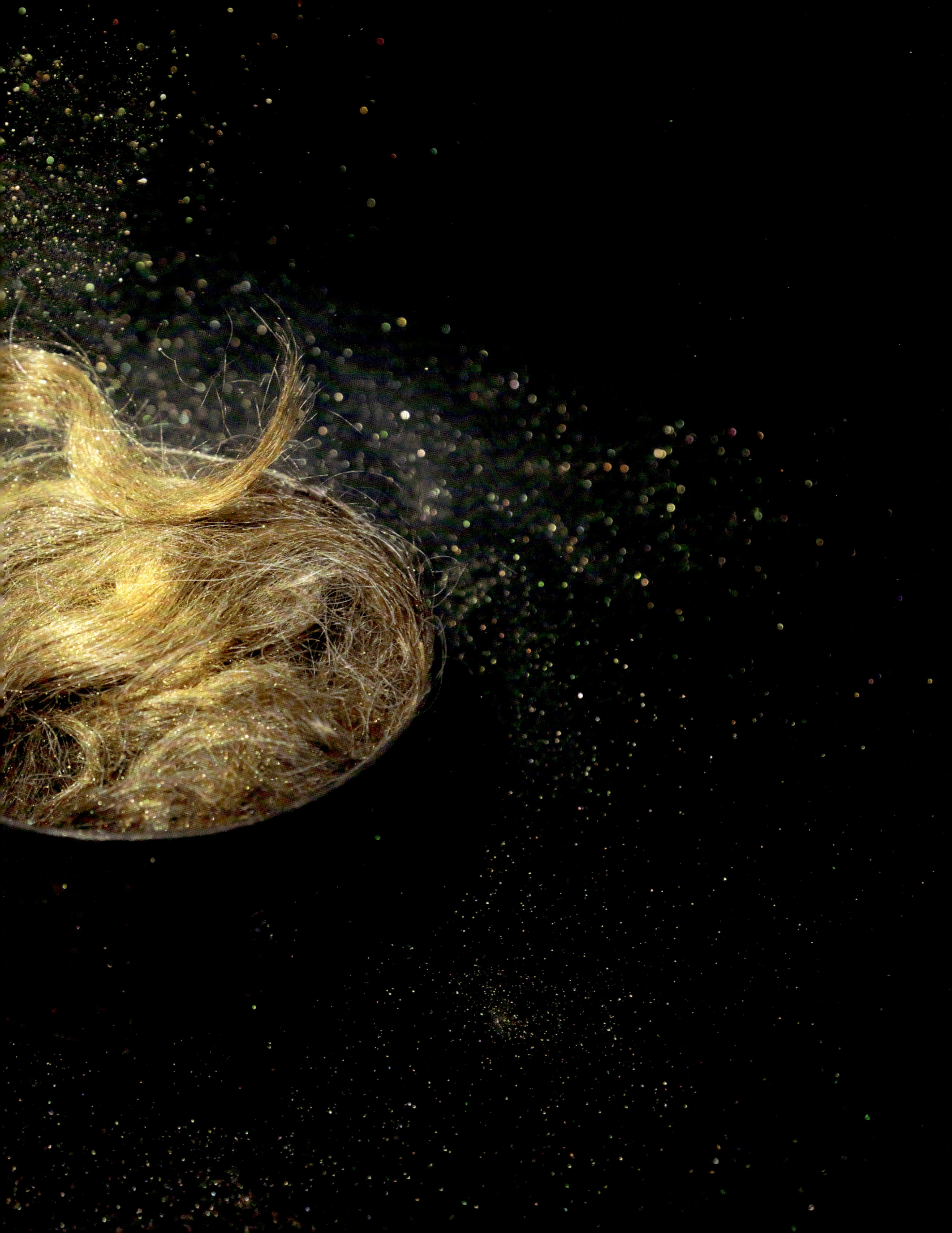

Going blind is one of my greatest fears.

In my twenties, I taught photography to a legally blind person. He could discern light from dark and would intuitively use the camera as he went about his day. Then later, he would hold up the prints an inch away from his better eye to discover what was actually there in the world.

I google *artists that went blind*. Although all of our vision shifts if we are lucky enough to get old, artists don't retire; they typically work until they die. It's strangely inspiring. Van Gogh developed xanthopsia from being prescribed a diet of foxgloves to cure his epilepsy. Xanthopsia, a color vision deficiency, means one primarily sees yellow, so of course sunflowers and stars spoke to him. Later in life, Degas and O'Keeffe both had macular degeneration and moved to different media to accommodate their shifting vision: Degas to pastels and sculpture and O'Keeffe to clay and charcoal. Monet developed cataracts in his sixties, forcing him into a warm orange world where he could no longer see his beloved purples. Leonardo and Rembrandt developed stereo blindness, their left and right eyes going in different directions. This is the reason why the *Mona Lisa* is so magnetic—you just don't know where to look.

## Why the Sunflowers Spoke to Van Gogh

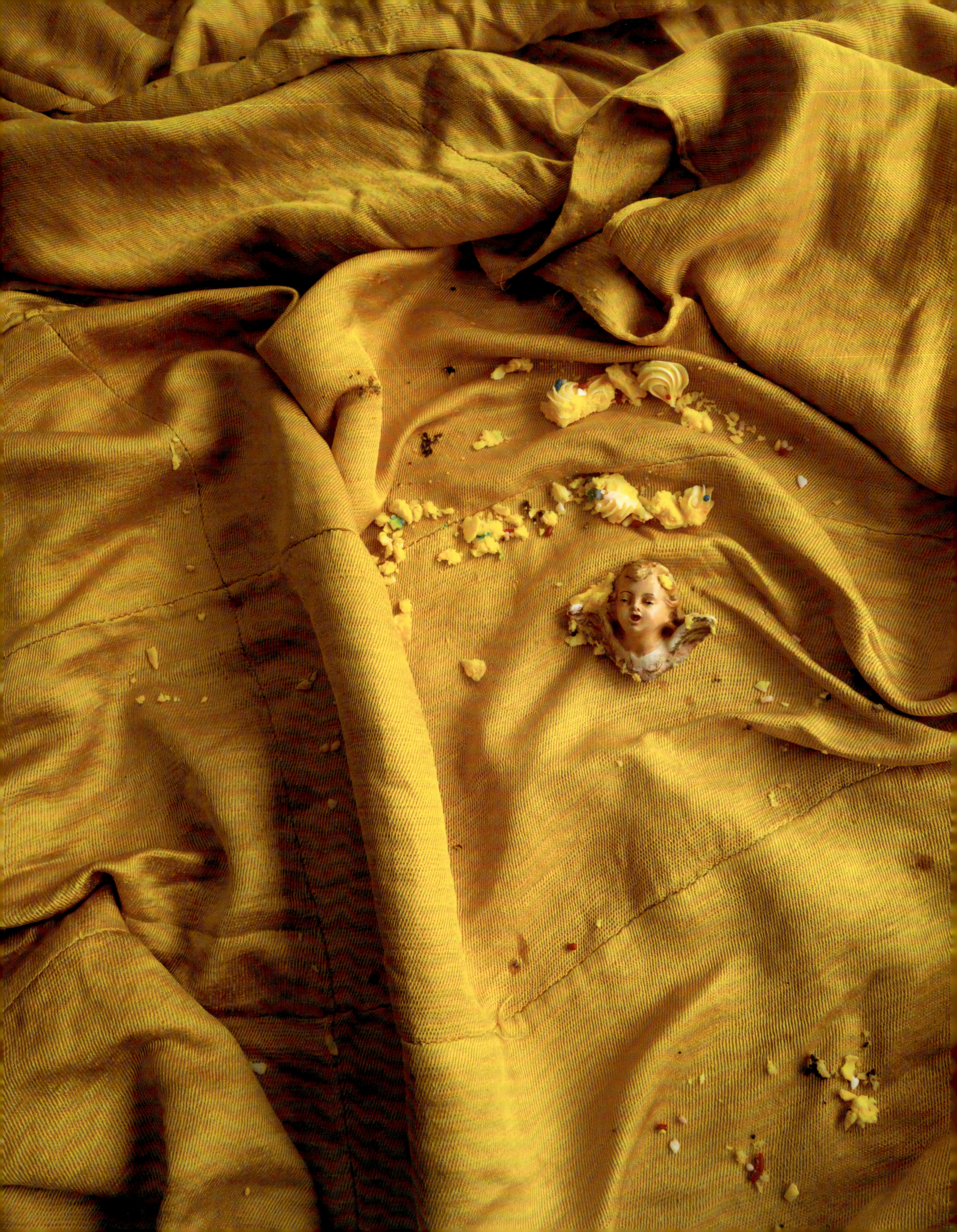

The late eighteenth century was known as the golden age of taxonomy: the naming, defining, and classifying of all things by white men. Abraham Werner was a German geologist and mineralogist who crushed gems and rocks to organize, standardize, and catalog all the colors he saw. Werner compared the deep color of *Copper Ore* to *Scotch Blue*. He likened *Red Orpiment* to *Aurora Red* and a *White Opal* to *Milk White*.

In 1814, the painter Patrick Syme expanded Werner's mineral data to create and publish the visual color chart known as *Werner's Nomenclature of Colours*—a list of real-world examples of 108 shades. Syme added a dollop of paint and further names and descriptions, including vegetables, animals, and more minerals.

This year, I added an extra column next to Werner's and Syme's titled WOMAN.

The White
of Human Eyeballs

| No | NAMES | COLOURS | ANIMAL | VEGETABLE | MINERAL | WOMAN |
|---|---|---|---|---|---|---|
| 23 | VELVET BLACK | | MOLE TAIL FEATHERS OF BLACK COCK | BLACK OF BLACK AND RED WEST-INDIAN PEAS | OBSIDIAN | RUTH BADER GINSBURG'S ROBES |
| | | | | | | |
| 85 | VERMILION RED | | RED CORAL | LOVE APPLE | CINNABAR | STAIN ON SIDEWALK BELOW ANA MENDIETA'S APARTMENT |
| | | | | | | |
| 41 | AURICULA PURPLE | | EGG OF LARGEST BLUEBOTTLE OR FLESH FLY | LARGEST PURPLE AURICULA | FLUOR SPAR | BRUISED EYE OF NAN GOLDIN |
| | | | | | | |
| 24 | SCOTCH BLUE | | THROAT OF TITMOUSE | PURPLE ANEMOME | BLUE COPPER ORE | TONI MORRISON'S BLUEST EYE |
| | | | | | | |
| 51 | BLUISH GREEN | | EGG OF THRUSH | UNDER DISK OF WILD ROSE LEAVES | BERYL | RACHEL CARSON'S SILENT SPRING |
| | | | | | | |
| 91 | CARMINE RED | | FLAMINGO | RASPBERRY COCKSCOMB CARNATION PINK | ORIENTAL RUBY | BLOOD STAINED SUIT OF JACKIE O |
| | | | | | | |
| 9 | ASH GRAY | | BREAST OF LONG-TAILED HEN TITMOUSE | FRESH WOOD ASHES | FLINT | POLONIUM STAINED FINGERS OF MARIE CURIE |
| | | | | | | |
| 7. | SKIMMED WHITE MILK | | WHITE OF HUMAN EYEBALLS | BACK OF BLUE HEPATICA | GRANULAR LIMESTONE | TEARS OF QUEEN ELIZABETH SITTING ALONE AT PRINCE PHILIP'S FUNERAL IN COVID |
| | | | | | | |

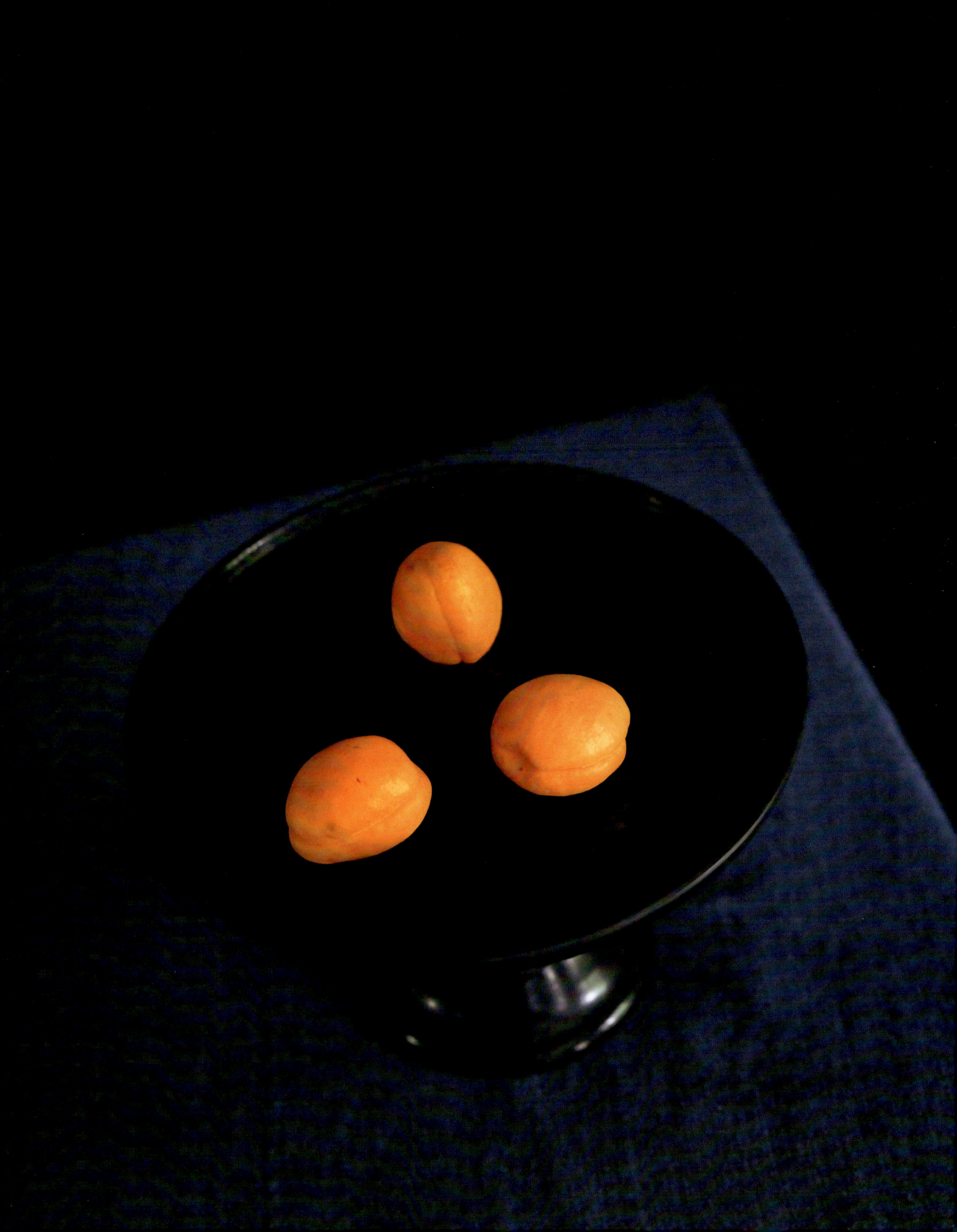

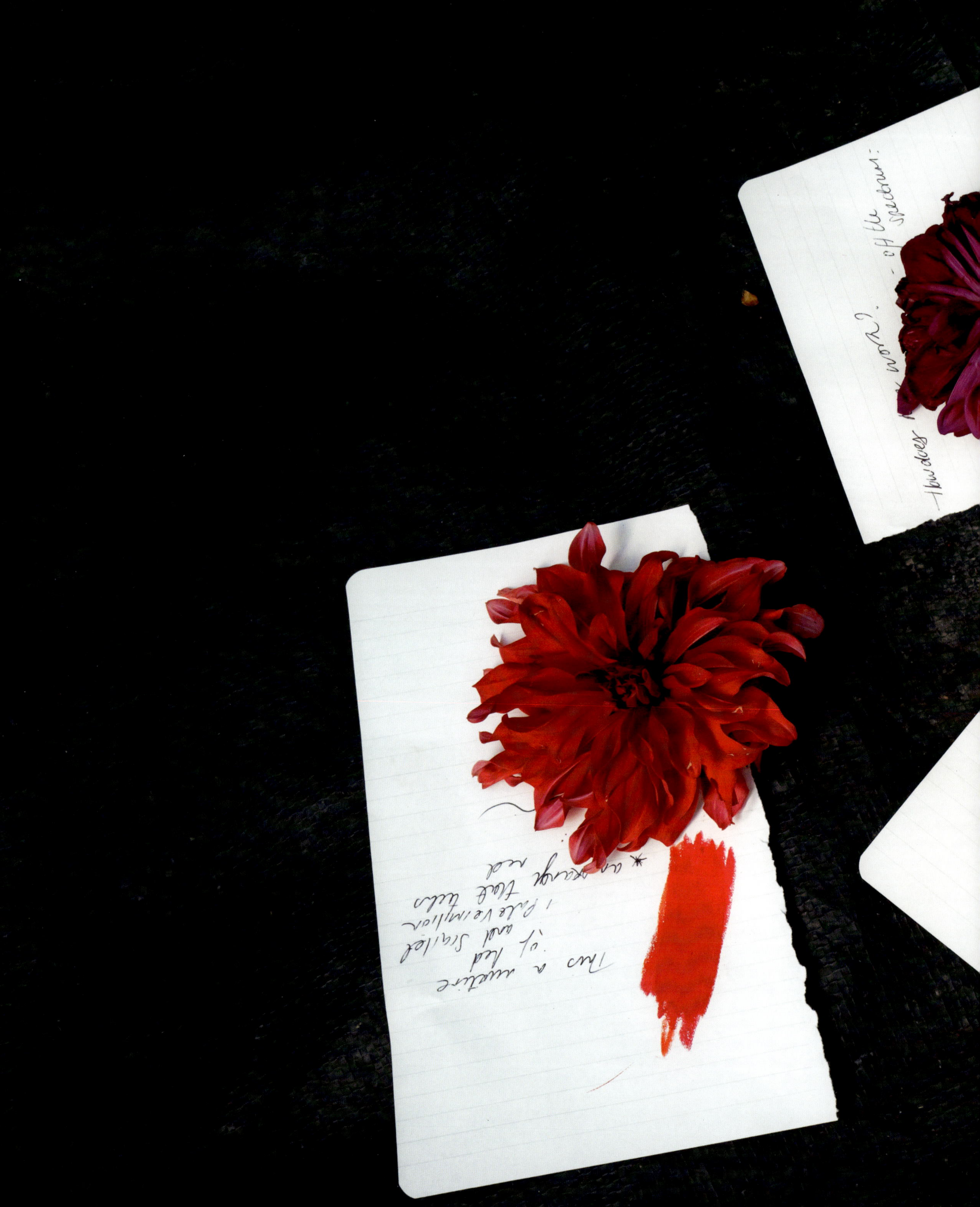
How does
work?
- of the spectrum:

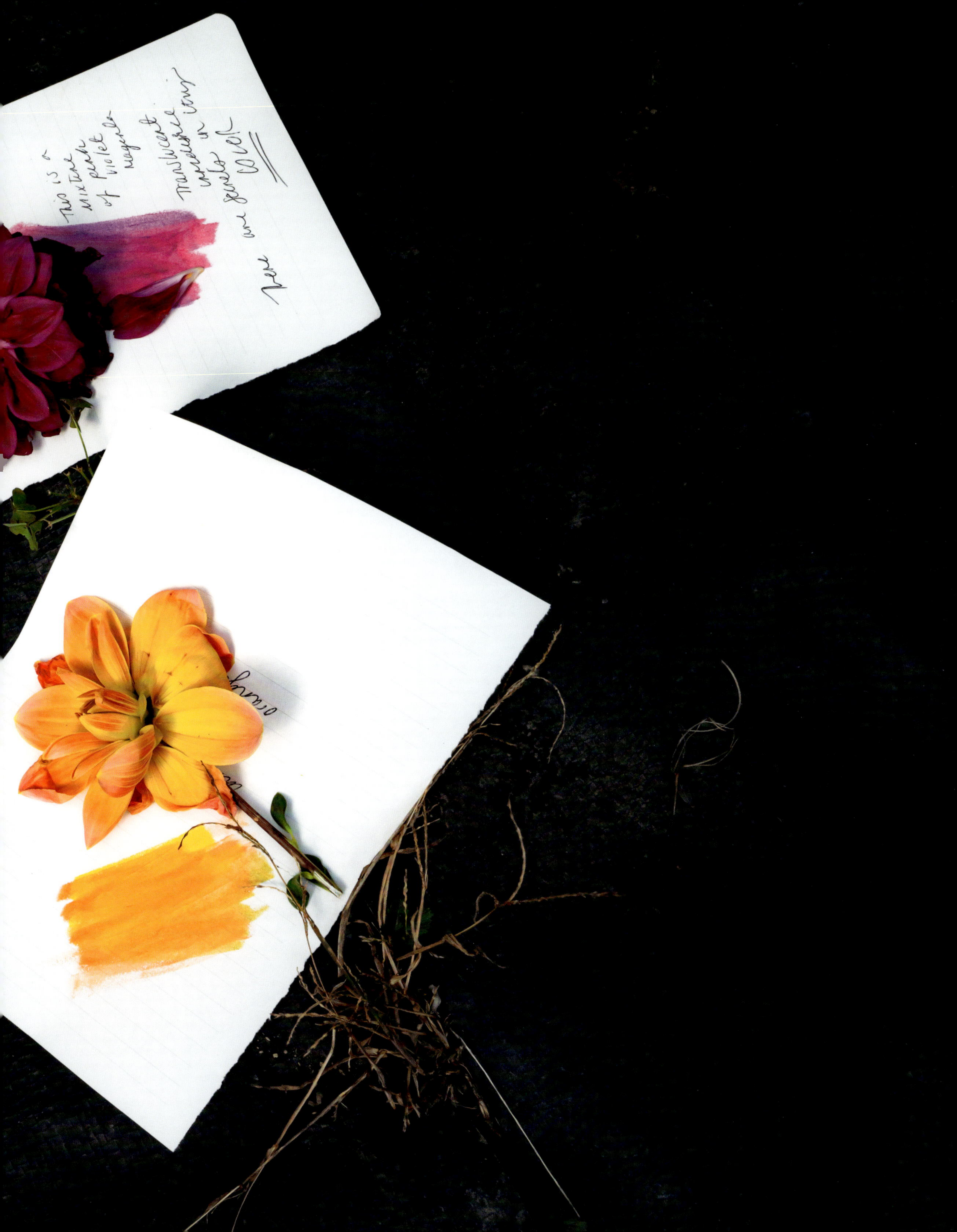
this is a
mixture
of pink
violet
magenta
translucent
color

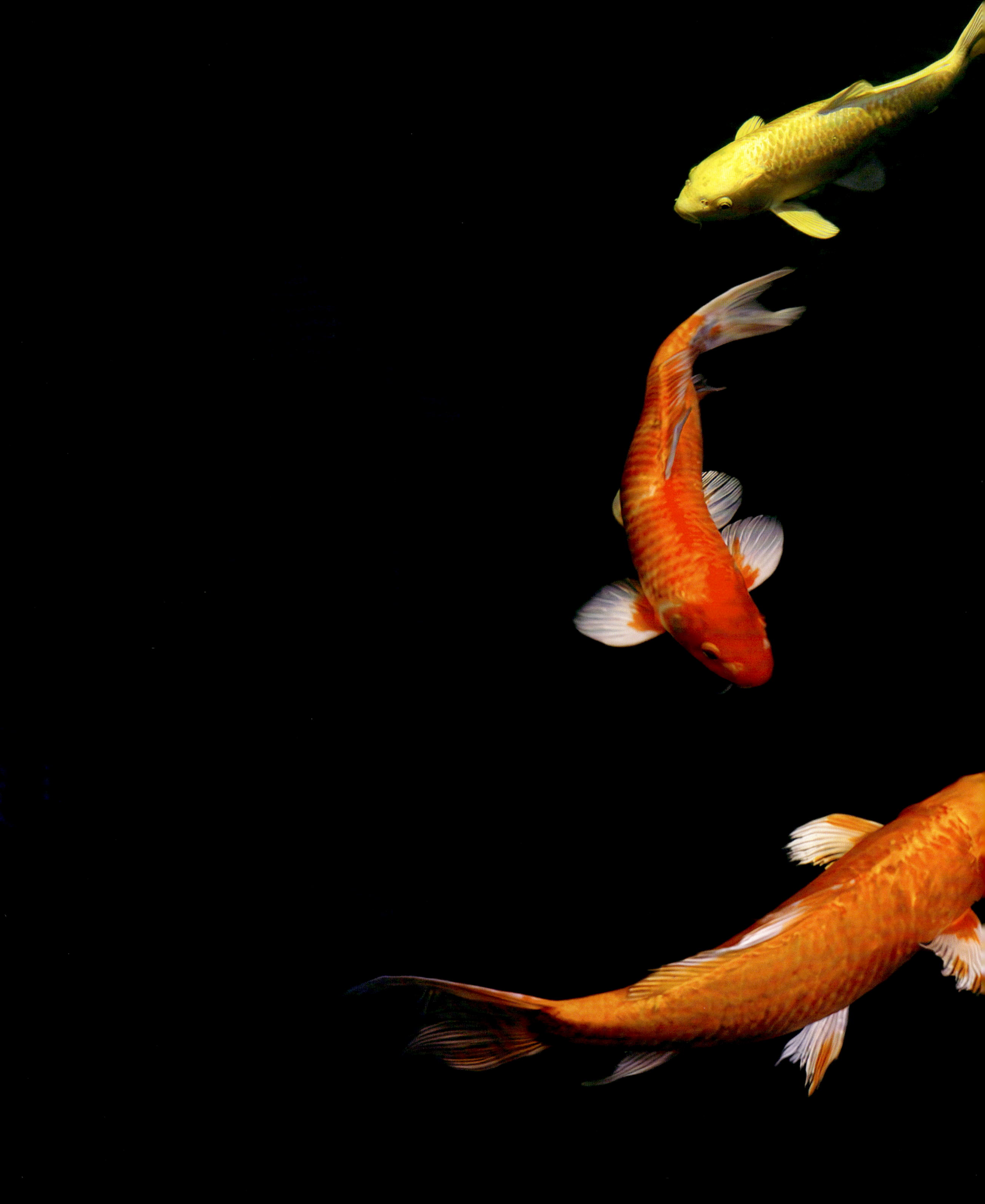

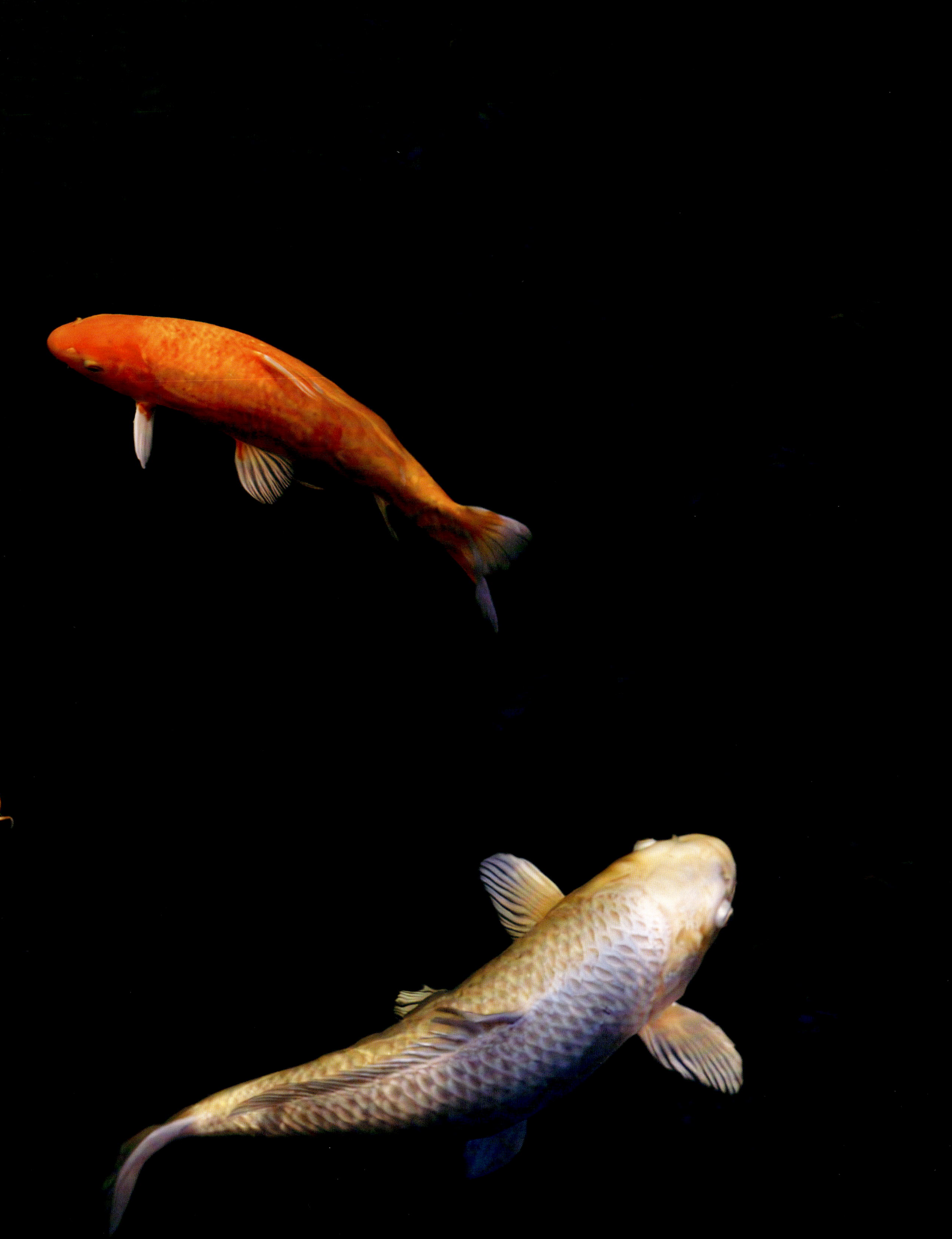

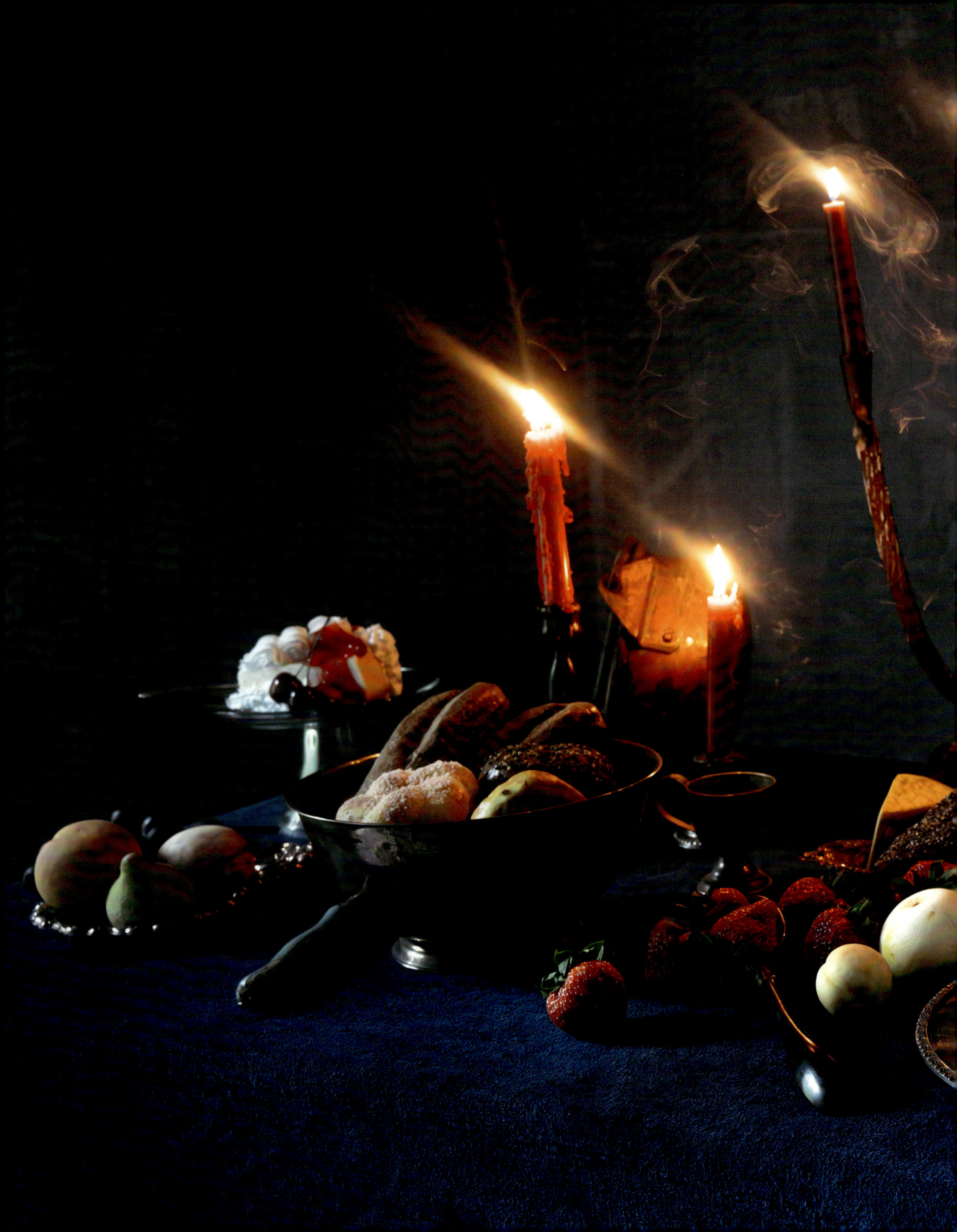

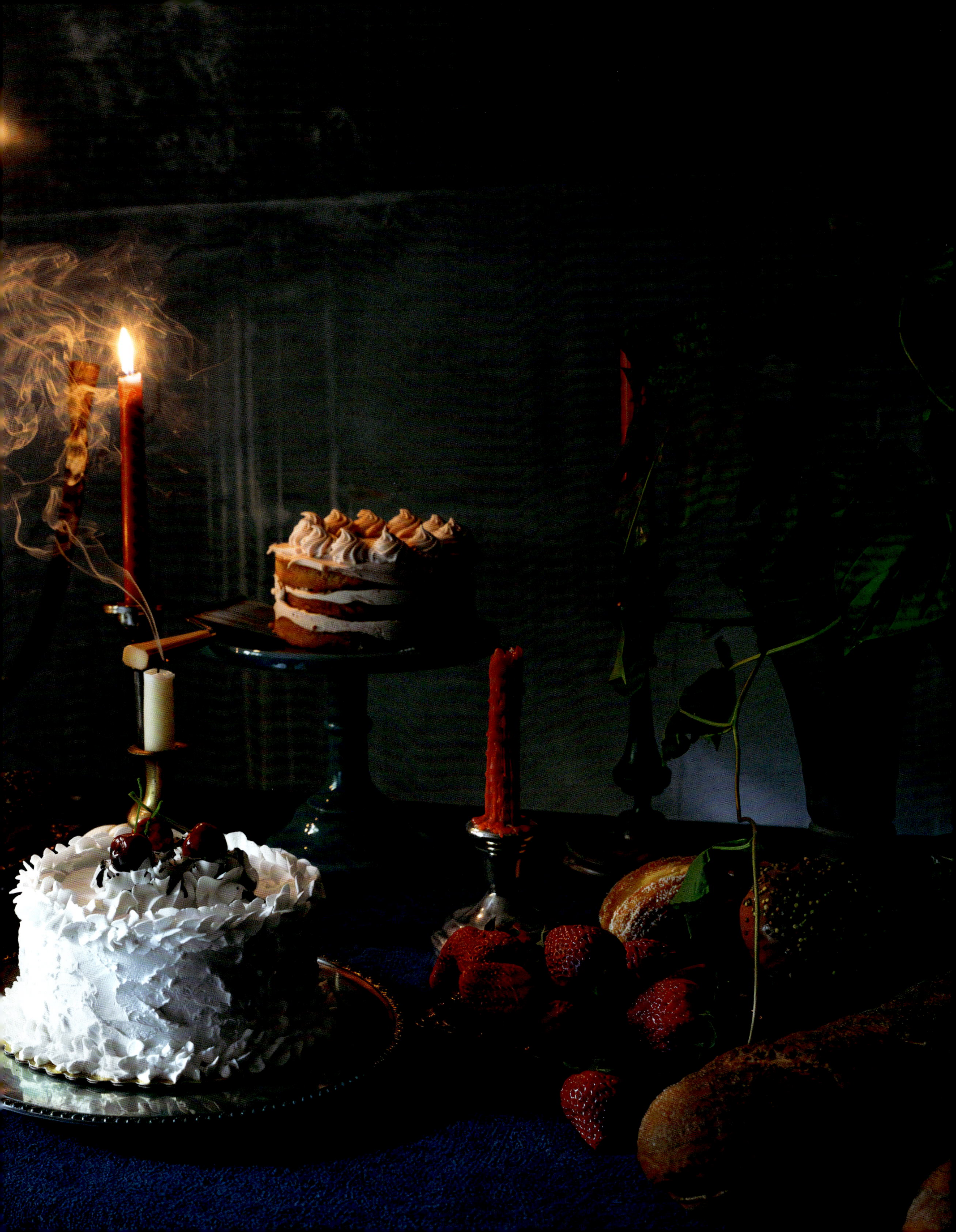

# Heaven Is a Tin of Canned Peaches

It's early March in Maine. Spring is still eight weeks away. It has been winter for months. All the trees are dead, nails and hair have stopped growing, bones feel brittle. Our tarnished eyes heave exhausted from a monochromatic landscape.

In search of color, I end up in the supermarket parking lot, waiting for the doors to open at 7 a.m. It's rained all night, but now the sun is breaking through the clouds. Hannaford, glowing in a tangerine light of sunrise, seems almost hopeful.

A still life is what I want to make: a deep violet Caravaggio glow near a window with vibrant persimmons, ruby red pomegranates, amethyst figs. I am seeking an ancient fire, a single wilting poppy, exotic fruit on black velvet—something rich and seductive, lush and decadent.

But here, in the fruit and vegetable section by the entrance, bathed in harsh blue fluorescent light, there's only kale, potatoes, celery, turnips, onions, parsnips, apples, and imported bananas-at-the-edge-of-a-fruit fly—utilitarian produce to fill the stomach, not the eyes.

Toward the back of the fresh produce at the flower stand, the dyed fuchsia carnations and bleached white baby's breath suffocate in plastic. I can't bear it.

*Cakes!* Cakes are luxurious. But the bakery fridge has only small blue round ones and flat rectangular lime-green ones, and lime green makes me shudder. I hit rock bottom in the dessert aisle, foraging on my knees for treasure in front of Duncan Hines. Rock bottom is where heaven is a tin of canned peaches and salvation a shaker of multicolored sprinkles.

At the checkout, I buy hot pink carnations with no smell, an ombré cupcake to match an August sunset, a glass jar of sliced bloodred beets, bright cherry tomatoes, a punnet of dark blackberries, one Galaxy apple, and a bottle of cabernet sauvignon to drink sooner rather than later. It is the red shopping cart of the desperate.

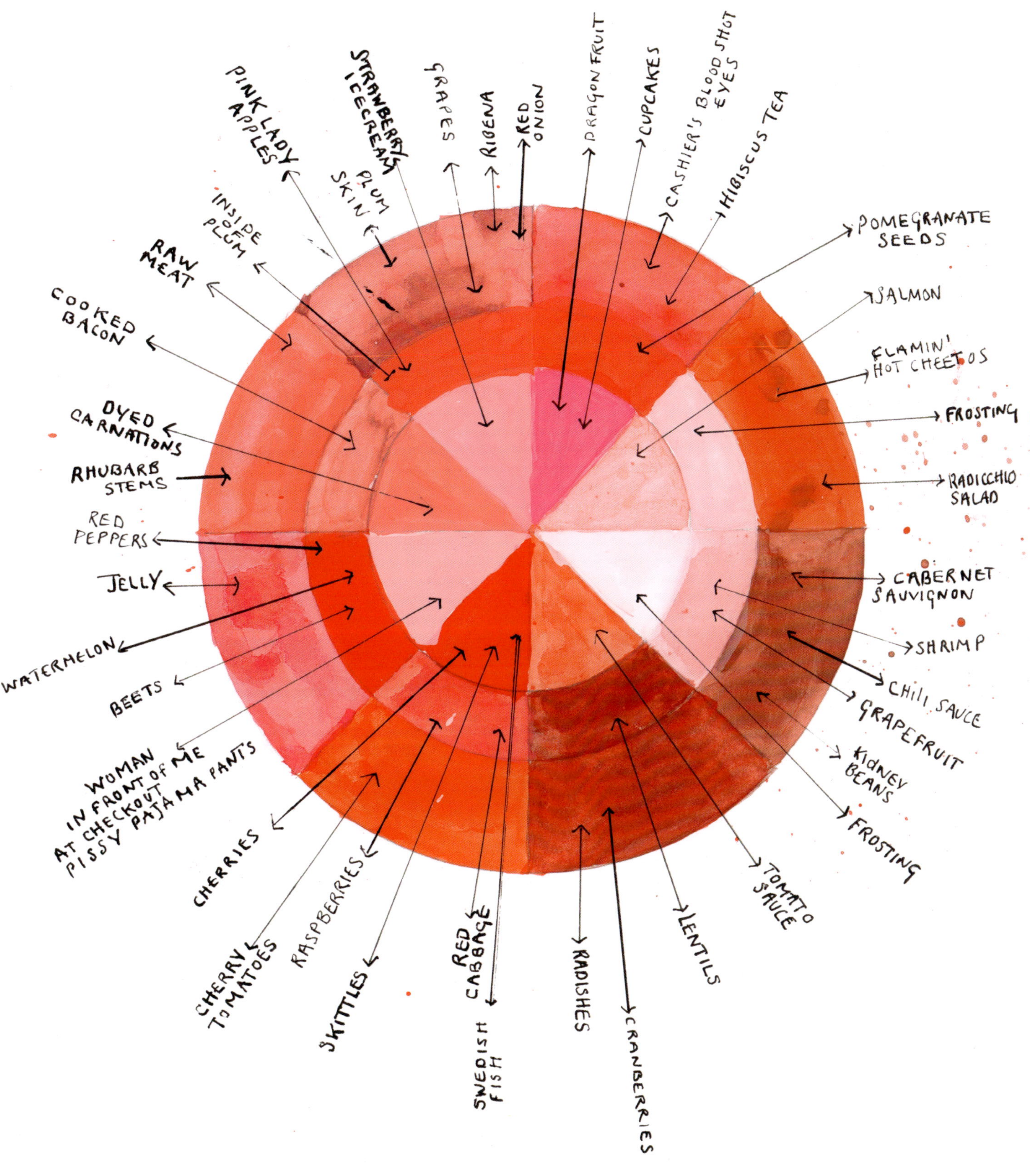

PINK LADY APPLES
STRAWBERRY ICECREAM
GRAPES
RIBENA
RED ONION
DRAGON FRUIT
CUPCAKES
CASHIER'S BLOOD SHOT EYES
HIBISCUS TEA
PLUM SKIN
INSIDE OF PLUM
RAW MEAT
COOKED BACON
POMEGRANATE SEEDS
SALMON
FLAMIN' HOT CHEETOS
FROSTING
RADICCHIO SALAD
DYED CARNATIONS
RHUBARB STEMS
RED PEPPERS
JELLY
WATERMELON
BEETS
WOMAN IN FRONT OF ME AT CHECKOUT PISSY PAJAMA PANTS
CHERRIES
CHERRY TOMATOES
RASPBERRIES
SKITTLES
RED CABBAGE
SWEDISH FISH
RADISHES
CRANBERRIES
LENTILS
TOMATO SAUCE
CABERNET SAUVIGNON
SHRIMP
CHILI SAUCE
GRAPEFRUIT
KIDNEY BEANS
FROSTING

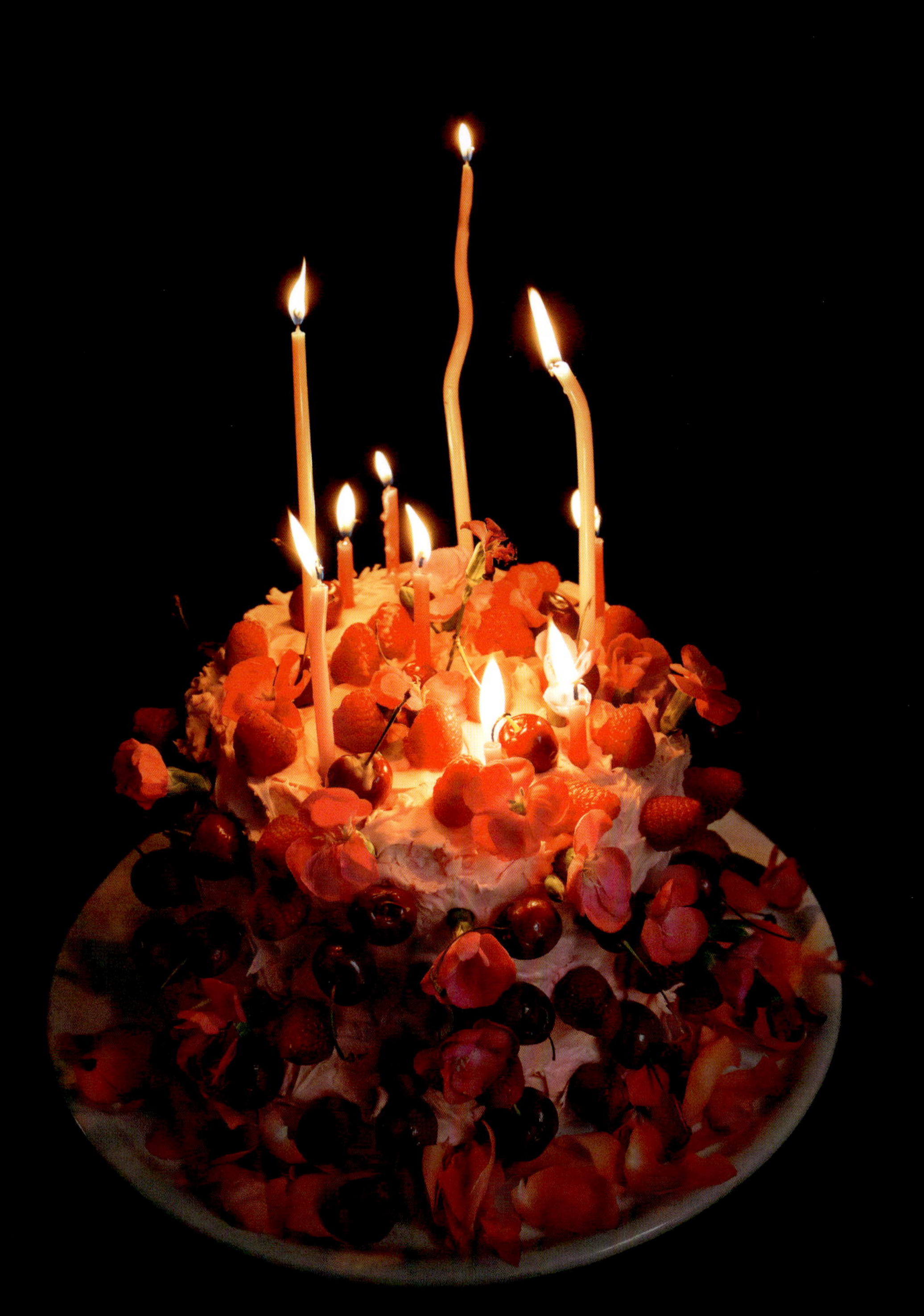

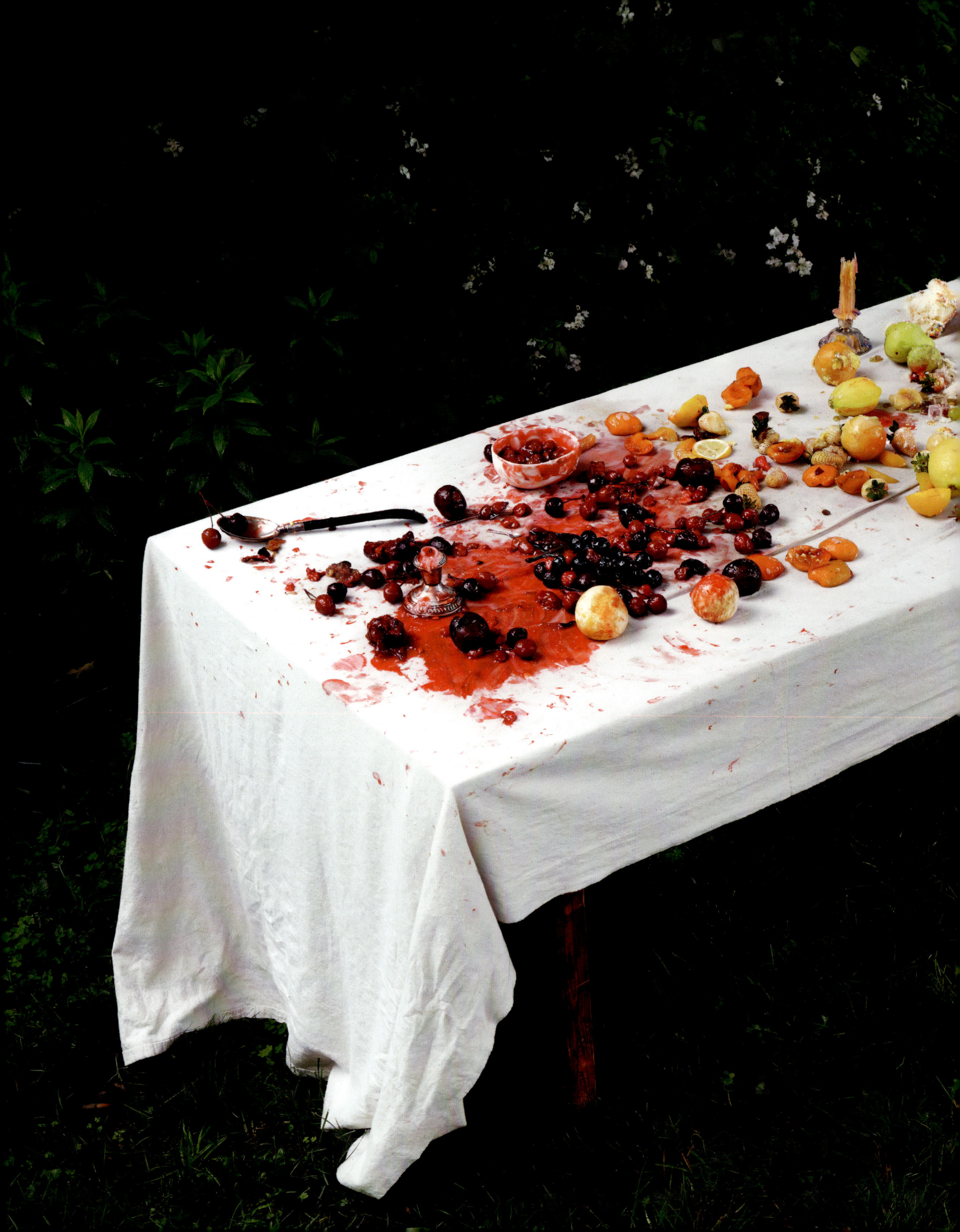

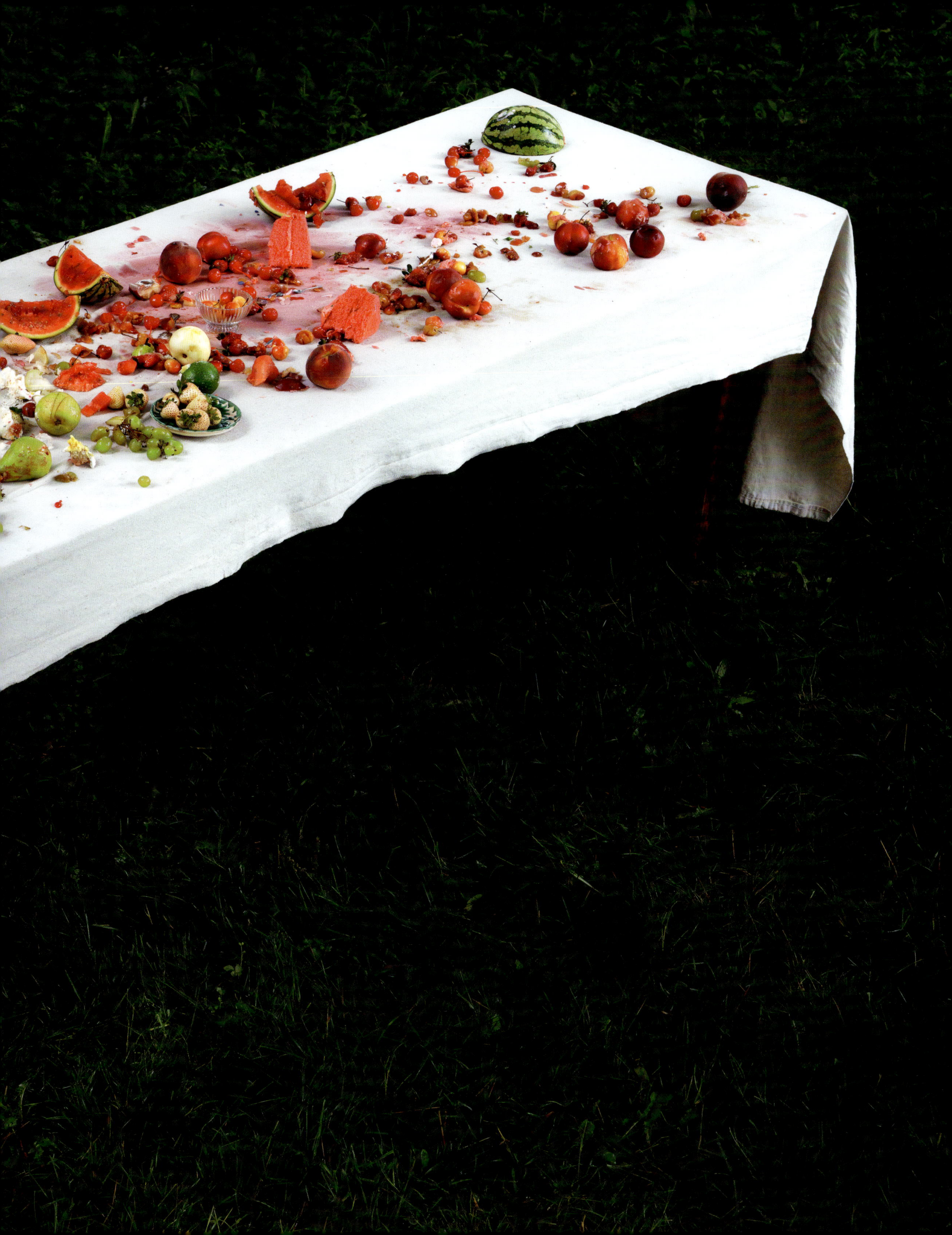

It is a scientific fact that color affects the body. This is the reason why cherry blossoms in spring are so dangerous. Beware: this pink near that blue sky is explosive—the memory alone is enough to get me through the winter. Every April in Japan, fearless picnickers gather under these trees to eat their strawberry sandwiches while contemplating the ephemeral nature of life. In the language of flowers, cherry blossoms are a symbol of mortality. It's that heartbreaking, short-lived beauty that makes us ask such existential questions of a flower.

The color pink sends love notes to the pituitary glands, the ones that regulate the hormones. In turn, the hormones regulate every decision we make—like whether to eat cake or go back to bed.

Color is a serious business.

Pink
Is a
Touch

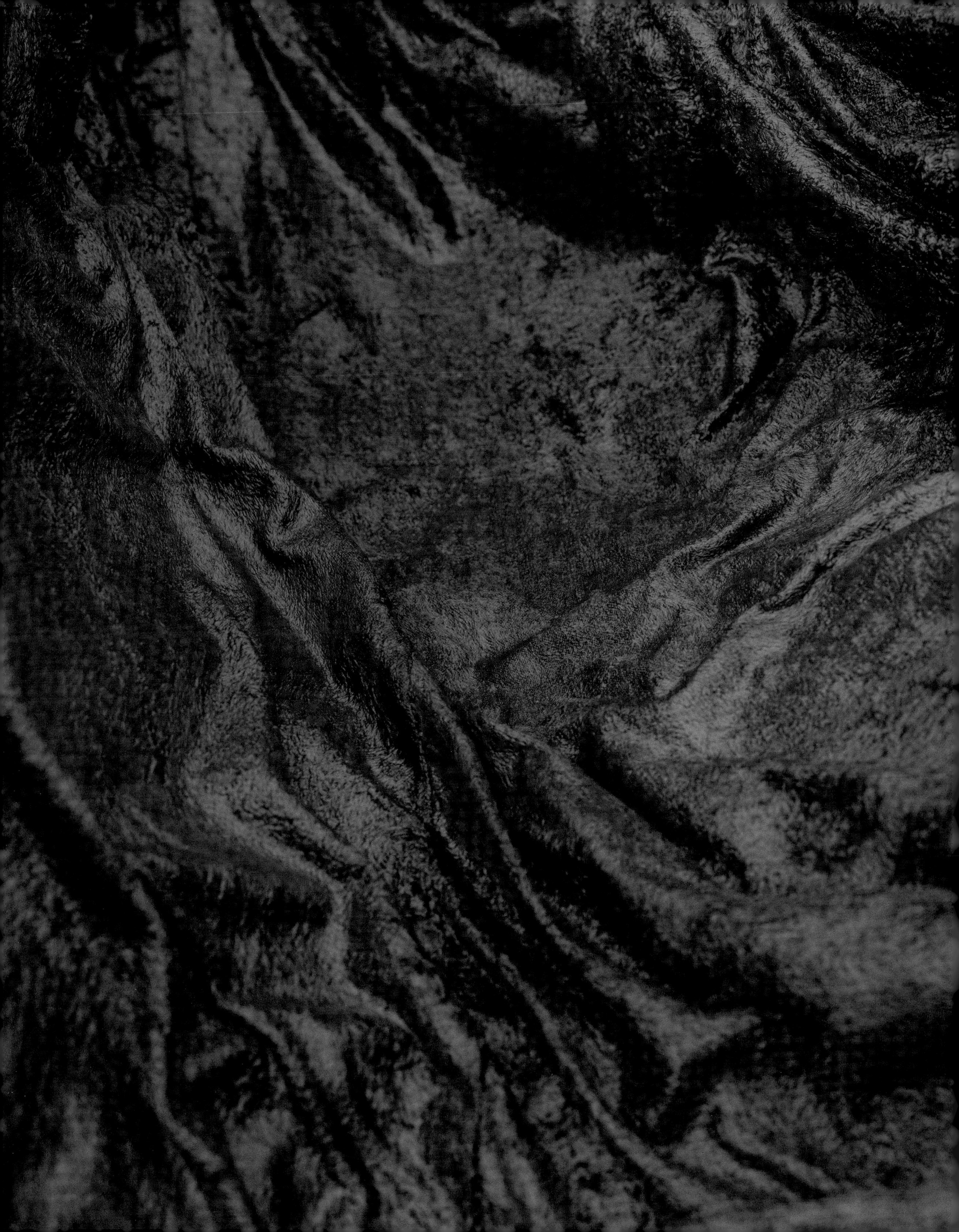

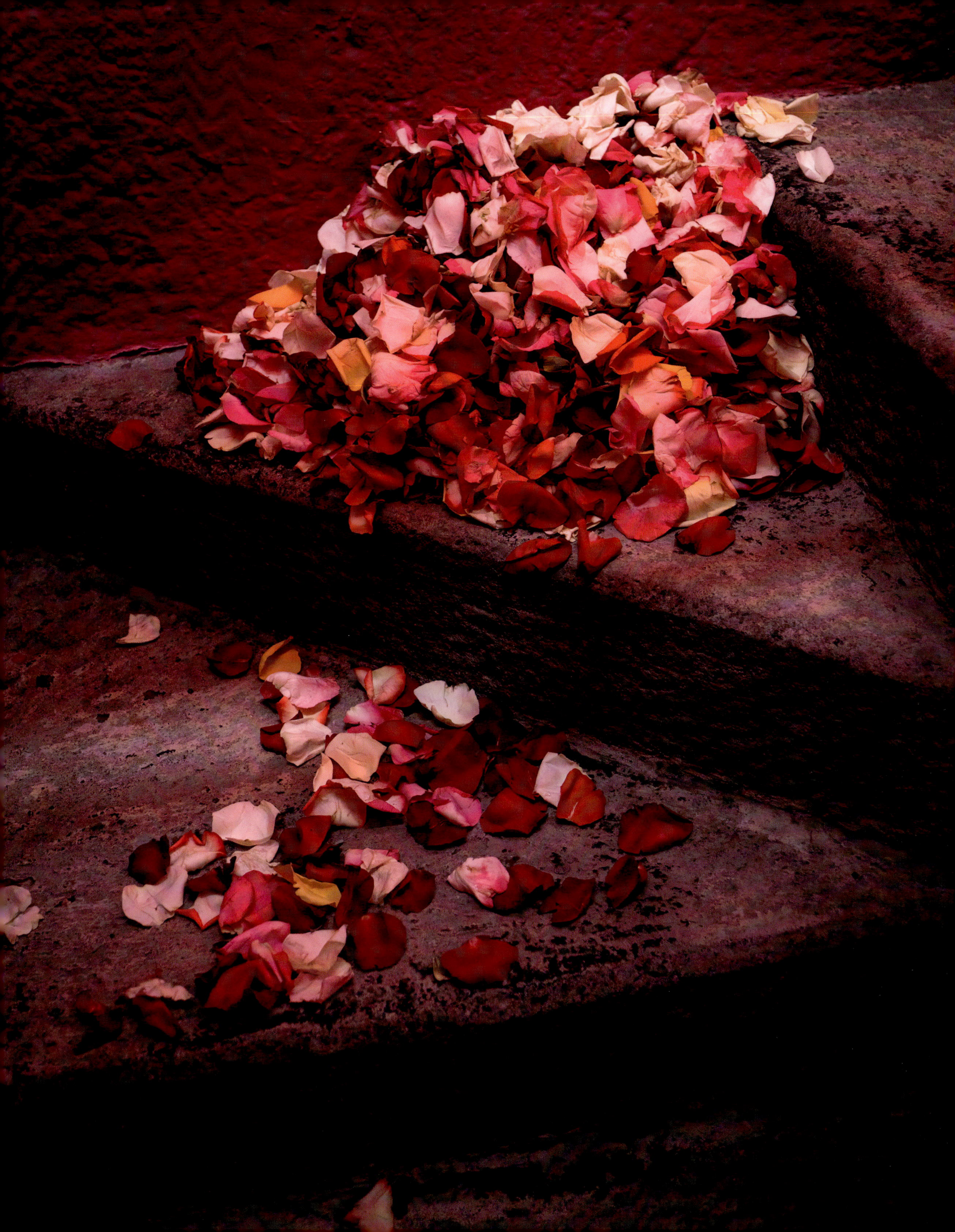

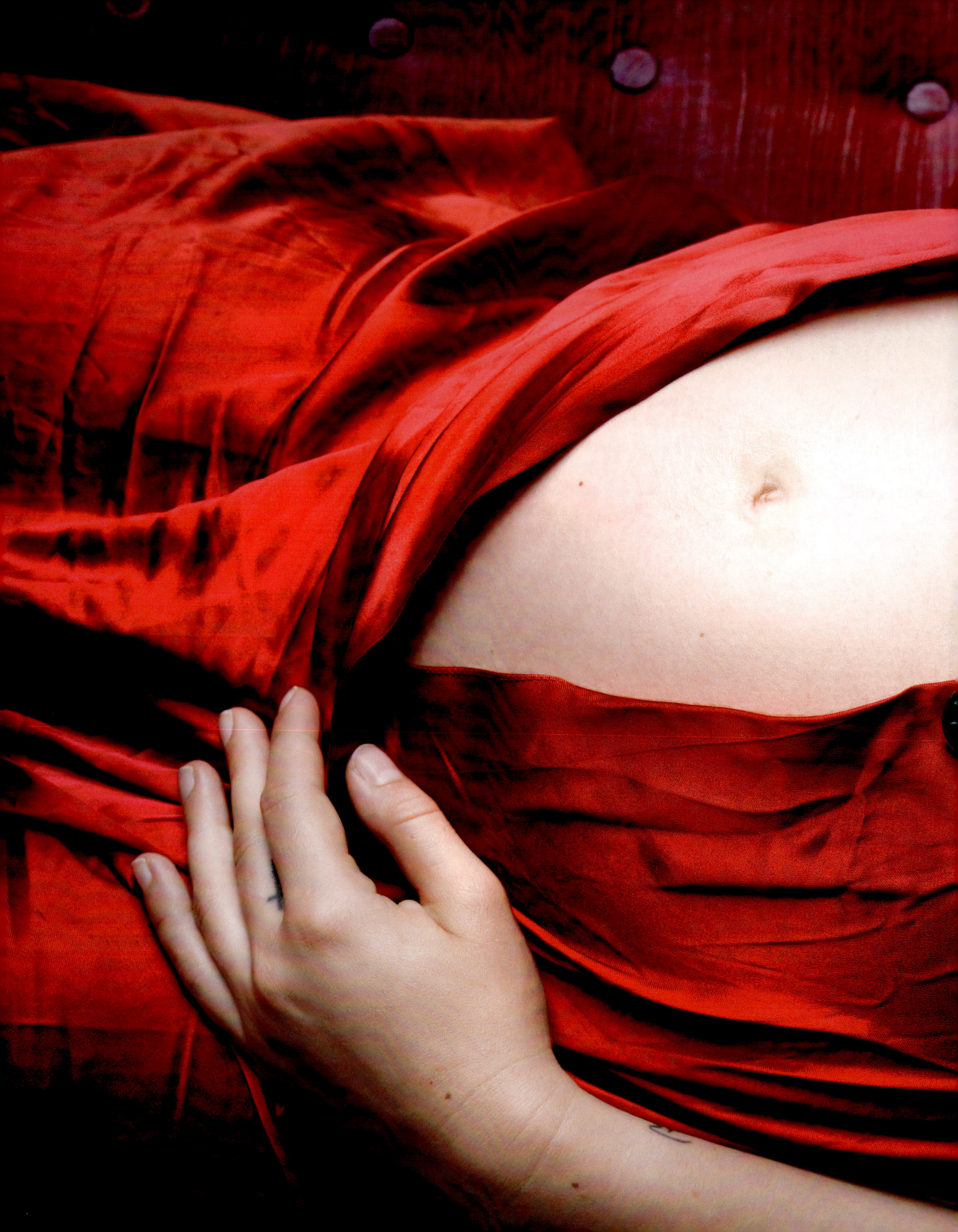

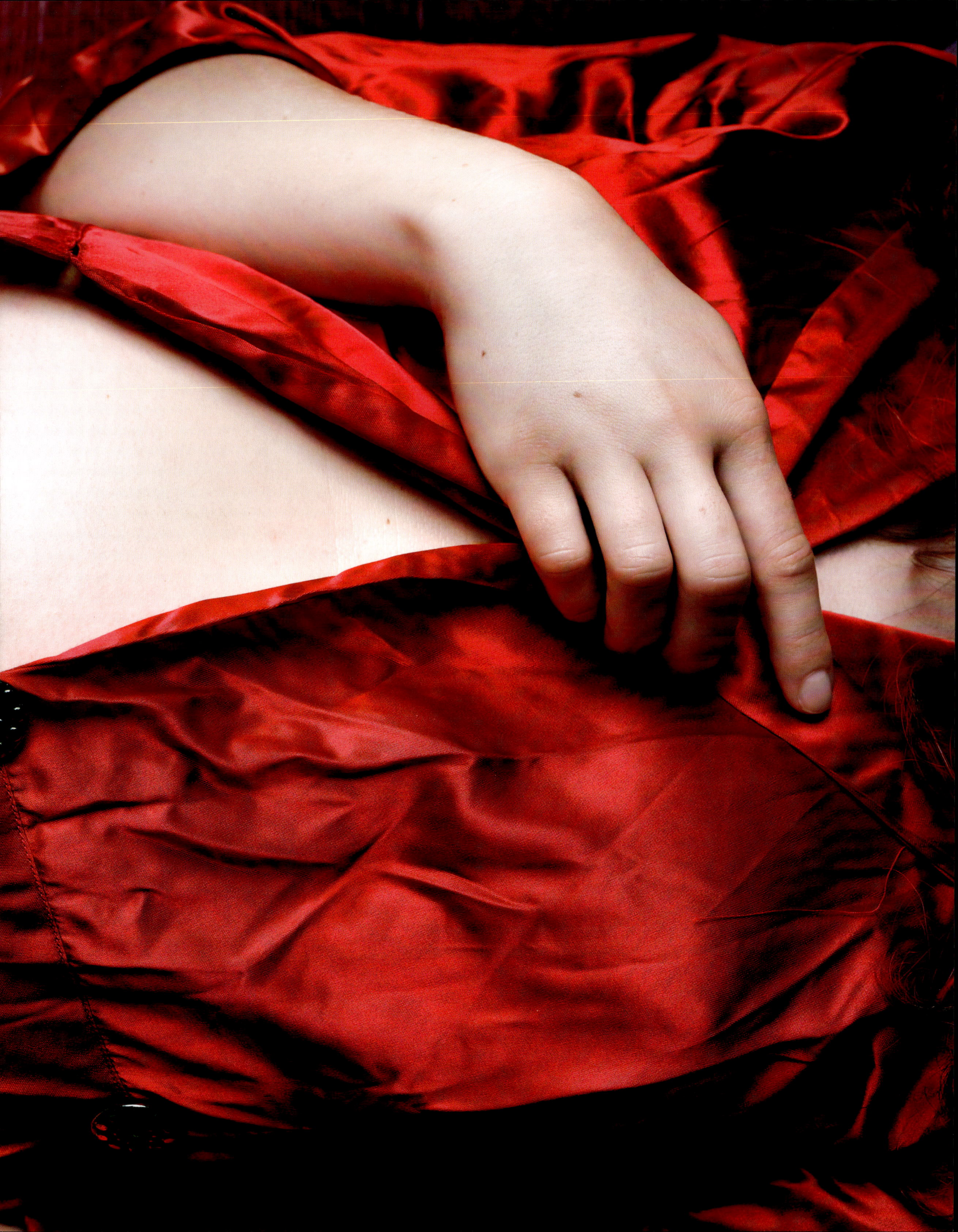

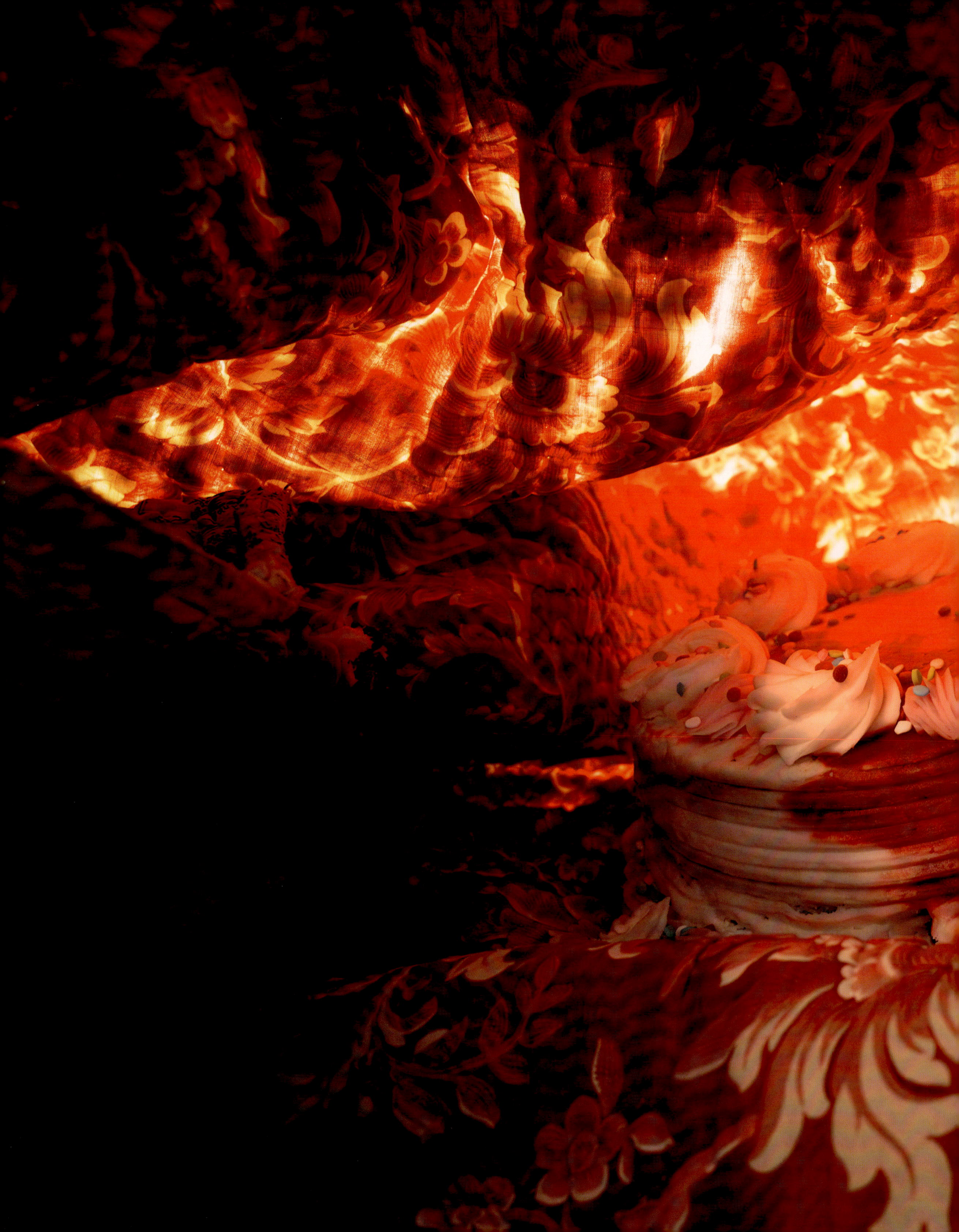

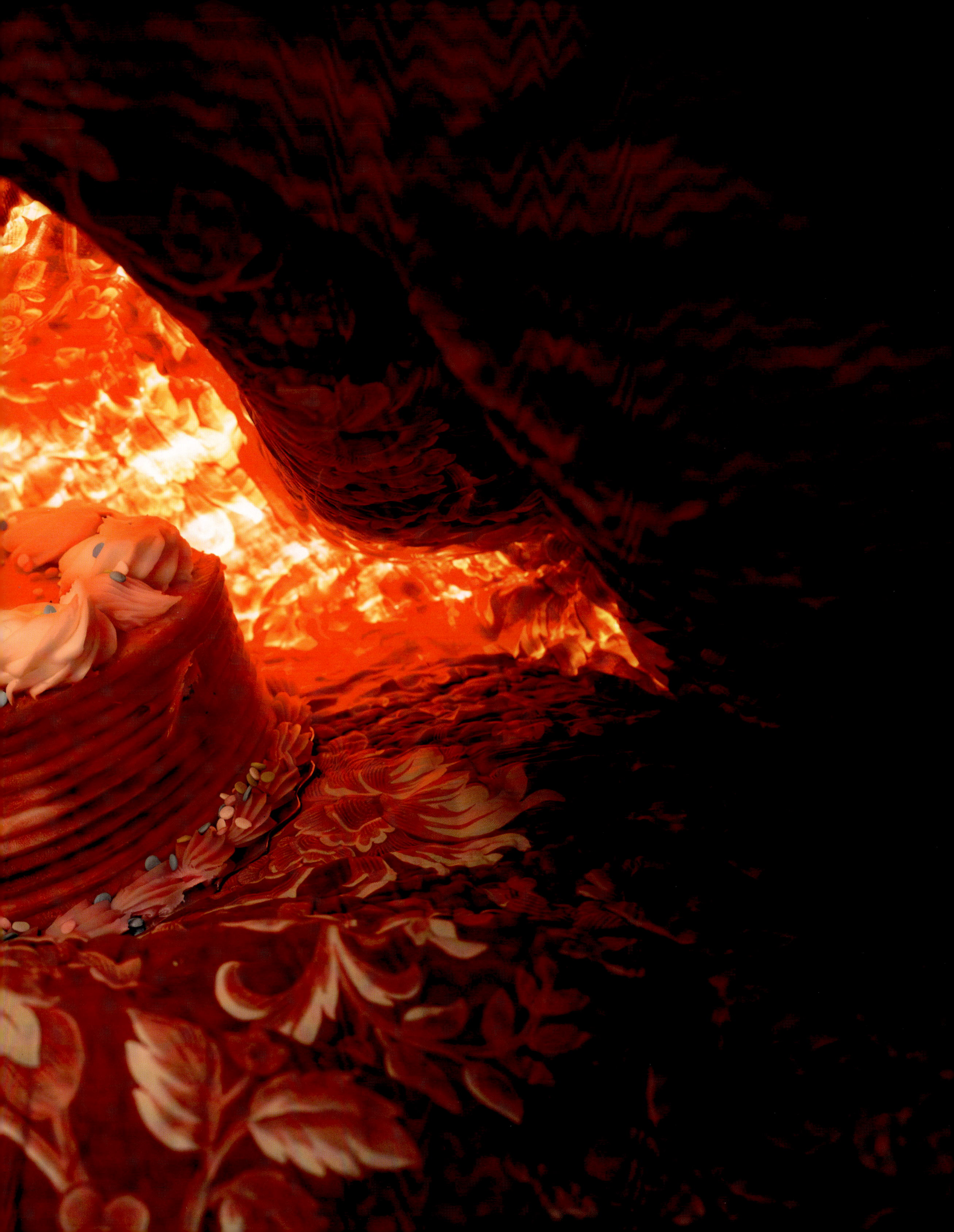

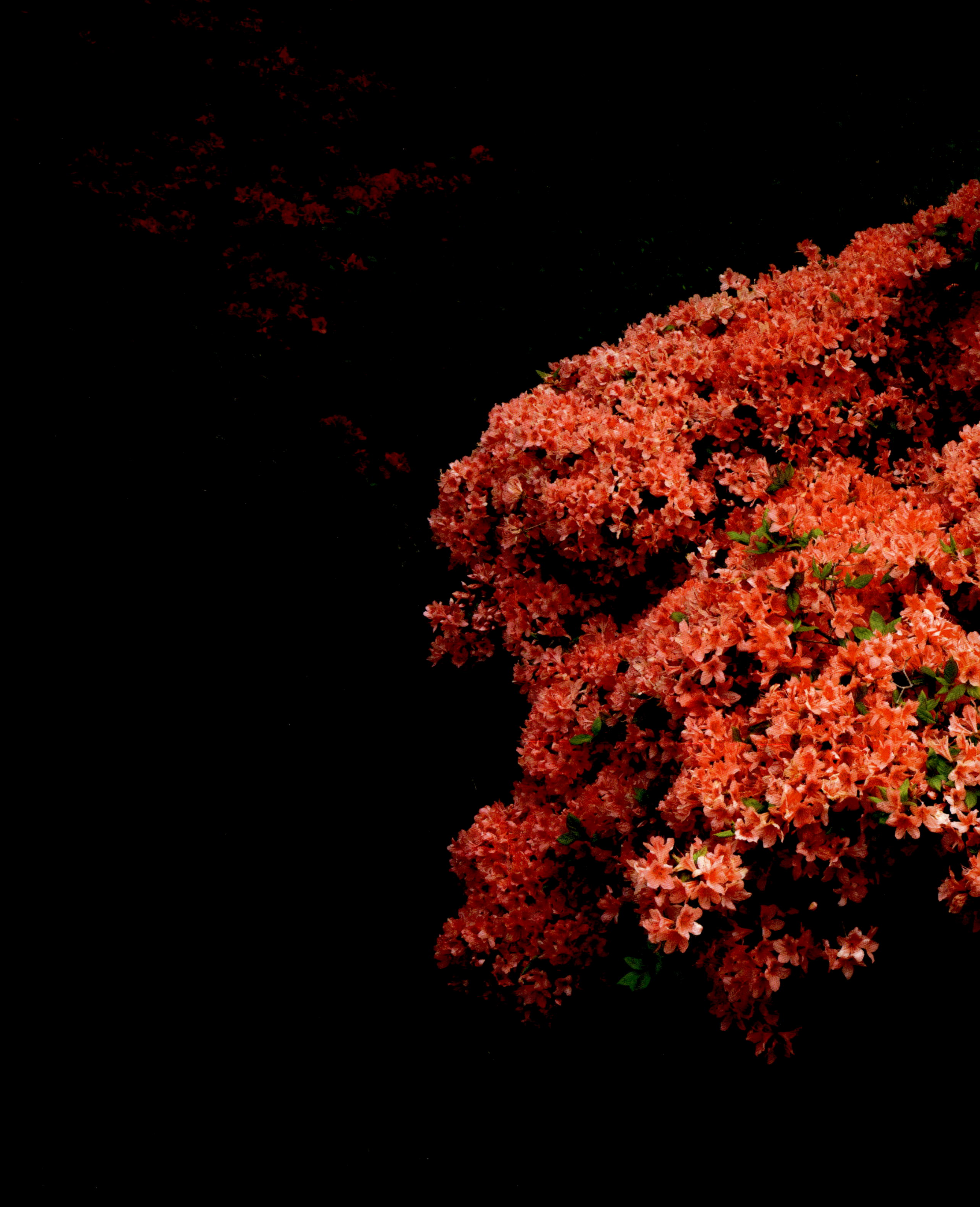

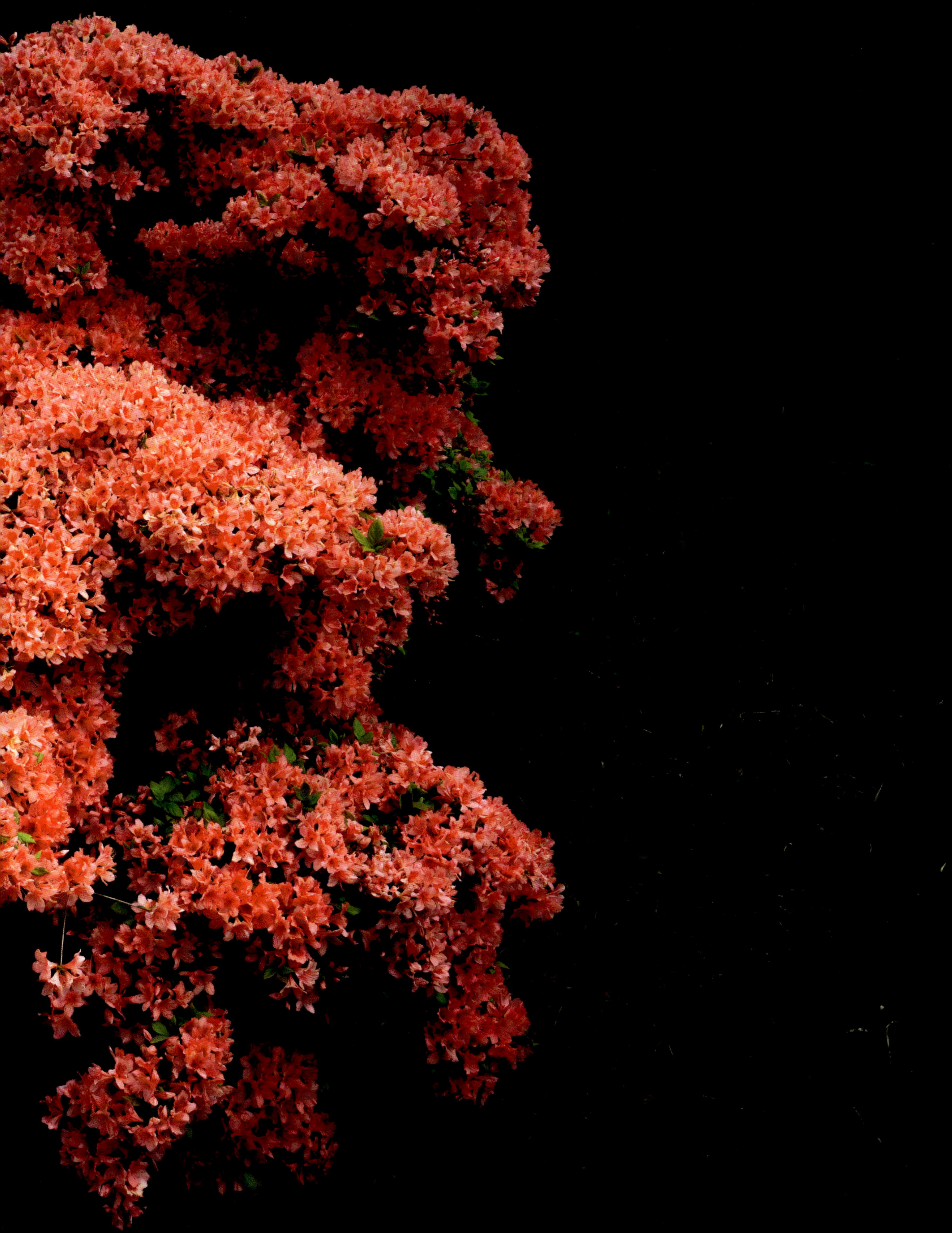

Off the coast of Maine, on the island of Vinalhaven, a small antique shop sits on stilts above the millpond. It's full of found treasures, everything and nothing you need. Drop me off in the morning, and I'll see you tonight. A verdigris whistle, a burgundy wine key with *Chateau de Chambord* engraved along the side, a small scarlet satin purse. Antique textiles and linens fill the tables and shelves, embroidered with initials and dyed in every color. Pinks and reds from madder and cochineal, a sea of blues soaked in indigo, blacks and purples from logwood, and my favorite, a radiant yellow dyed with goldenrod flowers.

Last night, I swaddled myself in a gold silk sheet like the woman in the Klimt painting and thought about the shaman I have been secretly seeing. She sings to me, *Surrender, my friend, surrender, that is only fear, my dear, surrender*, while she sweeps my body with a broom of feathers. The gold holds me, and I finally find sleep.

This morning, I google the painting *The Kiss* and am surprised to remember there's a man in the bed with the woman and he looks exactly like my husband Doug. I am having a lovely sleep, flushed and rosy-cheeked with sex, all warm in my golden blanket covered in swirls and clusters of scarlet and cobalt flowers.

## Last Night, I Slept in the Goldenrod

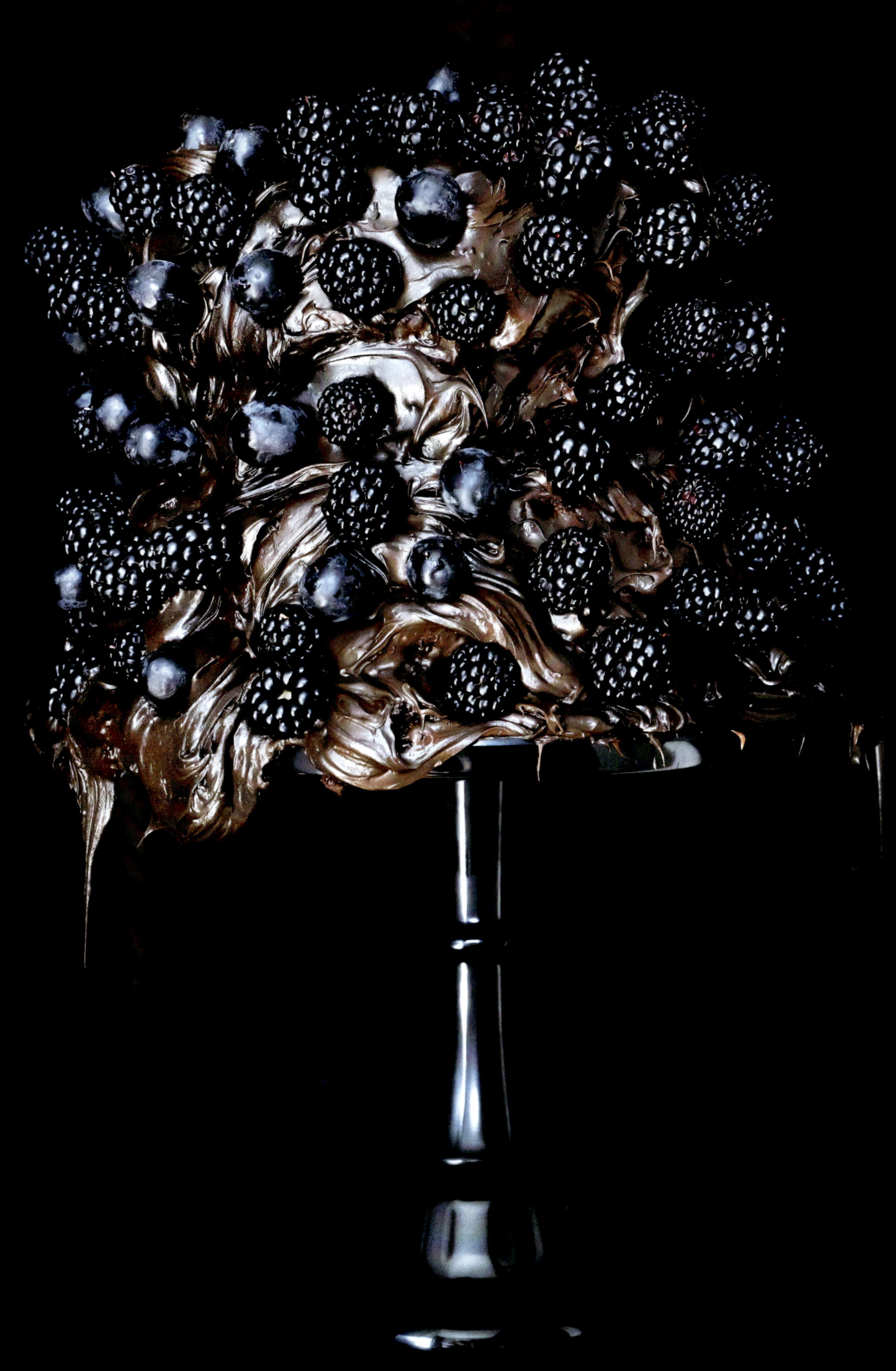

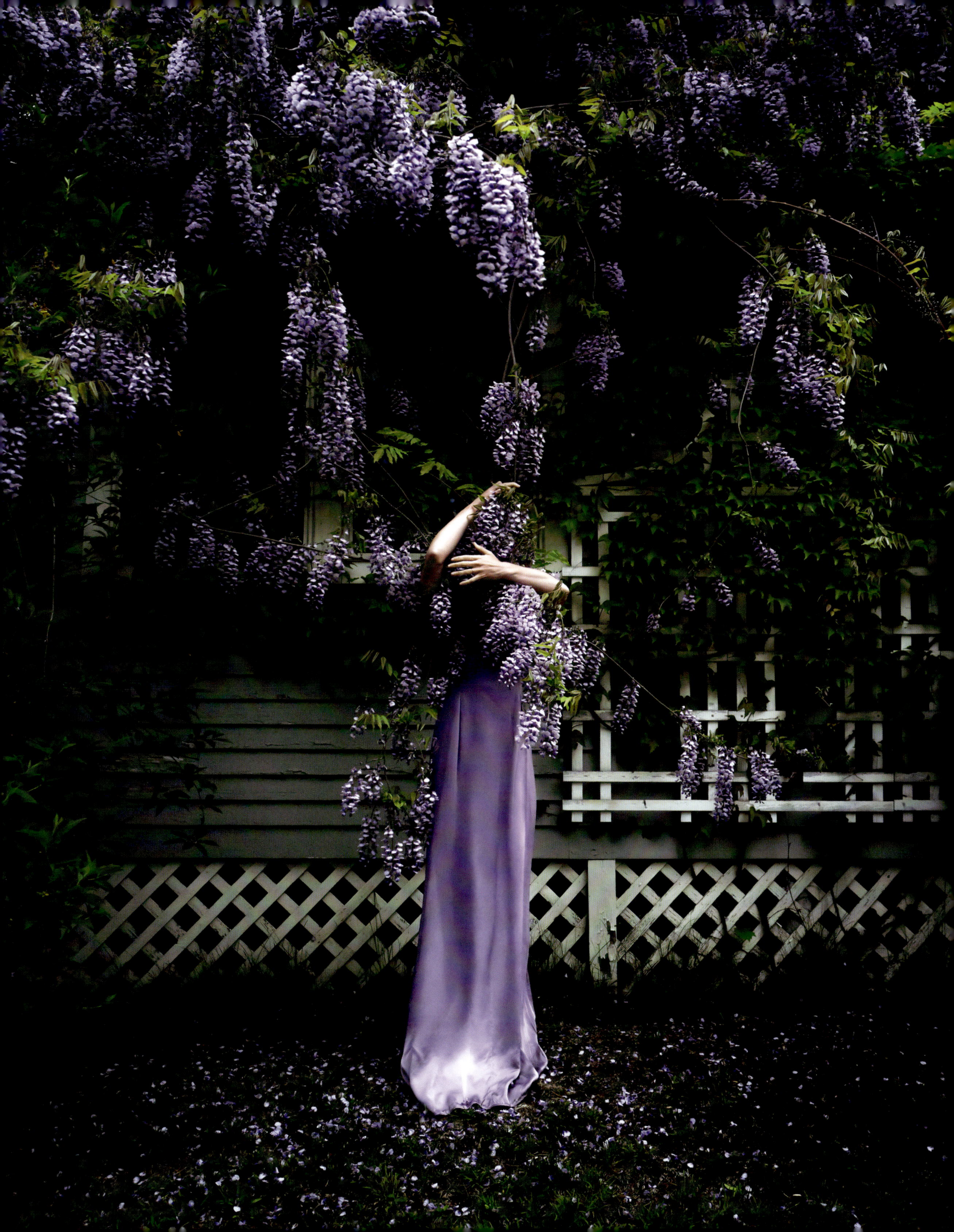

At the height of summer, the roses are climaxing. They are so alive, they can never be dead. Interior pinks writhing, bloodred lips licking, violent oranges ripping, throaty purples panting, breathless soft yellows, all gripping the flagpole, asphyxiating the fence, relentless in their demand to be on top.

Nature is screaming her own name tonight.

Roses have always been linked to excess, sex, and love. Julius Caesar would send a shipful of roses as a thank-you. Nero dropped thousands of roses from holes in the ceilings at parties, the original foam rave.

And every night, Cleopatra would leave her yellow saffron-infused bath for a bed covered in rose petals. I tried this once, but my wet body on the flowers made an orange paste and permanently stained the sheets. Gertrude Stein said *a rose is a rose is a rose. Yes,* I thought, *that's it*, as I later did the laundry.

Arterial<br>Blood<br>Red

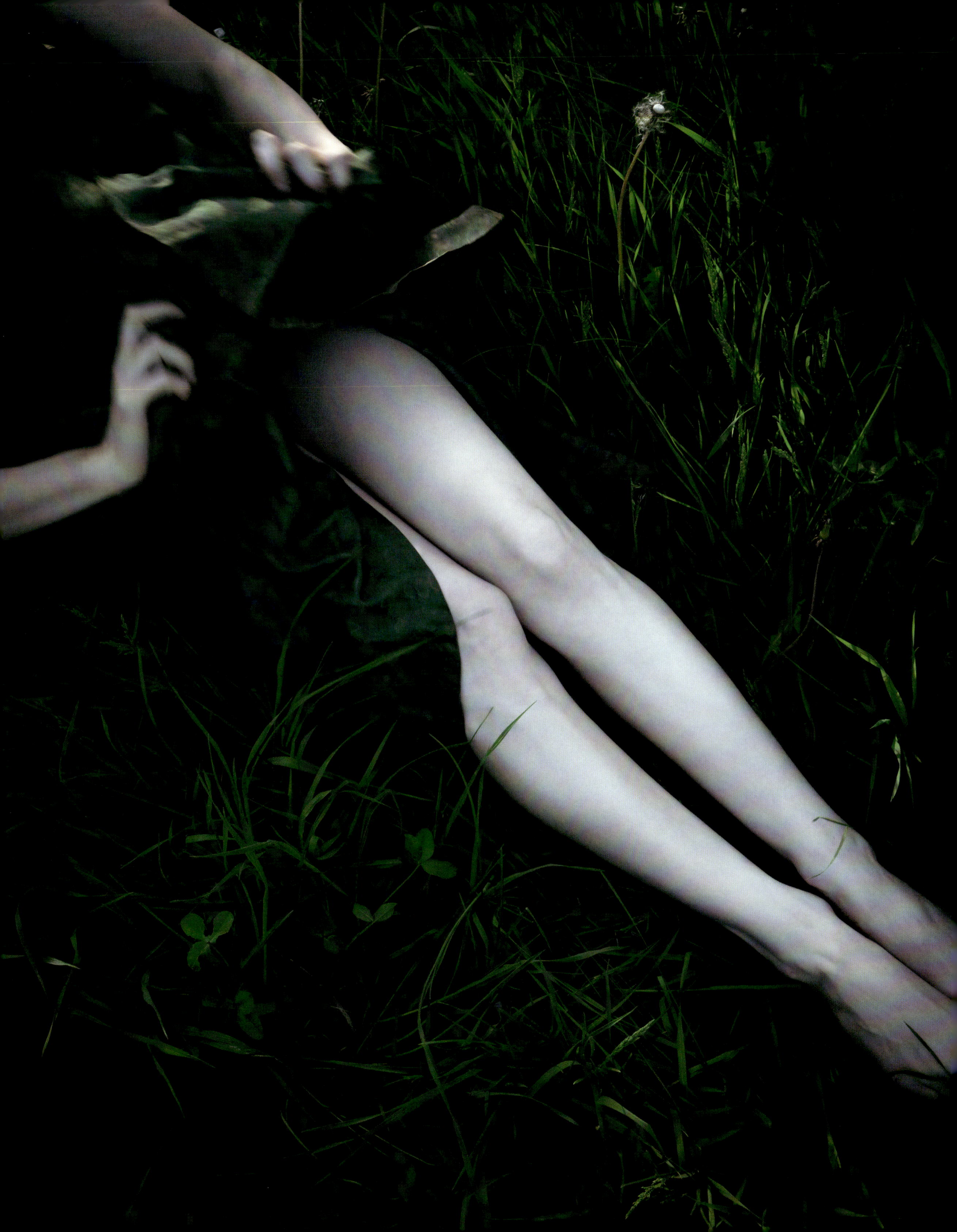

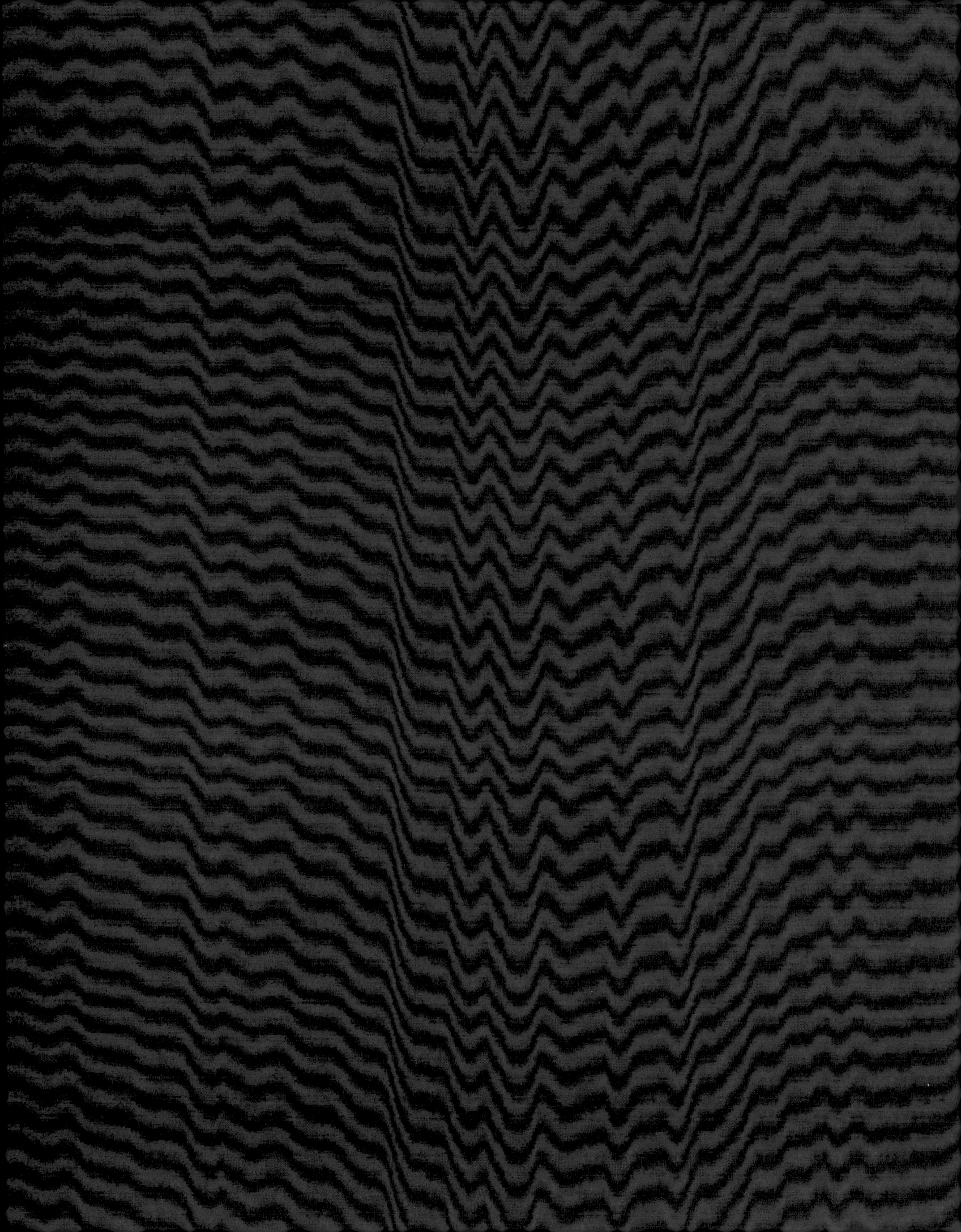

Nature is screaming her own name tonight.

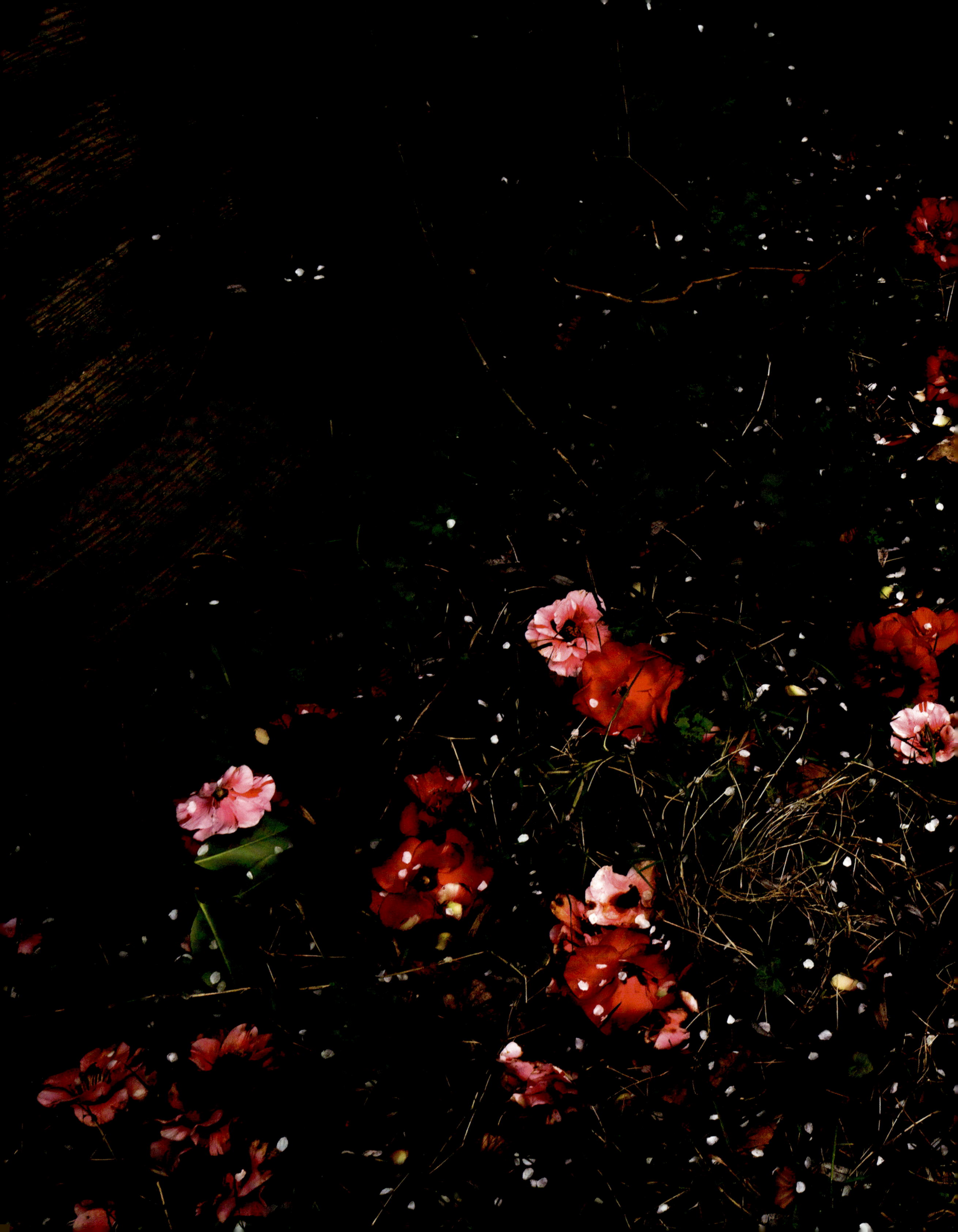

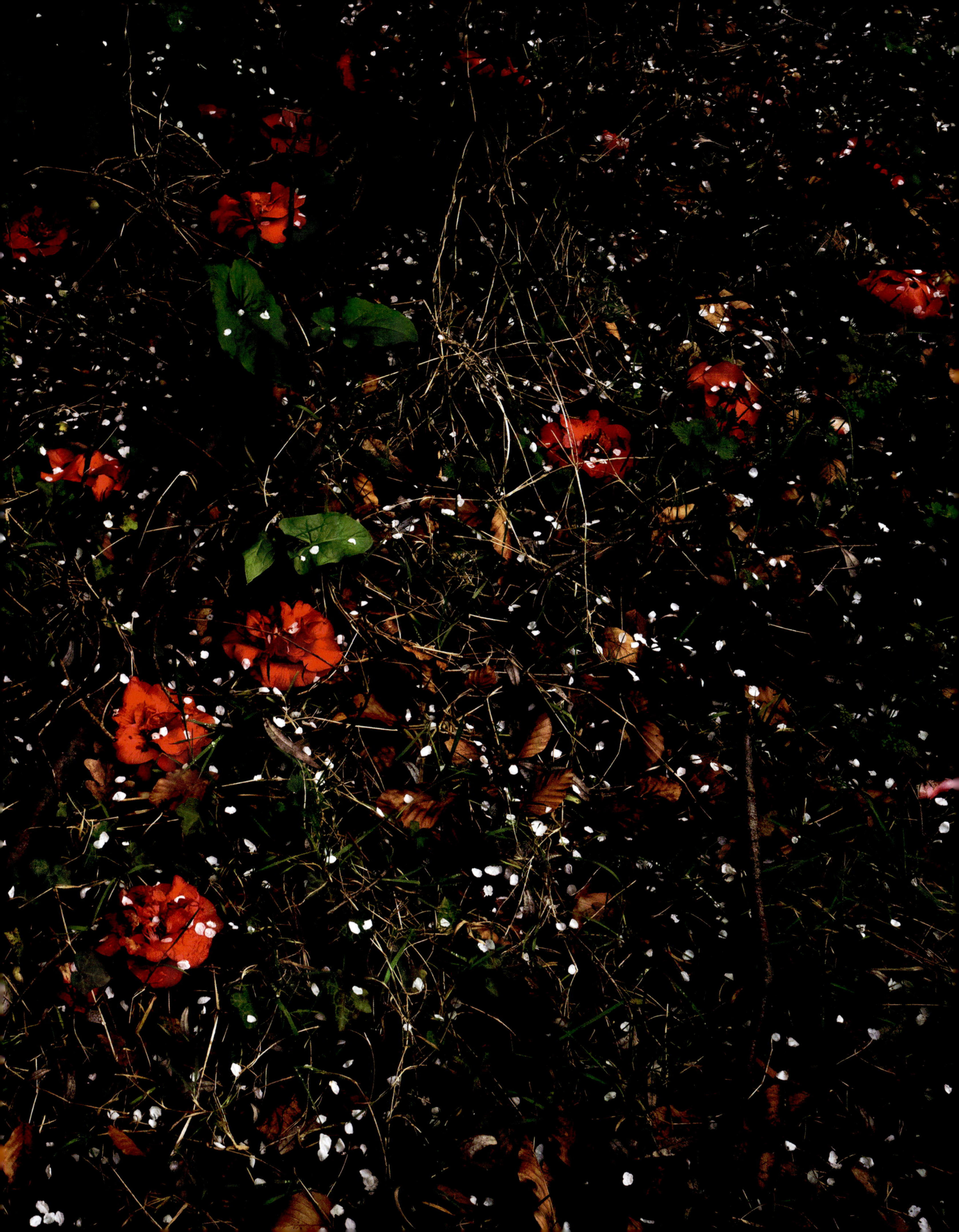

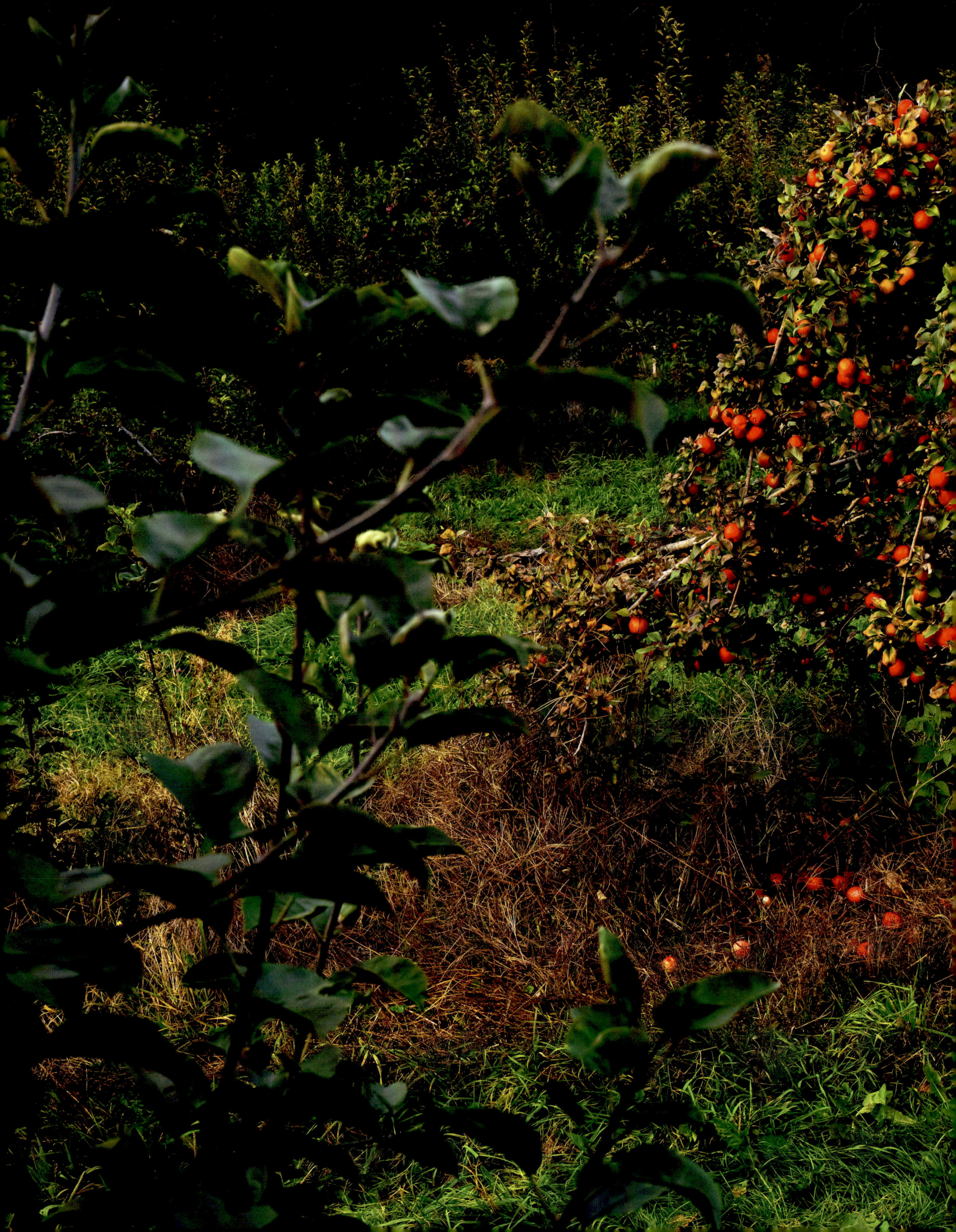

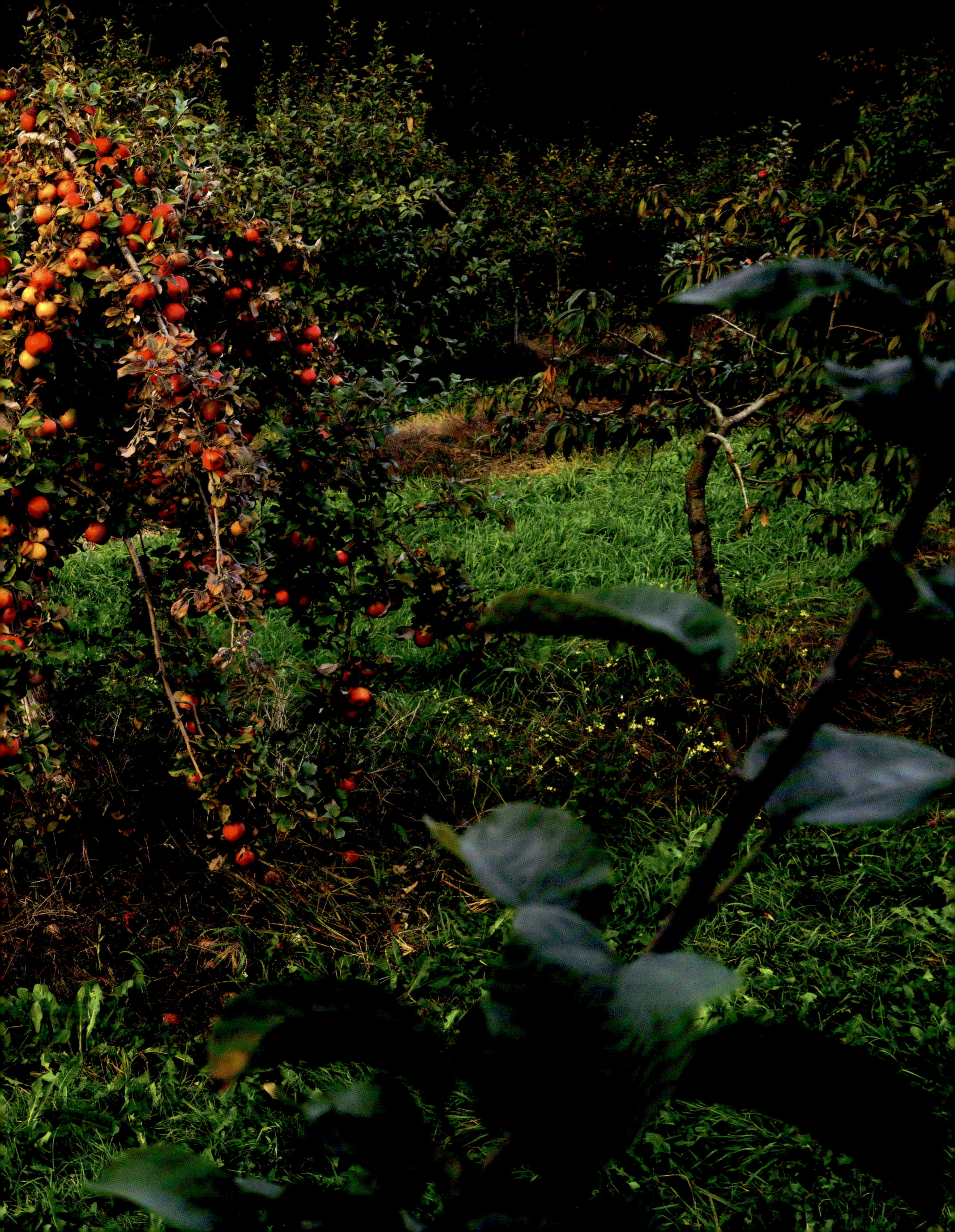

# Pink Cakes and Yellow Cakes

There is something so pleasing about the word *cake*. The sound is complete in the mouth. It's like the word *fuck*—two hard consonants right up against each other. Cake is definitive.

A few years ago, my friend Jesse taught my daughter Scout how to make a cake just like her mother Elizabeth had made them. Jesse's mum was the queen of the cake pile, and Jesse grew up in a world of wild cakes. There were no rules and no mistakes—cakes stacked in multiple layers, smothered with berries, flowers, and fudge sauce, oozing with icing, chocolate, and ice cream.

Cakes have been used since the beginning of time to celebrate, commemorate, and commiserate. We map our lives in cakes: birthdays, graduations, weddings, funerals. Good or bad, everyone has a cake memory.

Traditionally in England, the joint cutting of a wedding cake symbolizes working together as a team and the top tier of the cake is saved until the christening of the first child. Doug and I left ours at my dad's house. One day the fan broke in his fridge-freezer, and without a thought, he threw everything away, including our cake.

In utero, cake is the only food. The word *placenta* comes from *plakous*, the Greek word for cake. As children, cakes are one of the first things we associate with happiness, with freedom from routine. We are all born pleasure-seeking hedonists, becoming only more restrained with age. A basic cake is affordable, and many of us already have all the ingredients to make one in our kitchens—butter, flour, eggs, and sugar. These now common cupboard items are a recent luxury. In the past they were only for the elite. Sugar arrived under the weight of colonization and the slave trade. Cakes are not innocent.

Cakes—like flowers, clothes, and colors—have often been linked to the feminine. The phrase *a piece of cake*, meaning *It's so easy*, originated from the British Royal Air Force, none of whom had ever actually made a cake. Making a cake at home means you're a domestic goddess. In the 1950s, an era of perfection and Valium, angel food cake was invented, a cake so spirit-crushingly complicated to make, what woman had the energy to strive for more than a domestic life? Angel food cake, made of air from earthbound ingredients, needs a custom kitchen utensil to cut it, an object reminiscent of an ancient agricultural tool. You can often still find these puzzling little rakes in antique stores. Thank goodness the sixties brought us Little Debbies, Ding Dongs, and Ho Hos. Women started to ice their cakes with italic script: *I'm on the Pill* and *You Suck, I'm leaving you*.

The Greeks and Romans knew the link between cake, gender, and sex and were the first to create novelty cakes in the shapes of boobs and dicks. Cupcakes became a craze at the same time that the corset was invented. For a few dollars, the tiny waist of a cupcake, topped with an explosion of frills and ruffles, is a perfect way to bring fantasy into the everyday. When my friend's brother's contortionist girlfriend was on *Britain's Got Talent* dressed in a negligee and singing opera while eating cake in an inverted wheel yoga pose, the theater held its breath for three minutes and then collectively rubbed its eyes. I think of it often.

Cake is the perfect metaphor for the extremes of human experience: light and dark, pleasure and repulsion, heaven and hell. Cakes have shaped our culture, embedding themselves in art and history. Cake is for desire and pleasure: that's its only raison d'être. But cake can also trigger guilt and shame. Even as children, we know cake is divisive. Who gets the bigger slice?

Cake is often used as a literary trope symbolizing how to live—or not live—a life. The Cat in the Hat eats cakes in an overflowing bath with all the taps running: a maximalist's dream. Alice is seduced by the EAT ME cake, which turns her into a giant. And we gasp with joy and repulsion as Bruce Bogtrotter is forced to eat a whole chocolate cake as punishment in *Matilda*.

So we are primed, but perhaps still not ready, for Miss Havisham's rancid wedding cake in *Great Expectations*: a black festering mound that seemed to be moving and, on closer inspection, was alive with spiders—a dark mirror of the protagonist's heart. It is the only part of my college English Lit class I remember.

Virginia Woolf loved cake because cake is sexy, and sexy is the opposite of dying. Cake even looks like sex: hard bits, squishy bits, drippy bits, woozy caverns and erect peaks, and dollops of cream. She said, *I want to dance, laugh, eat pink cakes and yellow cakes... the older one grows, the more one likes indecency*. And then she filled her pockets with stones and walked into the river.

Sylvia Plath's favorite food was a vivid, blood orange tomato soup cake. She loved its color. Her journals were full of recipes, notes, and descriptions of cake. More cake than interior life, really. She baked a cake every single day, even on the morning she decided she could not go on. Her last smell was cake when she sealed the kitchen door and windows and replaced the cake with her head, the oven still warm and fragrant.

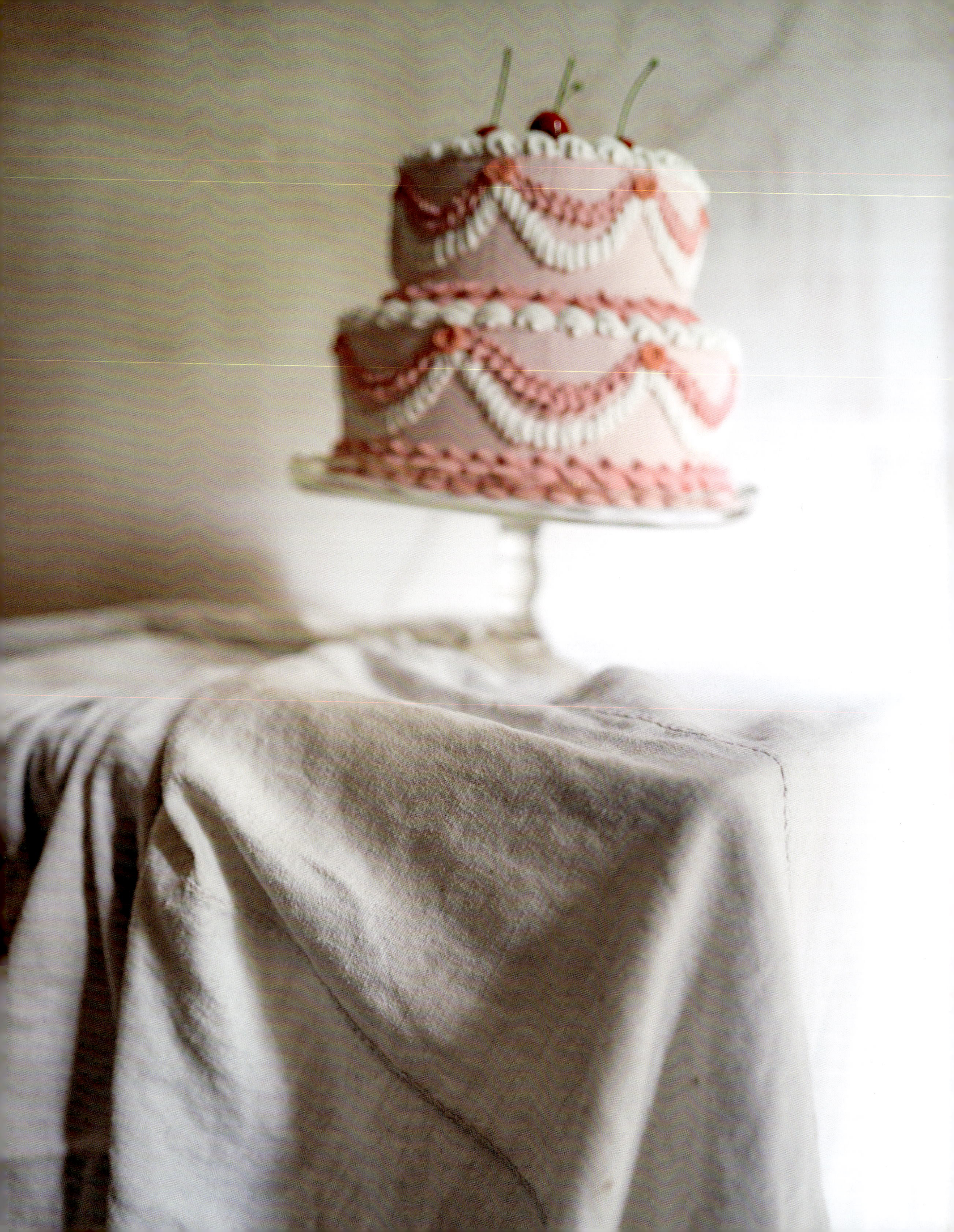

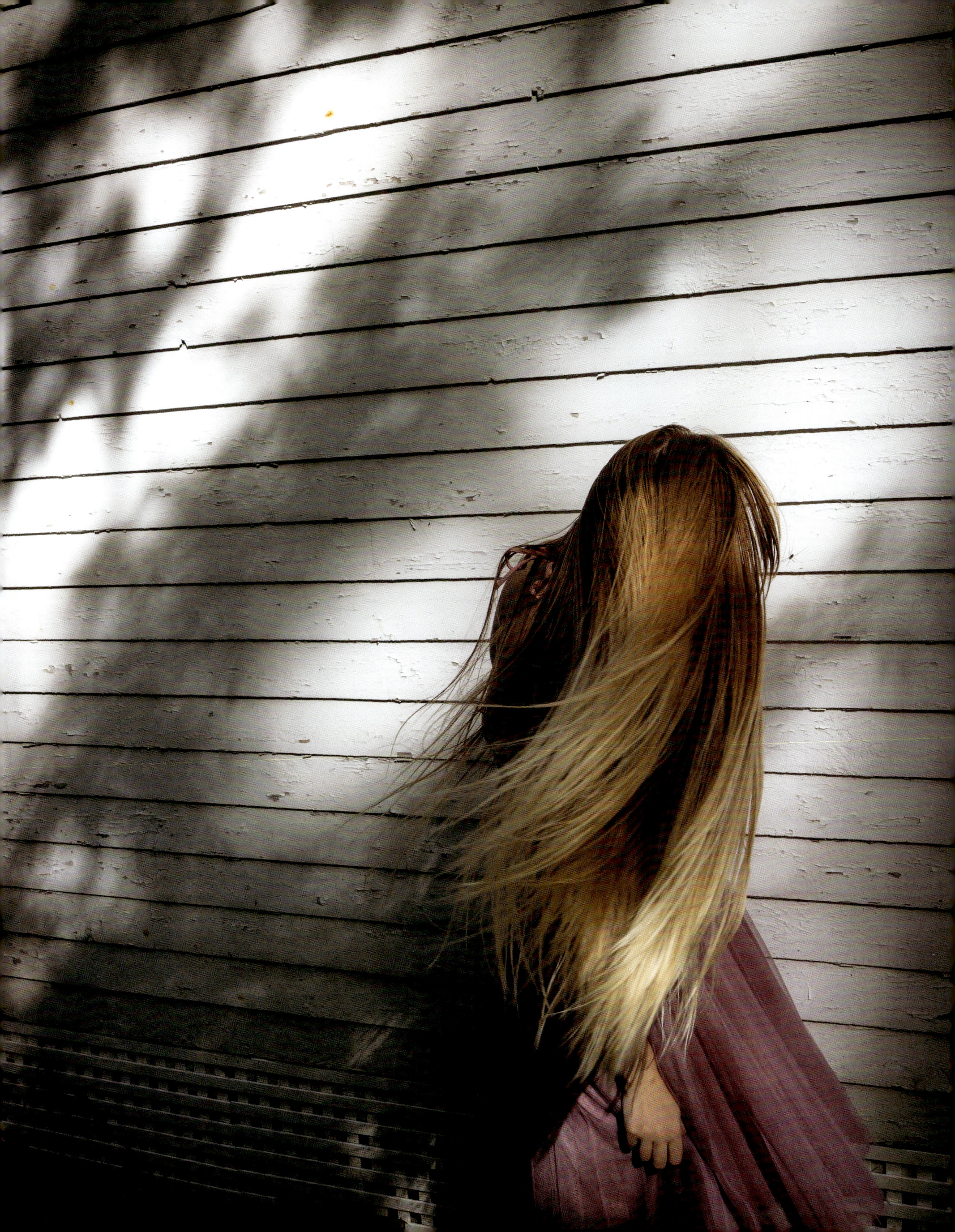

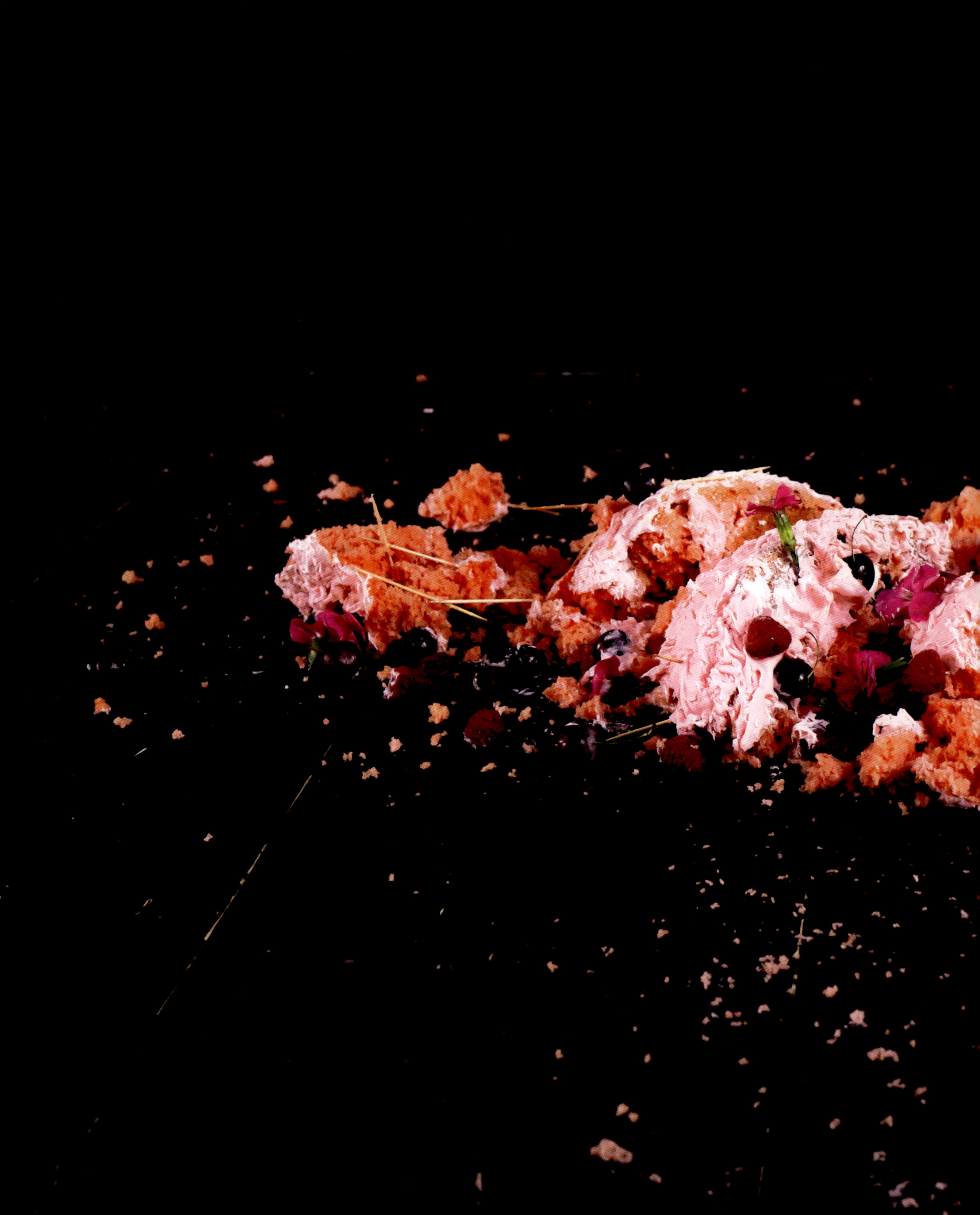

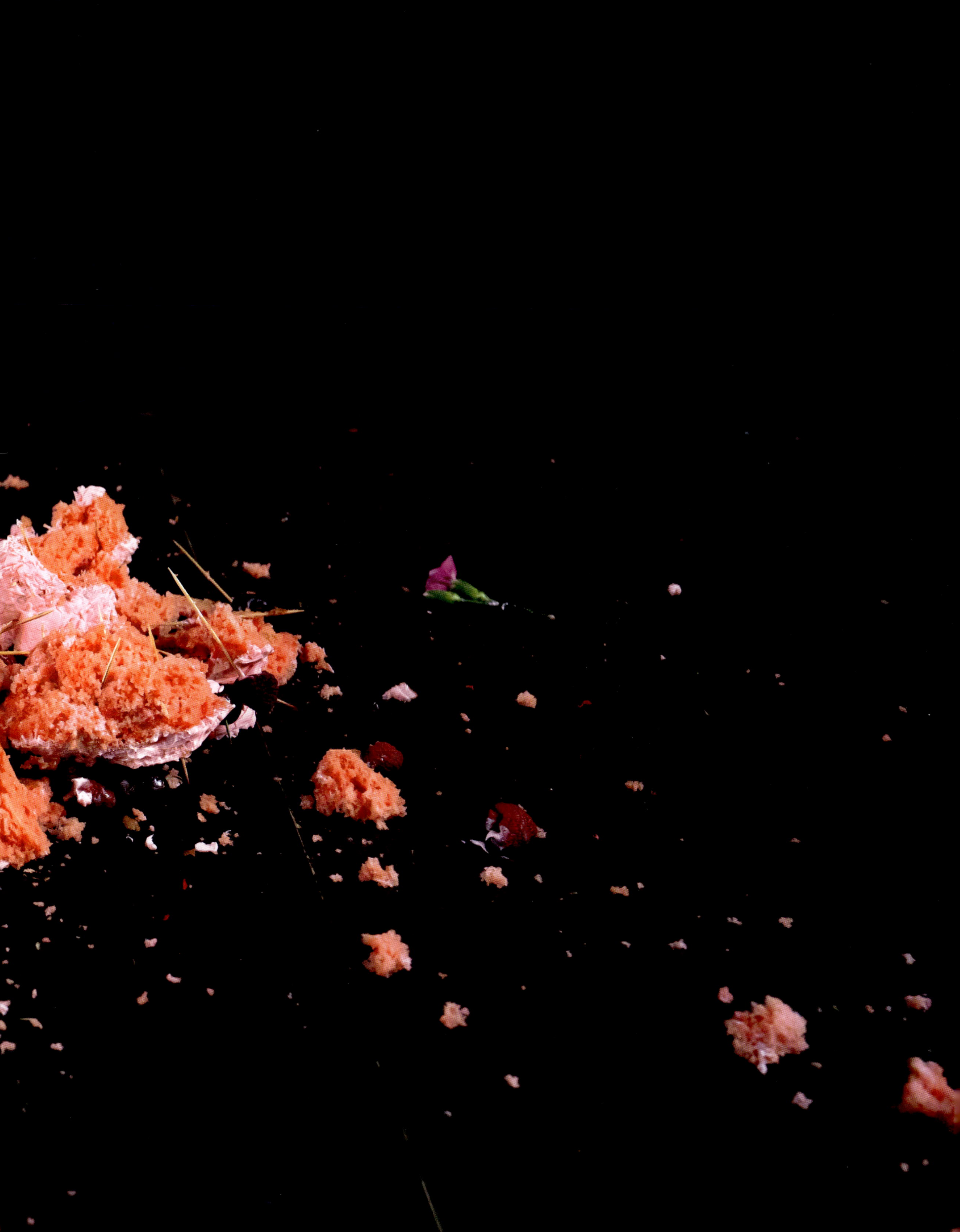

My friend Jean loves both color and cake. Lemon cake, strawberry shortcake, carrot cake, coconut cake, the white spiral of a Swiss roll, the pink and yellow grid of a Battenberg, Mississippi mud pie with its geological layers of earth browns, pound cake, cheesecake with its wounds of red, kaleidoscopic marble cake, the fireworks of Funfetti. After she's done eating, she picks up the plate, closes her eyes, and licks it clean. Her body shudders. Taste is her primary source of pleasure.

Last year, she was diagnosed with vascular dementia and then her husband left. Her mind is melting.

When I visit the care home, she is lying on a lilac-colored La-Z-Boy in front of the TV, listening to a country music channel and watching a slideshow of better times on a loop. On the nightstand there are two books someone has gifted her. The first, *How to Welcome the Unwanted*, and the second, an empty journal meant to record her thoughts and activities. I open it to the first page and the only word she has written is CHOCOLATE in large wobbly letters. She doesn't want either of these fucking books. She wants pleasure, and she wants it now. Cake, red lipstick, the feel of velvet under her fingers, a pink coat, a purple shawl, coffee ice cream, and stories of Paris.

When dying, beauty is the only language worth speaking.

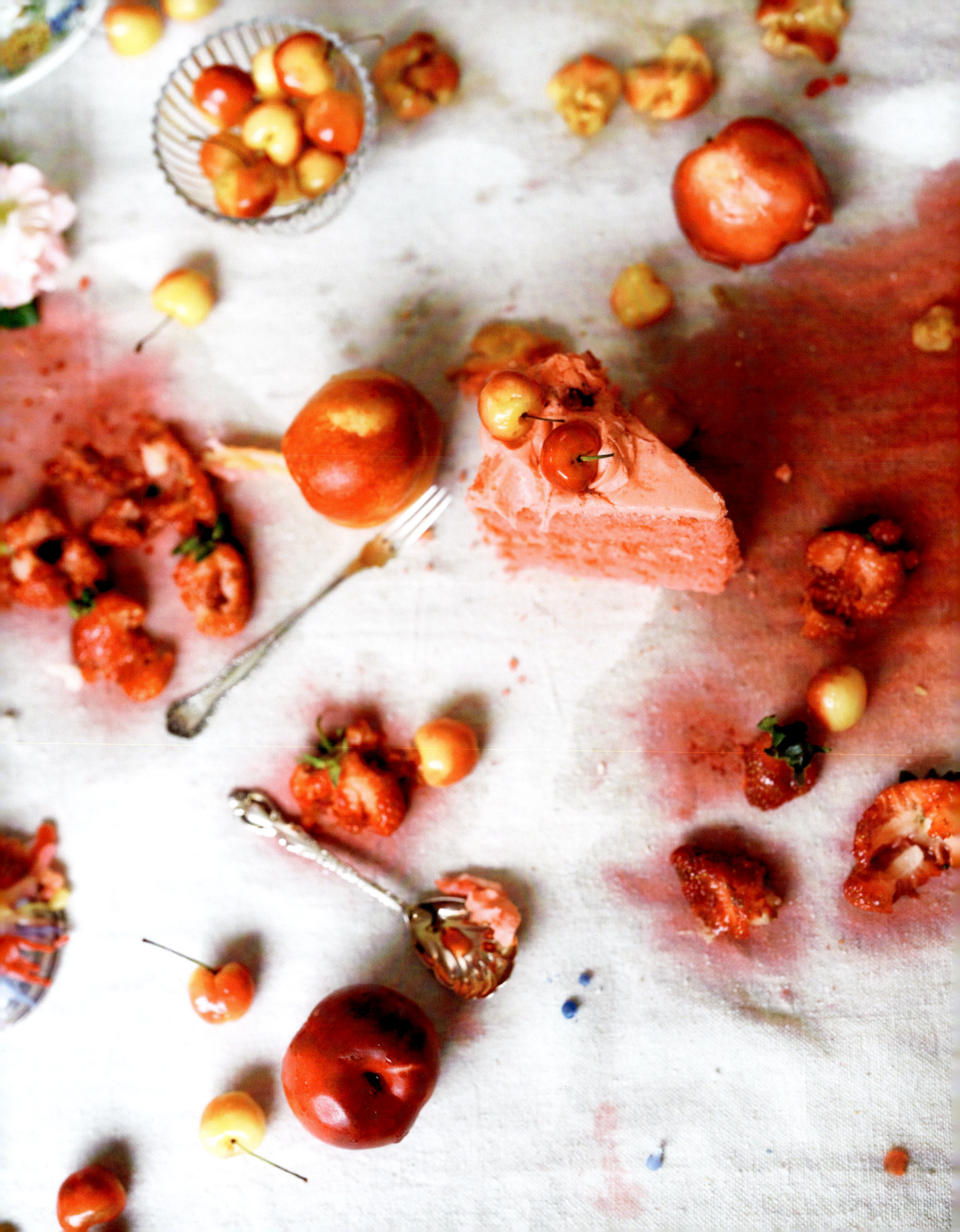

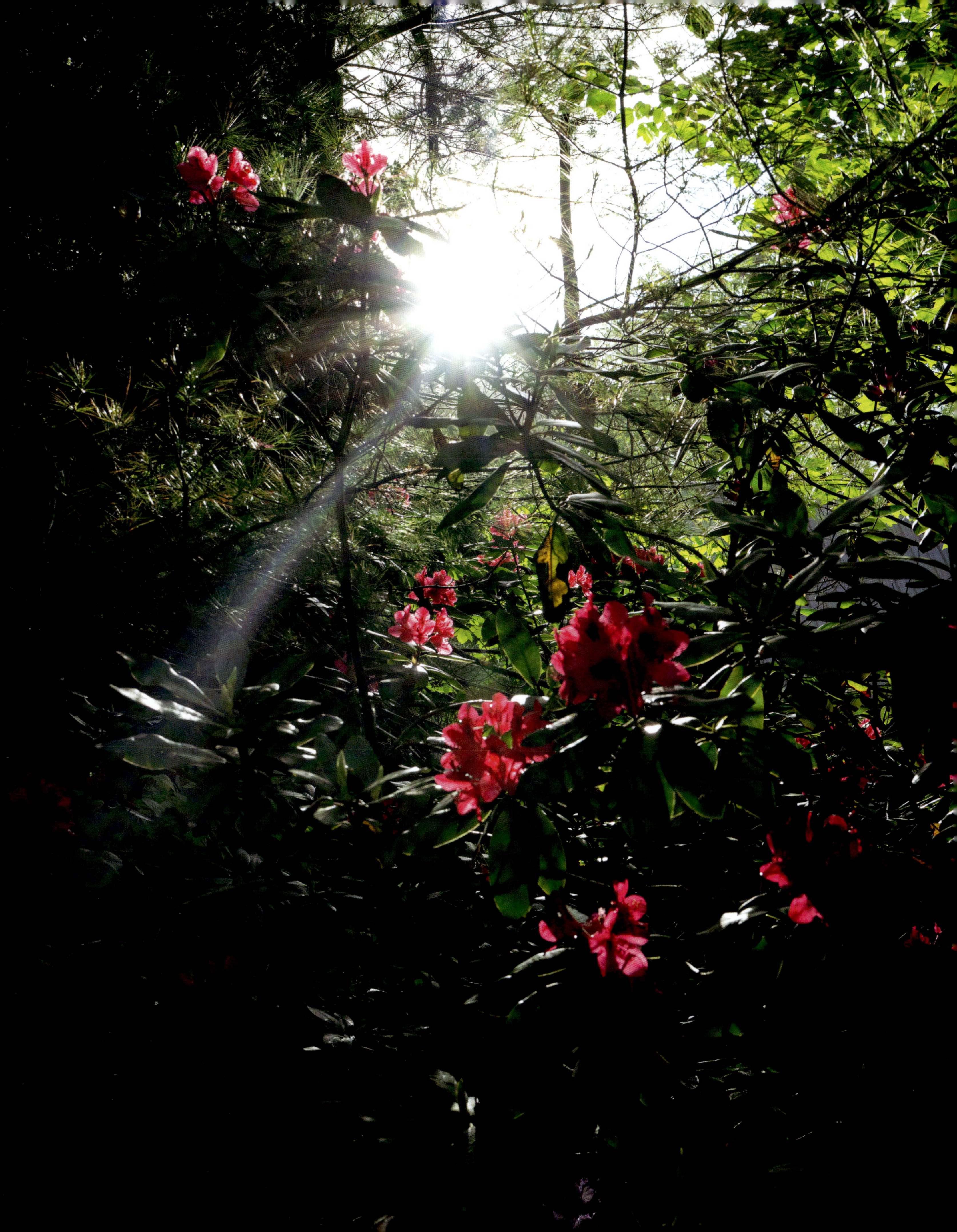

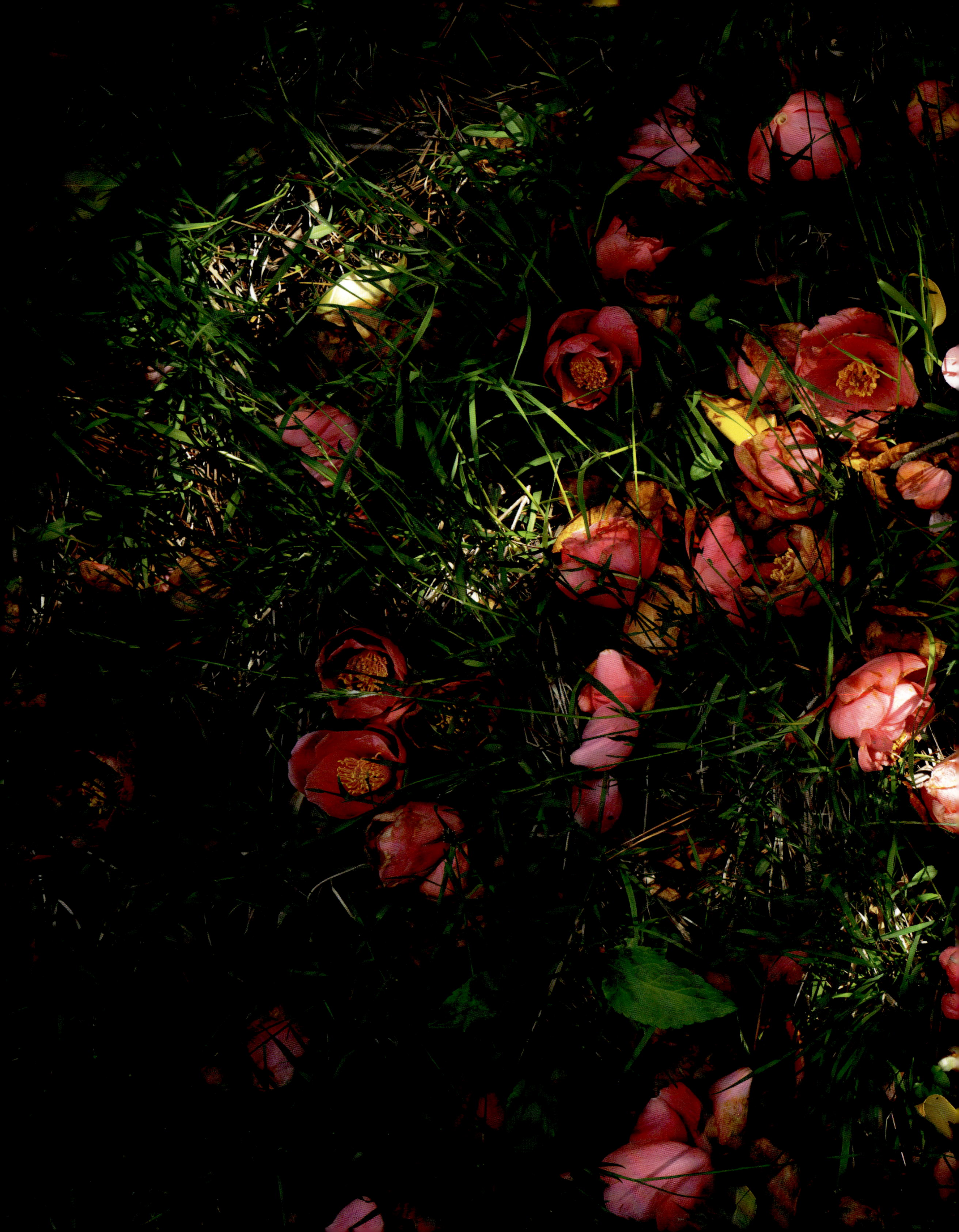

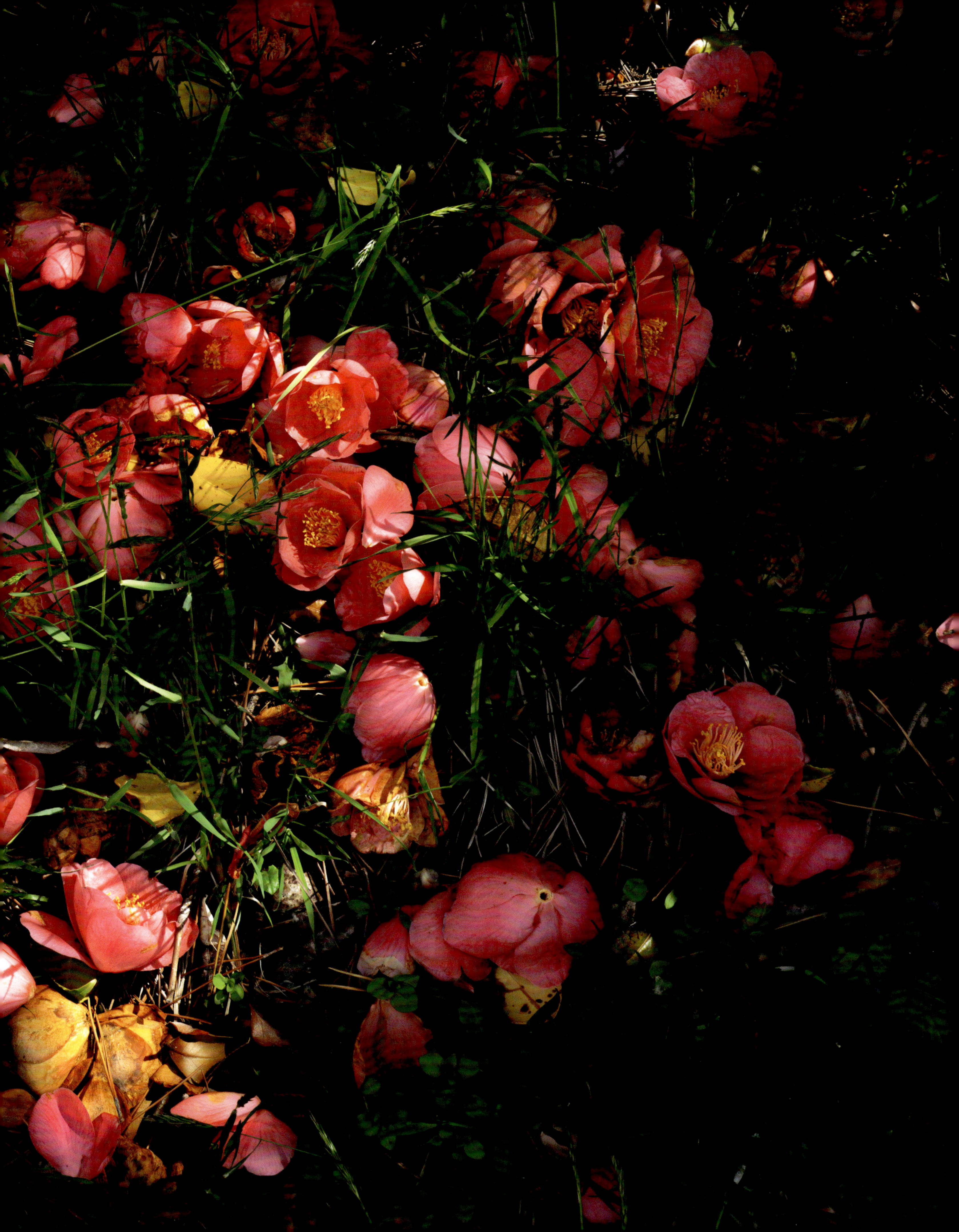

# The
# Color
# Wall

I keep a twenty-by-eight foot wall in my home studio empty and paint it the color I want to be surrounded by, the color I need in my pictures, the color I want my body to absorb and reflect—a color that clashes or balances my outfits, skin, and mood.

The paint gets thicker and thicker each year. By the end of my life, the wall will be out into the middle of the room, the years cataloged and marked. We can never move.

When I was pregnant, I painted the wall a soft pink to match my baby, but it felt too sweet: it wasn't the rope I needed to pull me through the monotony of the first year of parenting. I kept adding darker and darker shades of pink until I ended up with Benjamin Moore's violent magenta Razzle Dazzle.

The following winter, I painted the wall gold, folded one hundred paper cranes, and pinned them in a *V*-shape flying south.

Six months later, I painted the wall silver, hung a disco ball in the window, and wrote short staccato sentences about time in a 2H pencil every morning.

As summer ended, I painted the wall a teal green (misnamed Aruba Blue) to match a dead cormorant I had found in the middle of the road. I arranged it in front of the green—a still life. Scout, then a toddler, shushed me, pointer finger to lips, and whispered, *Why is the birdie always sleeping?* Cormorants are one of the only birds whose wings become waterlogged to help them dive deeper, so they must dry their wings at dusk, a sight that chokes me every time.

After that green, I decided to paint the wall a deep sapphire blue because sitting in front of that color makes me feel like a rich woman. (I usually only feel that rich when I have a box of forty Tampax, a case of Spindrifts—preferably pineapple—a pack of AA batteries, a book of stamps, an E-Z pass, and a full tank of gas.)

A few years later, after my best friend Mary died, I painted the wall her favorite color—a shade of warm saffron that will always be—Mary's Yellow. I would lean my cheek against that color to soothe myself when I couldn't stop crying. Color is a balm.

The year COVID hit, I dripped an orangey-red paint all over the walls and floor to make the room a vibrant tomato womb. I dragged my computer in front of it and started to dress only in pink, so the screen lit up like a beating heart on my daily Zooms.

And last winter, obsessed with Flemish eighteenth-century still lifes, I painted the wall a rich plum, but it dried to black. Each word I wrote became more and more internal until I was underground, digging deeper and deeper into the dark.

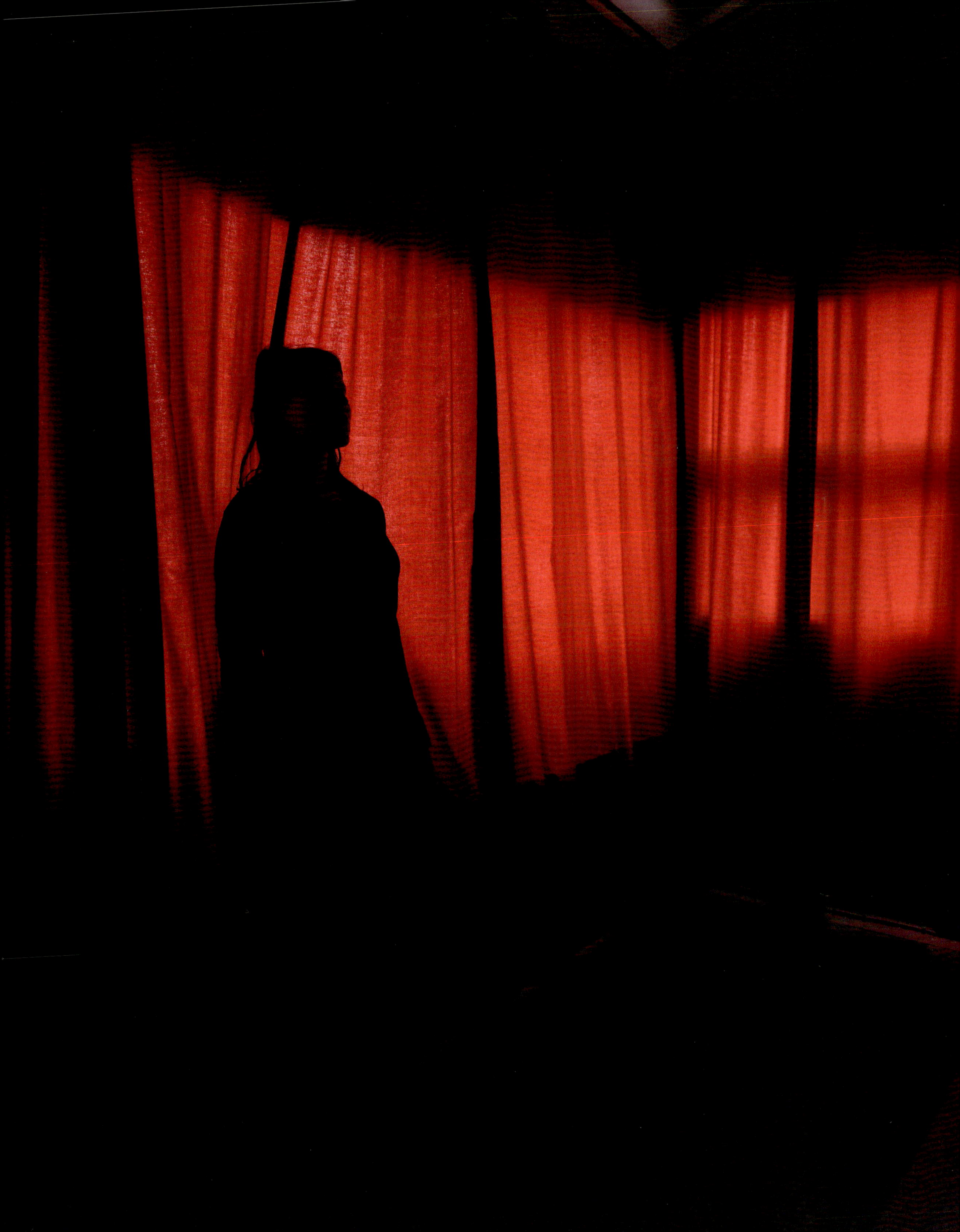

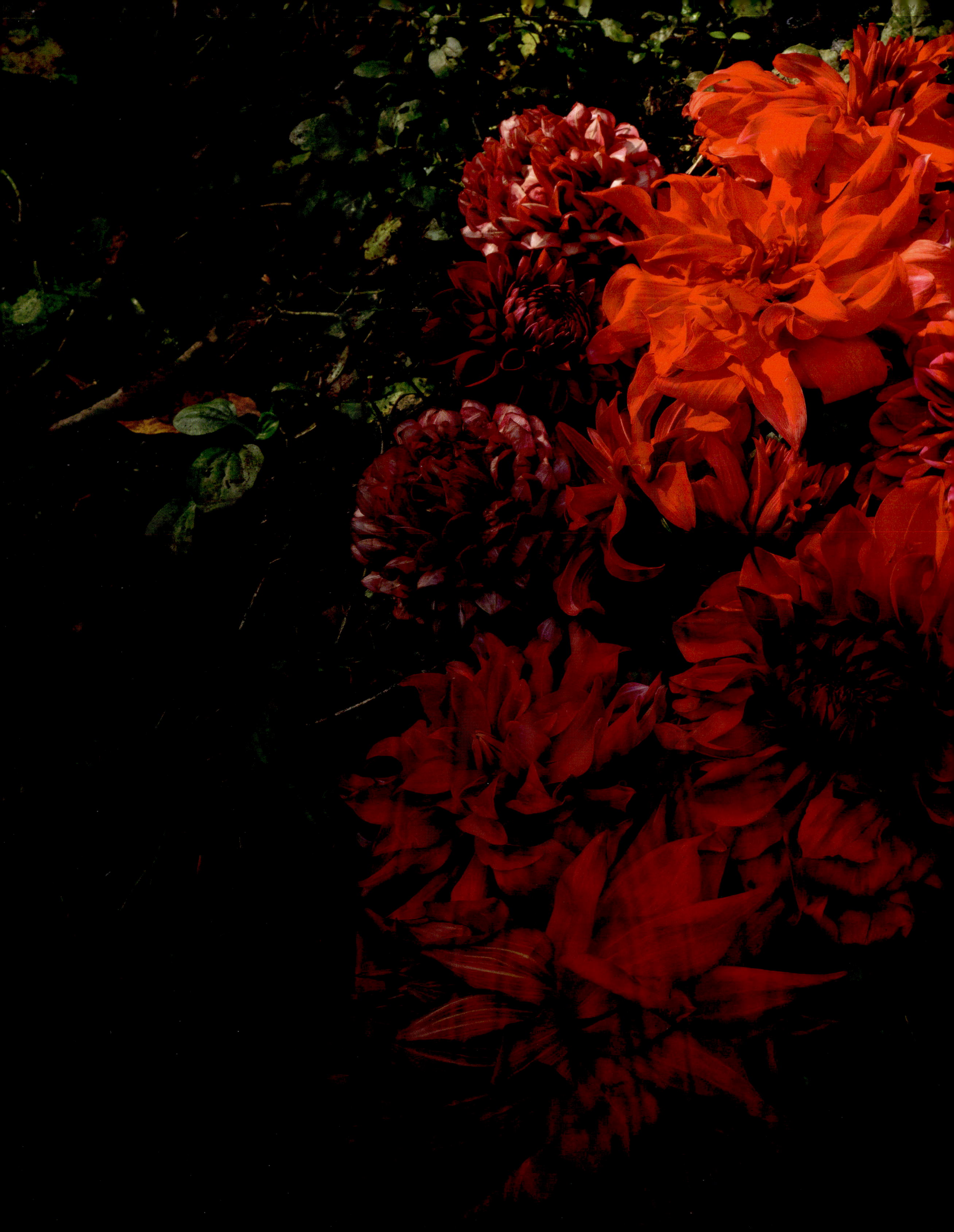

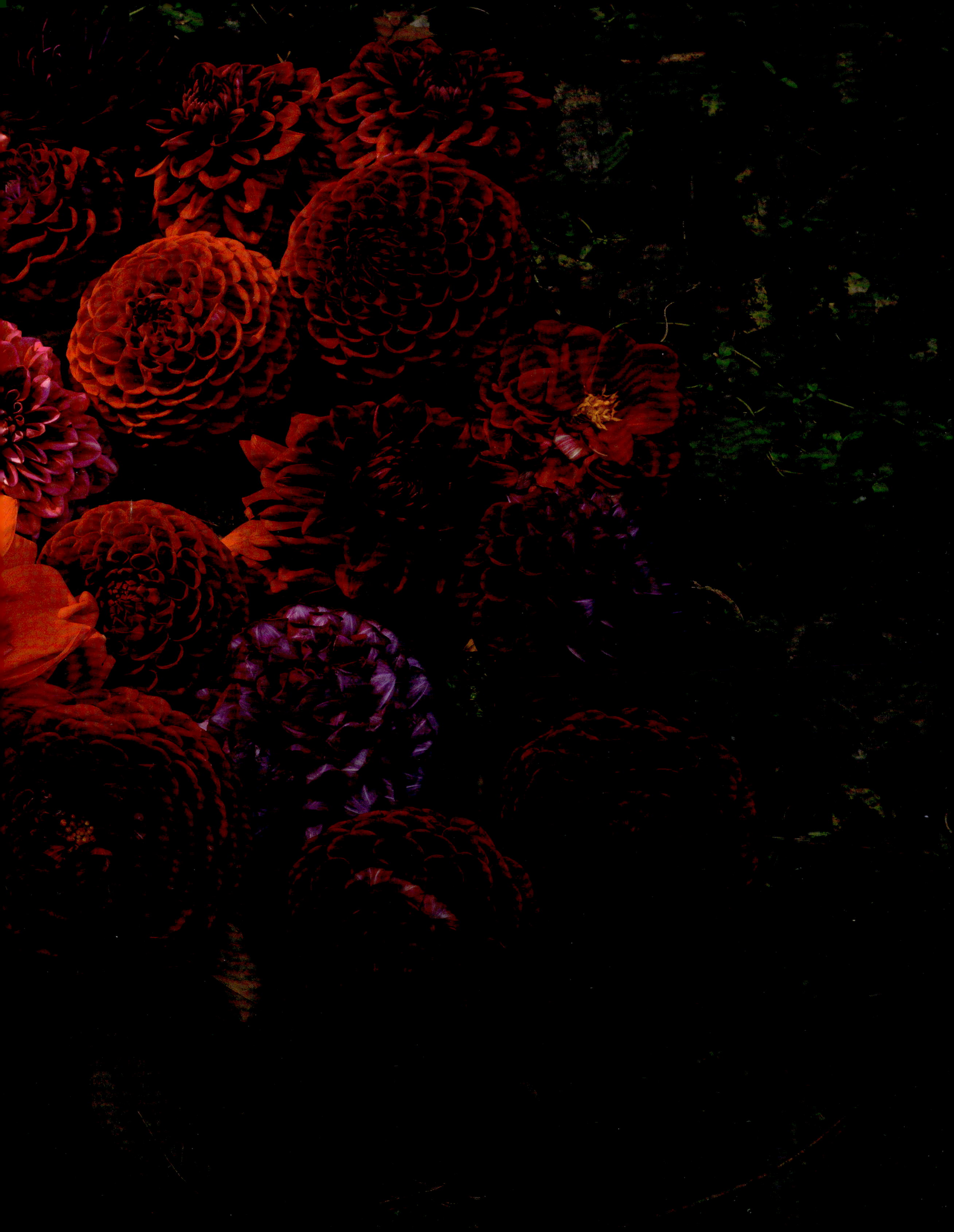

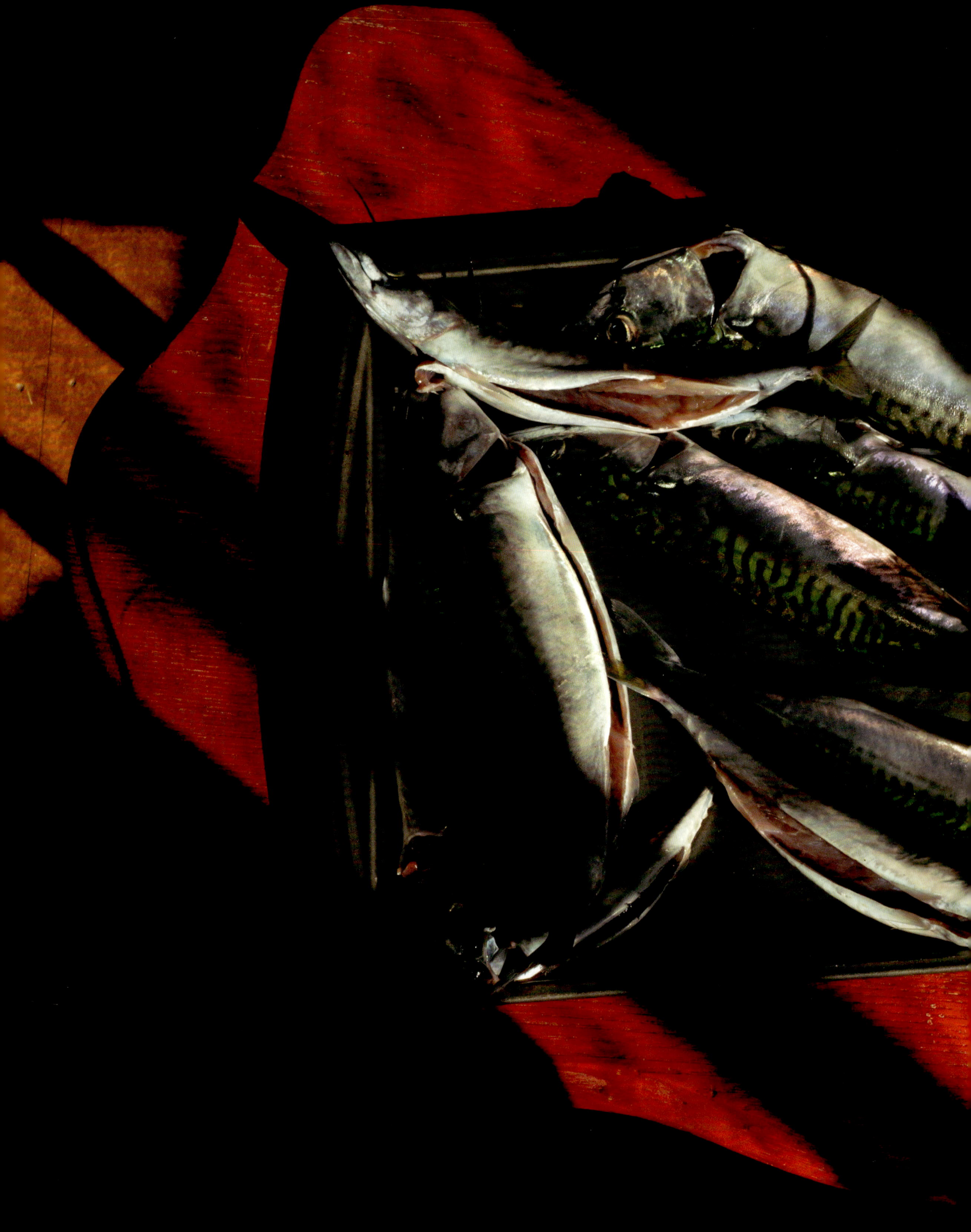

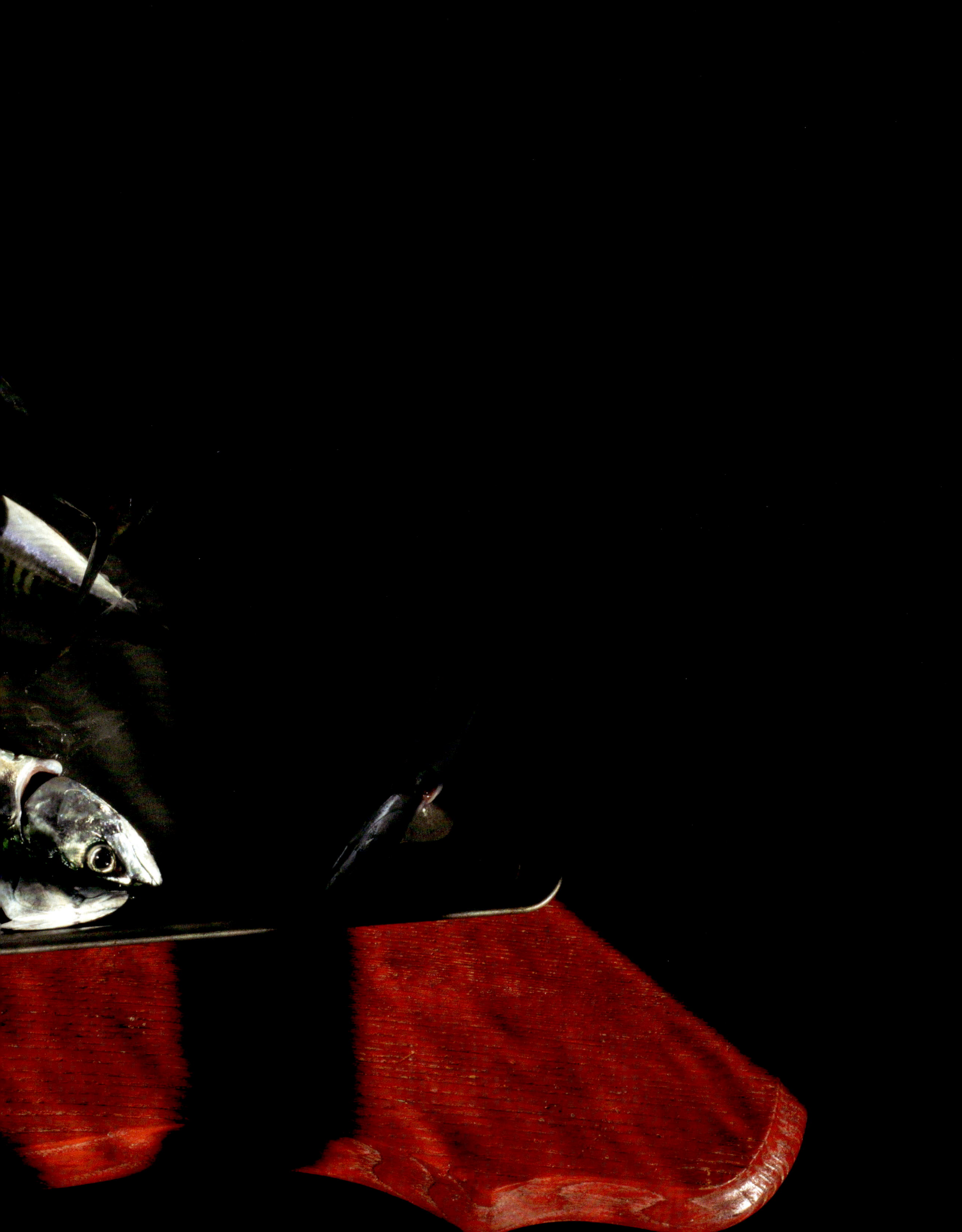

# Light-Bearers

Incandescent light refers to light energy created from heat and is the usual light we see—the sun, a light bulb, fire, car headlights on a moonless night, a lover's face lit up at sundown.

We get fluorescence when light energy is absorbed as one color and reflected back as a glow while the atoms try to stabilize. In Maine, the orange buoys stacked at the side of a driveway in winter are an eyesore, but on a foggy ocean in the Penobscot Bay, the beauty of the glowing orange causes grown men to touch the corners of their eyes and look away.

Phosphorescence is similar to fluorescence but reflects back the light for longer. Like the stars on your bedroom ceiling as a kid, which is when you first learned that you can make your own magic.

Bioluminescence differs from fluorescence: one needs dark and the other light. Bioluminescence is light created through chemical interaction, not heat. Animals use it for defense as well as sex. Squids flash green to stun their attackers, giving themselves an extra second to dash away. And in the daytime, they make the darkness come early by exploding their ink sacks, leaving their predators in a thick cloud of night. A firefly is just a plain old beetle, but at dusk, with bioluminescence, that firefly becomes a little golden god.

In the daytime, plankton are see-through-mostly-invisible-colorless nothings. But plankton, from the Greek word for drifter, own the night. Plankton contains *luciferins*, from the Latin *lucifer*, meaning light-bearer. These light-bearing drifters ignite when the water is disturbed by waves breaking or naked night swimmers. They light up the world's oceans with electric blues and emerald greens while simultaneously creating up to 50 percent of the oxygen we need to breathe.

Iridescence has nothing to do with fluorescence, phosphorescence, or bioluminescence. Iridescence, from the Greek goddess Iris of the rainbow, is the result of direct light hitting the broken surface of an object and reflecting back other colors when viewed at different angles. Iridescence is unrelated to pigment. The common blue jay and the morpho butterfly, famous for their dazzling blue feathers, have only brown pigment in their wings. Lots of things are iridescent: bubbles, fish jumping in sunlight as they fight the lines that will kill them, beetles in formaldehyde, bird feathers sticking out of fascinators, male peacocks, seashells on the seashore, opals stripped from the land, *Exxon Valdez* oil slicks floating in the ocean.

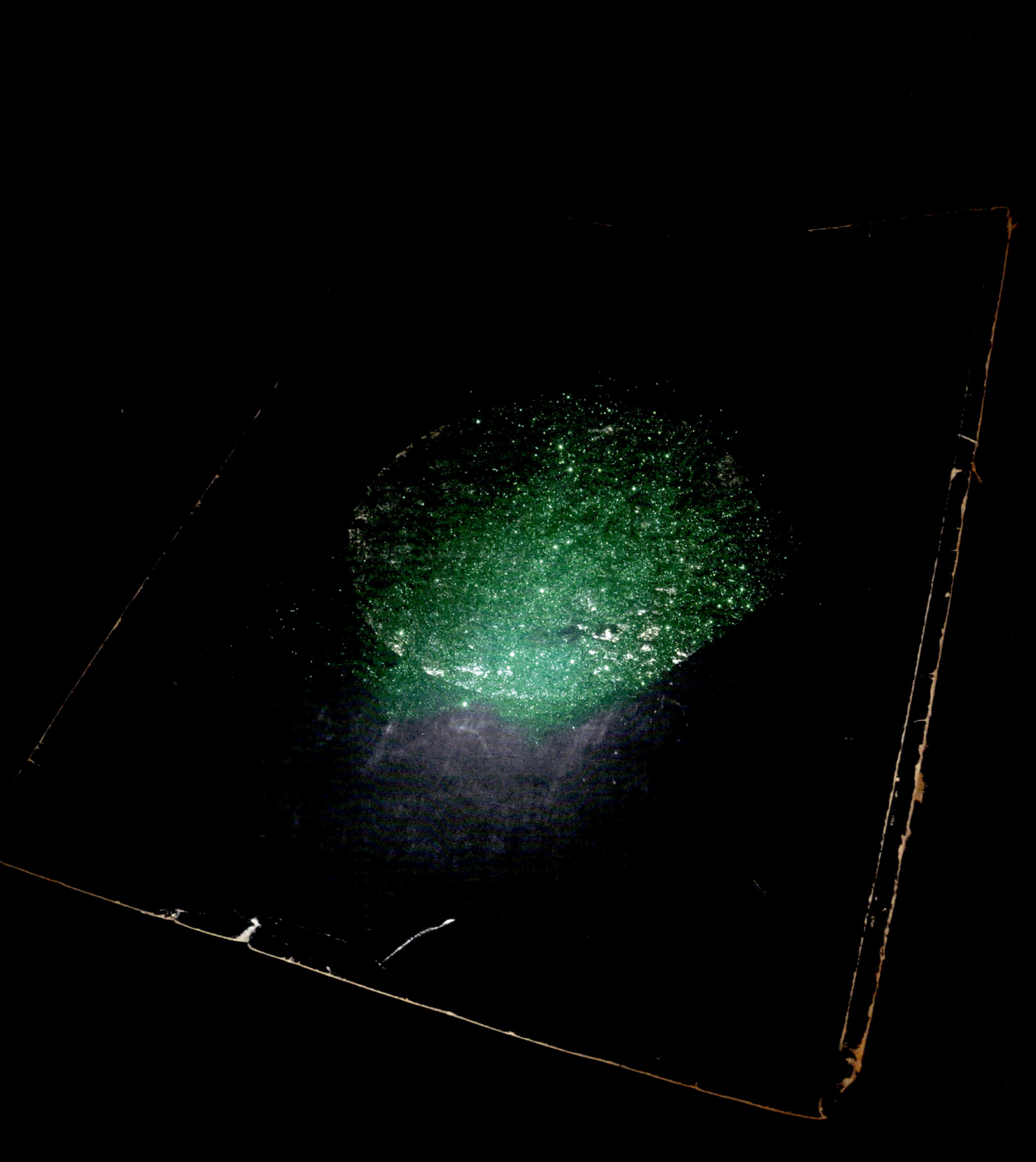

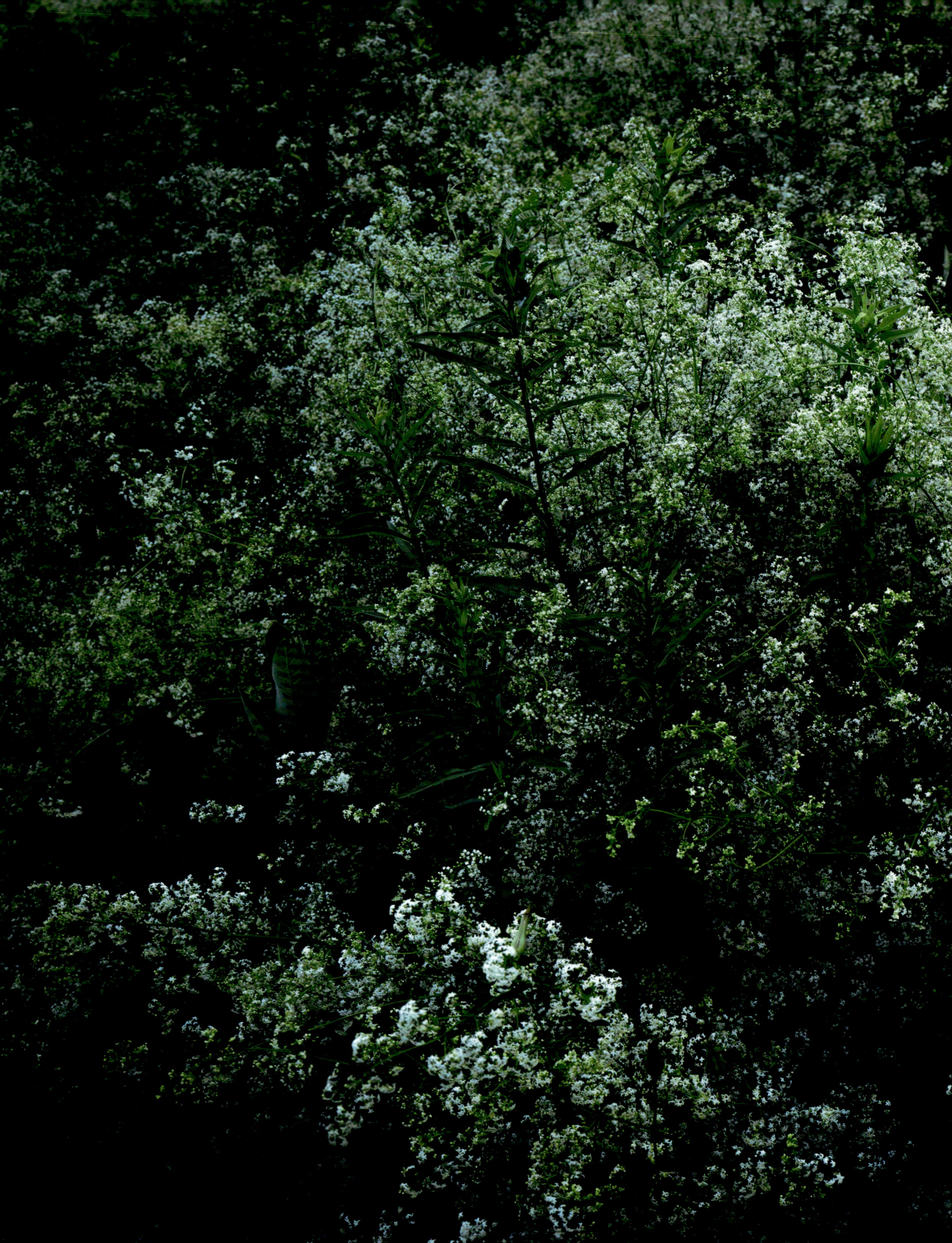

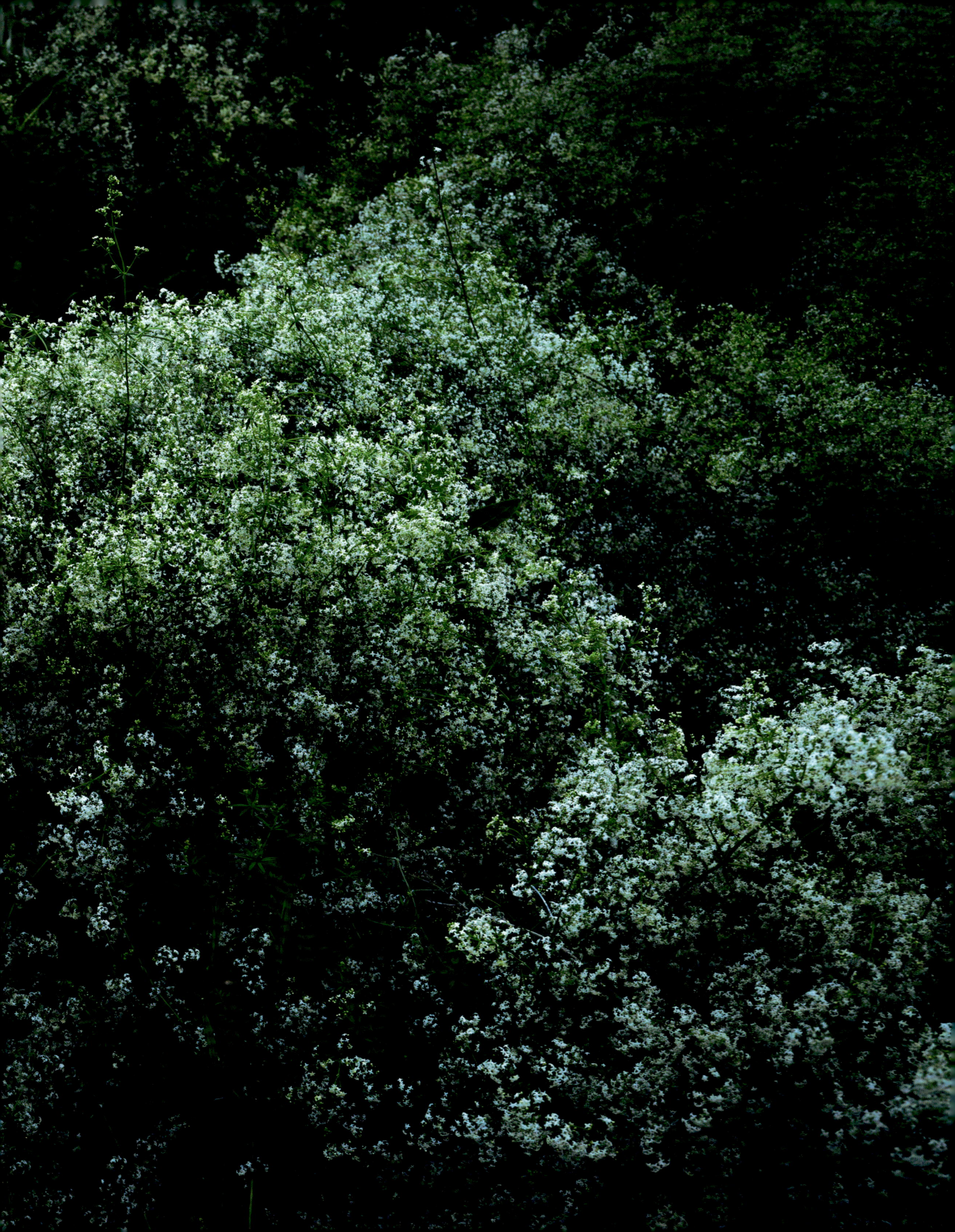

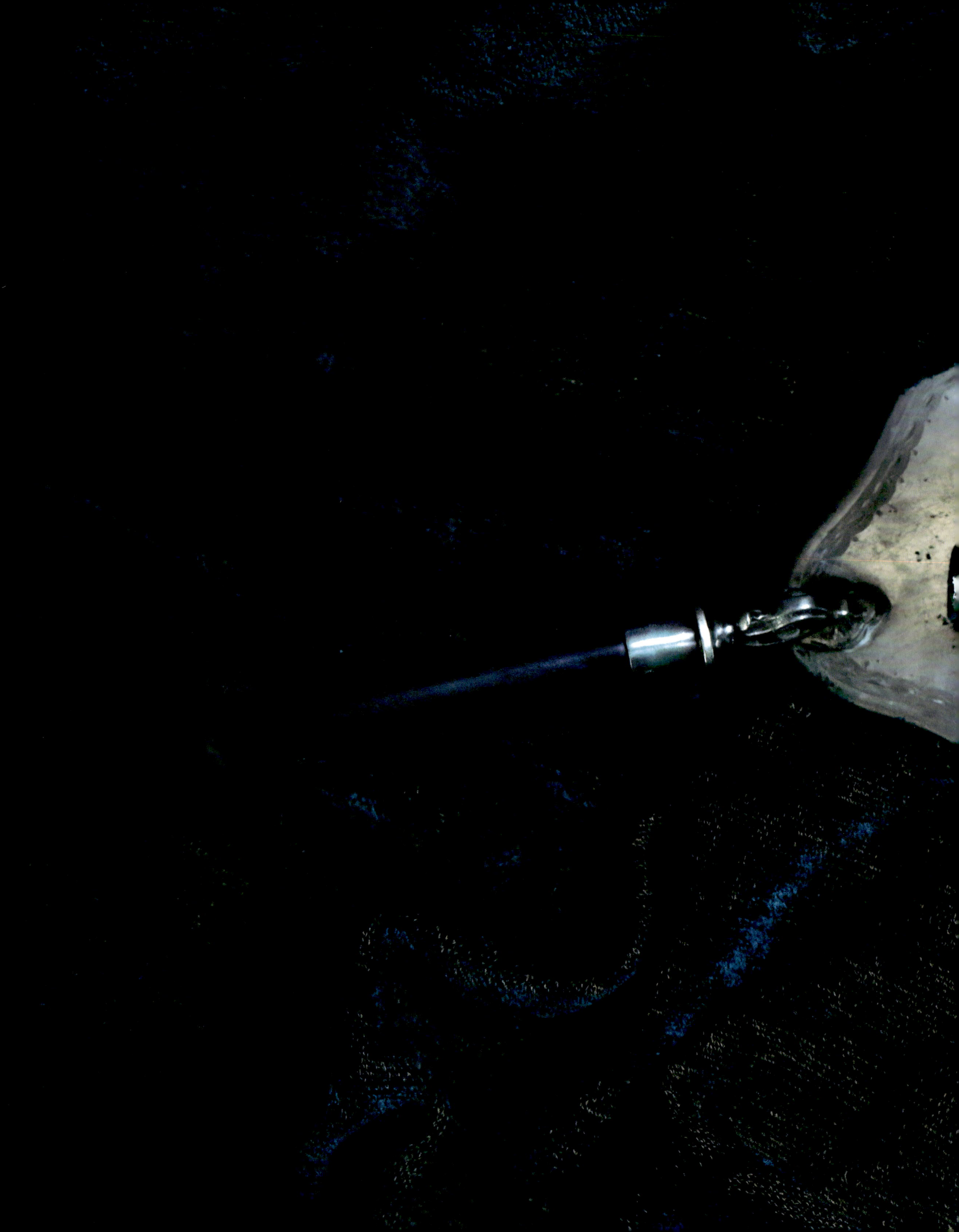

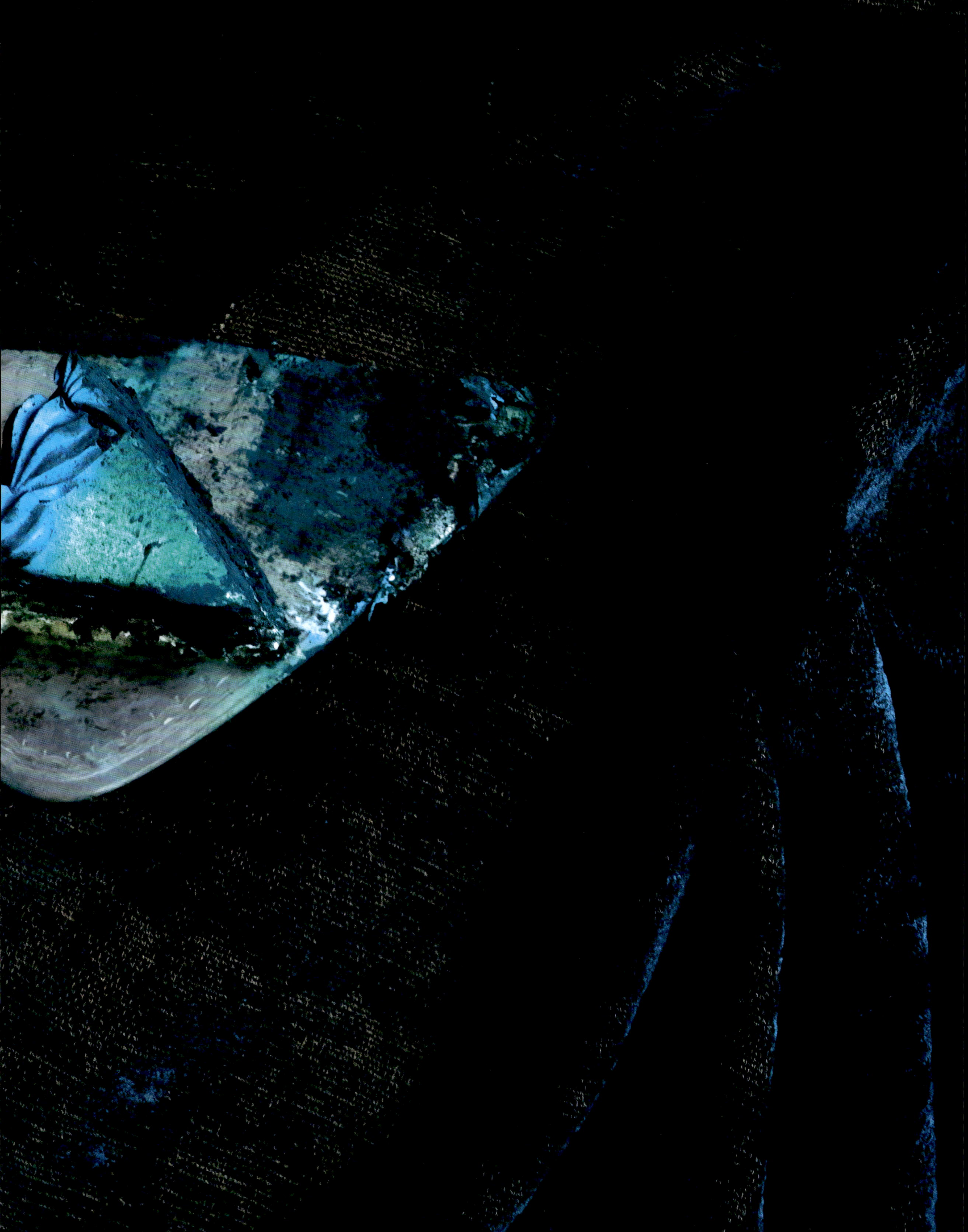

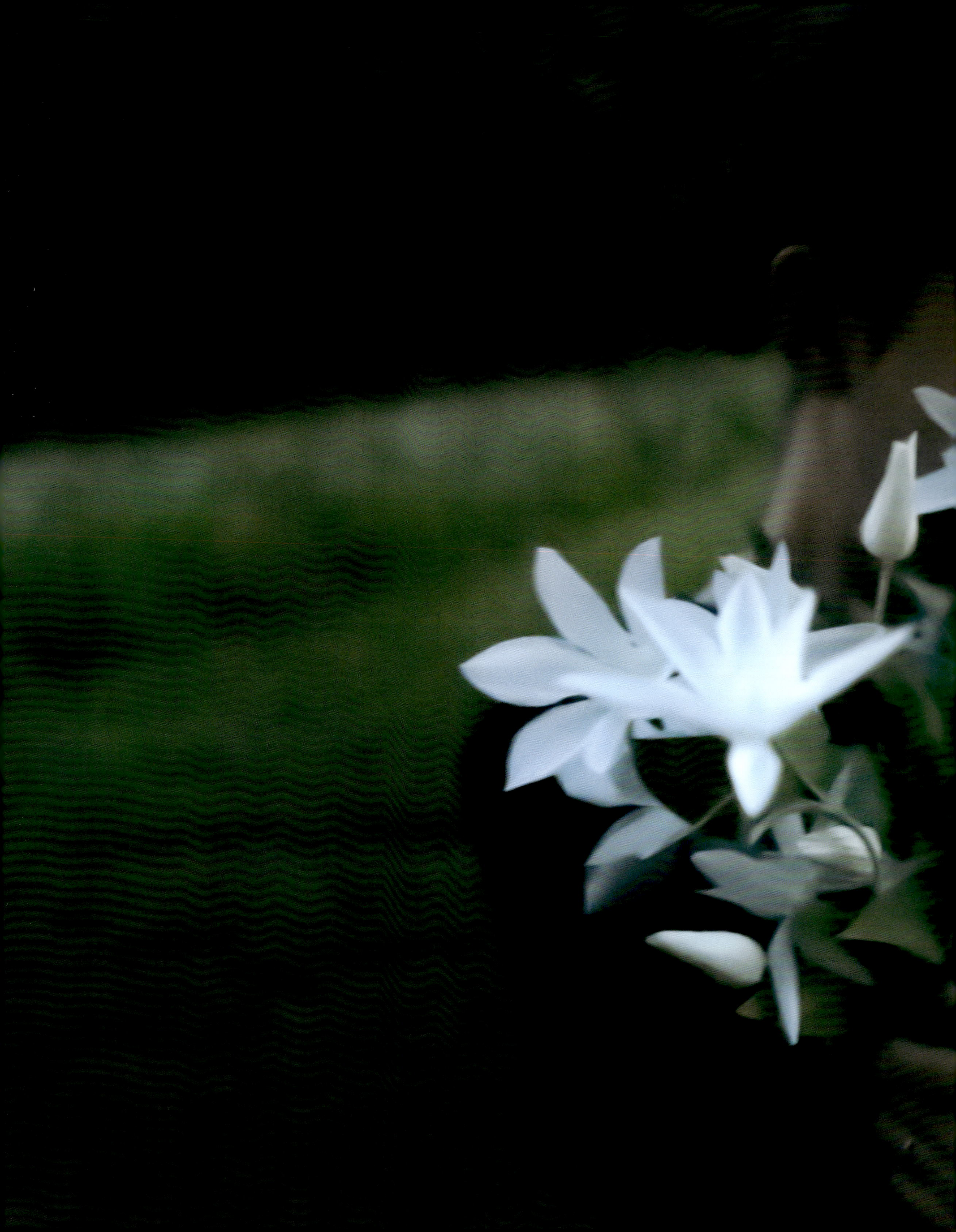

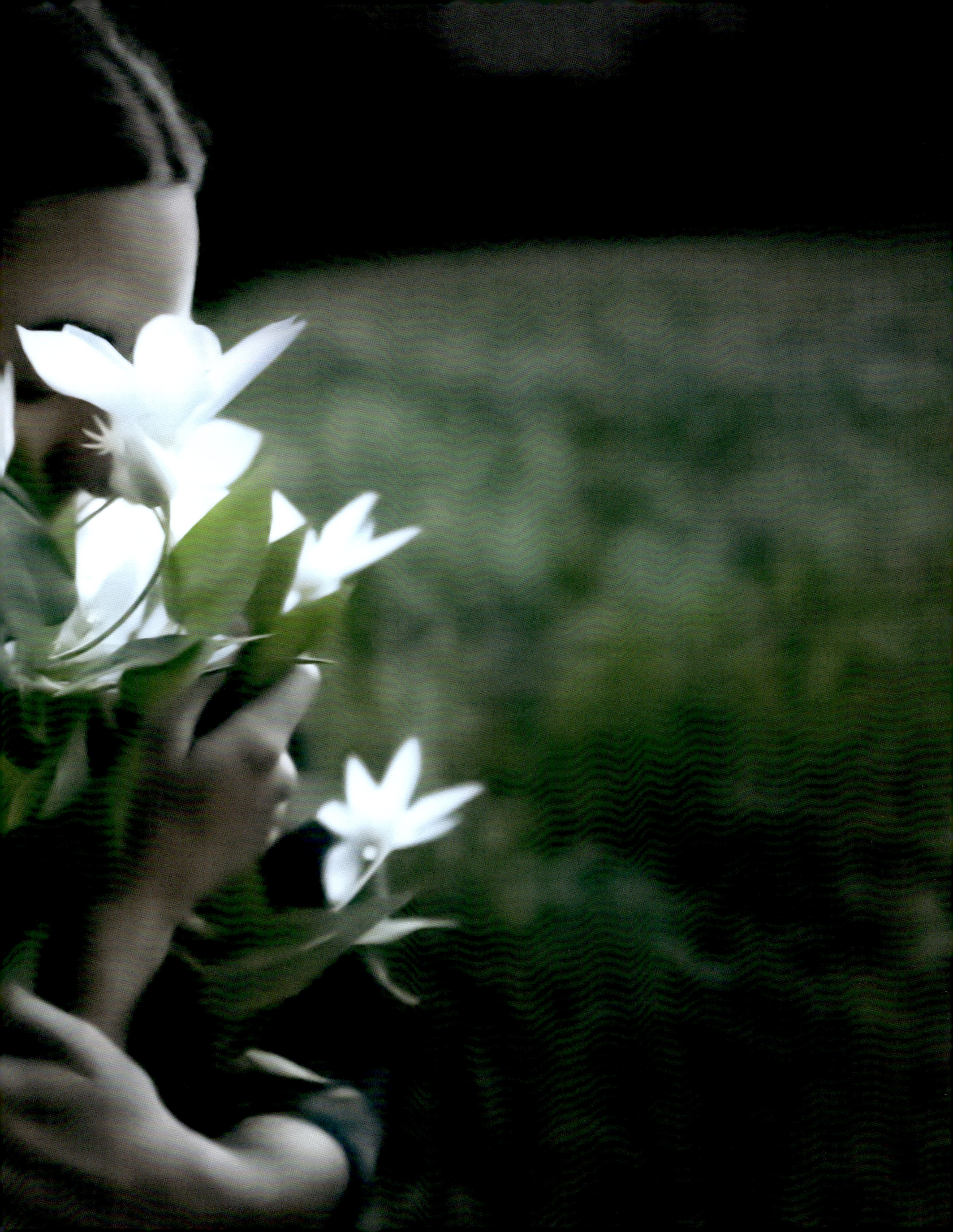

## The Sublime and the Beautiful

In 1797, the German philosopher Immanuel Kant made two columns in his notepad, dividing aesthetics into the sublime and the beautiful. Under the first heading, *Sublime*, he wrote: mountains, oceans, grand vistas, oak trees, the night, stars, and the masculine. In the second column, headed *Beautiful*, he listed flowers, sunshine, meadows, the small, and the feminine. The sublime was to be revered as majestic, important, multiple, and monumental. The beautiful became the decorative, insignificant, singular, and superficial.

I hate rules and prejudice around beauty and color. On holiday last winter, I read *Chromophobia* by David Batchelor, a book about the cultural hierarchy of color. It turns out that some people fear certain colors. I relayed this to Scout and Doug, and they laughed, pretending the color green was chasing them. It is more sinister than that.

Deep systemic prejudice around color pervades our culture. In art school, one professor told me that no good art comes from hot climates. And there it is: racism, the bias toward the north, the minimal, the white, the masculine.

In contemporary Western culture, bright colors are often thought of as less sophisticated, dismissed as primitive, garish, childish, and frivolous. It wasn't always this way. Gothic cathedrals were once a rose pink, and the ancient Greeks painted their marble statues in vibrant colors. Originally, Aphrodite of Milos was fuchsia but faded to white with time. Look at the reverence for neutral palettes in interior design, fashion, and architecture. Shades of Scandinavian whites and creams with names like Ecru, Salt, Mist, and Gravel are considered classic, elegant, clean. To like vivid color is somehow a question of taste. It is better to have midcentury modern homes with ivory plaster walls, pale gray rugs, and beige throw pillows stacked high on an alabaster couch, with just a glimmer of gold in a lamp or the legs of a taupe kitchen stool.

In the face of such neutrality, I want to tear my eyes out.

Contrast that to the bright colors of Mexican and Caribbean homes: blood orange, turquoise, canary yellow, hot pink. Luis Barragán's buildings in Mexico City made me run around the magenta courtyards in tears with arms wide open like I had just scored a goal. Color is joy. Hinduism dedicates an entire holiday to a festival of color. During Holi, millions of people celebrate the end of winter by mimicking the childhood play of Radha and Krishna, whirling into euphoria, exploding different-colored pigment clouds in each other's faces. A state of ecstasy reached in a food fight of color to honor the start of spring. Play is a serious business.

Some people think that color, like fashion, is frivolous, purely decorative. They think we should not waste our time with such trivial matters when we could be thinking more serious, utilitarian thoughts. But both color and style can be armor, to reflect and protect. Ancient people the world over have layered on paint, talismans, and auspicious clothing as a ritual before going to war. Humans have been adorning themselves for thousands of years.

Secretly, we all strive for beauty in art and our lives, but it is best not to talk about it. Elaine Scarry calls this *the silent use of beauty* in her book *On Beauty and Being Just*. If we bring up beauty, we seem shallow, uninterested in politics and the world's injustices.

So beauty and justice became opposites. And yet Matisse said he wanted to make all his paintings so *beautiful that suddenly, all problems would subside*.

And therein lies the problem. Academia worries that if we welcome and nourish beauty, how can we respond to injustice? But the truth is, women have been multitasking since the beginning of time: cooking meals while giving birth. We can handle holding more than two concepts simultaneously. We can plant a garden of hollyhocks while at the same time fighting for gun control in America, finding a cure for AIDS, and proving the existence of dark matter in space. We know beauty and justice are entangled: both are concerned with harmony and balance.

Beauty creates a somatic response. The senses melt together. In at the eyes and out of the fingers in the form of an oil painting. In at the ear, out of the throat through song. When we see, hear, taste, feel, and smell something beautiful, we want to replicate it: take a photograph of the face, make perfume from that jasmine flower, write a poem about the waves. Some people stargaze every night to extend the presence of beauty around them. When we see something beautiful, the body is shaken.

A rainbow can be dismissed as too pretty. But that is not the fault of the rainbow—it is the fault of bad reproductions, the fault of consumerism in a capitalist society. The image of a rainbow in a picture on a mug replaces the actual rainbow: a free, accessible, and awe-inspiring phenomenon.

Beauty multiplies itself. Beauty makes people better: better neighbors, better lovers, better custodians of the planet. I have dedicated my life to this idea.

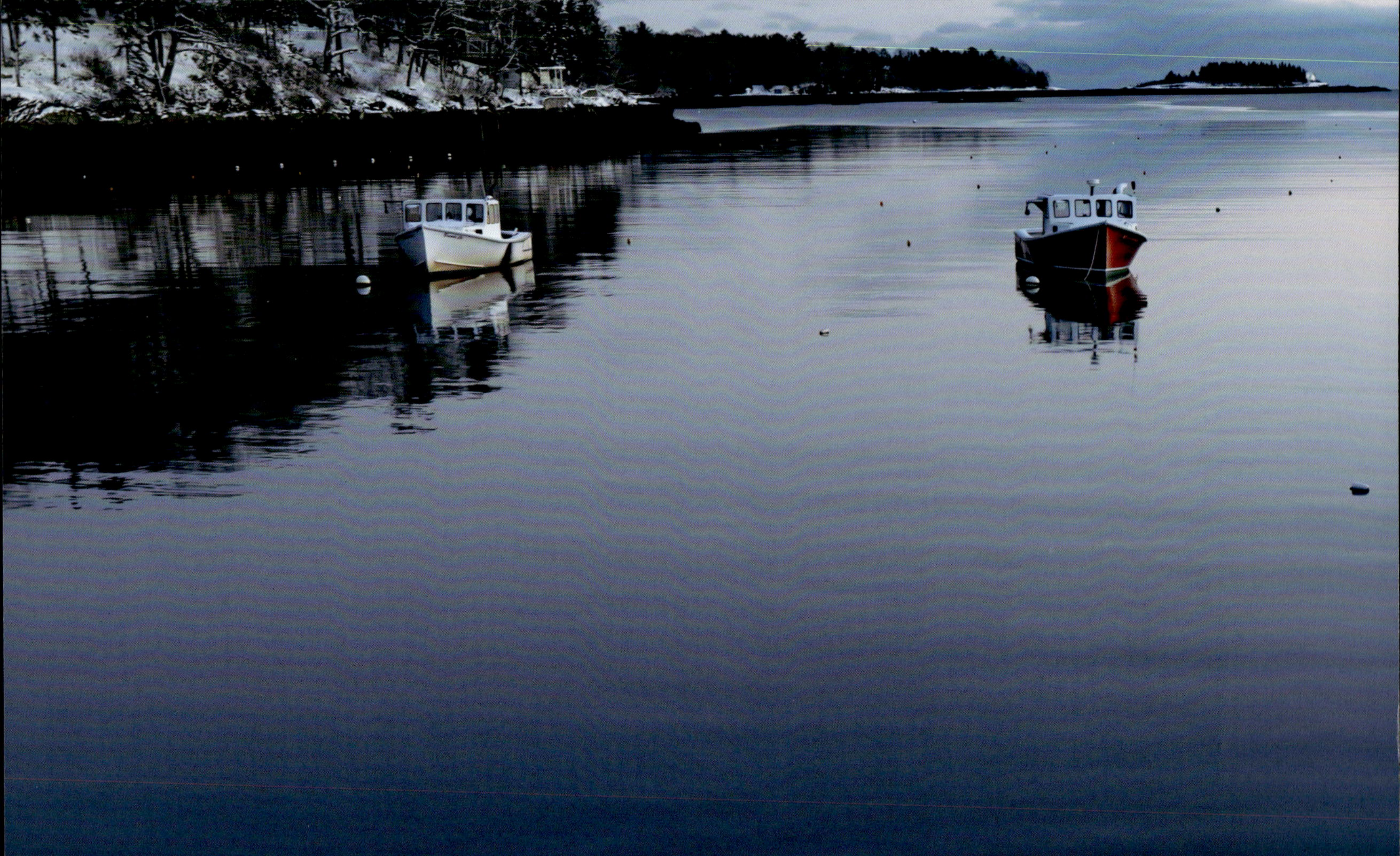

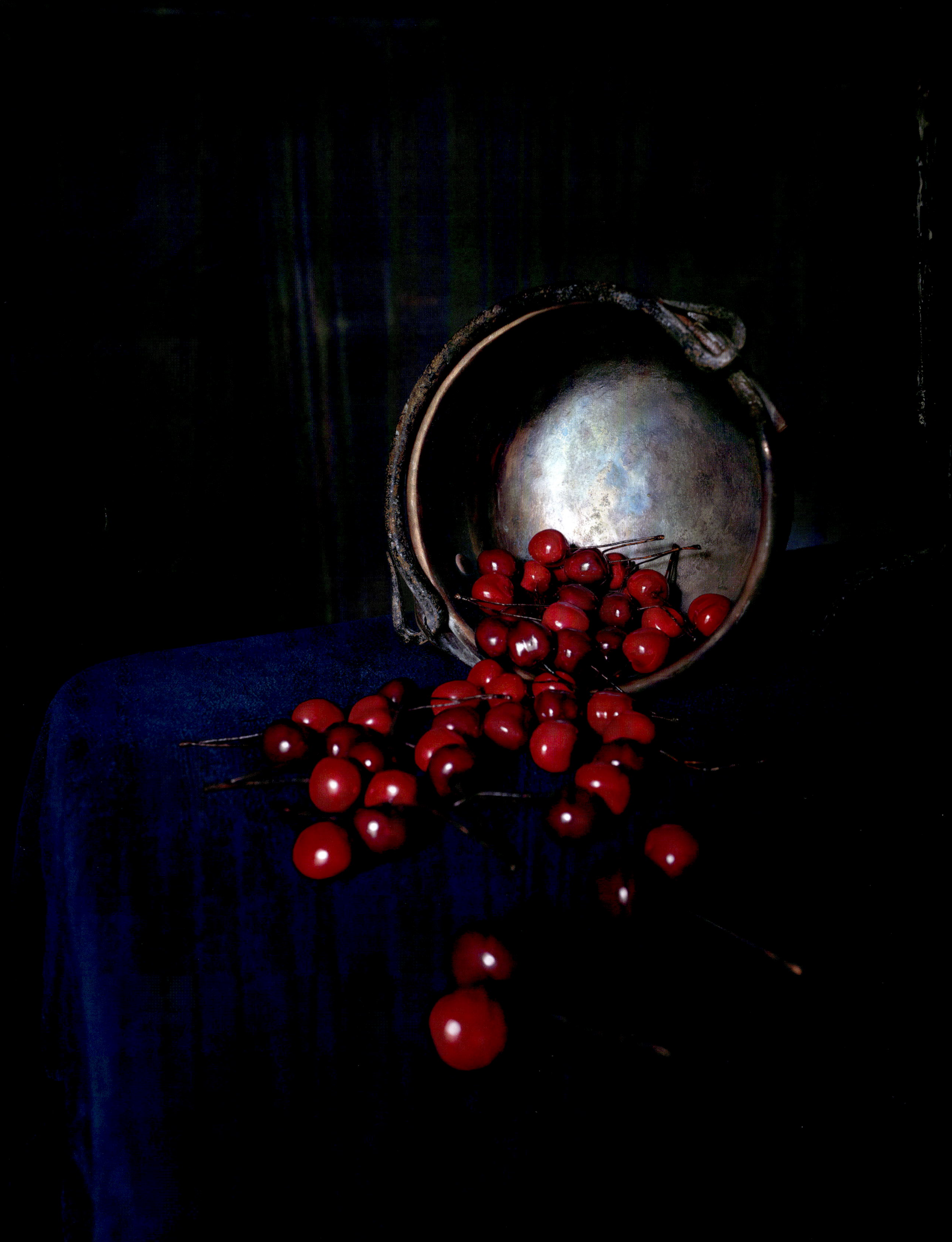

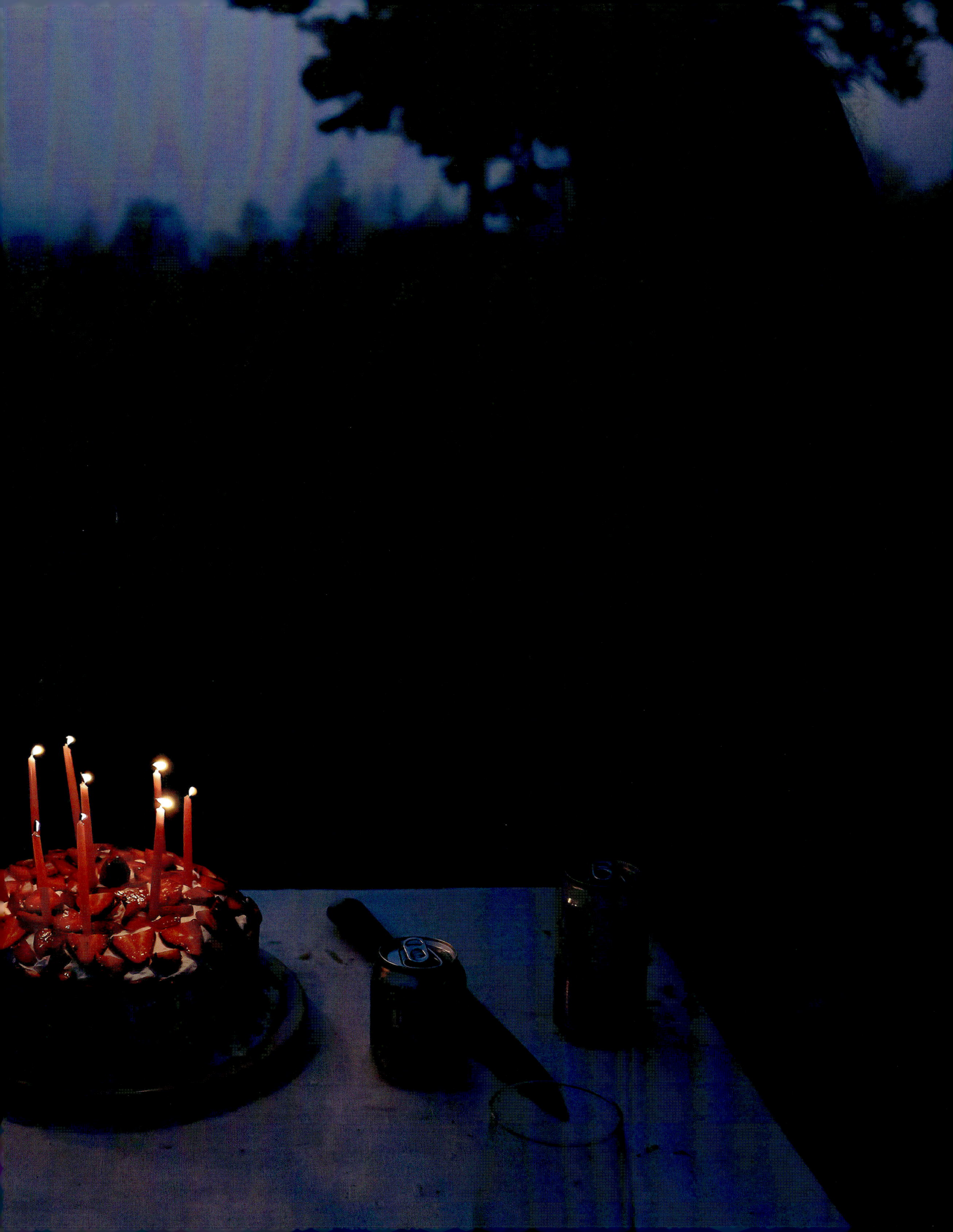

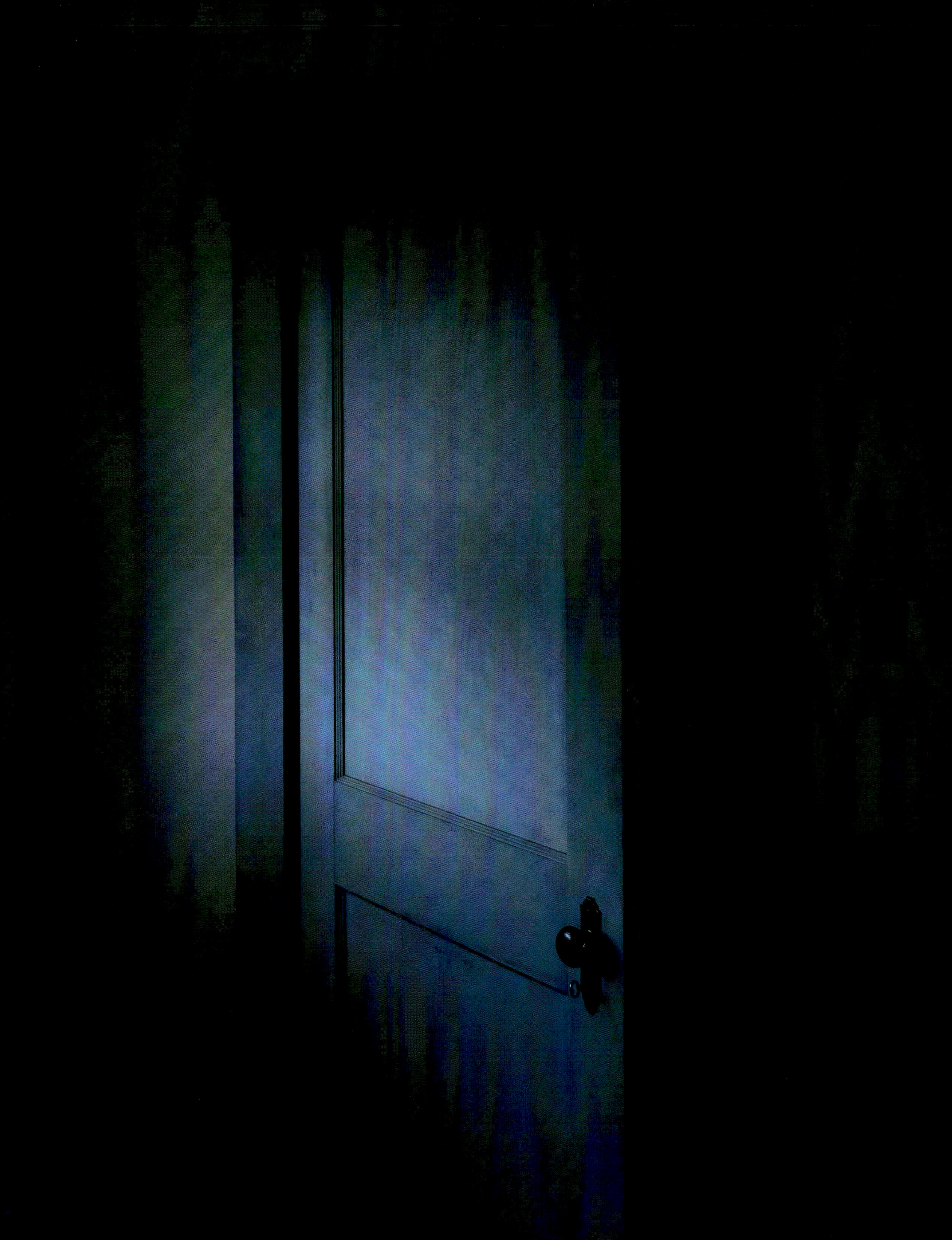

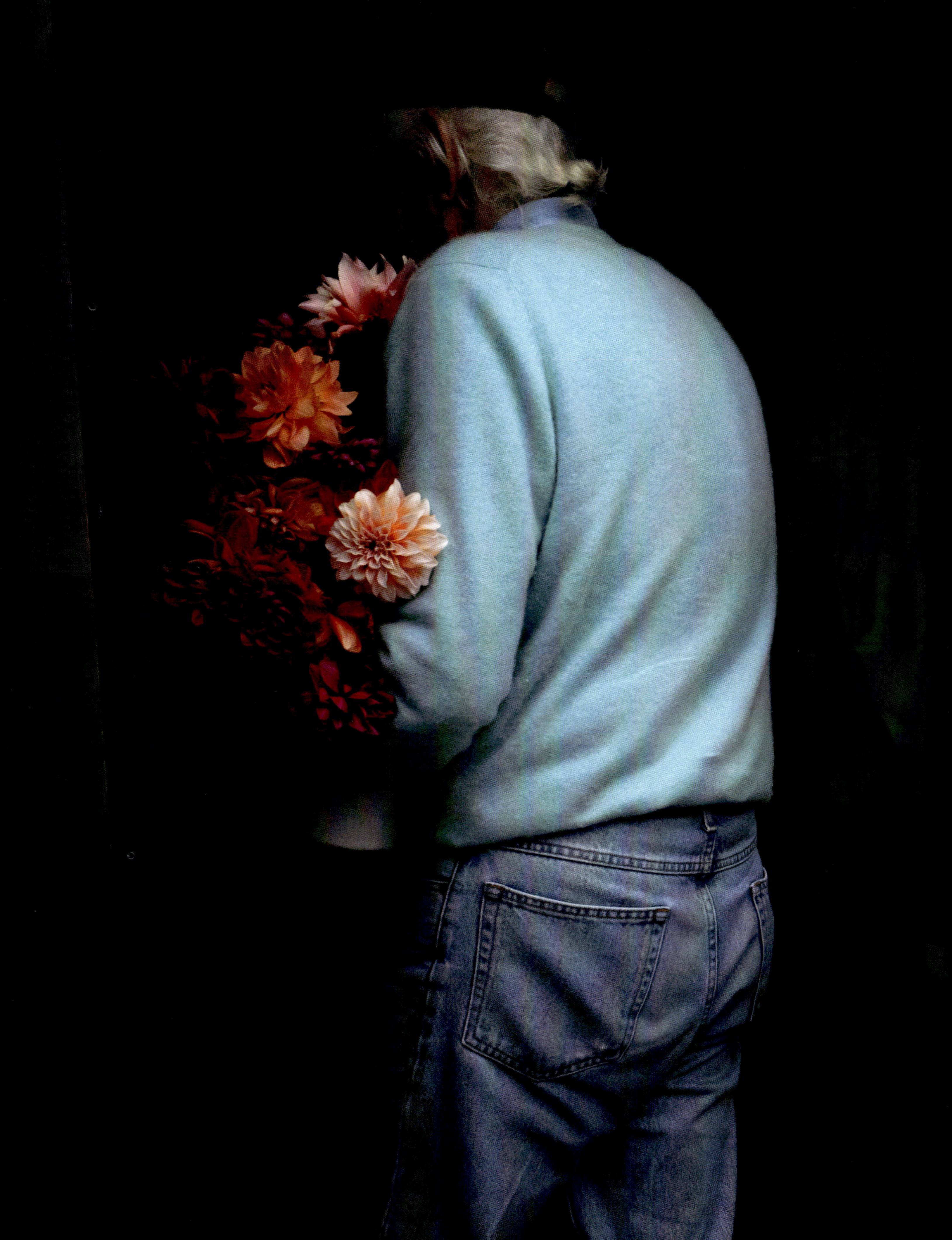

The day they thought Mum was dying, I bought a gleaming white pavlova from the supermarket.

She was supposed to be getting better. But in the ward, just as the doctor was telling me of her progress, she started having seizures. The room lit up a bright red, pulsing in time with angry alarms shouting *Code Blue, Code Blue*. It was as if we were in a strange nightclub in Berlin searching for the zeitgeist.

The nurse pushed me into a waiting room because no one likes to see the body going wrong, especially when it's your mother's. I lay on the floor as the janitor mopped around me, leaving an outline of a doubled-over sobbing me in a watery-yellow bleach solution on the linoleum.

My sister was doing the weekly food shopping, when I called to say, *Come immediately; Mum is crashing*. She abandoned her half-full cart in Aisle Three. Later, while the doctors tried stabilizing Mum, my sister went back to finish the shopping. We all deal with trauma in different ways. I went with her but only got as far as the bakery section. I found comfort, mesmerized by the beauty of the cakes. Row after row of curved iced treats, each with a pop of red cherry bringing order to the chaos of the day.

My mum always had a flair for the dramatic. When we were kids, she would sometimes eat part of a premade frozen raspberry pavlova for dinner and then finish it off the next morning for breakfast: layers of creamy white tufted meringue sweeping upward and then, in the center, a brilliant caldron of strawberries and raspberries, each gutted into quarters and mixed with sugar to intensify the red. It was a sight so beautiful it entered my mother's dreams at night. First thing in the morning, she would pull it out of the fridge and kneel before it on the countertop, and I imagined her making a mark of the cross in the sticky scarlet paste on her forehead before she dipped her fork into its heart.

To put such a color and taste in your body at 7 a.m. is a sign that you are desperate to live a more extraordinary life.

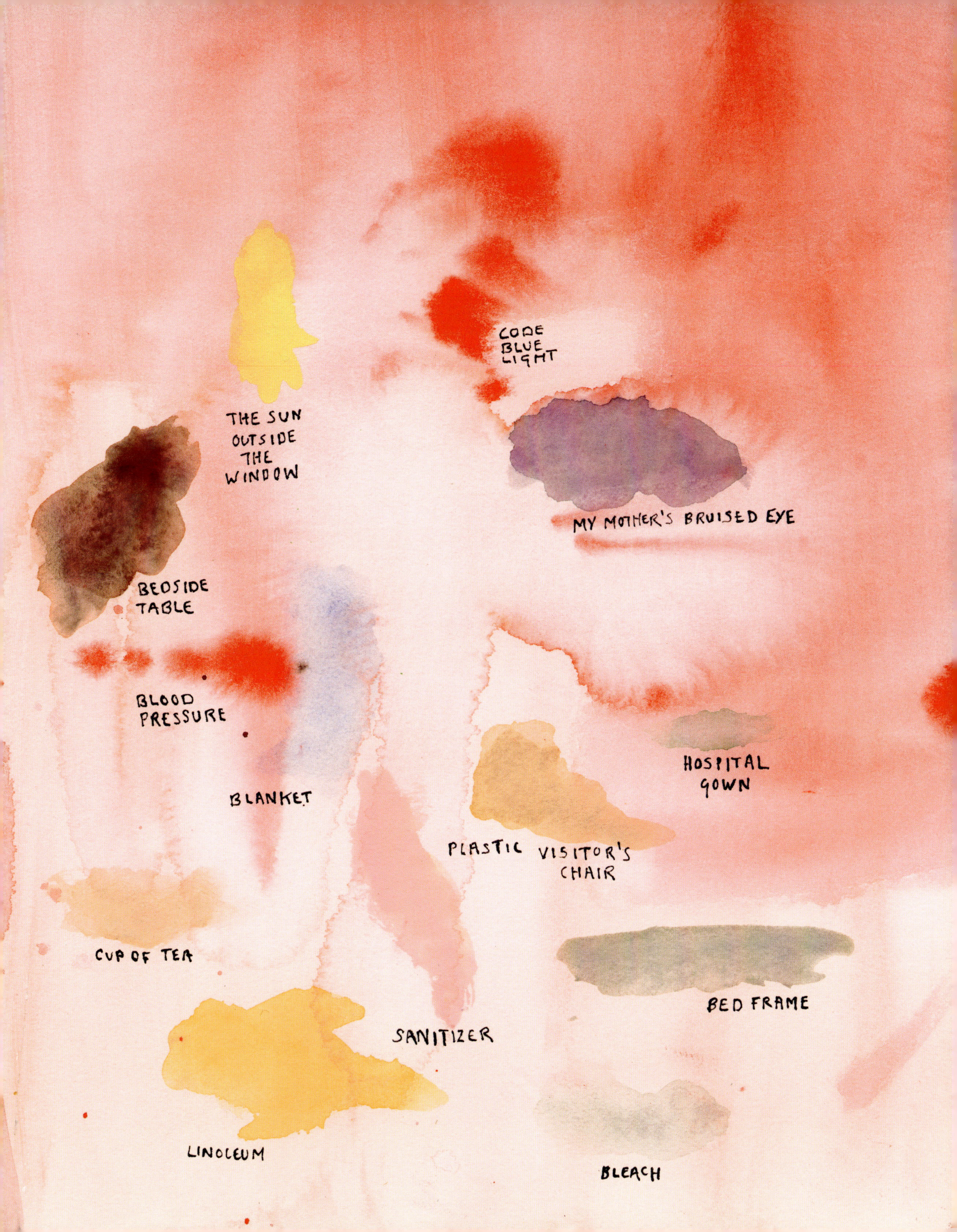

CODE
BLUE
LIGHT

THE SUN
OUTSIDE
THE
WINDOW

MY MOTHER'S BRUISED EYE

BEDSIDE
TABLE

BLOOD
PRESSURE

HOSPITAL
GOWN

BLANKET

PLASTIC VISITOR'S
CHAIR

CUP OF TEA

BED FRAME

SANITIZER

LINOLEUM

BLEACH

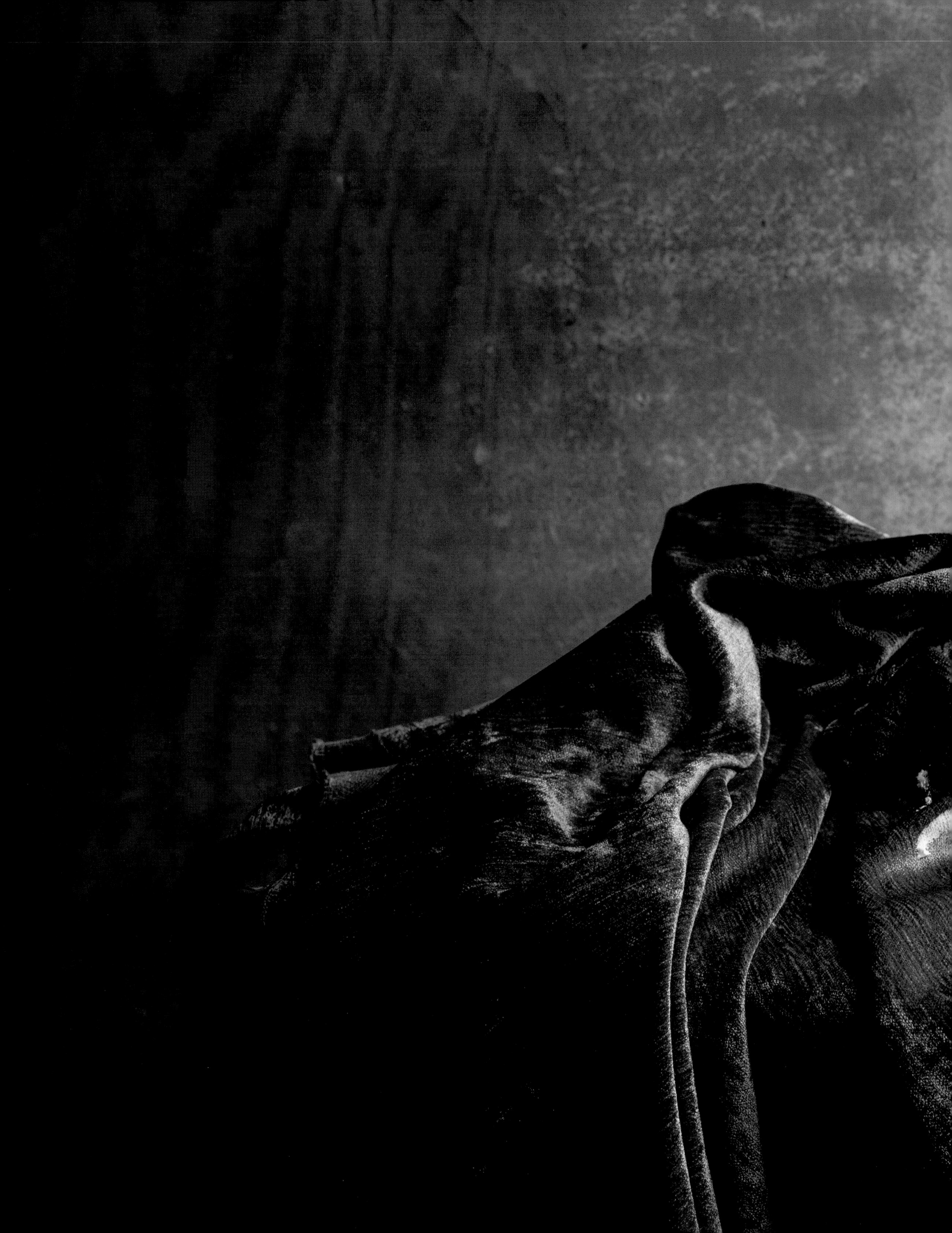

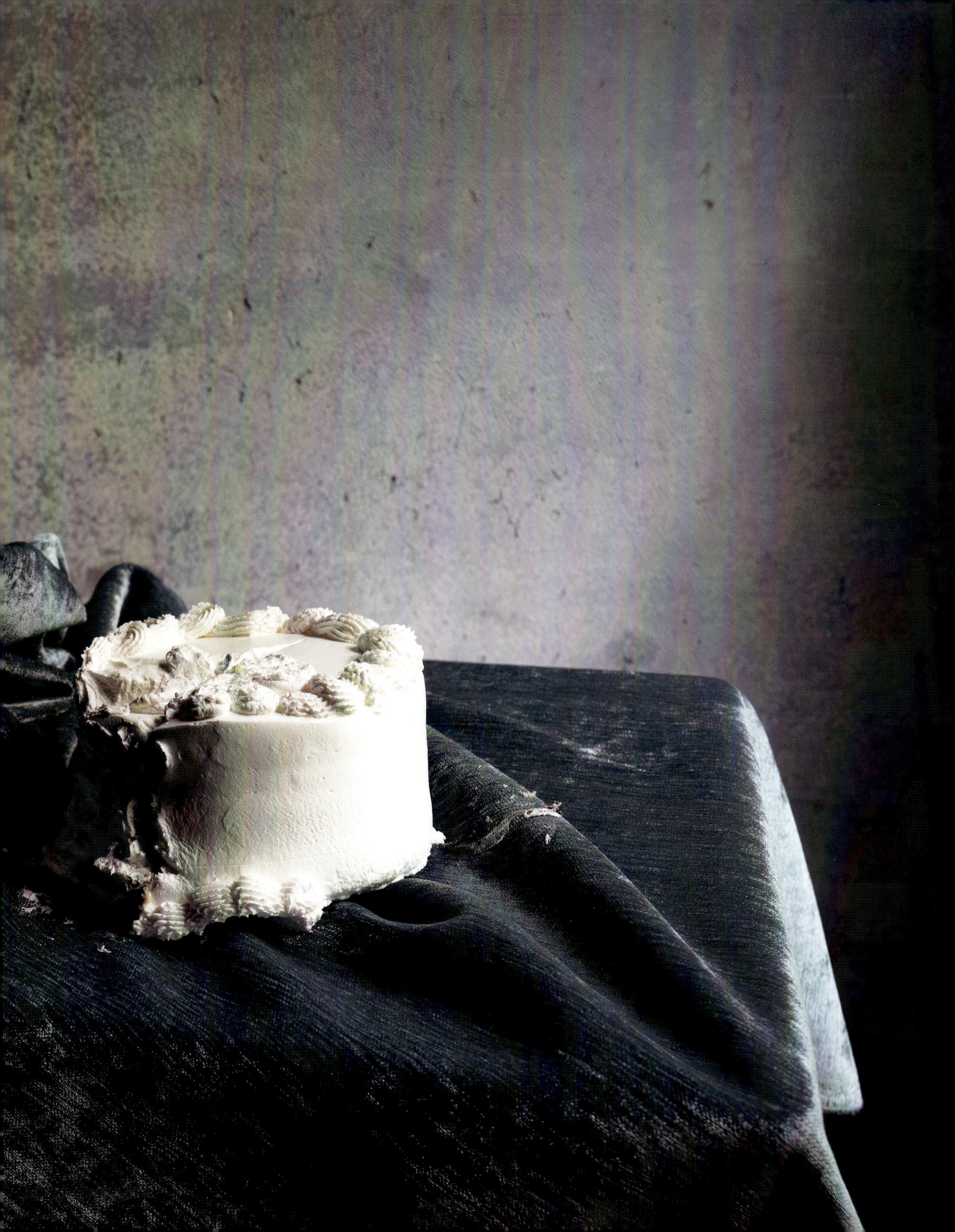

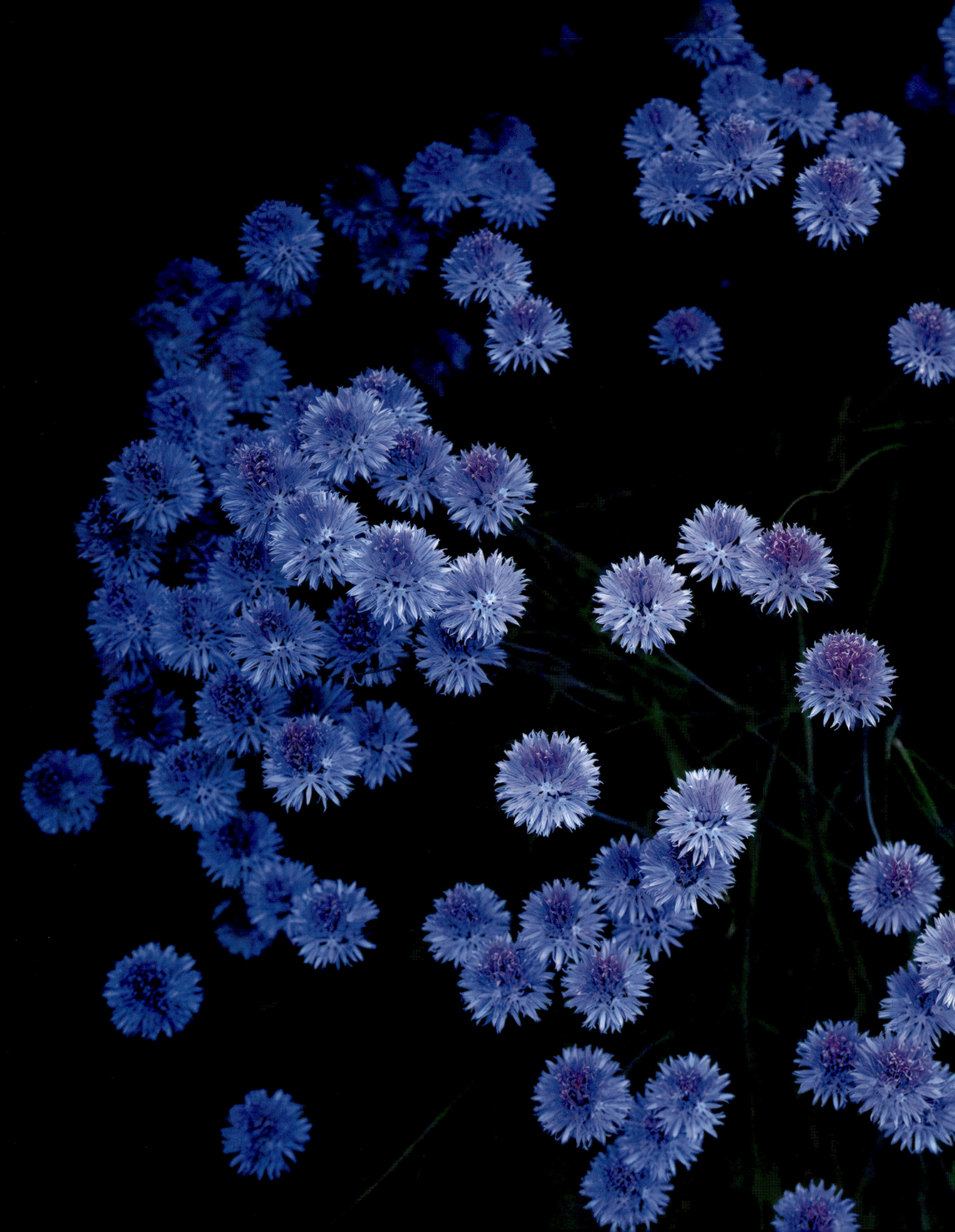

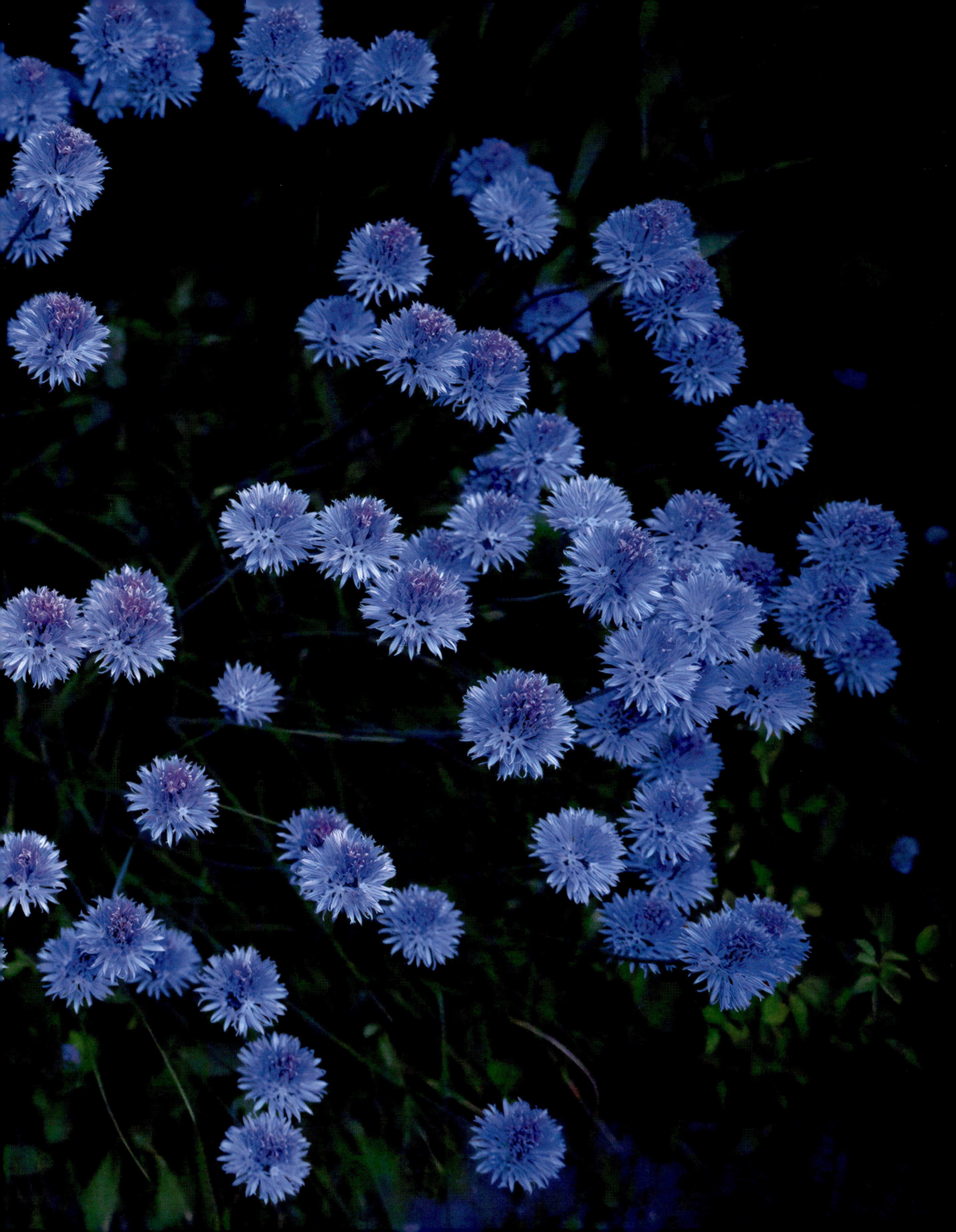

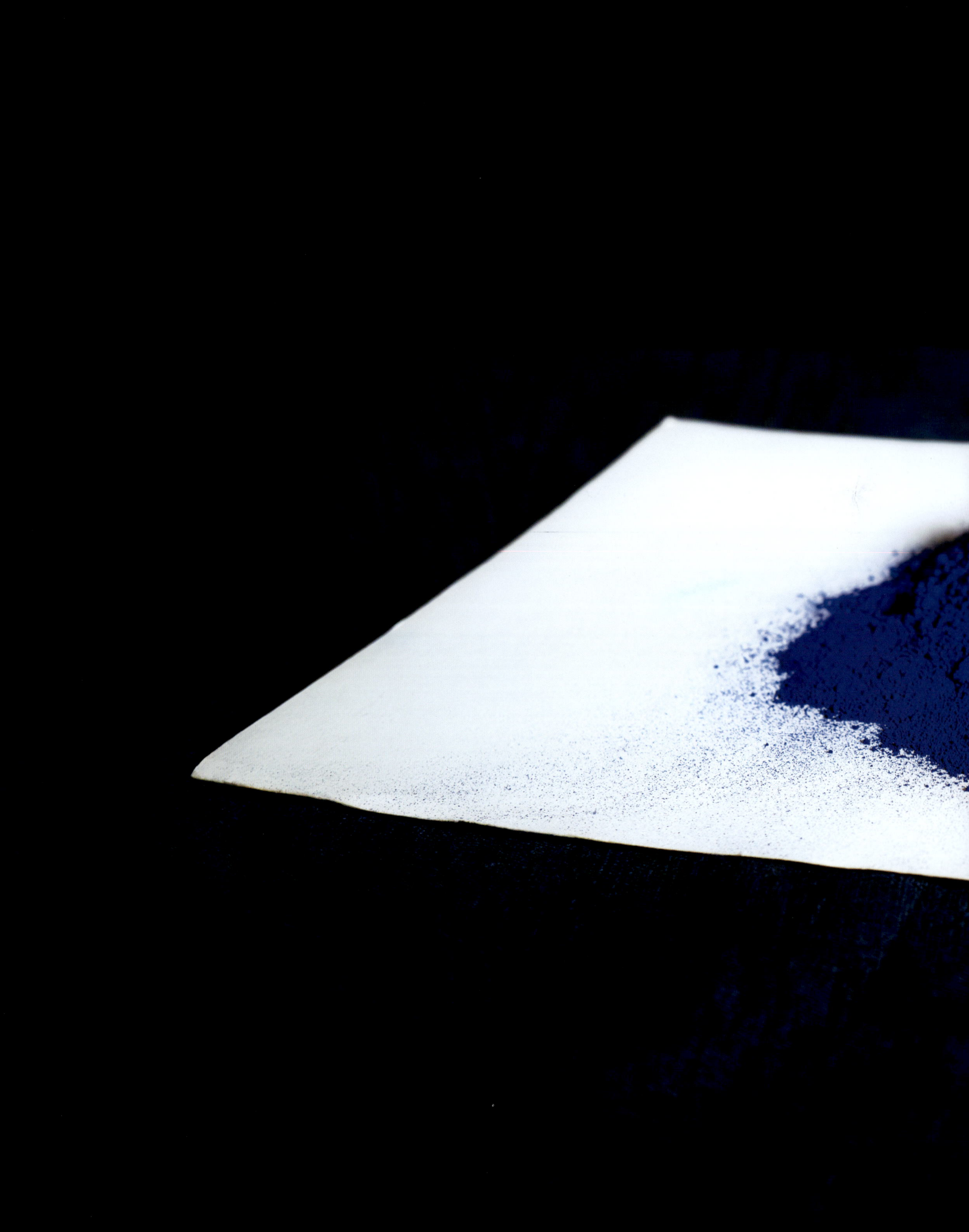

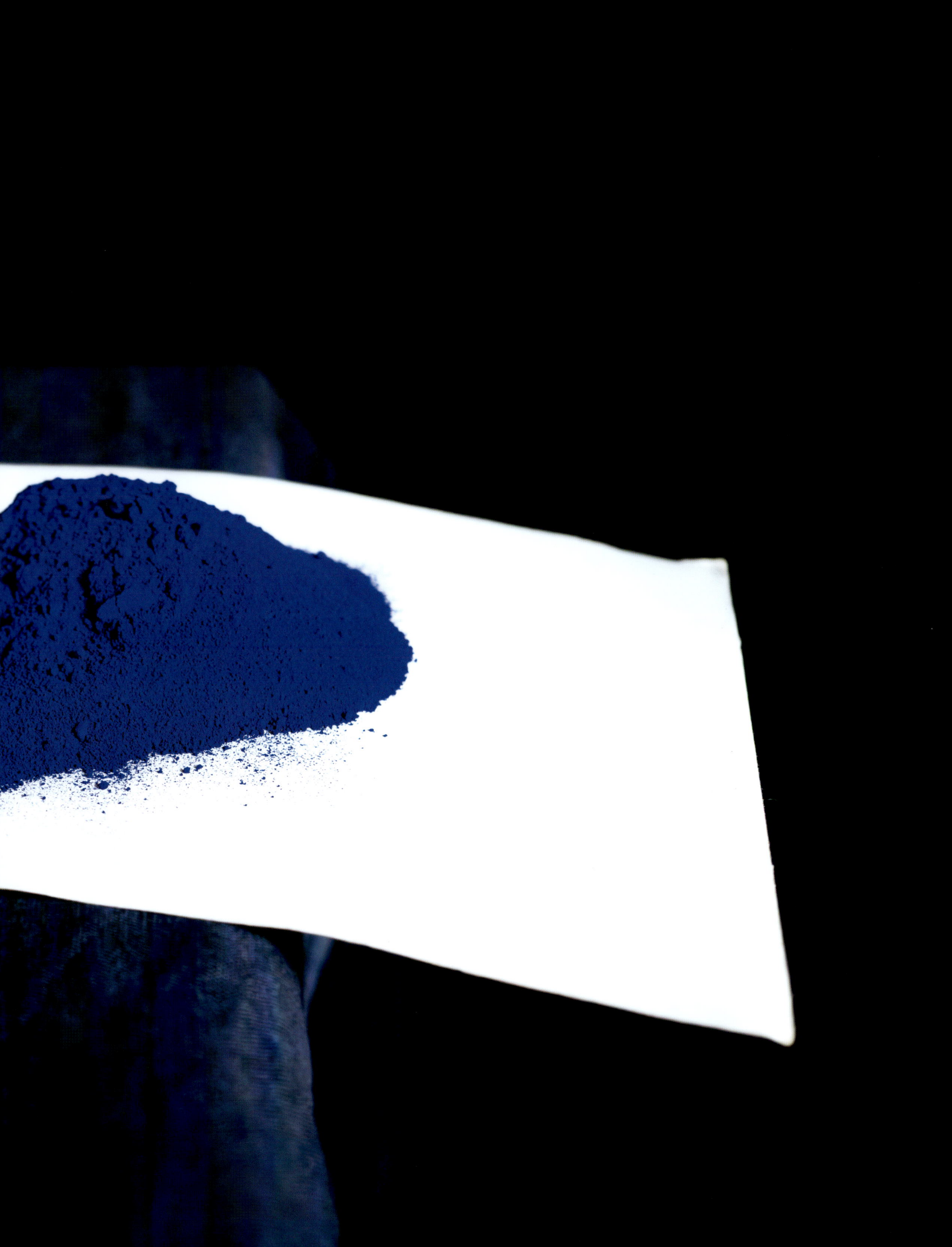

# Blue Violet to Scarlet Red

I'm a bride of the spectrum. I believe in color with a blind faith. Color is my god.

As a child, I swam three times a week at the local indoor public swimming pool just to be surrounded by pastels, all those cool tones interrupted by the lifesaving circles of orange. Later, as a teenager, I would smoke Silk Cut because of the lush plum packet.

In my early twenties in Barcelona, Antoni Gaudí was part of my everyday experience: I passed La Sagrada Família on my way from the subway to work. We think of Gaudí's impossible forms and shapes, a building-sized pavlova in the sky, but what about the colors of the mosaics? The oil slick hues of his tiled buildings kept me living there for almost three years.

My heart was broken for the first time at twenty-six, its pieces held together by the layers of blue in the Bermuda ocean. Looking at all those blues helped me make sense of the world—a blue therapy, and I knew things would get better.

Seven years later, Doug and I bought our first house in Maine because of the lustrous yellow forsythia blooming a cathedral in the backyard. Most of the year, forsythia are just dirty bushes, but for two weeks in April, they are a source of awe and wonder.

For a couple of years, orange was my favorite color. Marigolds. Clementines. Sunsets. Cheetos. Coral. Fire. Hermès. Tigers. Taxiing on a runway, watching the orange wind socks inflate always makes me want to burst into the chorus of *Love Lifts Us Up Where We Belong*. Orange was Kandinsky's favorite color, too. He said *orange is like a man convinced of his own powers*. Kandinsky had synesthesia and felt his relationship with color was spiritual. Orange is a pulse, a stab, a warning.

At thirty-eight, I spent a month's mortgage payment on a brilliant hot pink skirt. Trying it on in the changing room was like putting on a starling: I could feel the potential of flight. I tried walking away, leaving the store, but the skirt was burned on my retina, and I only made it five blocks before I turned back, Amex in hand. I needed to own that color, possess it: a shattering pink, as if I had slipped into the skin of a freshly caught mackerel.

A few summers later, I picked every pink flower in my garden for a still life. Halfway through photographing, I had to sit down because of heart palpitations. I could see the thick fist of my heart muscles squeezing and releasing as I dropped each flower in place.

Last year, I flew to Japan to take a picture of a red apple. In the markets there, apples are singular—each selected for its size and markings, polished by hand until it glows, and then wrapped in a pink foam skirt. This red sitting in the soft pink is worth the fourteen-hour flight.

At the end of April in Maine, we woke up to a foot of snow falling like table salt. After digging out my boots, I drove through the bone-gray mist putting brilliant red birthday cakes in my neighbor's mailboxes, a red so intense that later, when the sunlight hit them, Alicia Keys's *This girl is on fire* filled the air.

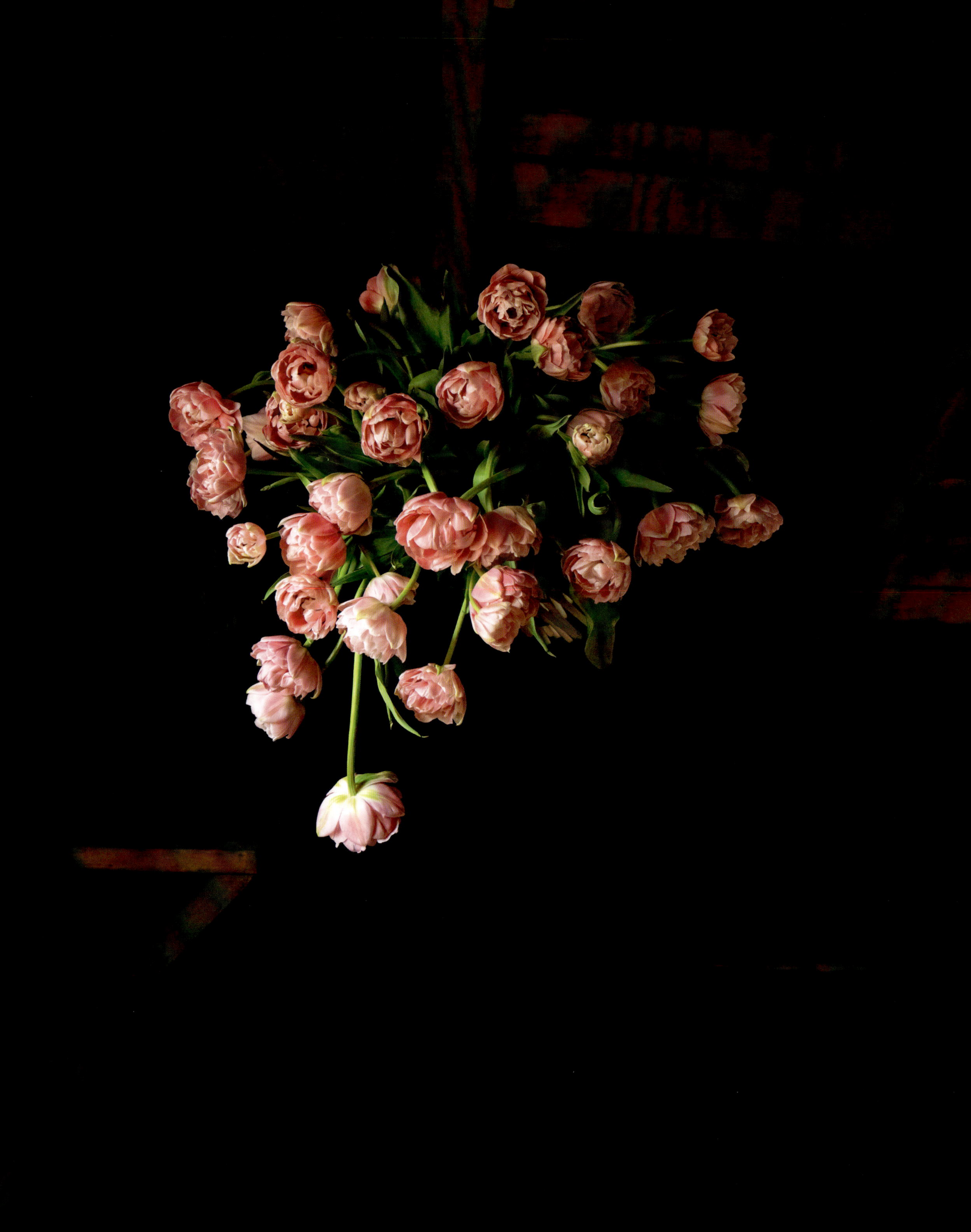

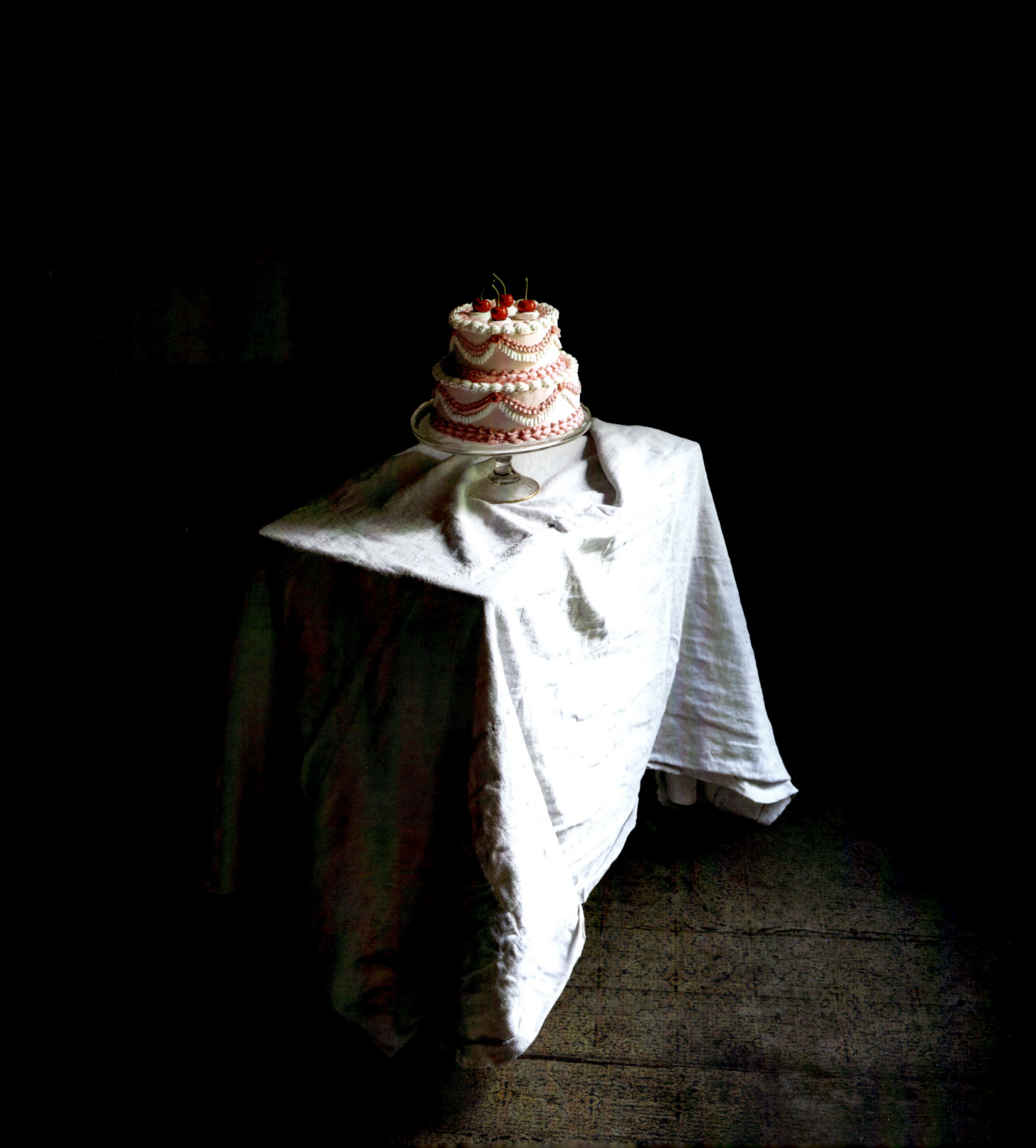

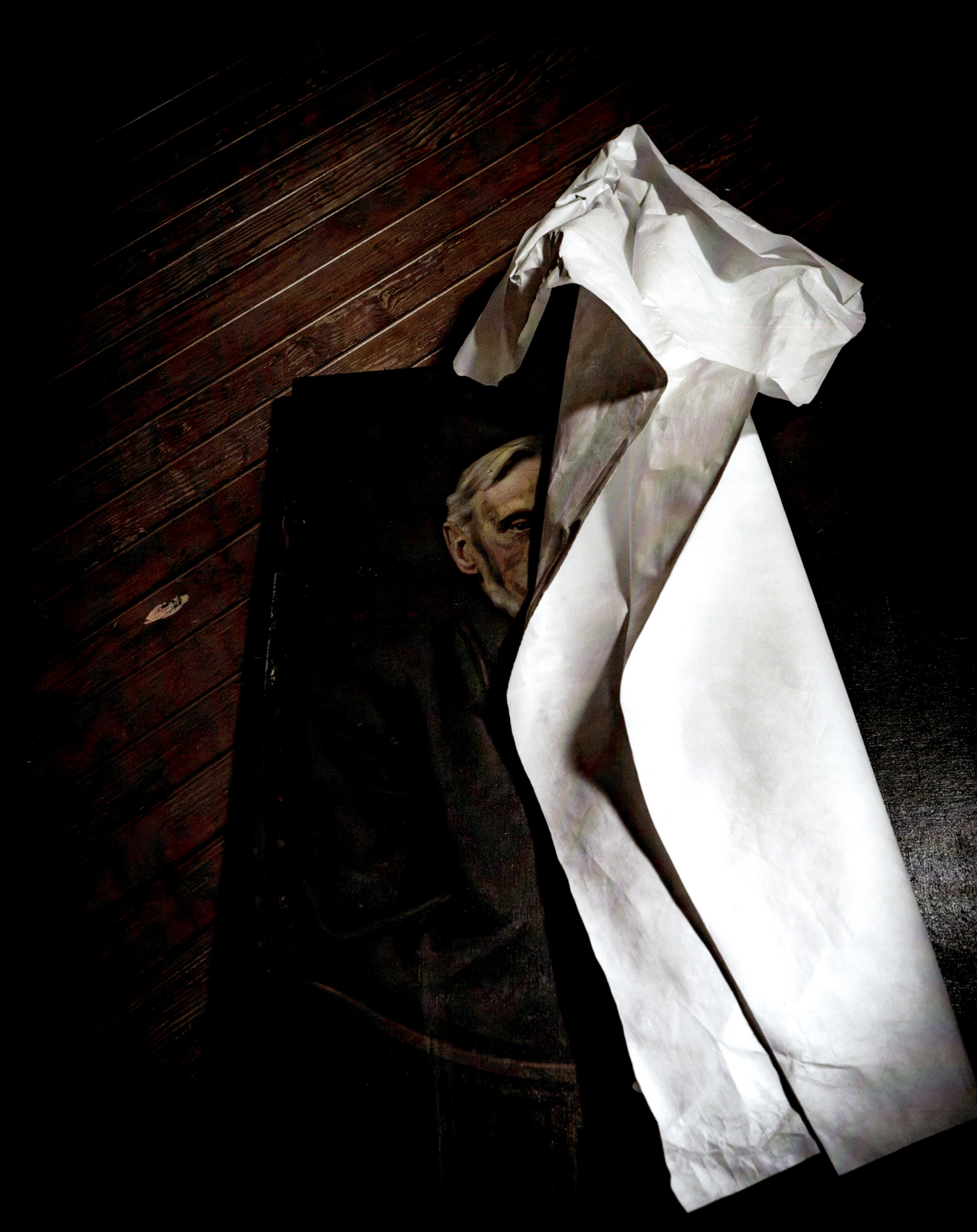

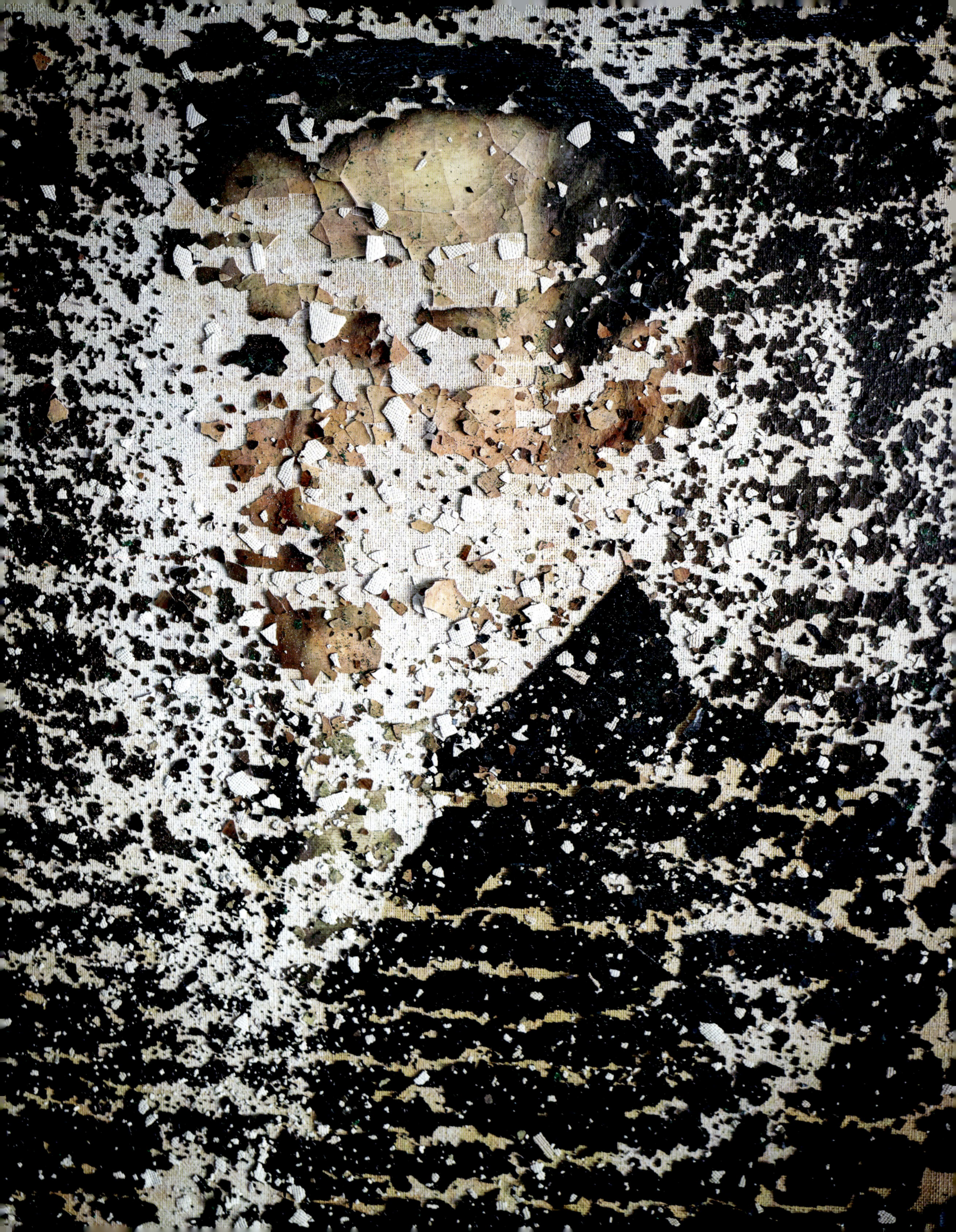

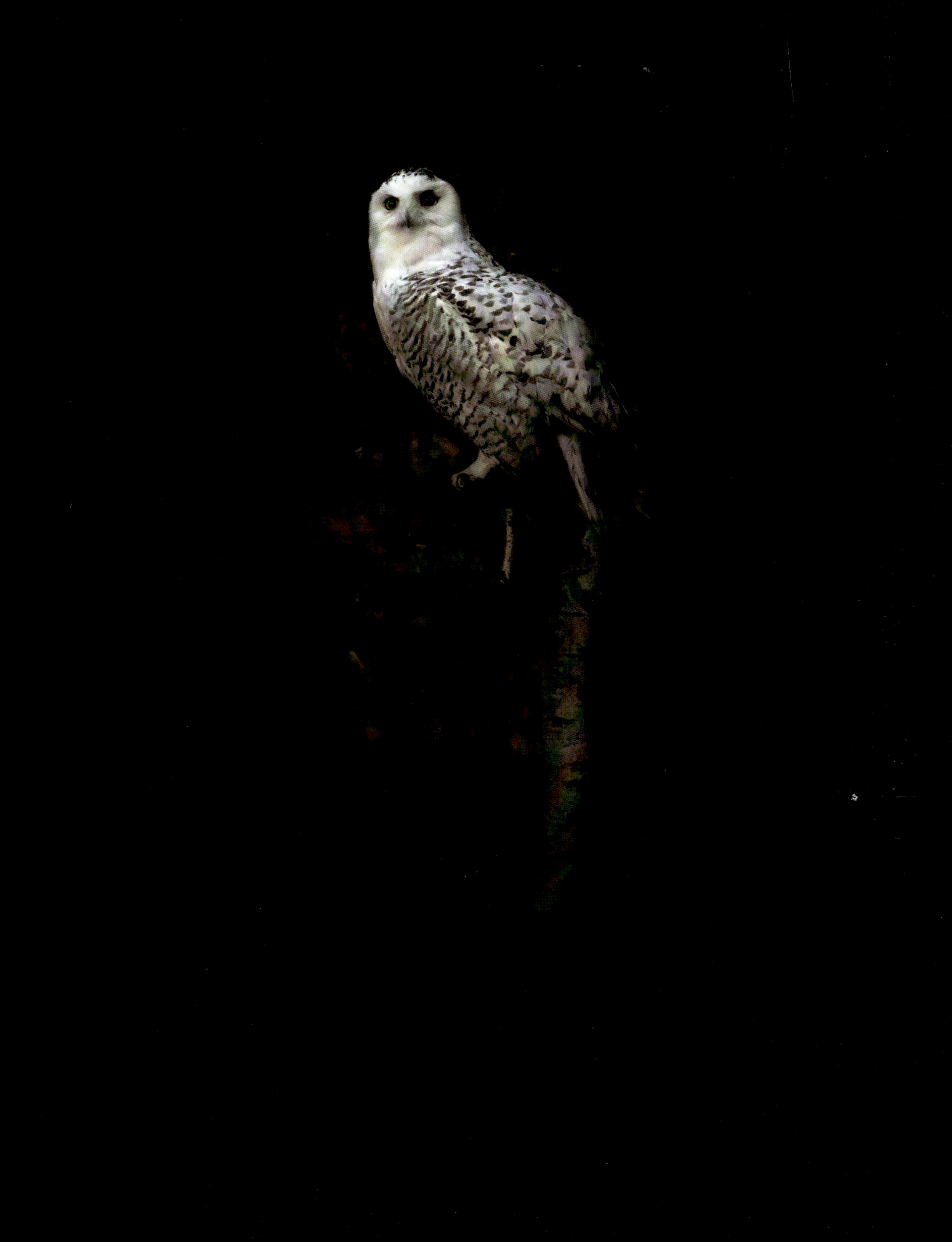

Gallstone
Yellow

In the fifteenth century, the physician Johannes de Cuba wrote *The Garden of Health* and invented one of the first color charts to compare the yellows of urine to diseases of the body, forever connecting color, art, and science.

Color charts, swatches, and samples are everywhere. Once you start looking, you'll find them in places beyond the obvious art and paint stores. They're in nail salons and hairdressers, car dealerships, furniture warehouses, and cosmetic counters. Butchers have color swatches displaying the amount of fat in meat, and dentists have their own color charts called *tentiers*, little incisors on sticks in varying degrees of white. For hundreds of years, the textile industry has understood the sensory pleasure of simultaneously seeing and touching fabric, producing leporellos of swatches to display seductive spectrums of silk, wool, leather, and feathers.

Color charts are sites of wonder, of order and balance, of experimentation and measurement and harmony—but also of racism. Shades of *nude* or *flesh* in stockings, underwear, and foundation sold only in limited hues of pink and light beiges for caucasian skin. So the Band-Aid becomes the cut. It is only recently that trailblazing beauty and lingerie companies founded by women of color have expanded the selections.

Color can also be an alert system, signifying pleasure or warning us of danger.

Just as a darkening sky is the prelude to a storm approaching, the body serves as a color chart of health. Gray skin means not enough oxygen in the blood. The body turns blue with hypothermia and pale with anemia. Eyes darken with sexual pleasure. Cheeks flush red with embarrassment and excitement. Graying hair results from no pigment being sent to its roots: just like leaves in autumn, the energy is better served elsewhere.

Vomit ranges in color from clear to black. The term *green with envy* comes from the Greeks, who thought an excess of bile in the body caused jealousy, turning the body and poop green. Science has since proven that BAM (bile acid malabsorption) is caused by eating too much fat.

I love color charts even when they skew toward the grotesque. The poop color chart on Google image search fills me with glee: celiac white to green to healthy brown to the charcoal tar black of peptic ulcers. I once made a drawing of all the colorful poops babies do in their diapers: the manta ray, the grape, the chipolata. Some days in winter I eat only beets for dinner, just to have a pink poo in the morning.

Blood leaving the human heart is a bright juicy red, but as it moves through the body, it decreases in oxygen and turns darker. The only creatures that have blue blood are aquatic animals like squids, lobsters, and octopuses. Leeches and worms have green blood, although some worms have purple blood—it all depends on the pigment in the respiratory system.

The Vedas, the ancient Indian philosophy of yoga, mapped seven colors to seven energy areas of the body in an upside-down vertical rainbow of the spine. This color system starts with red at the base of the spine, orange in the lower belly, a yellow solar plexus, an emerald heart, blue at the throat, indigo in the middle of the forehead and violet at the top of the head, predating Isaac Newton's splitting of the prism by three thousand years. But Western scientists still say that chakras don't exist.

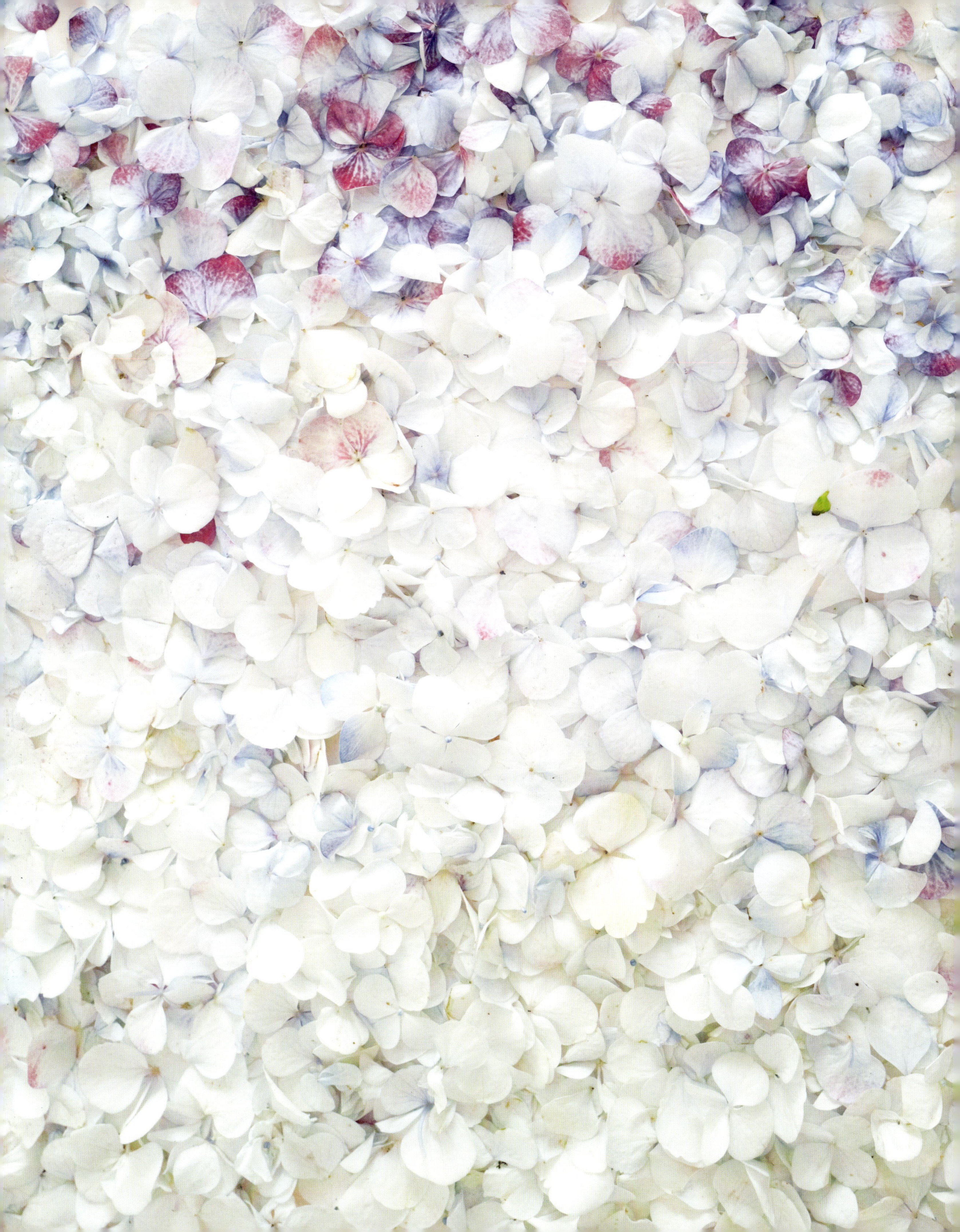

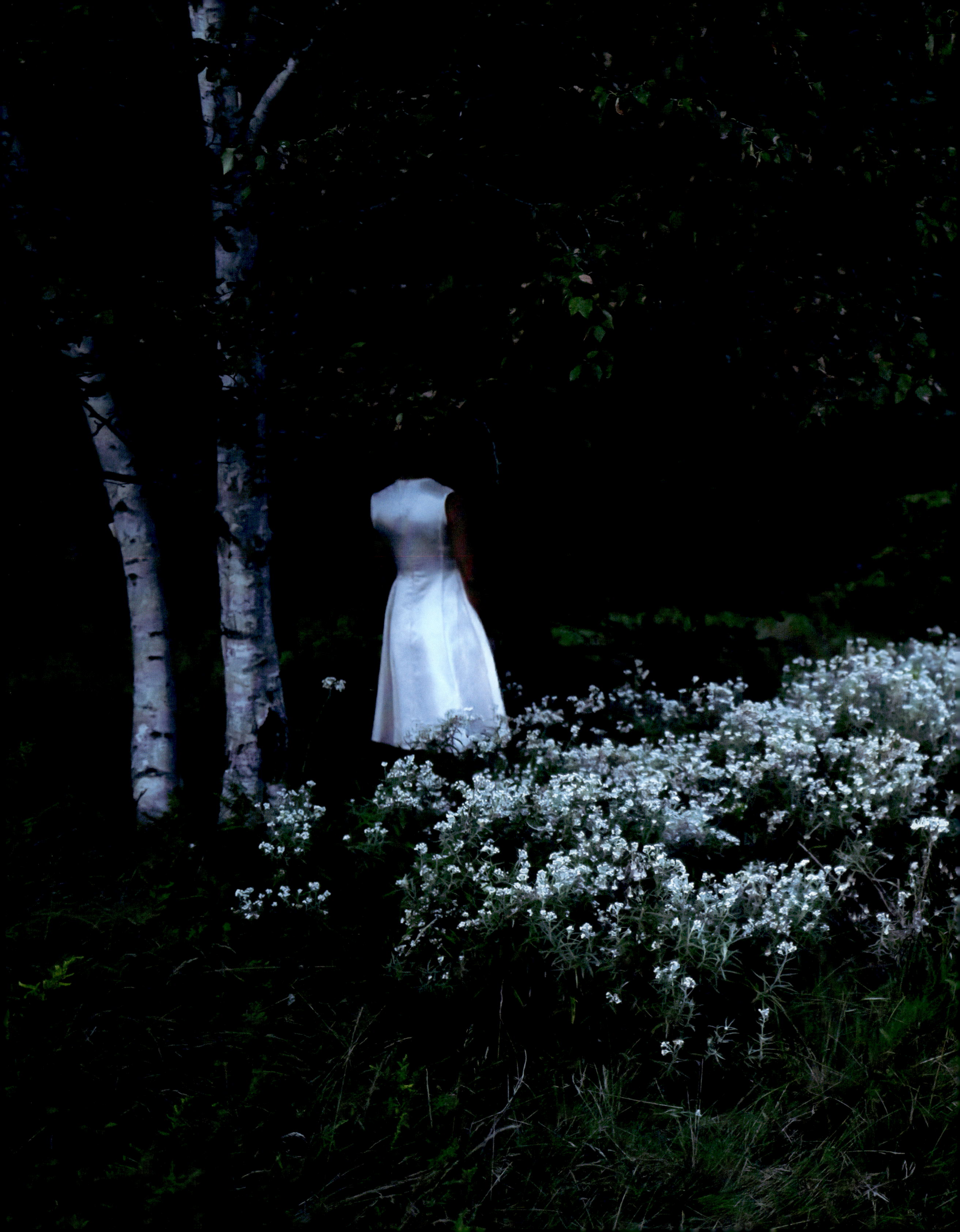

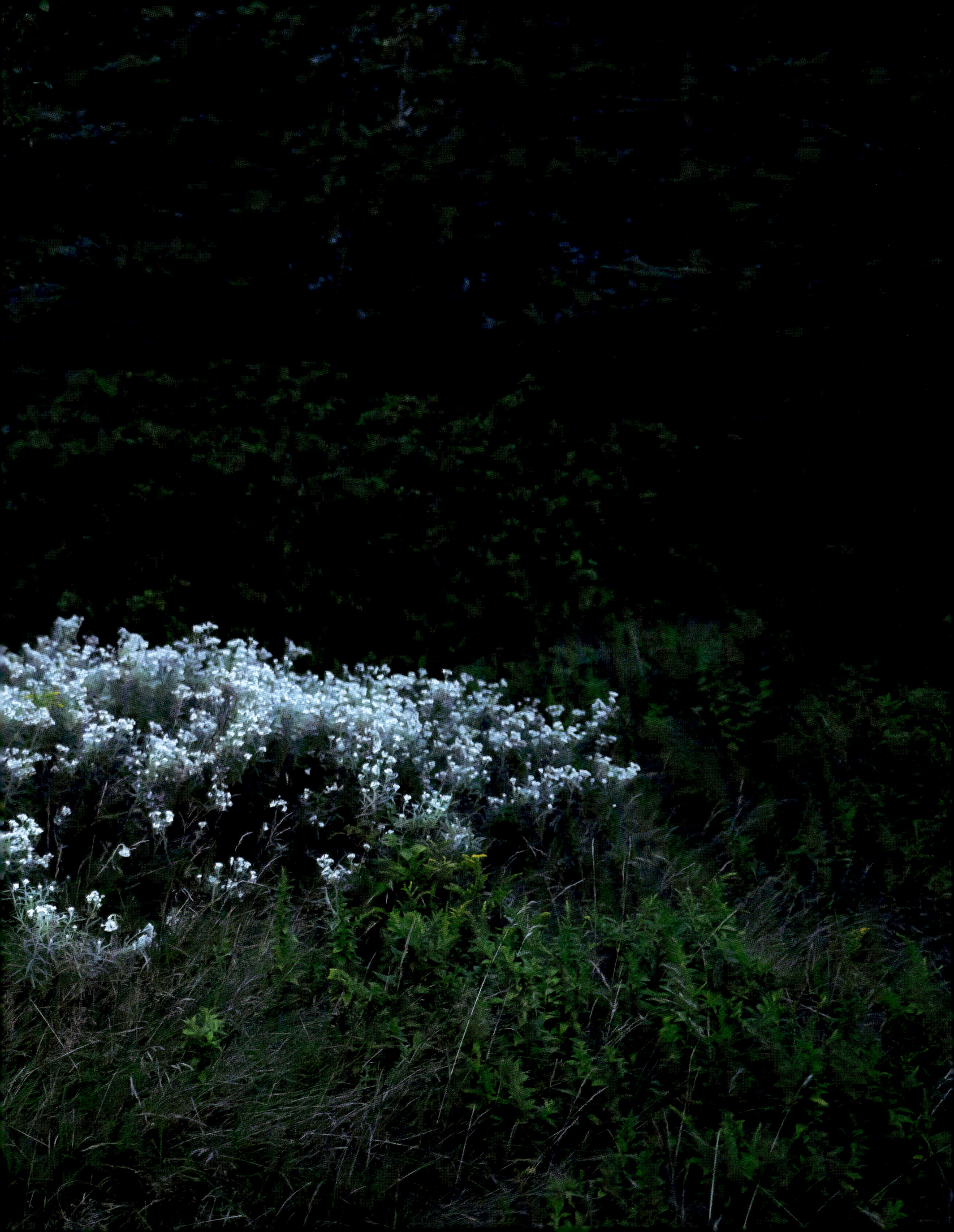

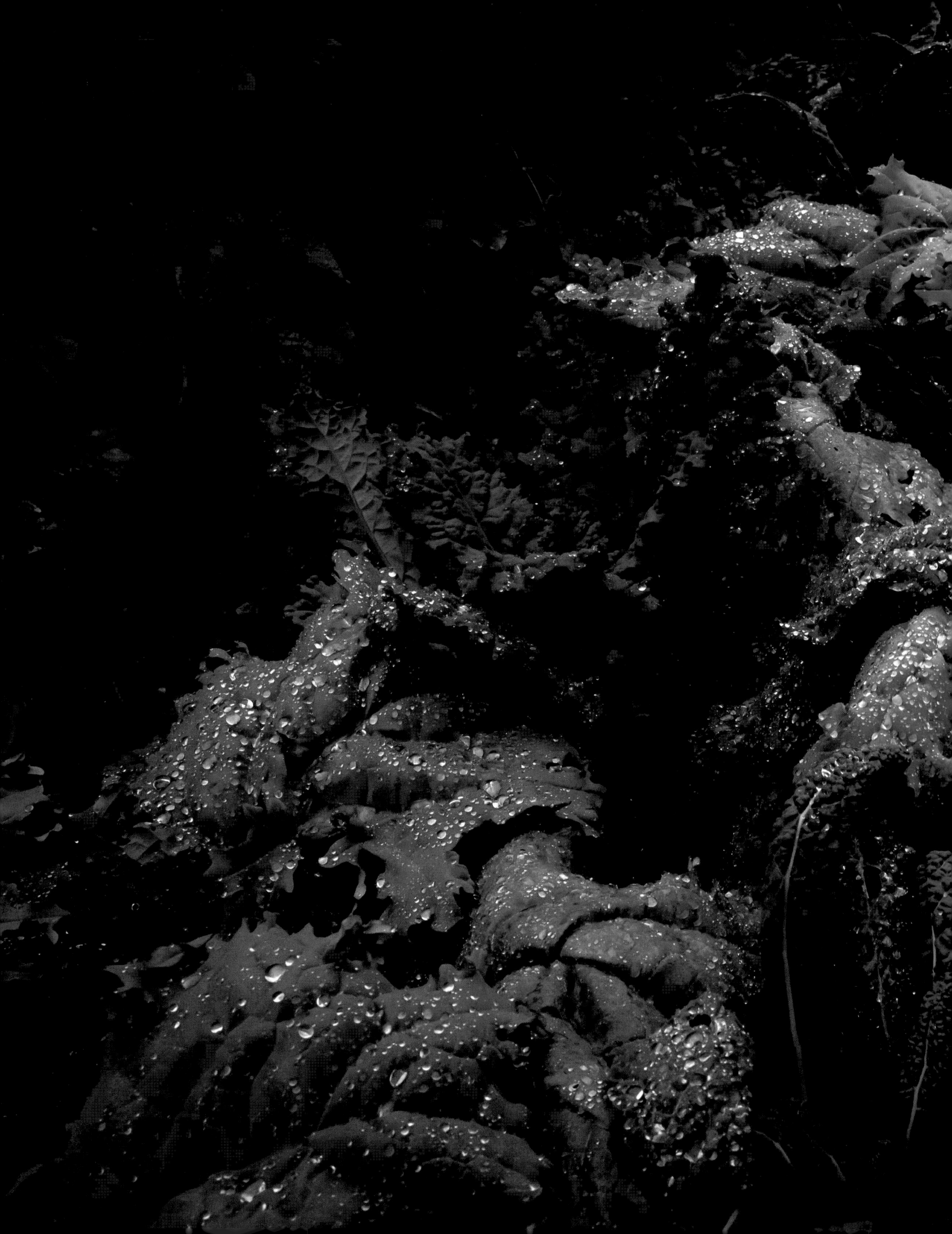

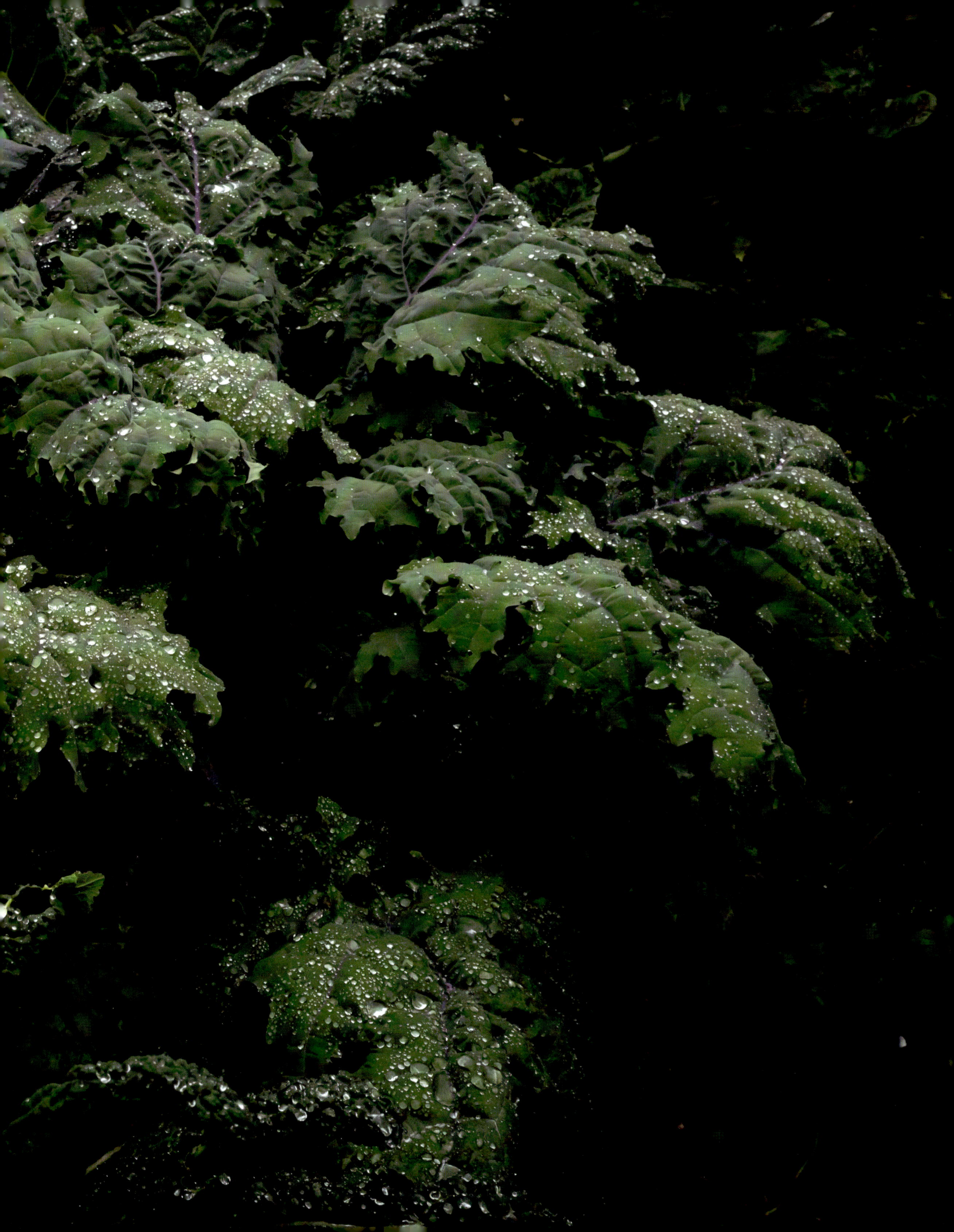

Until recently, men have always fought over the color purple. Purple dye was hoarded by the Roman Empire because it was so rare and expensive, costing an aristocrat a year's allowance for a pound of pigment. Tyrian purple was the color reserved for kings, emperors, and bishops: their robes, togas, and sashes dyed in the tears of crushed sea snails, clothes steeped in sadness.

It is not what the cave dwellers imagined when they blended animal fat and dust in the caves of France to make that first purple paint. They covered their hands in maroon paste and pressed them against the walls as they learned to stand upright.

Homer said the sea was purple, a *wine-dark* color. Monet said that purple was his favorite color and that *fresh air is violet*. And Prince loved purple because of its perfect blend of pink and blue, the color of androgyny.

In 1856, the scientist William Perkins invented the first synthetic purple dye from coal tar, a by-product of coal mining. He was trying to find a cure for malaria but instead ended up creating the color mauve and unwittingly starting a fashion craze. Perkins's work creating this dye led to the invention of chemotherapy.

Although I love a deep amethyst, the softer purples scare me. When I was out west, the blackened eye of the mountains at dusk was a color that haunted me. I couldn't shake the feeling of a dark history in those shadows—one of land theft, violence, greed, and corruption.

Imperial
Purple

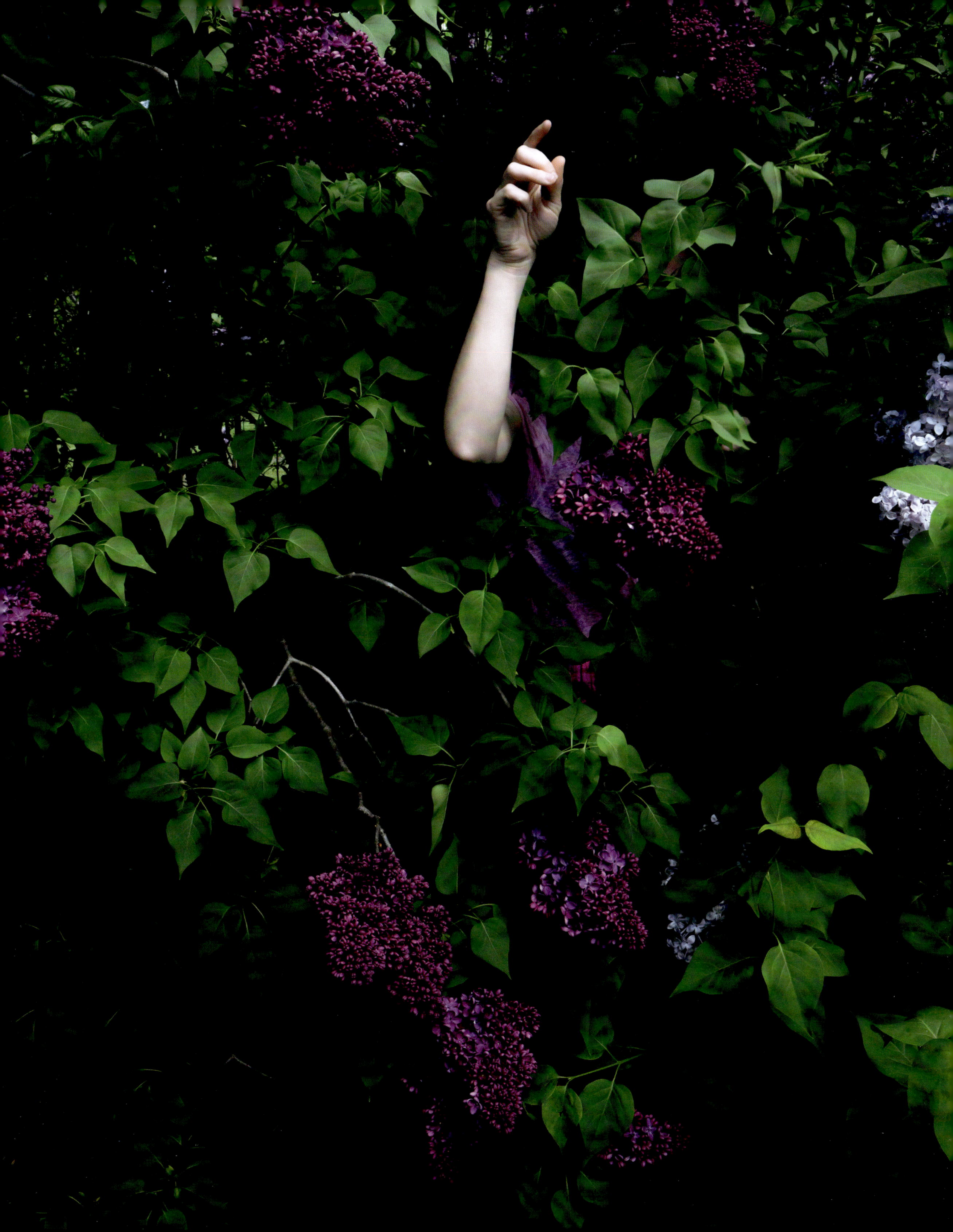

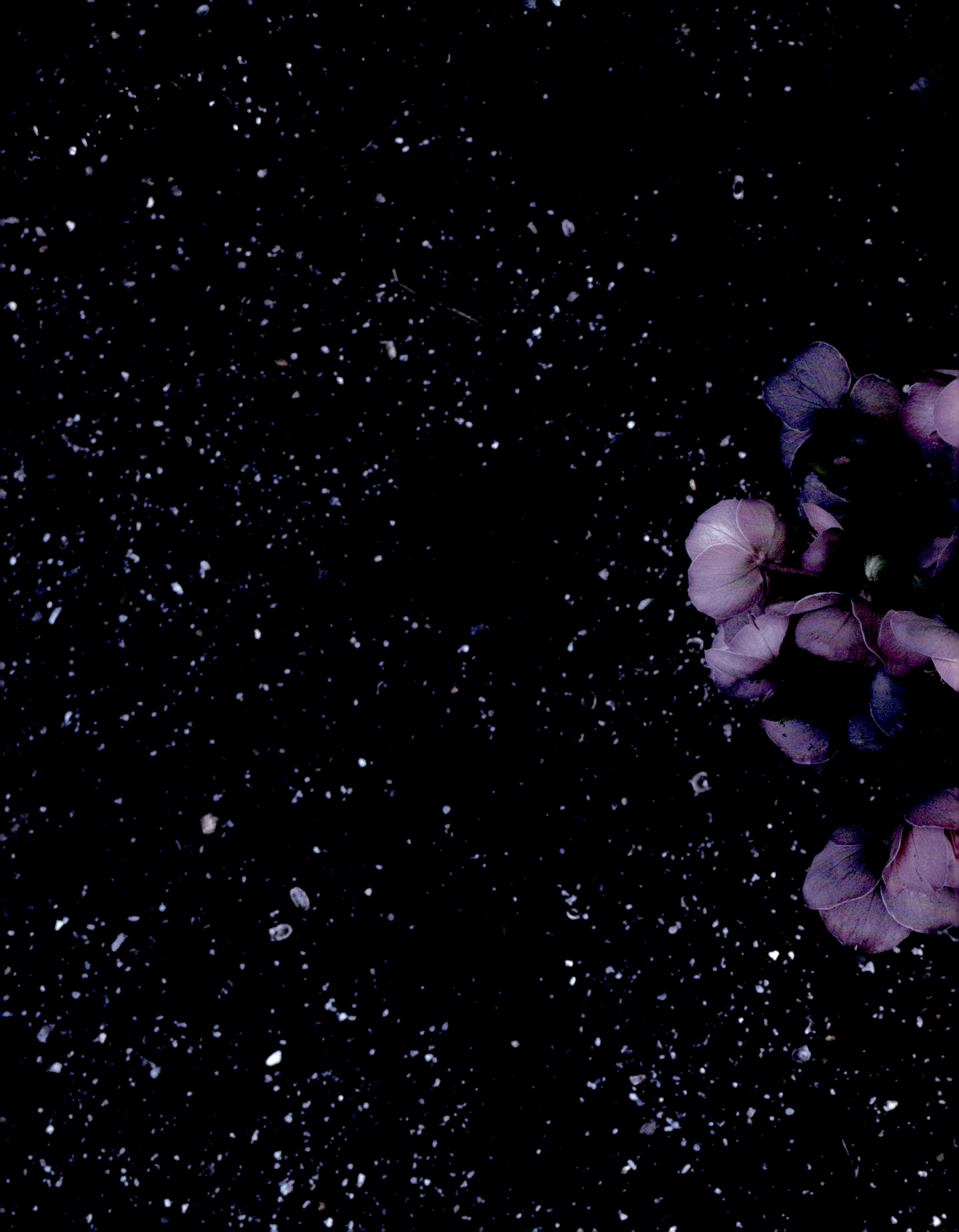

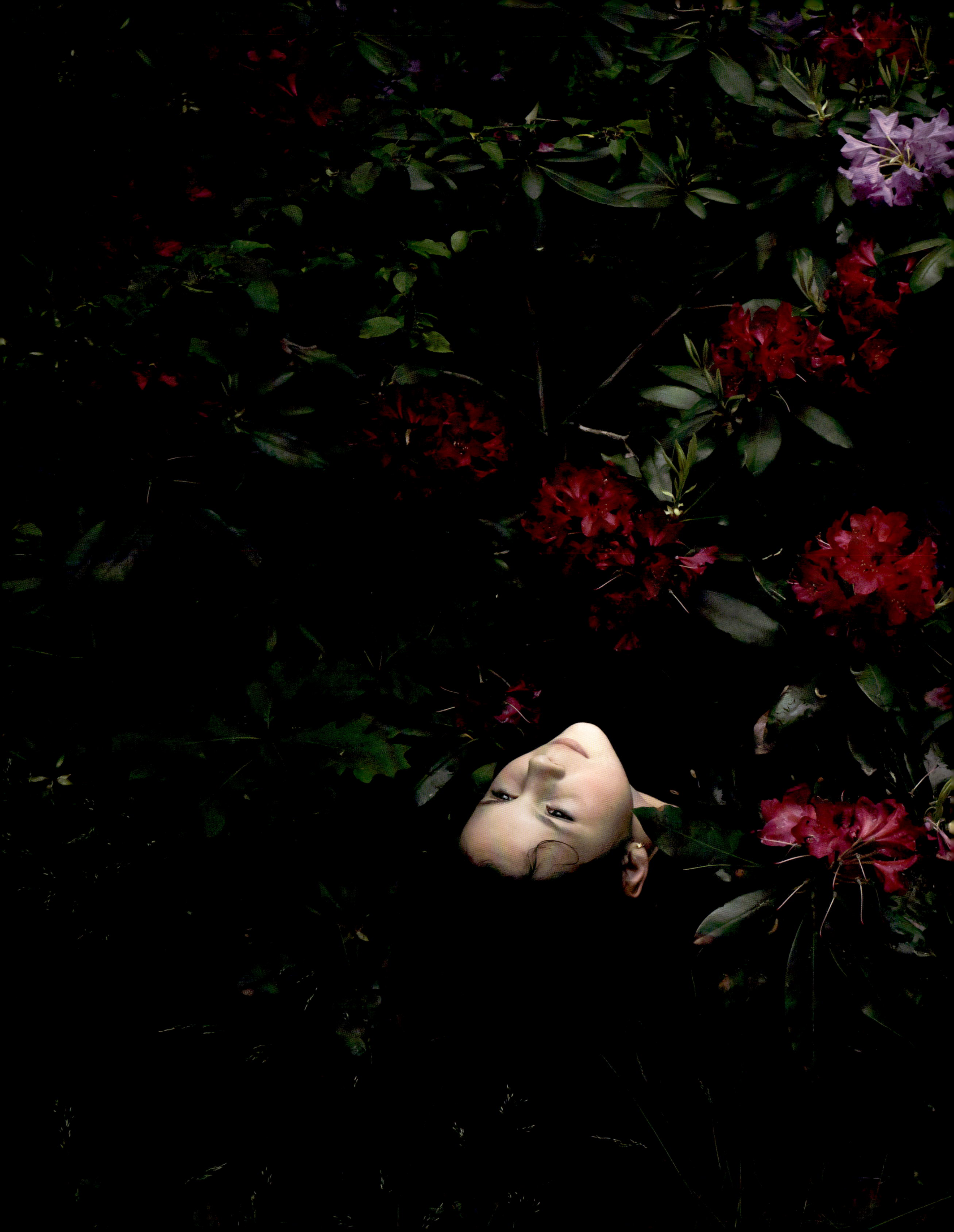

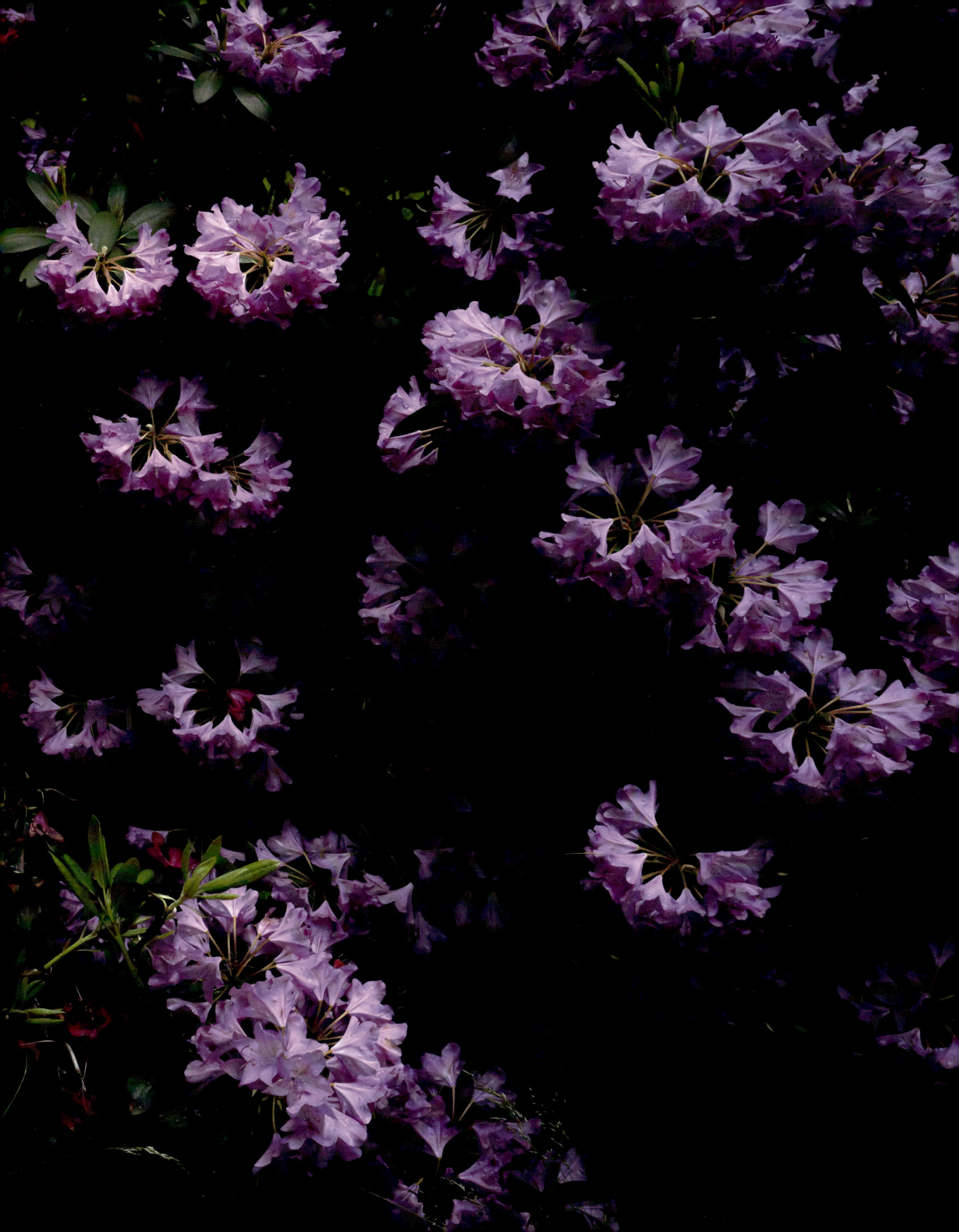

Driving Scout to school this morning,
the maples were dropping their pollen,
and it was as if the sun had shattered onto
the dark tarmac.

This yellow is a flaming Baked Alaska.
Each mouthful is a jolt to the central nervous
system. A combination of flavors and textures,
hot and cold, soft and crunchy, rich and light,
sweet and salty. Every bite, a blend of your
greatest love and your worst heartbreak.

This yellow is J.M.W. Turner's *The Angel
Standing in the Sun*. Its thick churning light
exploding, fingers spread through the viscous
yellow, layered like the air is on fire. All
the beauty and the pain of D minor, painted
from Indian Yellow—a gorgeous, lit-up
color straight out of the tube, made from
the piss of cows that live on a painful diet
of only mangoes.

This yellow is minute two of Diana Damrau
singing Mozart's Queen of the Night aria:
my mother's favorite song. When I was a kid,
she would watch our VHS copy of *Amadeus*
over and over again. I've heard that hearing
is the last sense to leave the body, so in the
hospital I play it for her on headphones and
her eyes blink wide open for the first time
in days.

On
Turner's Yellow

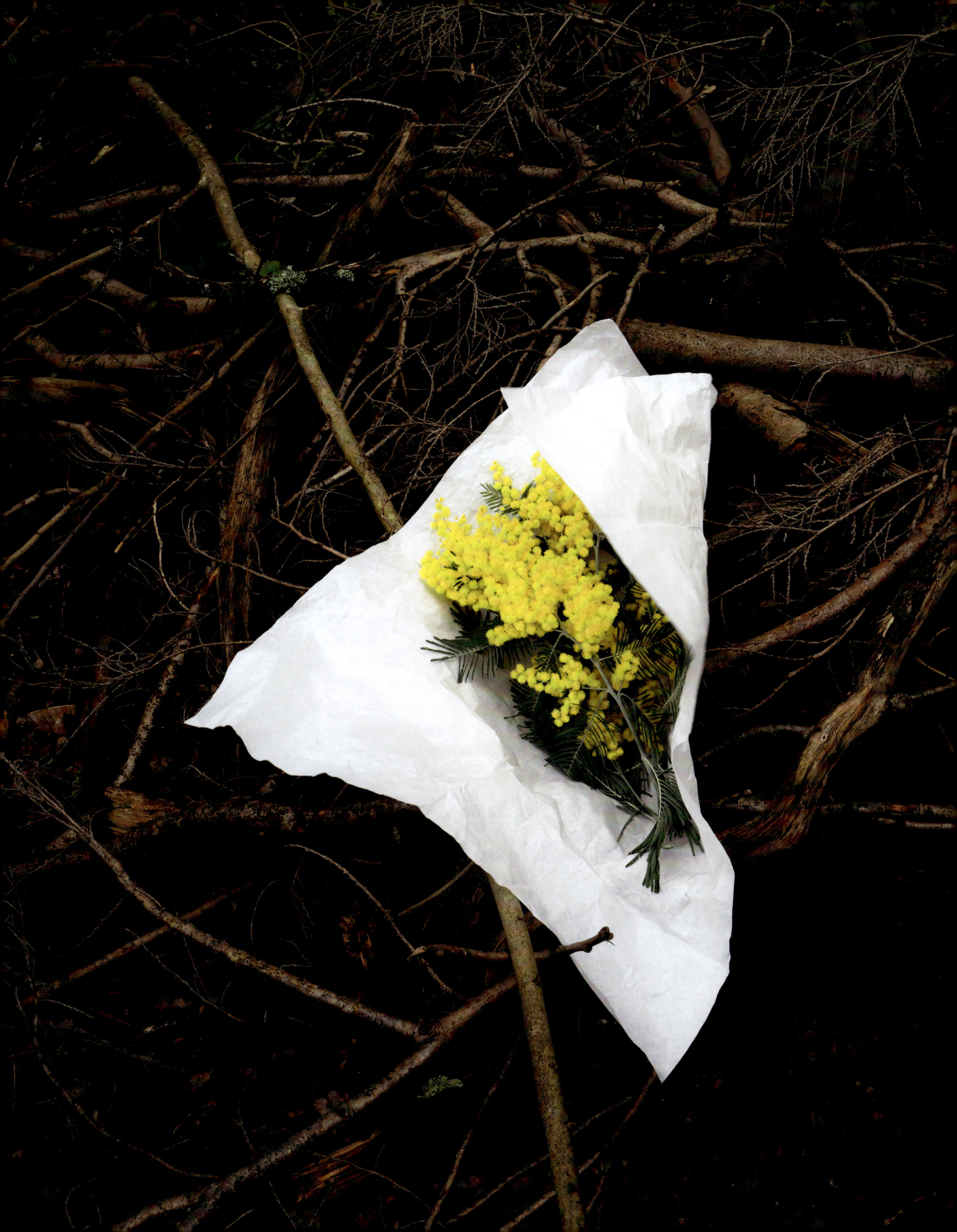

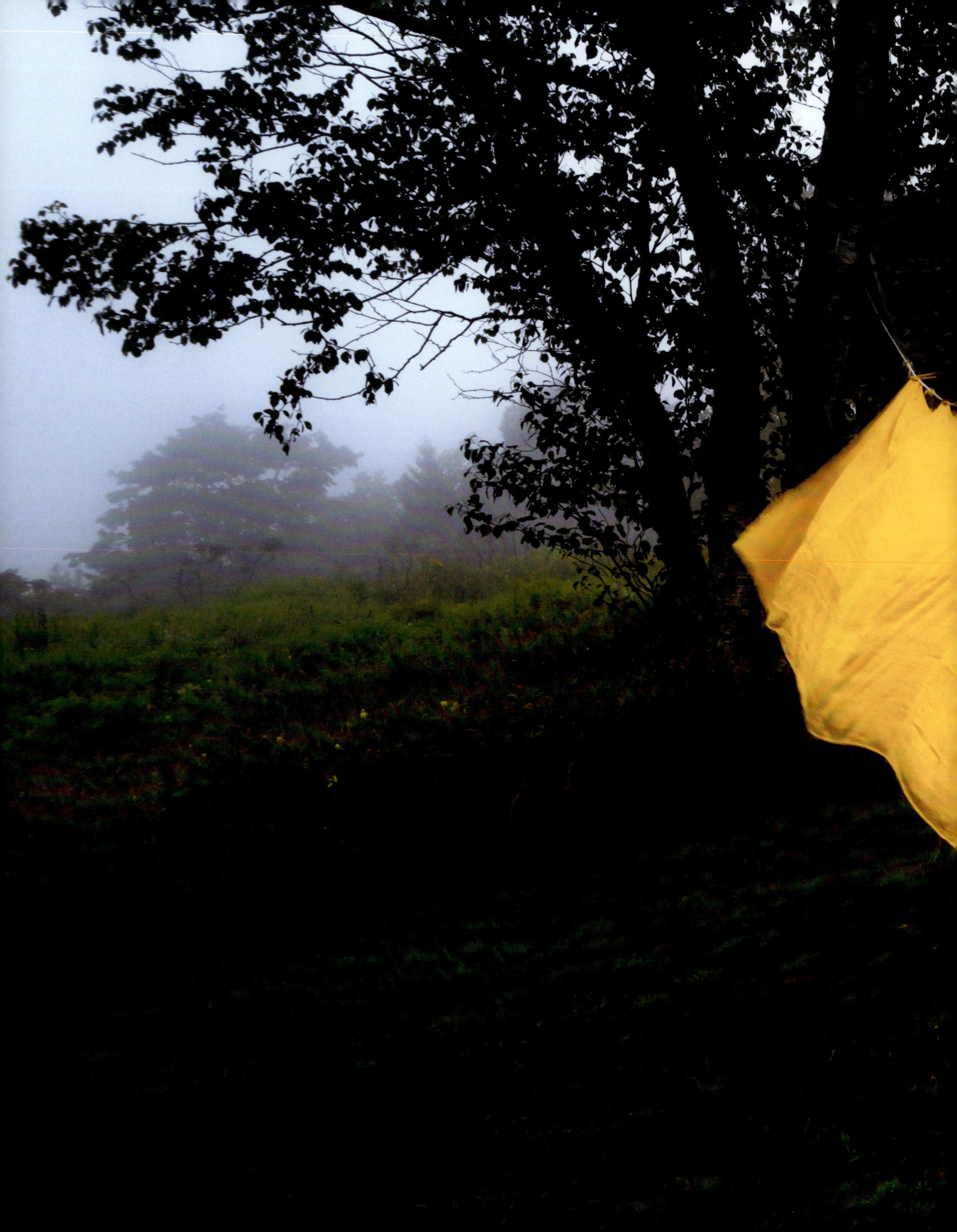

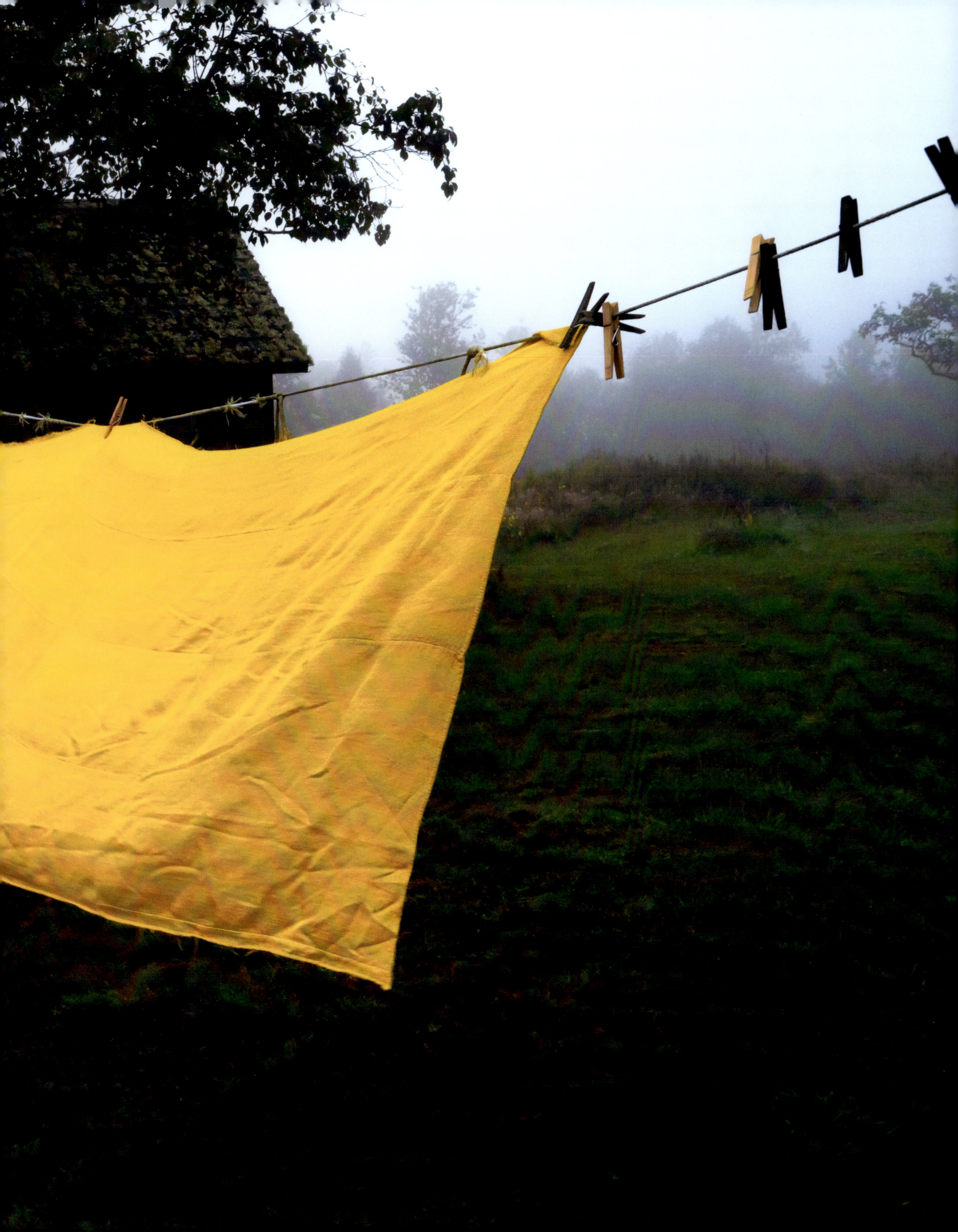

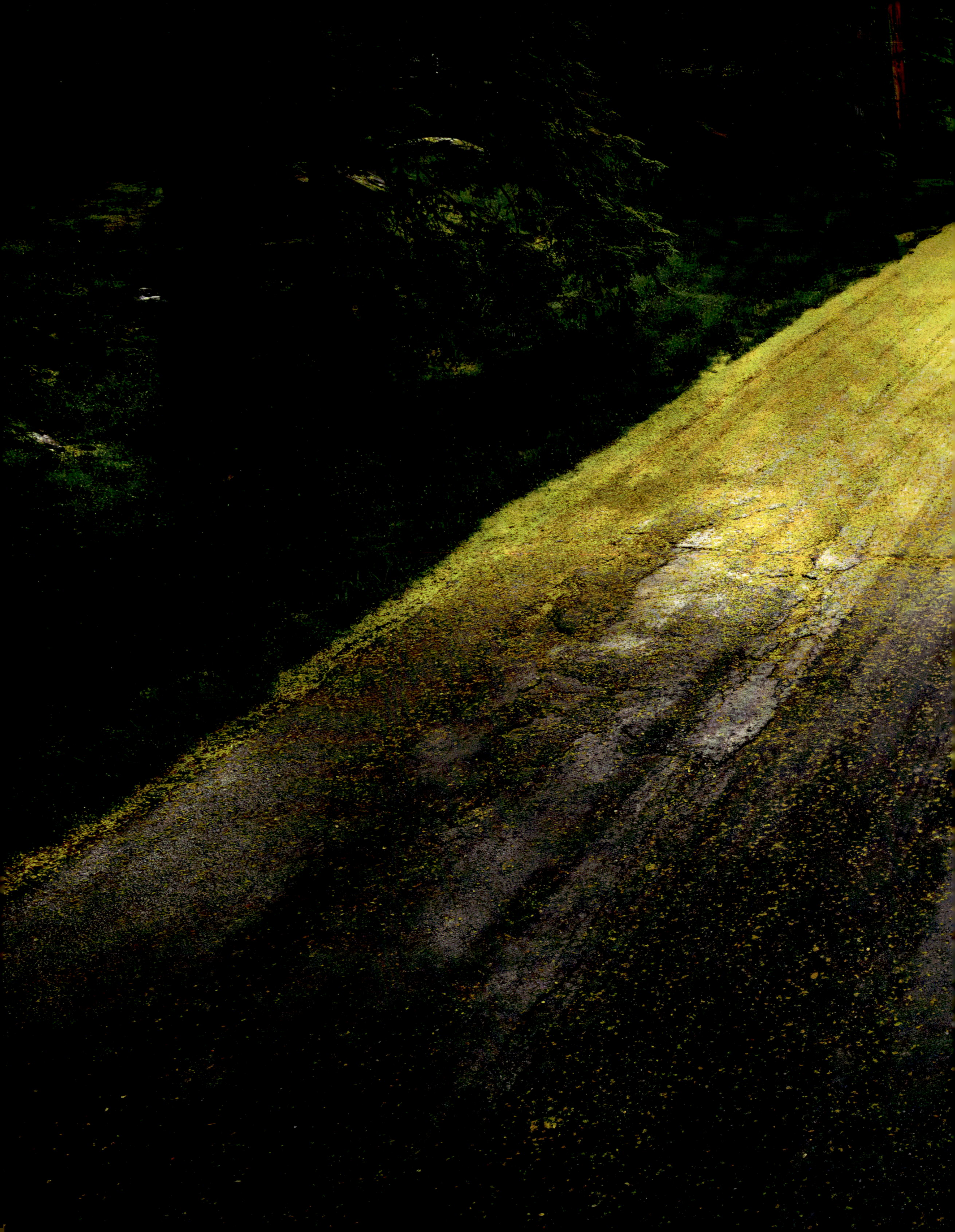

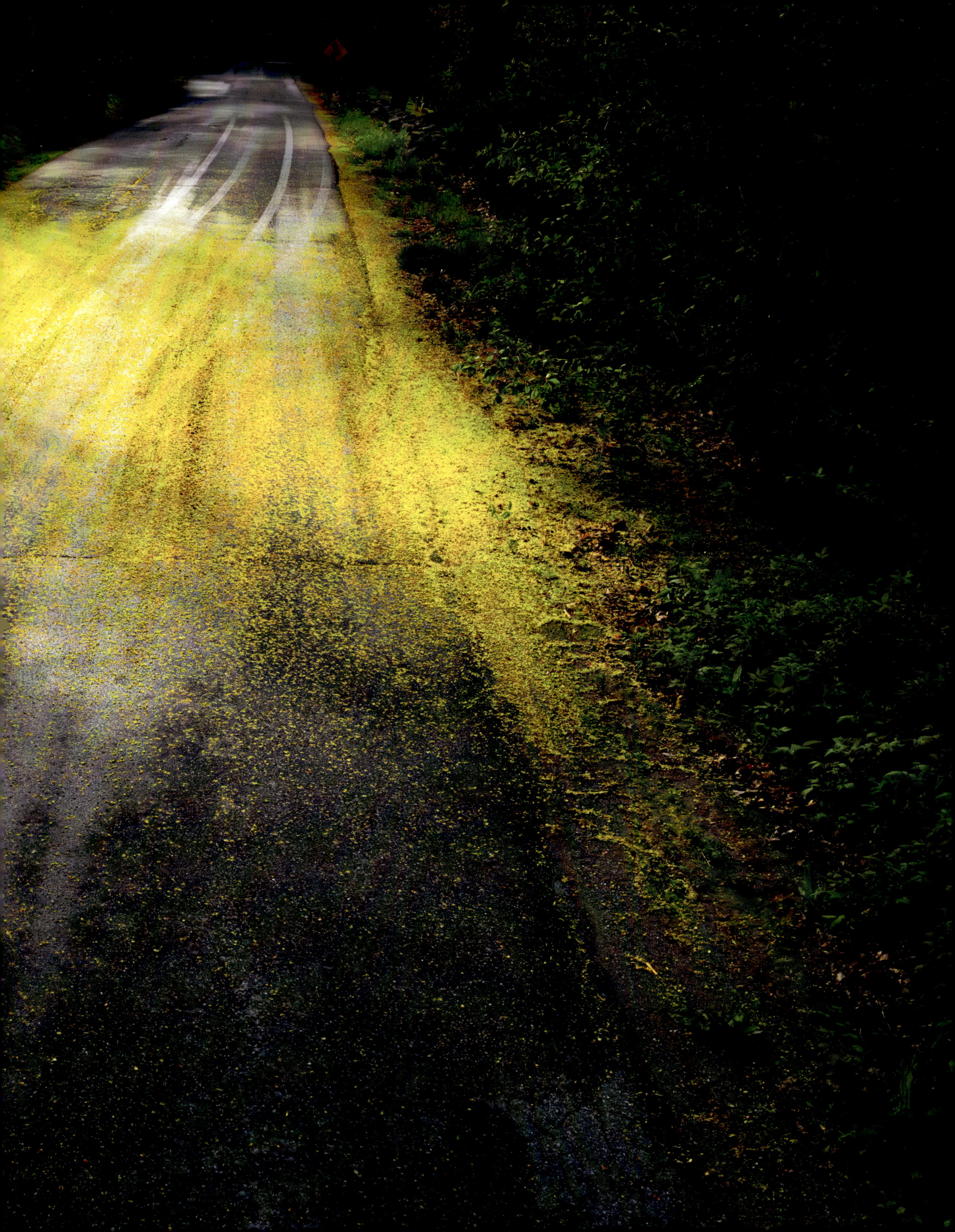

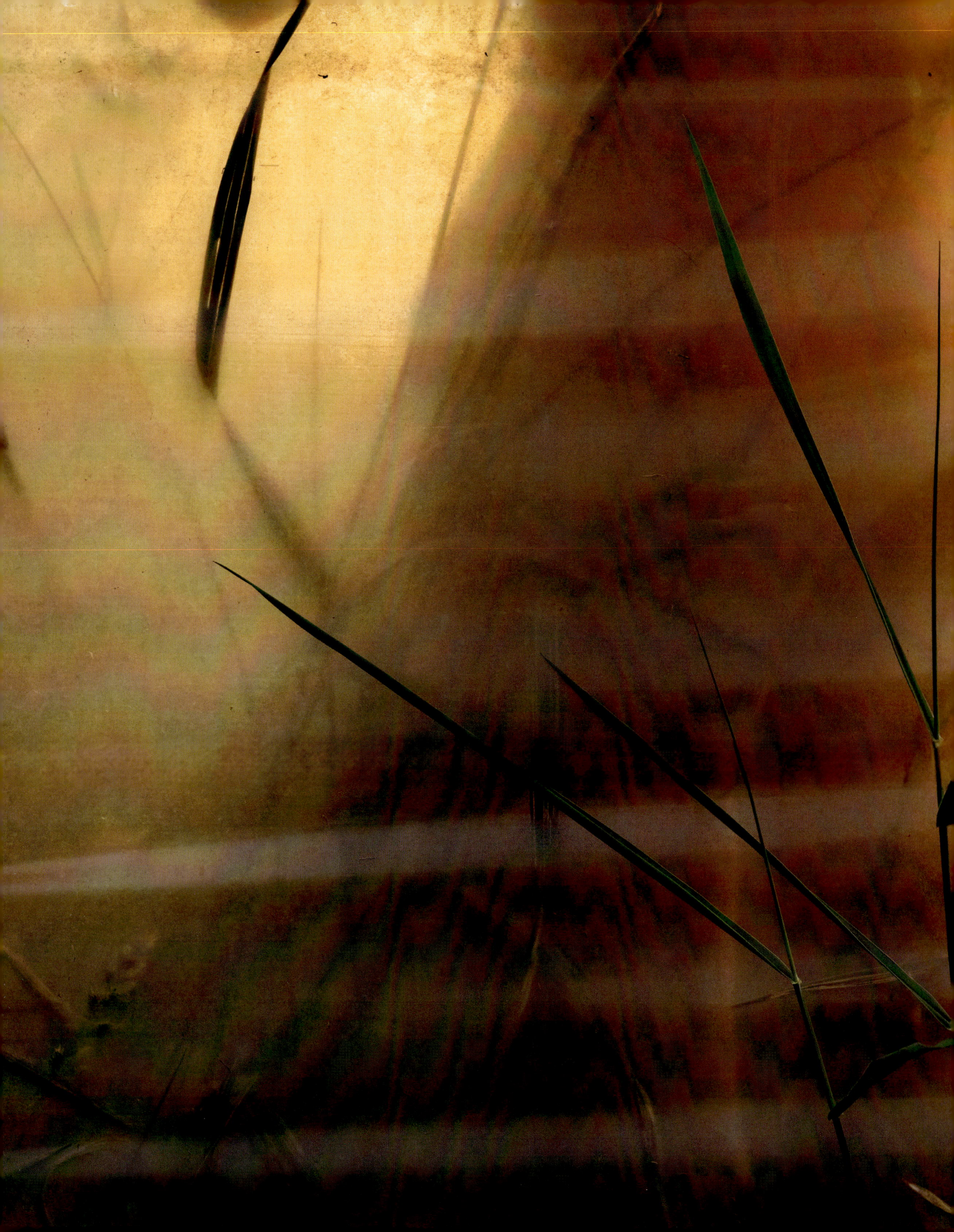

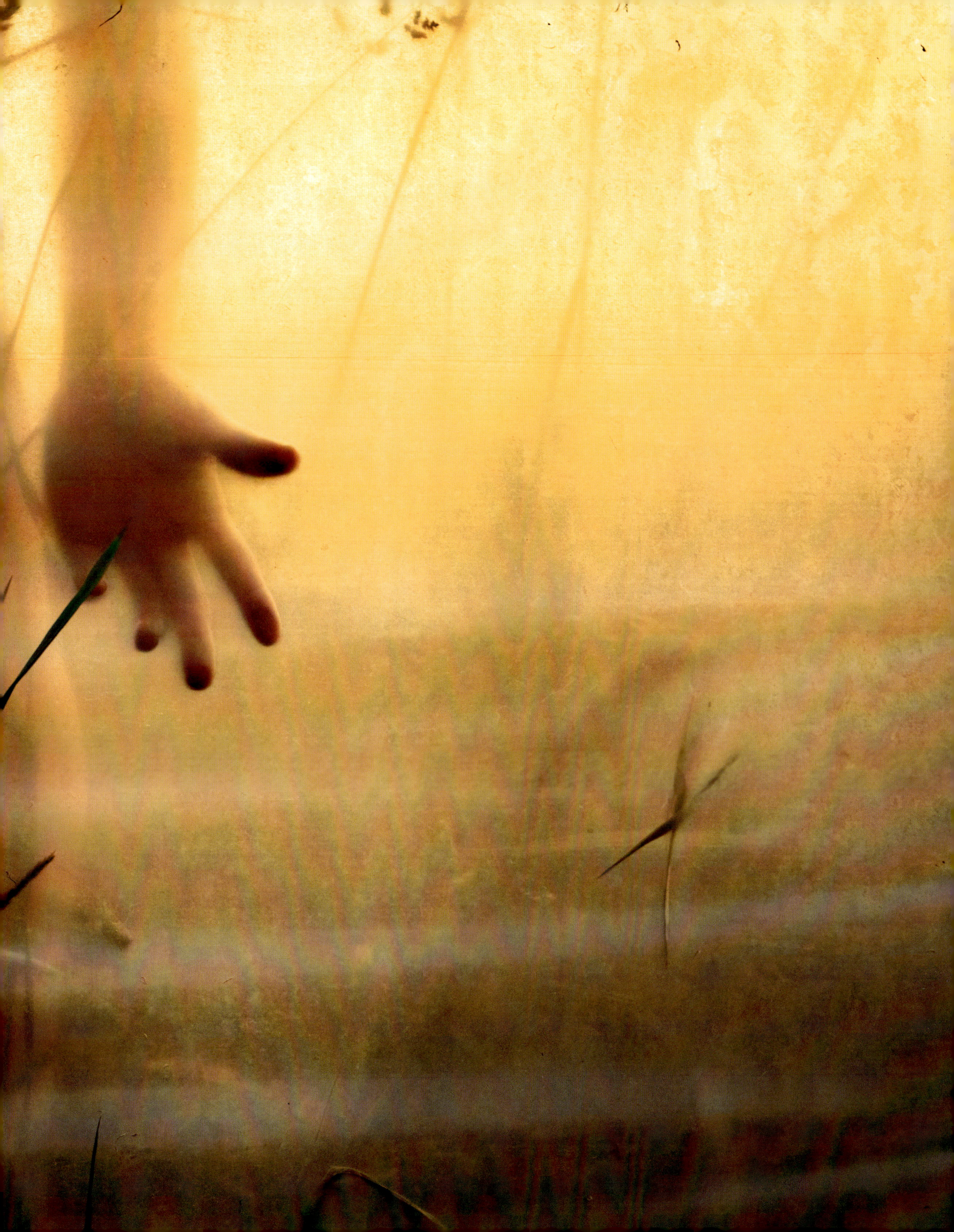

On November 4 at 10:32 a.m., Scarlet lies down under the maple in the backyard for the last time. Here, she says, and I lay down next to her. It's unseasonably warm, but still, Doug covers us with blankets. As Scarlet sleeps, moving in and out of this world, the maple throws its yellow leaves all over us like we just got married. Slow leaves, slow time, slow breath. The earth is claiming Scarlet back, calling her into the ground. The tree is also saying goodbye. The sun moves across the sky. Yellow against blue. Yellow is the opposite of blue. Dead is the opposite of alive.

When I was pregnant with Scout, I groaned at night during the last month because she lay on my organs when I reclined. Scarlet responded to my groans by throwing up. *She is internalizing your pain*, the vet told me. So, for the last month of my pregnancy, I slept upright in a chair, suppressing my moans so my dog would have ease. There's a *sea* in *ease*.

At 4 p.m., the vet's footsteps through the leaves mean there is no more time. I want to pick Scarlet up and run in the opposite direction, but there is nowhere to go. The vet injects adrenaline into her front left paw while I rest my head on her, listening to her heart. In liquid form, adrenaline is a pale yellow, a smooth gold path from here to there. And just like that, her heart stops. Nothing faster or slower than before. Just a breath and then not another.

Doug carries her to the back of the vet's black Subaru, laying her down on the ripped upholstery, and we arrange her like she is sleeping on a road trip to the beach. The vet asks us if we want her cremated. She fills out an index card, *What type of wood would we like Scarlet's ashes in? The carved rosewood is nice*. Her body will be kept in the freezer until Tuesday. I feel a steel gray shutter sliding down behind my eyes.

In the weeks that follow, the lack of Scarlet's physical presence is a black onyx cube that engulfs the house. Being home is unbearable and coming home a bitter disappointment. I'm used to a celebration every time I walk through the front door, even if I've just been to the mailbox and back. Now there's no point in walking. For once, I don't care why the sky is blue.

The house is too quiet. The bed's too clean. There is no one to talk to, and the floor has food on it for the first time in fourteen years.

People text me pictures and videos of Scarlet, and it's gutting each time I see her face in the palm of my hand, knowing that from now on, it will only ever be this version of her. The messages say she will always be with me in spirit, but I don't want her fucking spirit. I want her warm body pressed against me in my sleep, the smell between her paws. The body is not nothing. The body is everything.

The clocks go back, giving an extra hour of sadness. Everything in the garden turns inward and dies. Sunrise is a bitch. In the evenings, I sit in front of the TV with Doug and Scout, binge-watching five seasons of *Glee*. I spend the whole time staring at the fire, trying to swallow salty lumps of sadness because we agreed *enough crying already*.

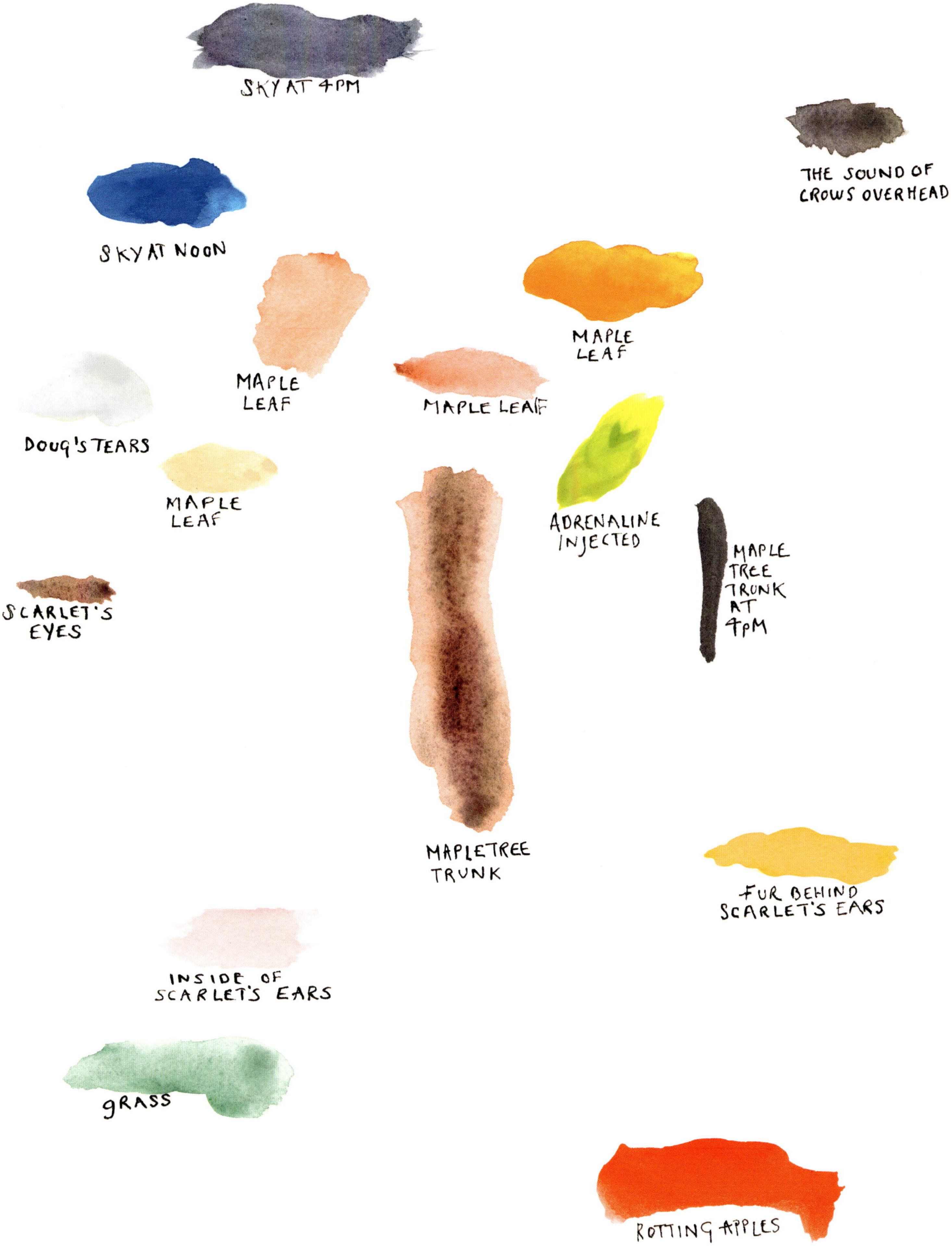

SKY AT 4PM

THE SOUND OF CROWS OVERHEAD

SKY AT NOON

MAPLE LEAF

MAPLE LEAF

MAPLE LEAF

DOUG'S TEARS

MAPLE LEAF

ADRENALINE INJECTED

MAPLE TREE TRUNK AT 4PM

SCARLET'S EYES

MAPLETREE TRUNK

FUR BEHIND SCARLET'S EARS

INSIDE OF SCARLET'S EARS

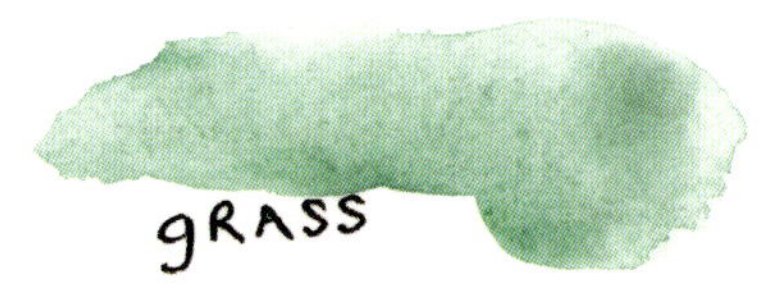

GRASS

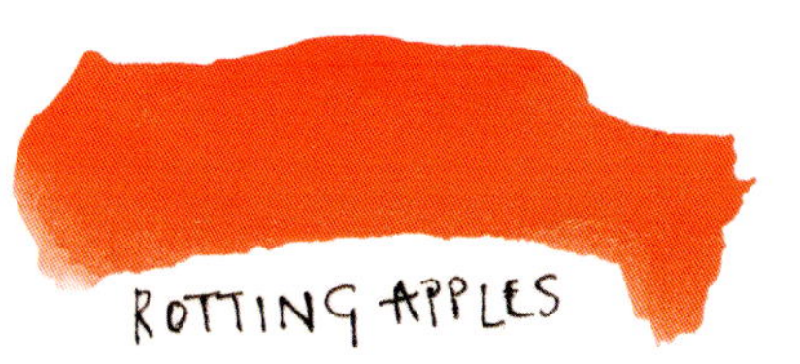

ROTTING APPLES

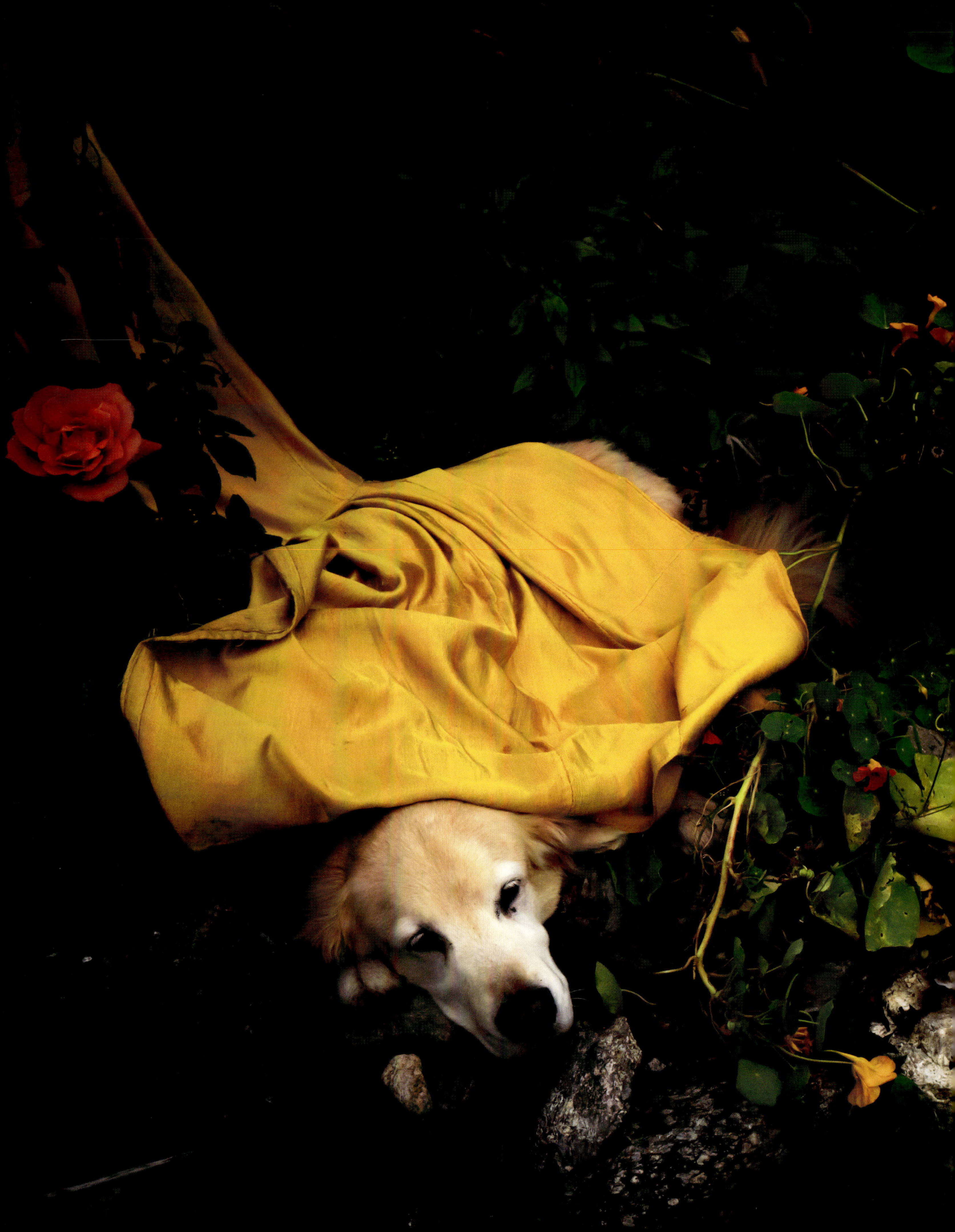

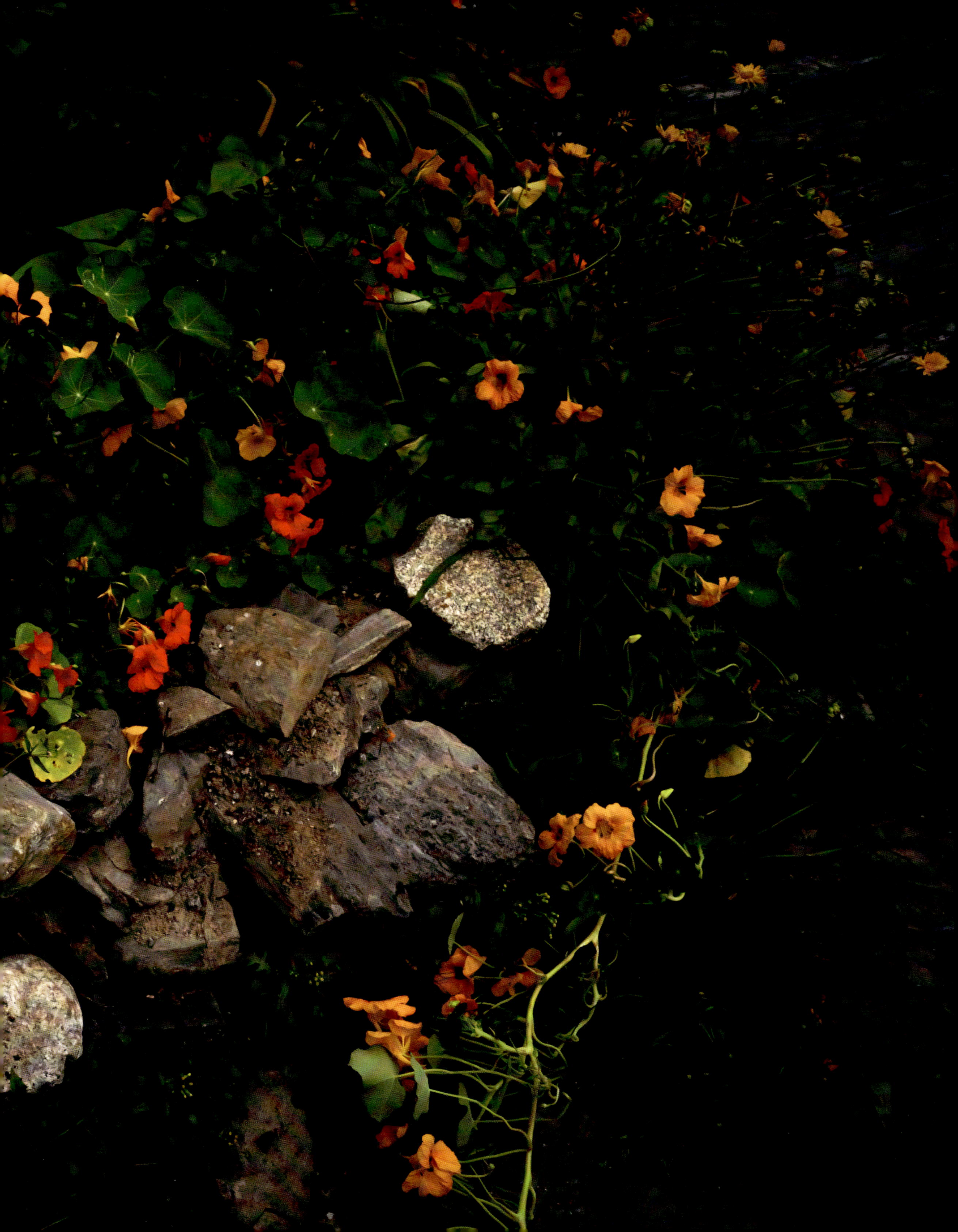

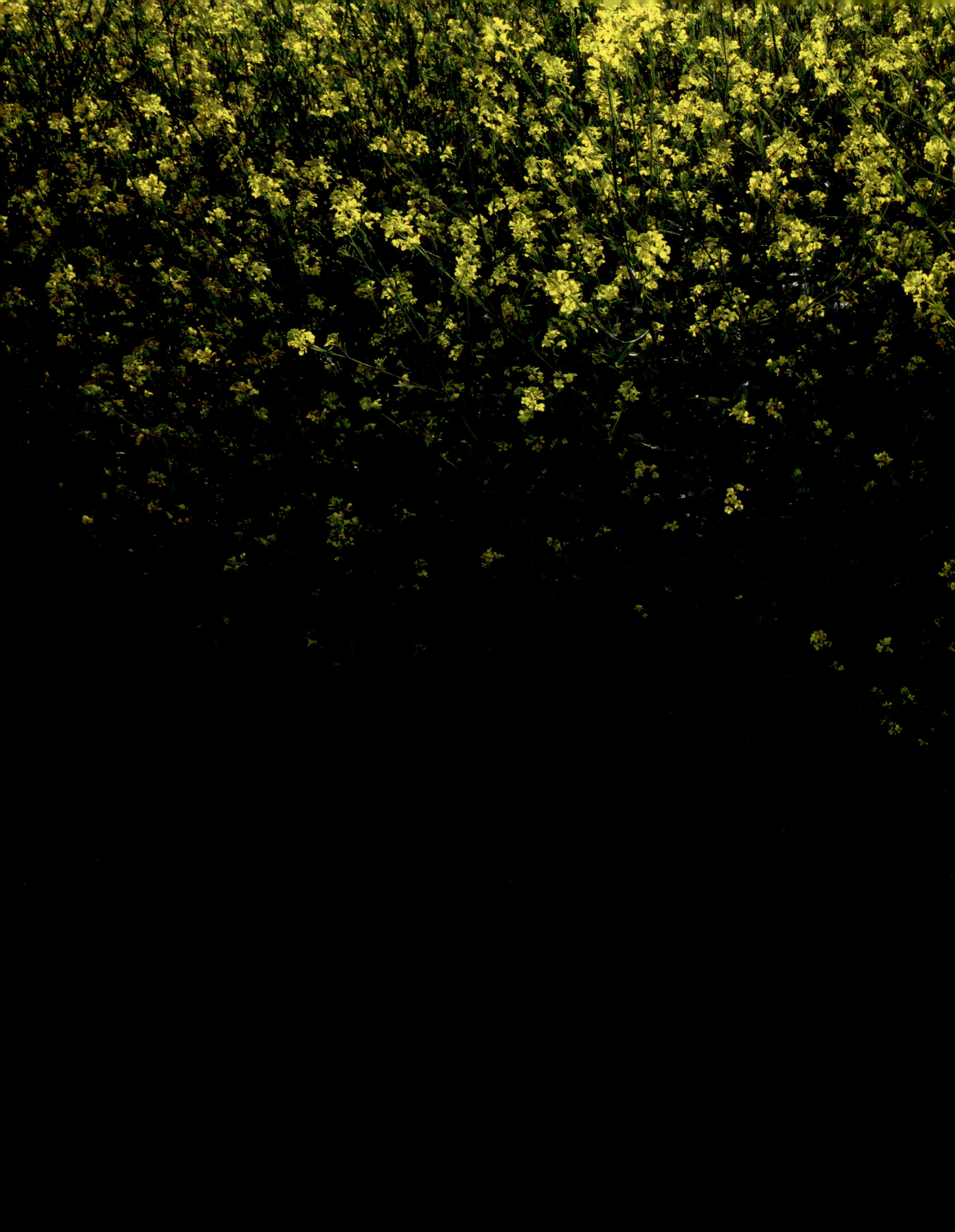

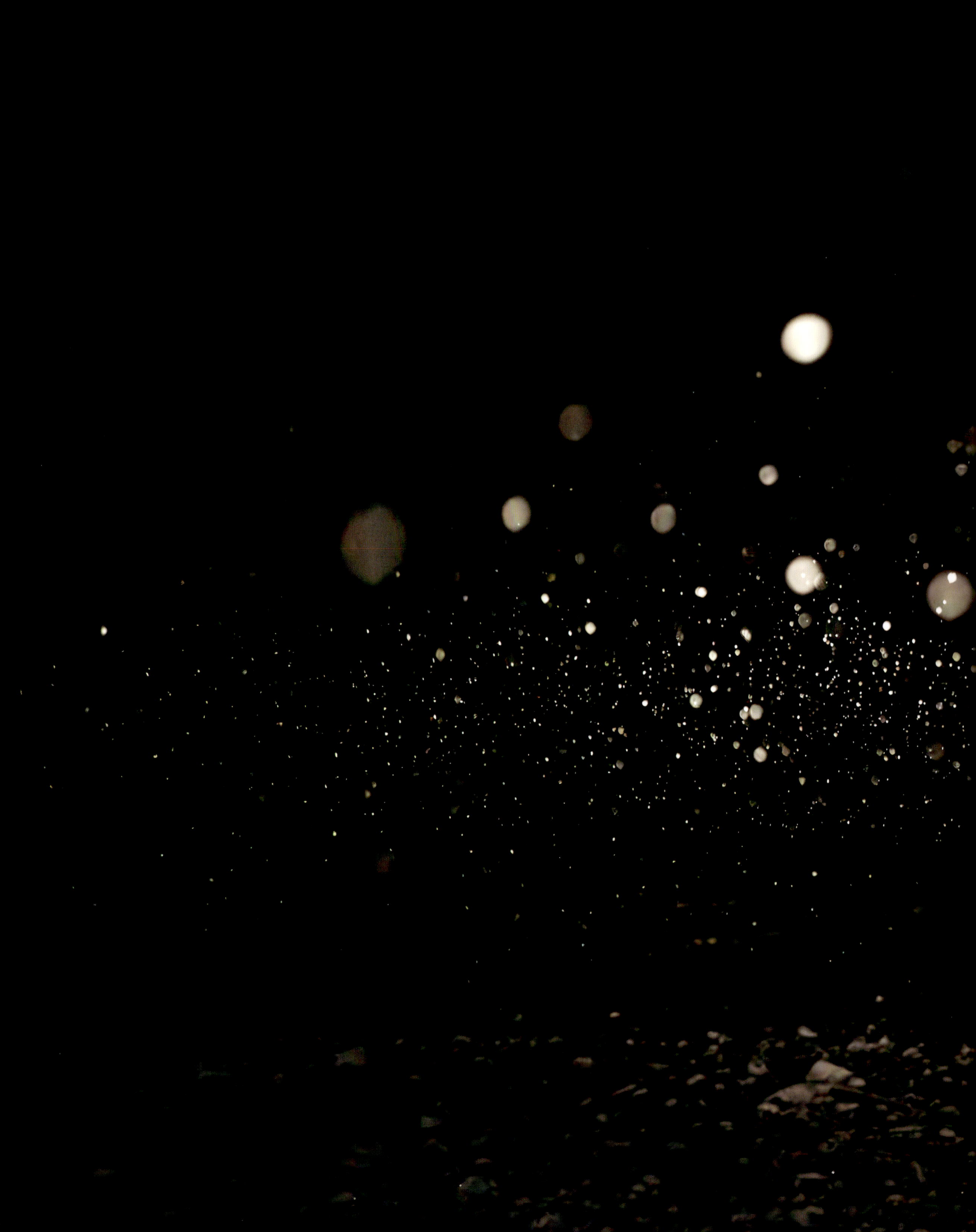

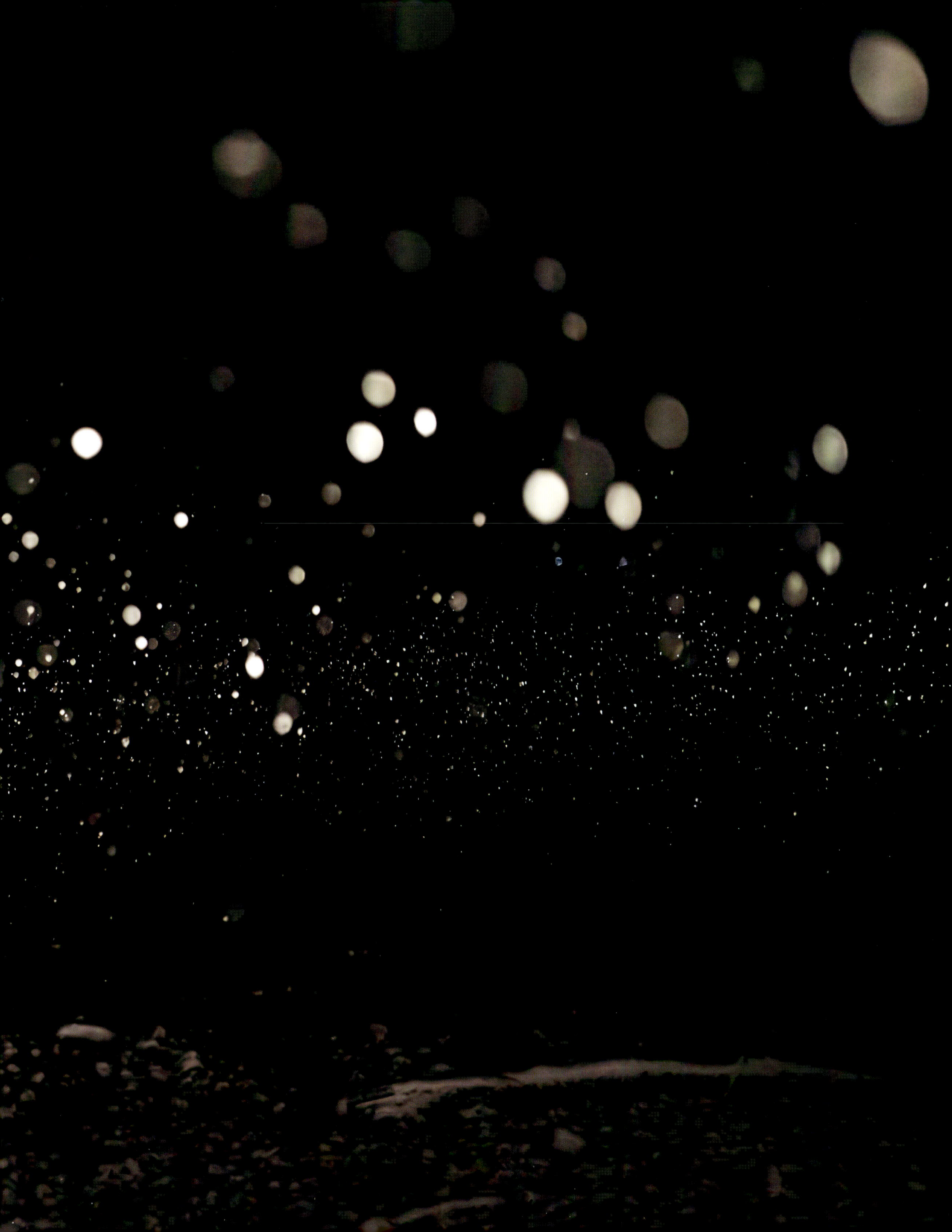

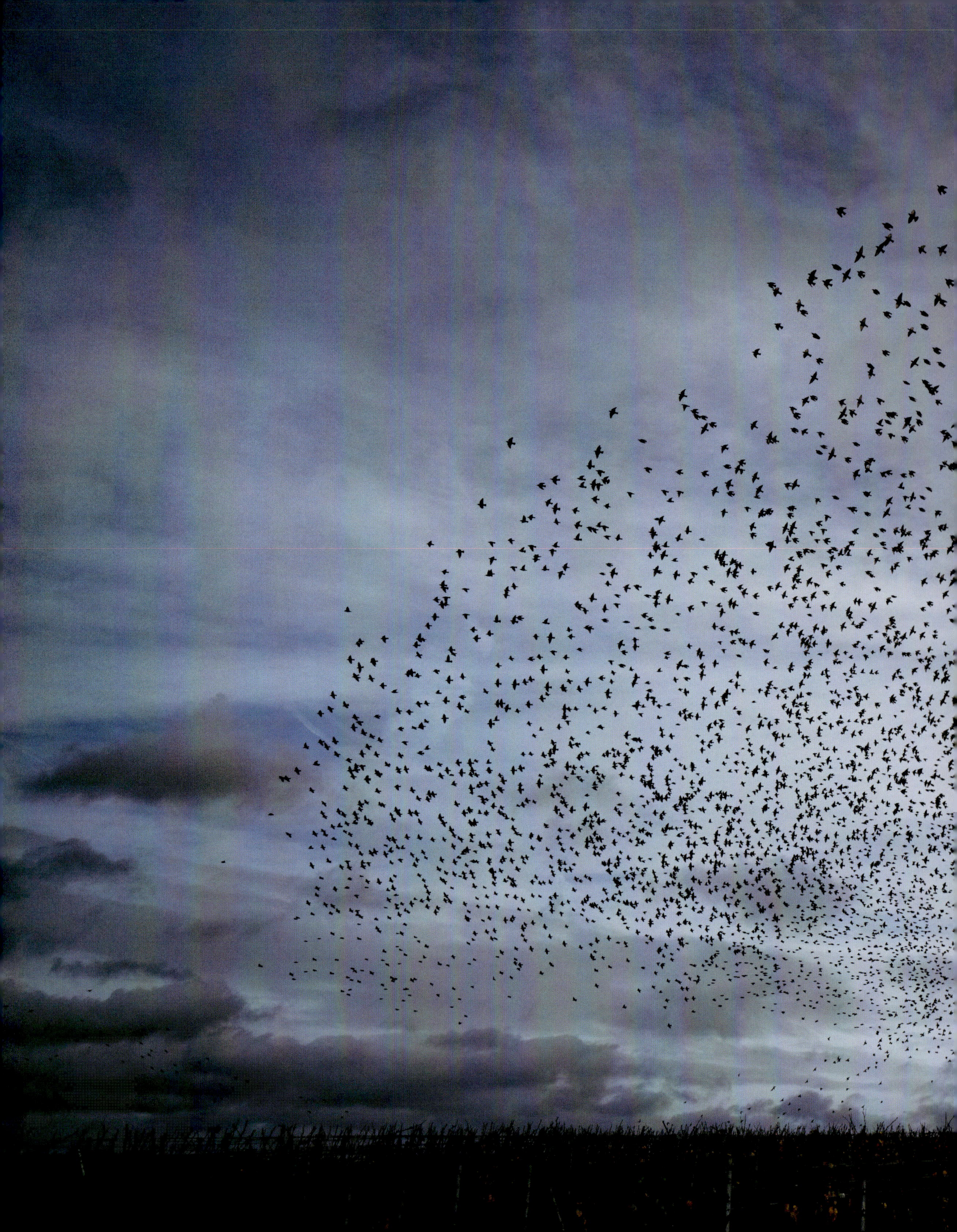

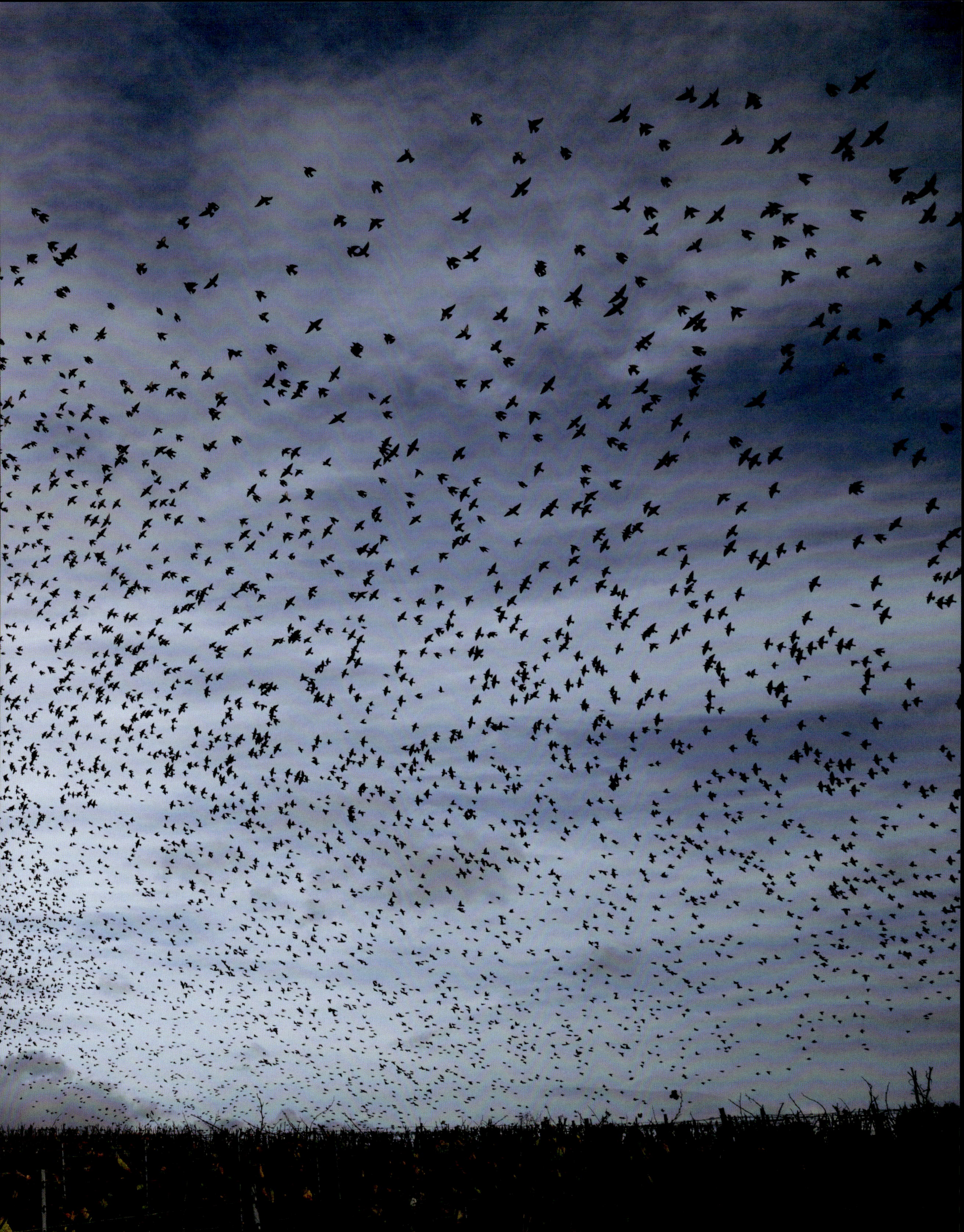

Oxygen, when frozen, is robin's-egg blue.

We live in a state of fight or flight, our panting brains drowning in oxygen. To reverse this and calm the central nervous system, inhale the midday sky—one, two, three, four—and then exhale the pale white clouds of carbon dioxide for eight, seven, six, five, four, three, two, one.

As you slow your breathing, the blue that is left inside of you intensifies.

Hold your breath between the ins and outs—a cobalt vibrates in the throat. Soon, the blue will seep into the neglected areas of your body, indigo staining the red heart, cerulean seeping into the gut, and ultramarine, that blue from beyond the ocean, settling into the bones. The body is sapphire.

## The Body Is Sapphire

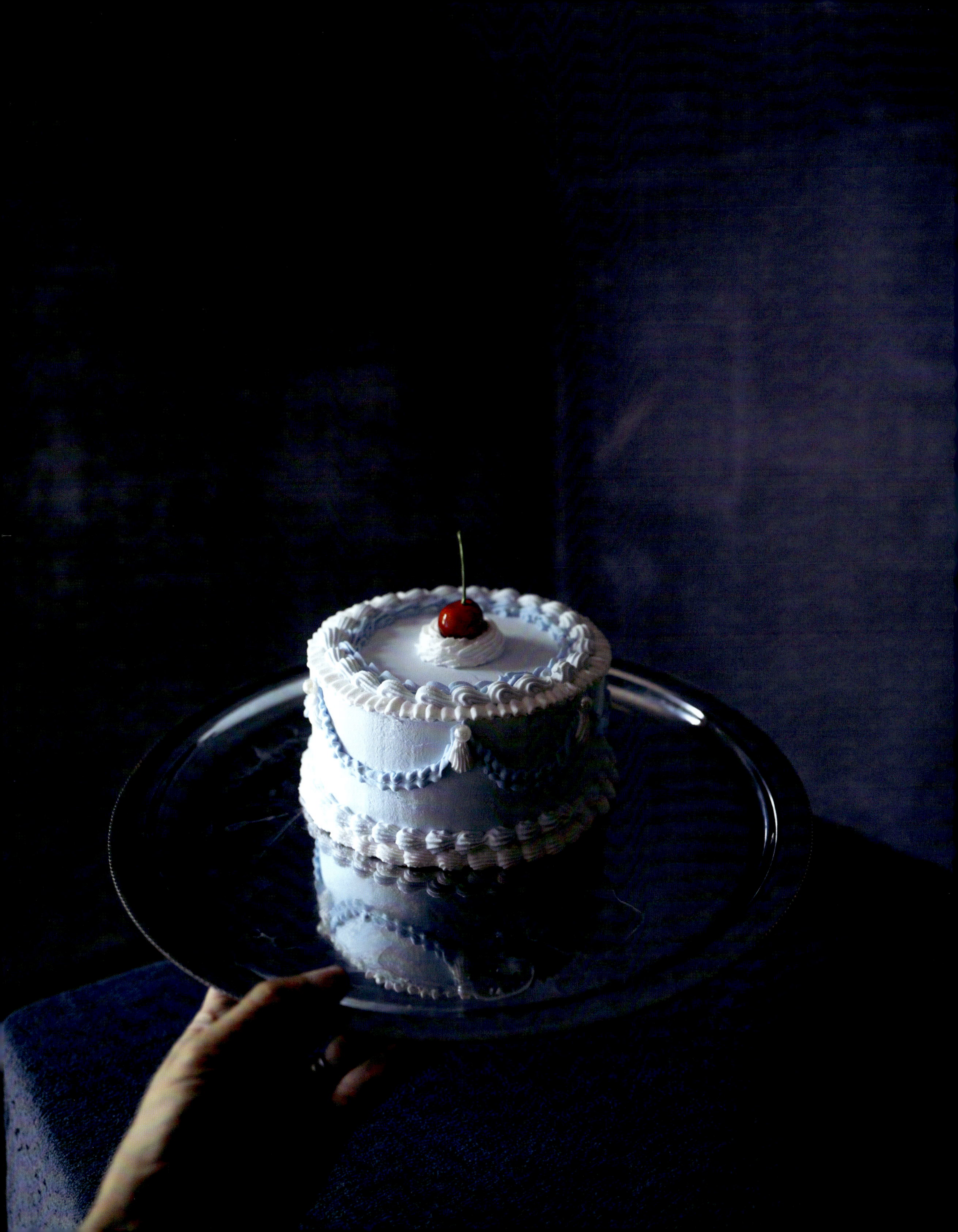

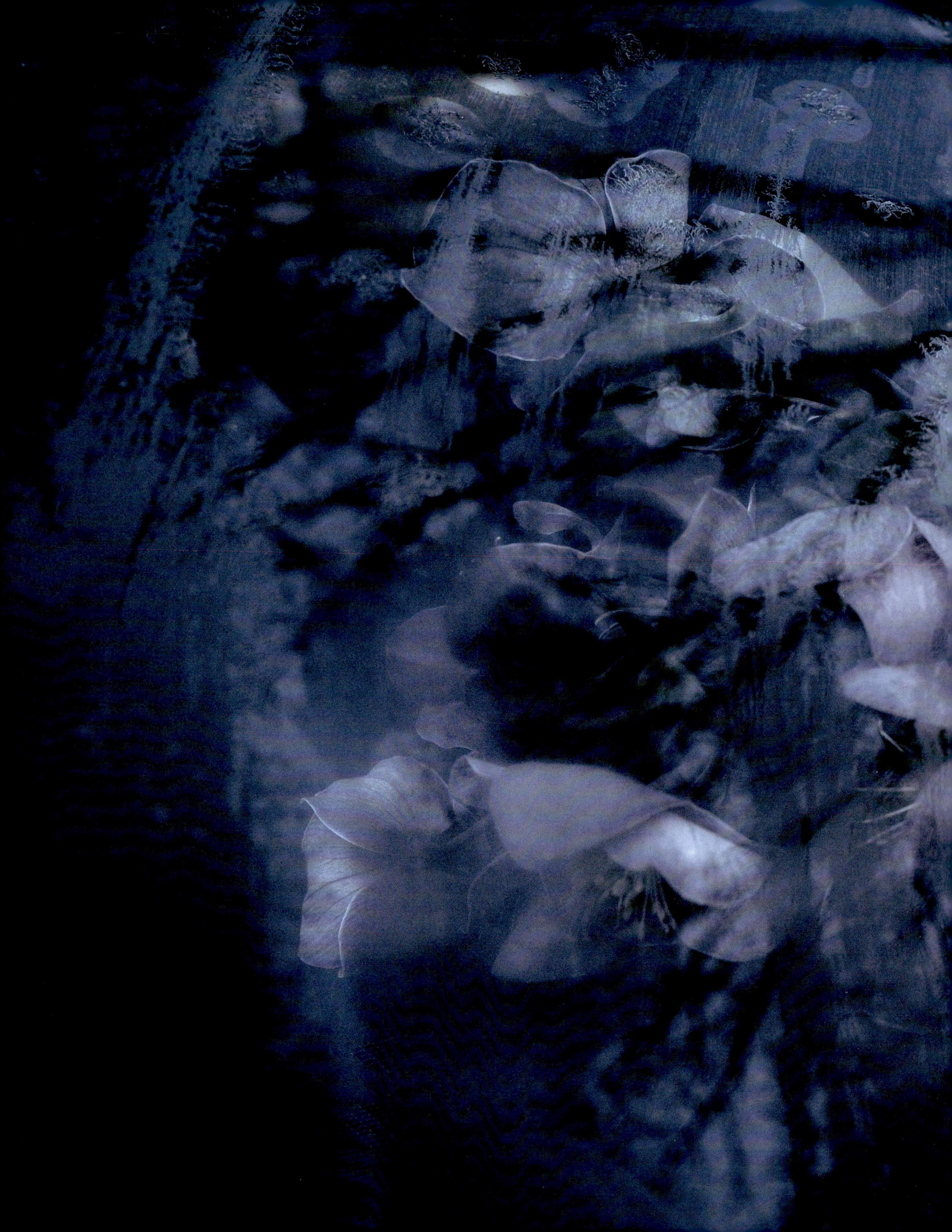

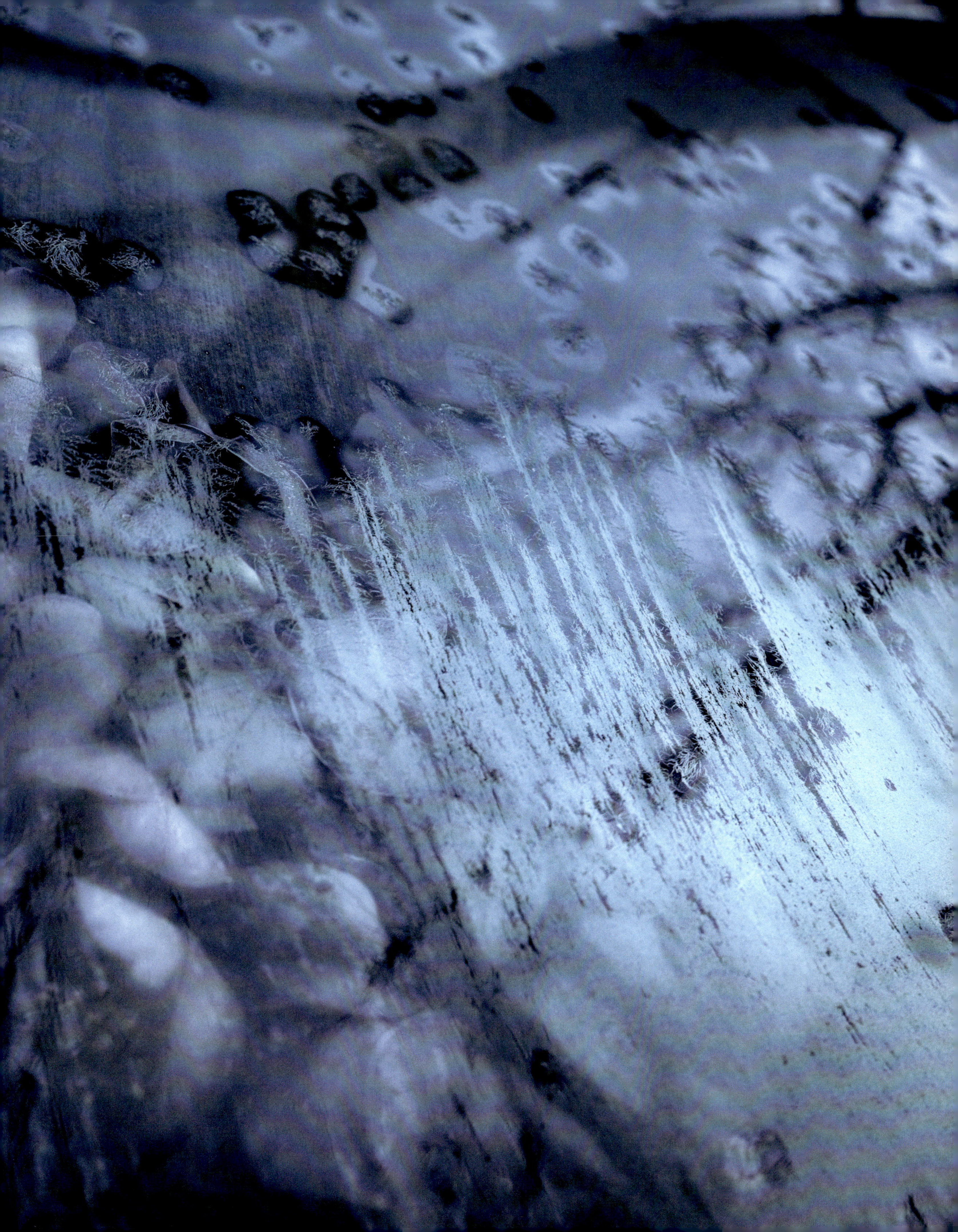

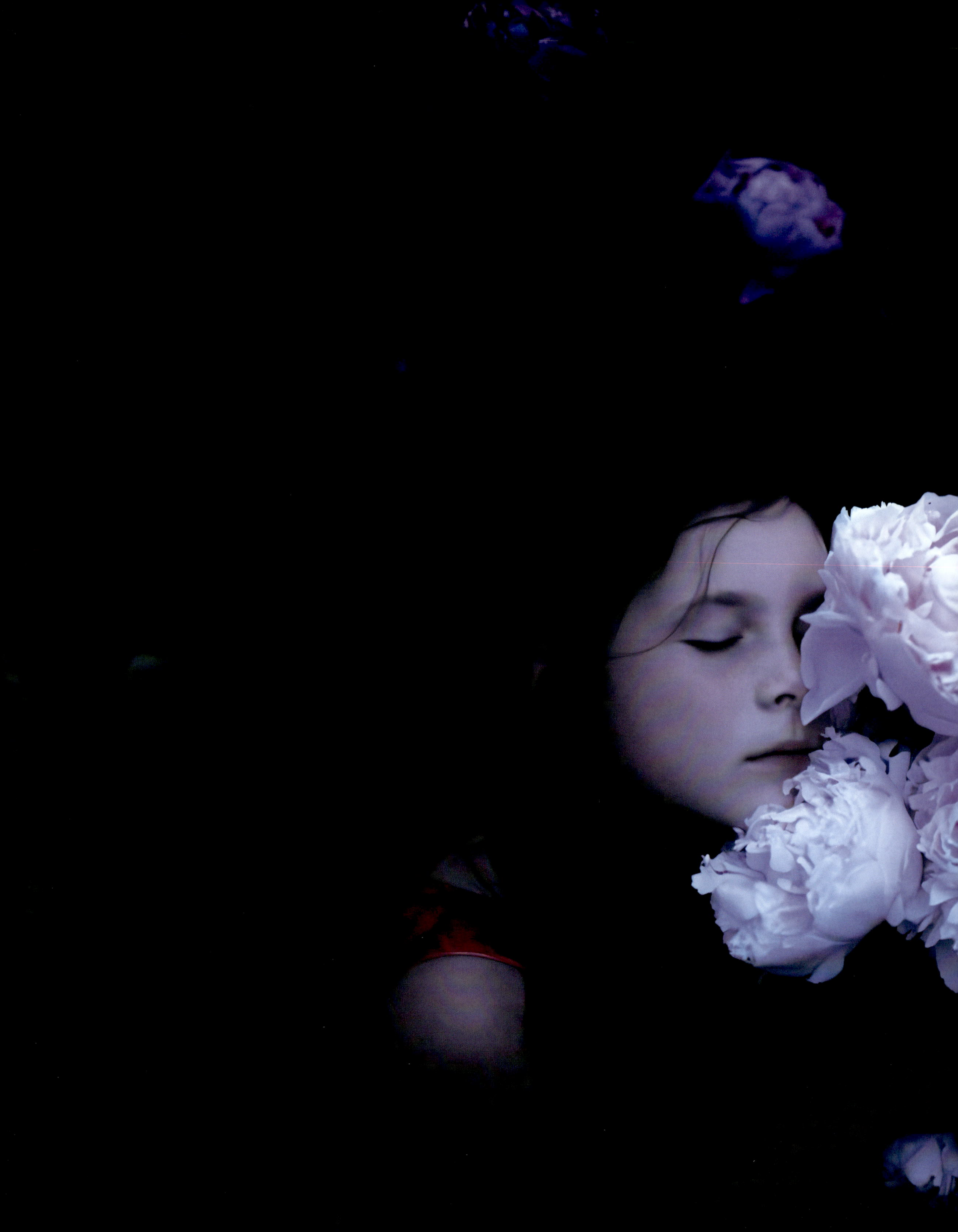

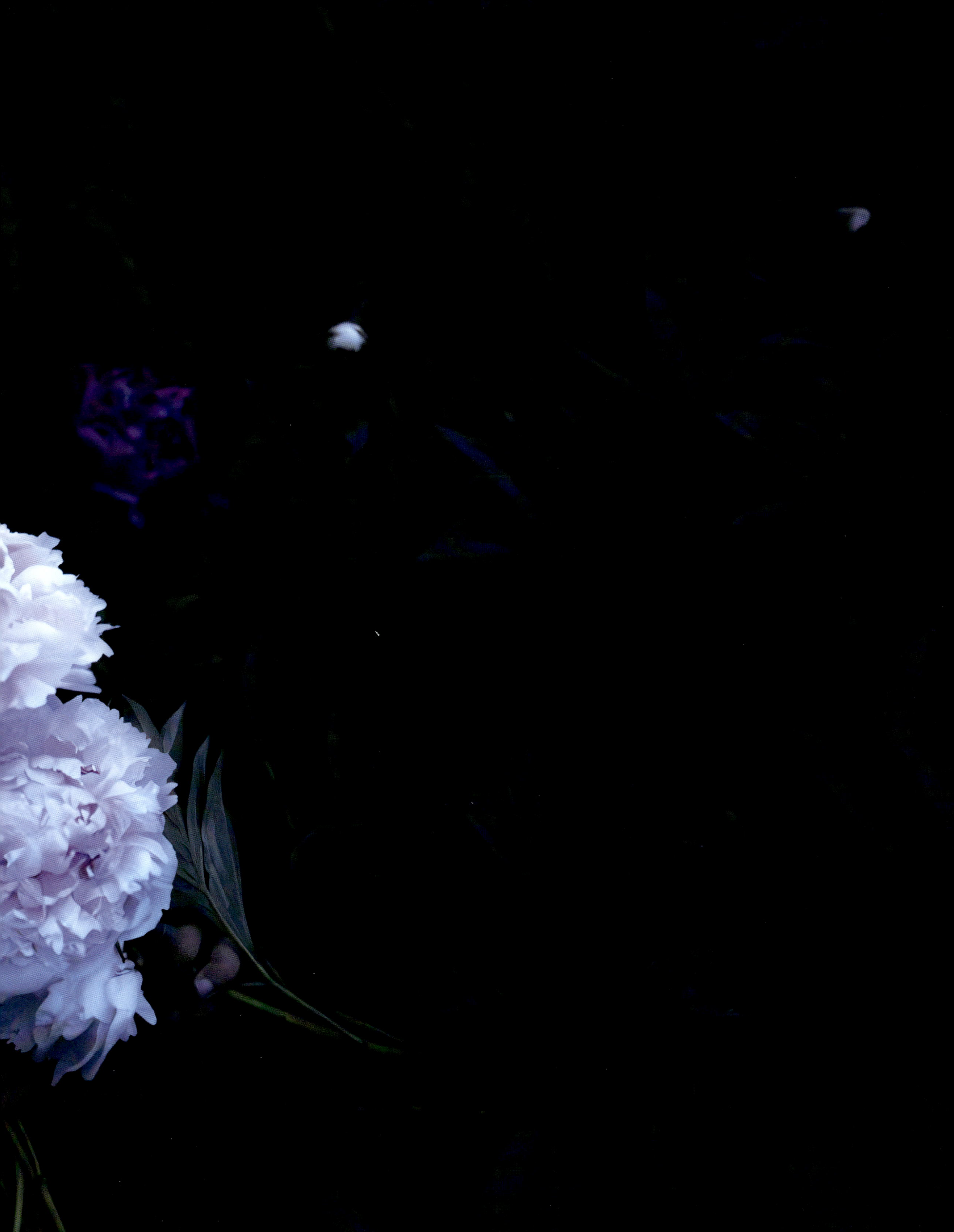

This past Christmas, my family went away for some winter sun, and my sister and I began a ritual of skinny-dipping at night. Fearless teenagers again, we left our clothes on the shoreline and slipped into the dark black of the ocean, the moon illuminating our naked bodies silver. Floating on our backs under the blaze of stars, I asked enormous questions of the night sky. *What am I doing here? What is my purpose?*

But everything in the night sky has already happened; the night sky is all in the past. The constellation Cassiopeia is four thousand light-years away. Four thousand light-years is four thousand human years. It's the Bronze Age up there: the wheel just invented on Wednesday, the first animal domesticated this morning. So what answers will I find there?

Here on earth, periwinkles know all about the power of time. If you bring periwinkles home to an aquarium in your living room, they will move up and down the glass walls in unison with the movement of the nearest tides.

In a dark, isolated cove at a place called Ferry Reach in Bermuda, three days after a full moon and precisely fifty-seven minutes after sundown, female glowworms rise to the surface and release a fluorescent teal orb of eggs. The males respond by ejaculating flashes of light through the neon cloud. When I lived in Bermuda, a teenager named Rebecca Middleton was raped and murdered at Ferry Reach. The details of her death are too awful to fully grasp, as is the disgraceful trial that ended with a double jeopardy verdict and the acquittal of the two guilty men. It is hard to comprehend so much pain and agony in such a beautiful place. In all the horror, I choose to imagine the glowworms lit an emerald path for Rebecca on her journey to the next world.

Life is the awe and the agony, the brutal and the beautiful.

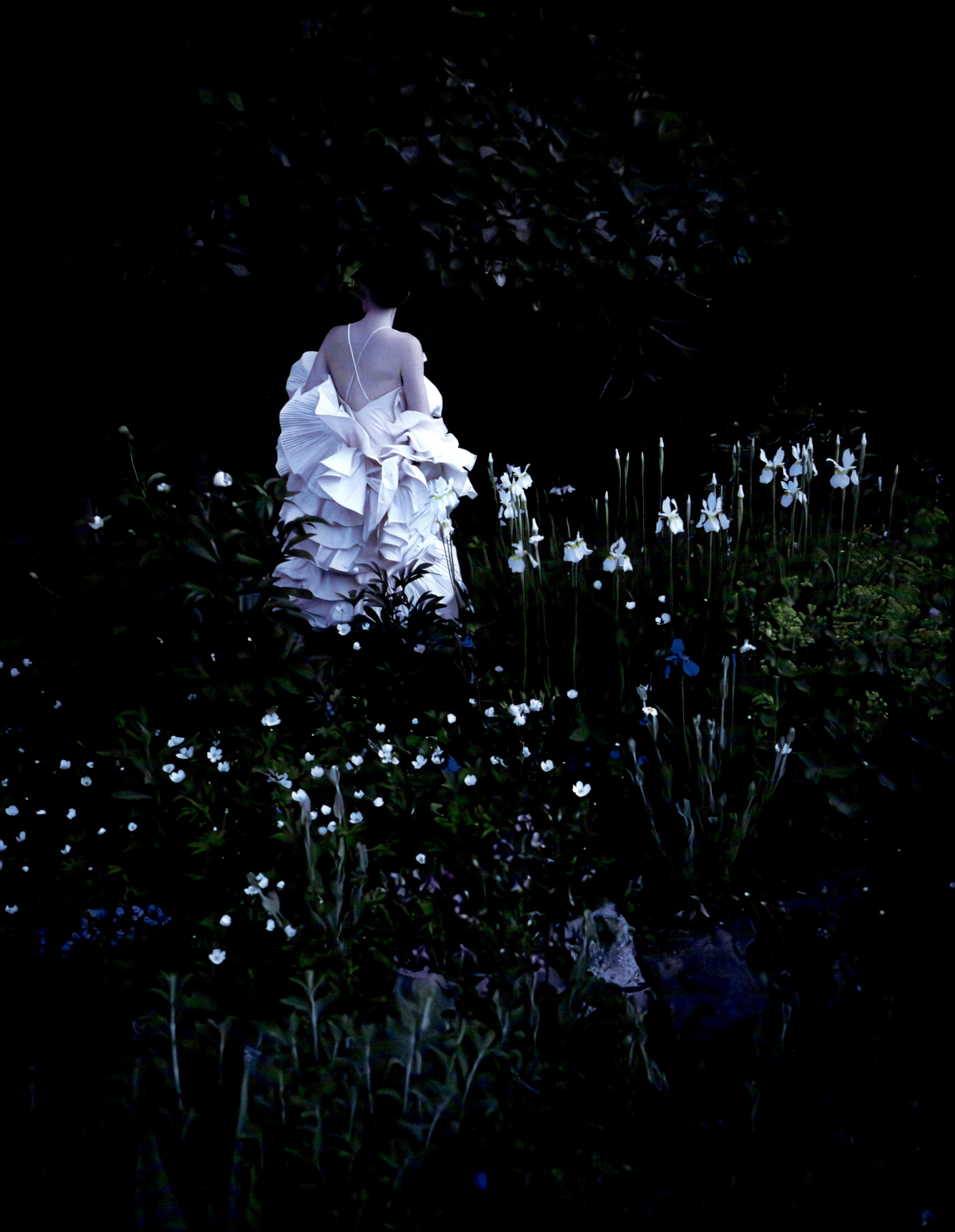

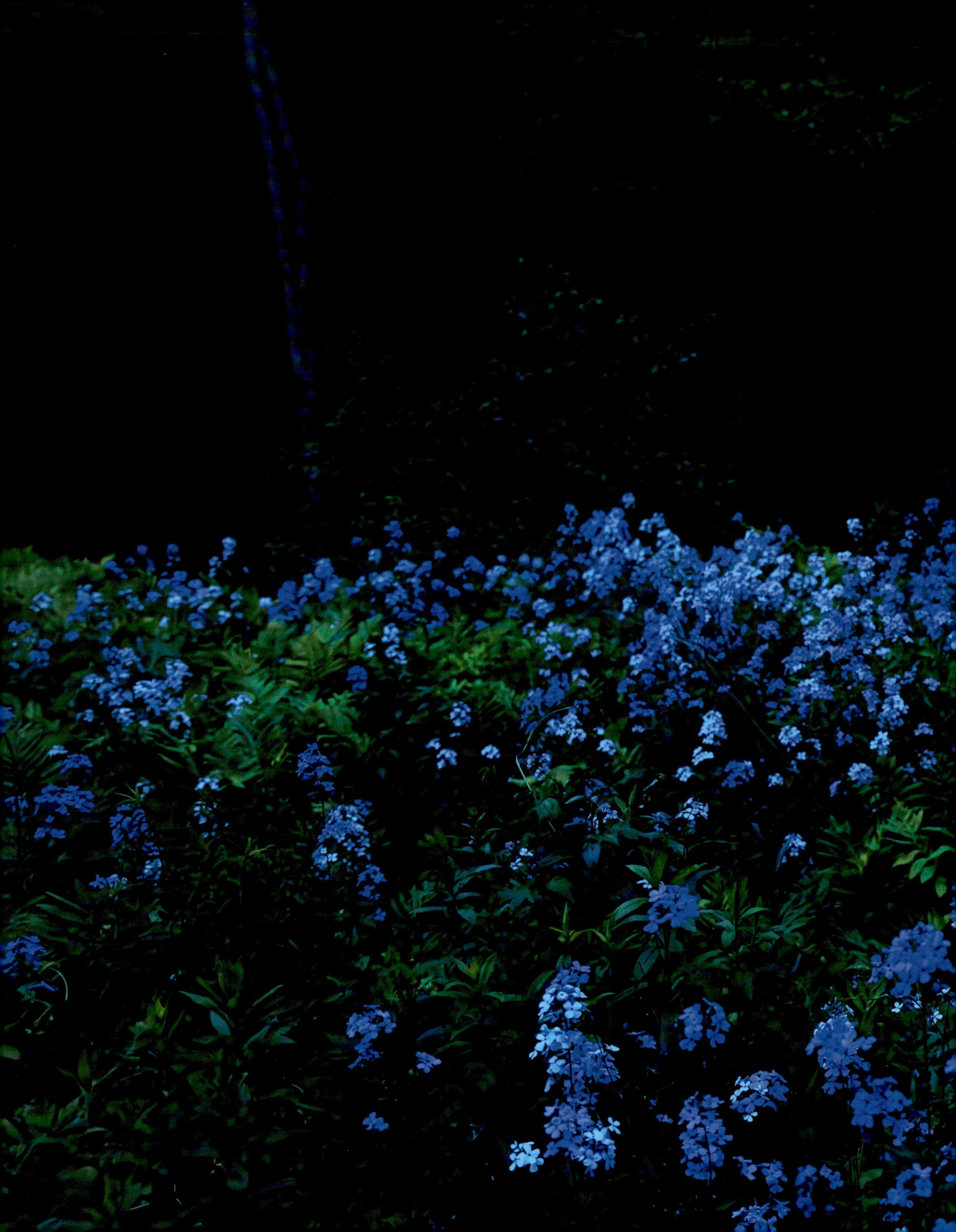

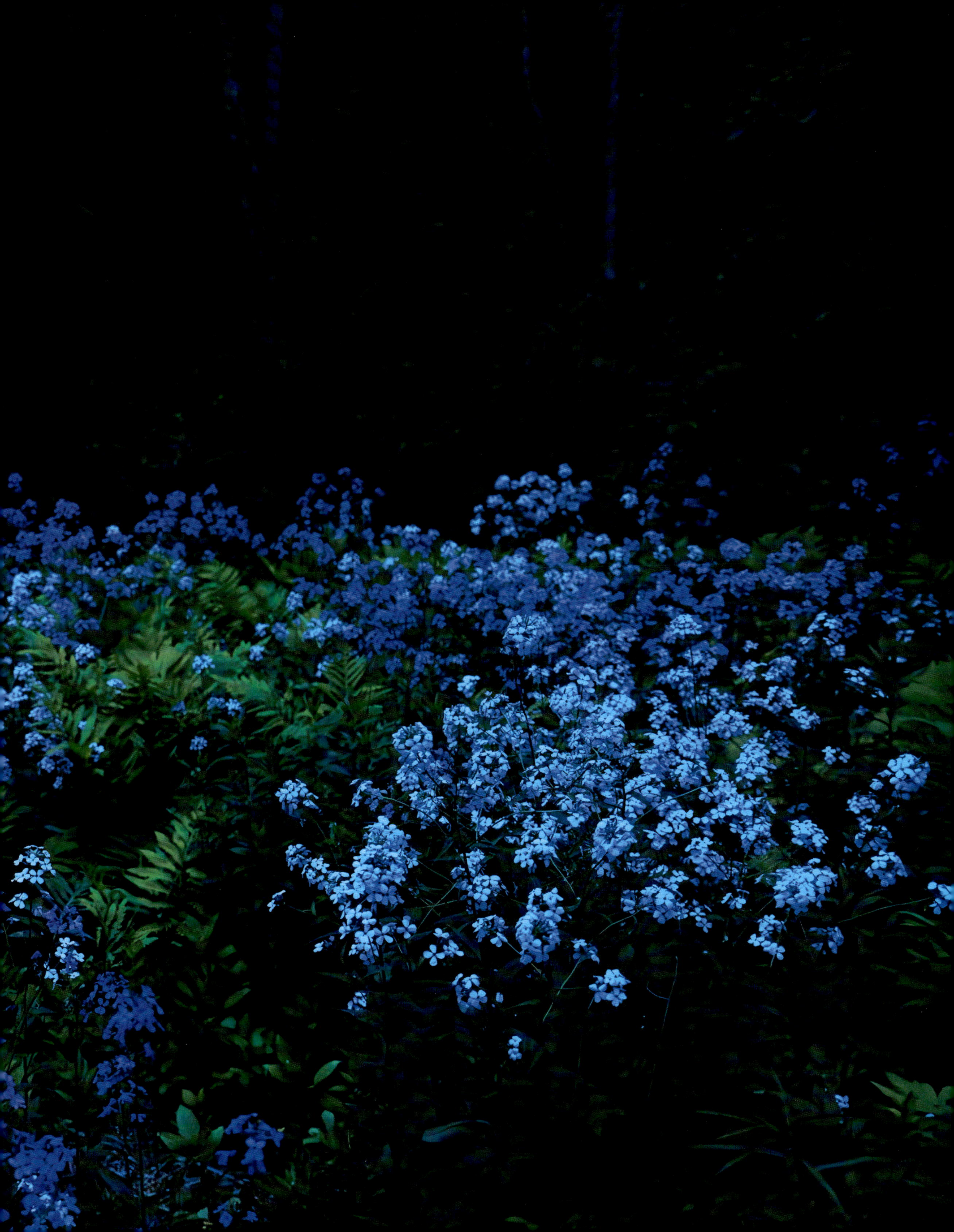

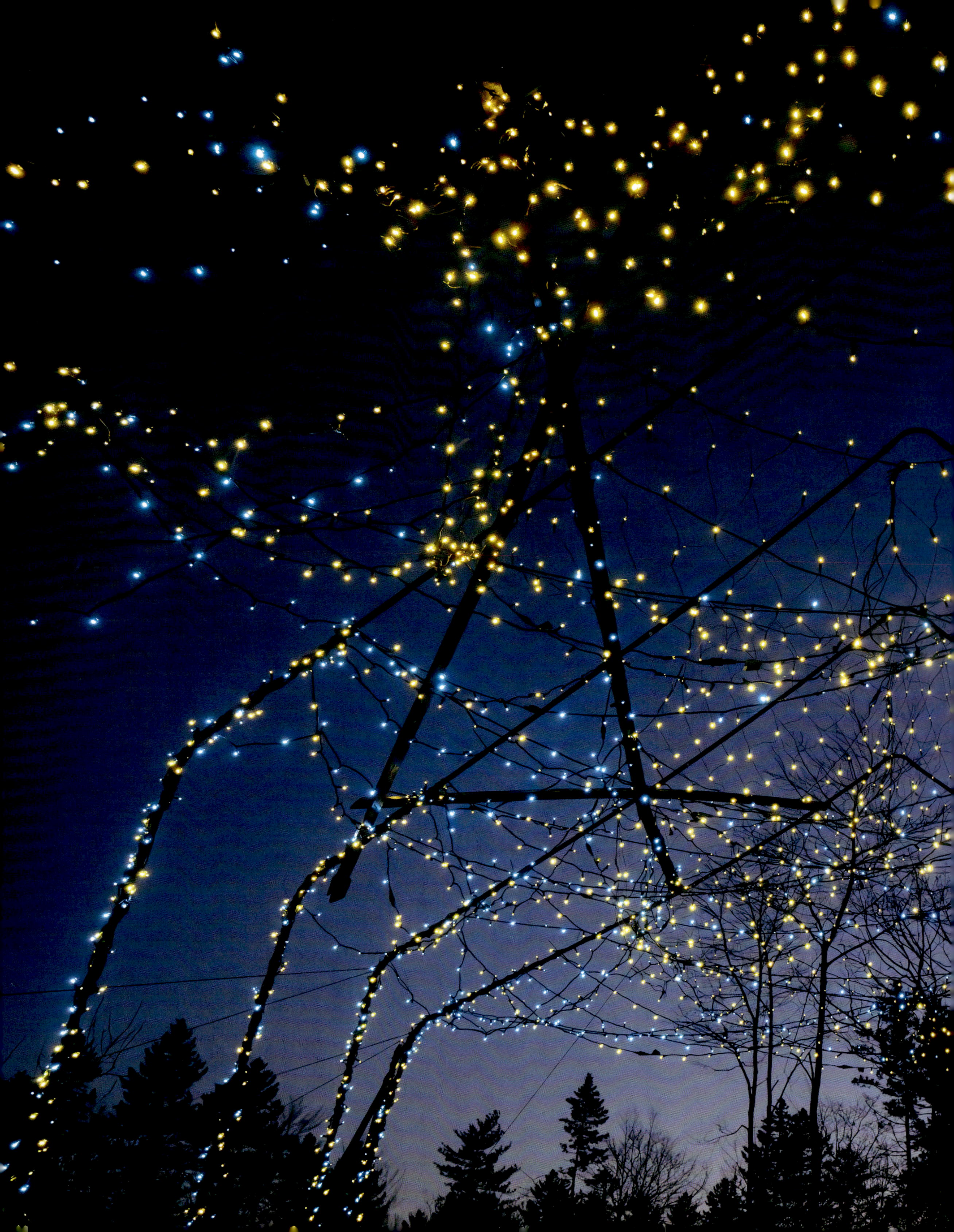

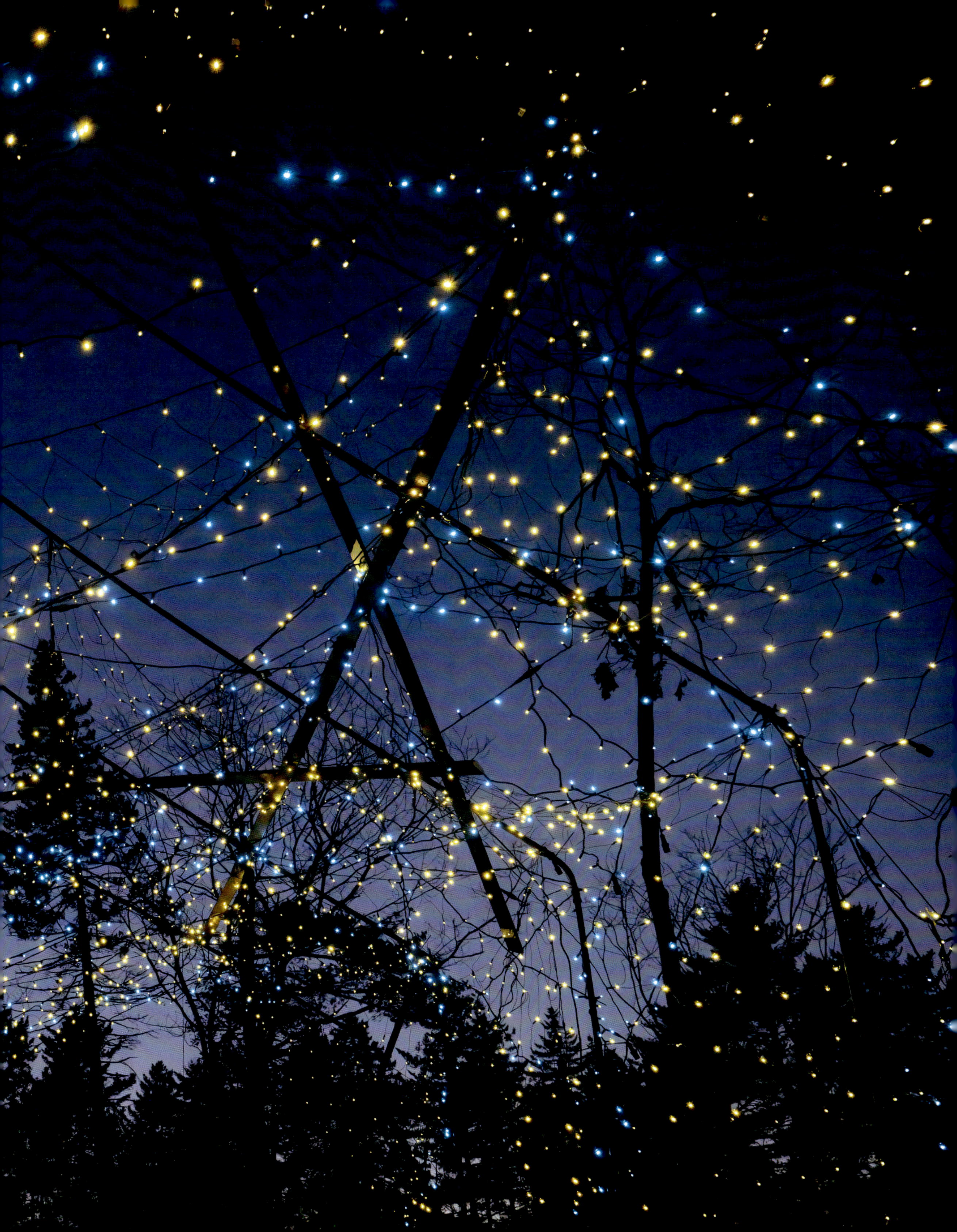

I want to see beyond the normal human range of color. There is a cube in the back of our brains called the occipital lobe full of the colors we know: red, green, blue, violet, cyan, magenta, yellow. But outside of this spinning rainbow block, deep in the rainforest of our minds, other colors are waiting, and you can only see them if you overexcite the brain by taking hallucinogens. You are now beyond the visible light spectrum into the realm of infrared, ultraviolet, radio and gamma rays—colors not yet named.

At night, behind closed alabaster eyelids, I discover a new color. In a one-room shack deep in the woods, a woman wearing a pale pink caftan releases the birds from the faded toile wallpaper. She is careful to leave the two figures frozen in time: a man fossilized on a knee with his arms outstretched and a woman twirling her way to deliver a jug of water. I take pictures as she brings the birds to life by touching their paper beaks, their eyes blinking open as they unfurl their wings. A flight of pink swallows, a murmuration of scarlet starlings, a siege of magenta herons. Some fly in slow motion, gliding in pale coral circles, while others make clouds of fuchsia with their frenetic wings.

When the bird woman leans in toward me to speak the name of the color, she breathes as close to me as my own skin, and I see a combination of every pink in the world sitting in her mouth. I know she will bite my cheek.

Colors Not
Yet Named

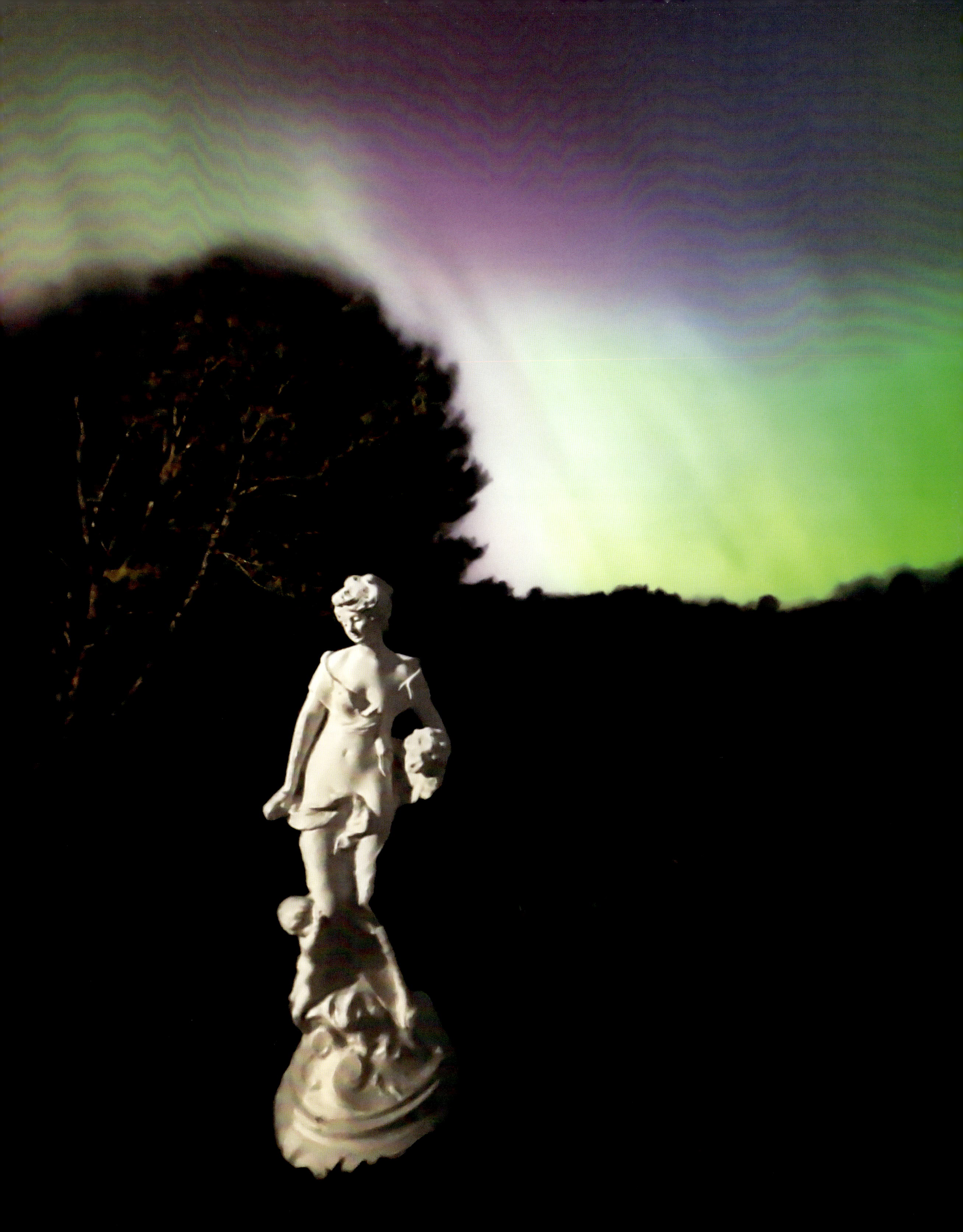

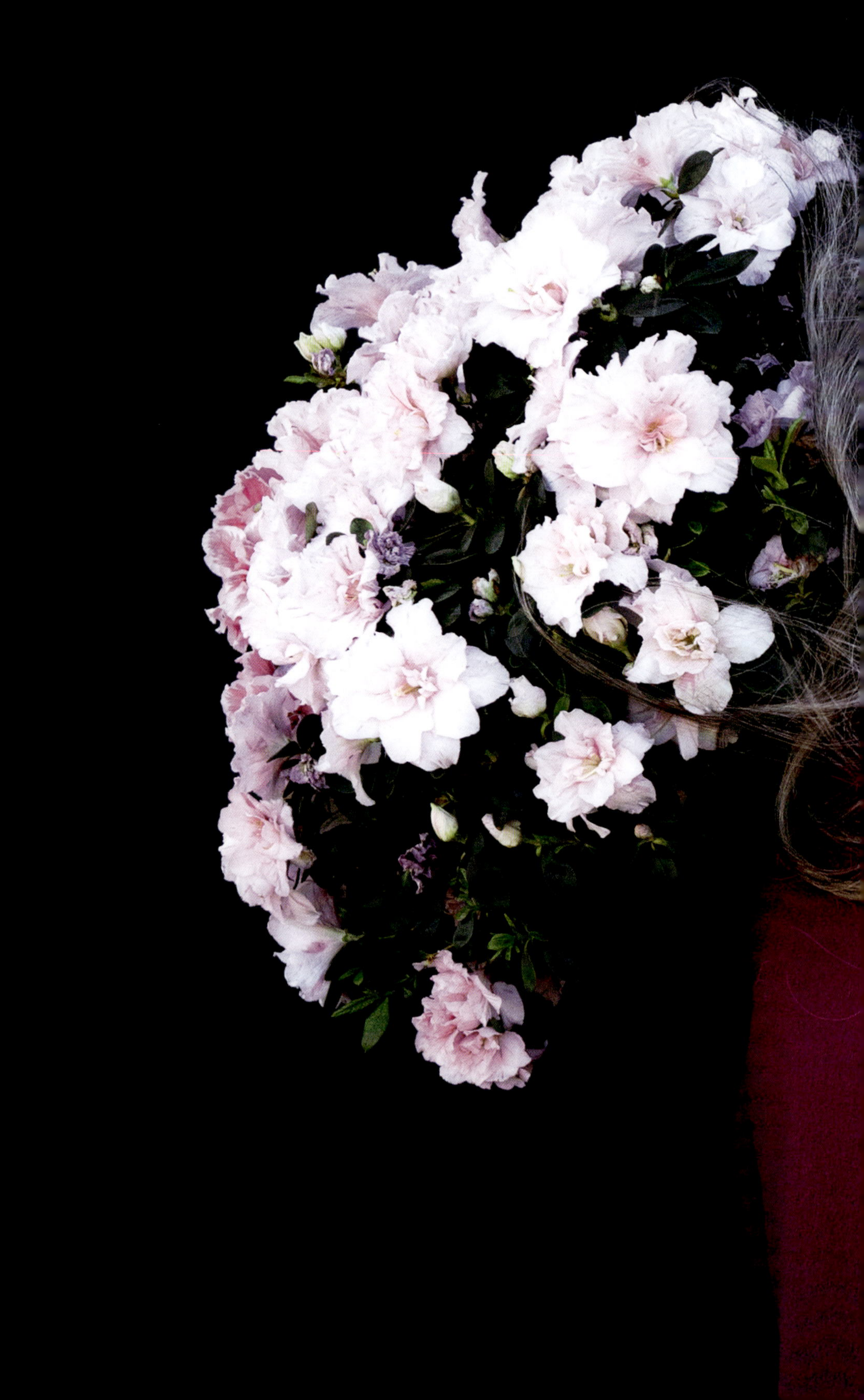

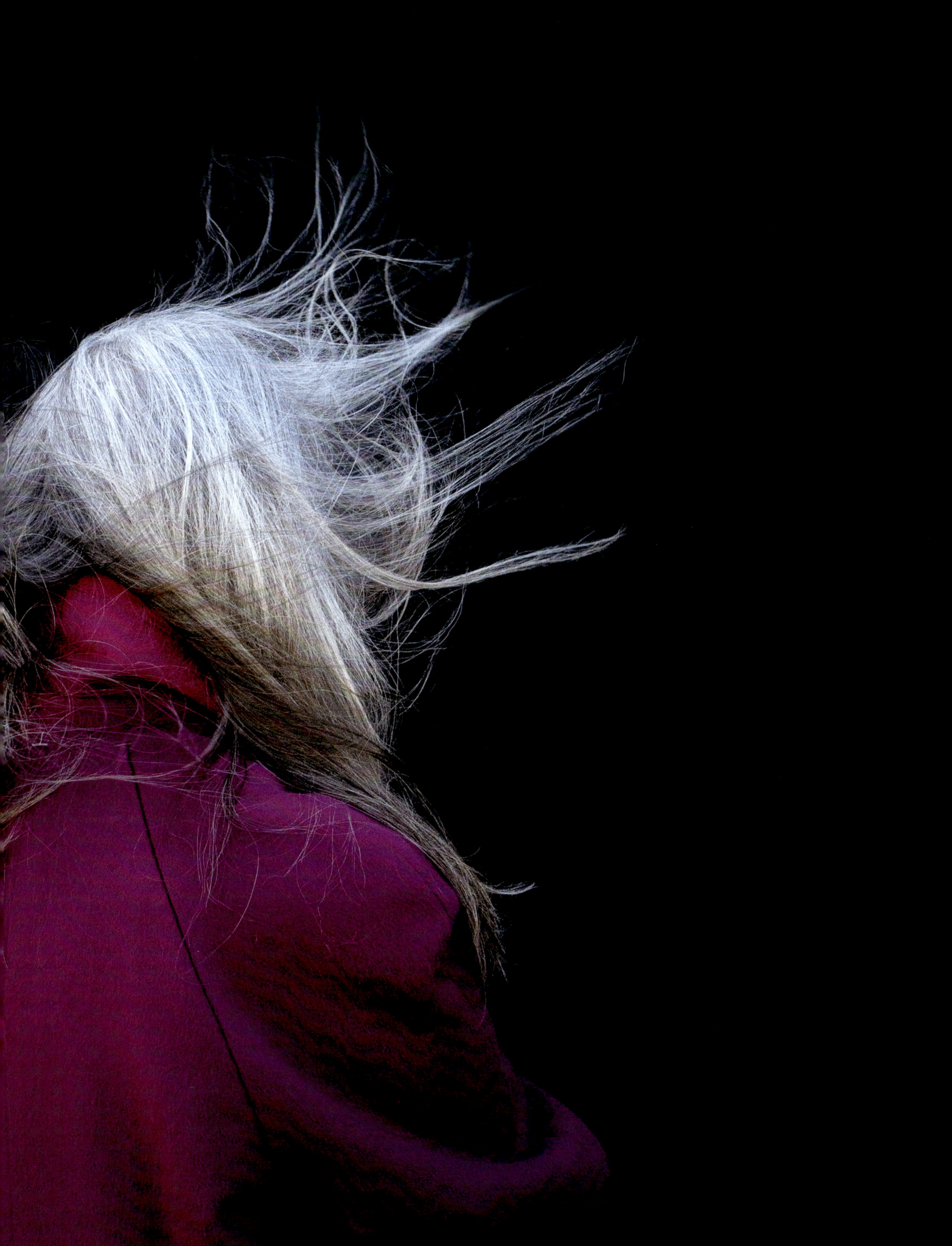

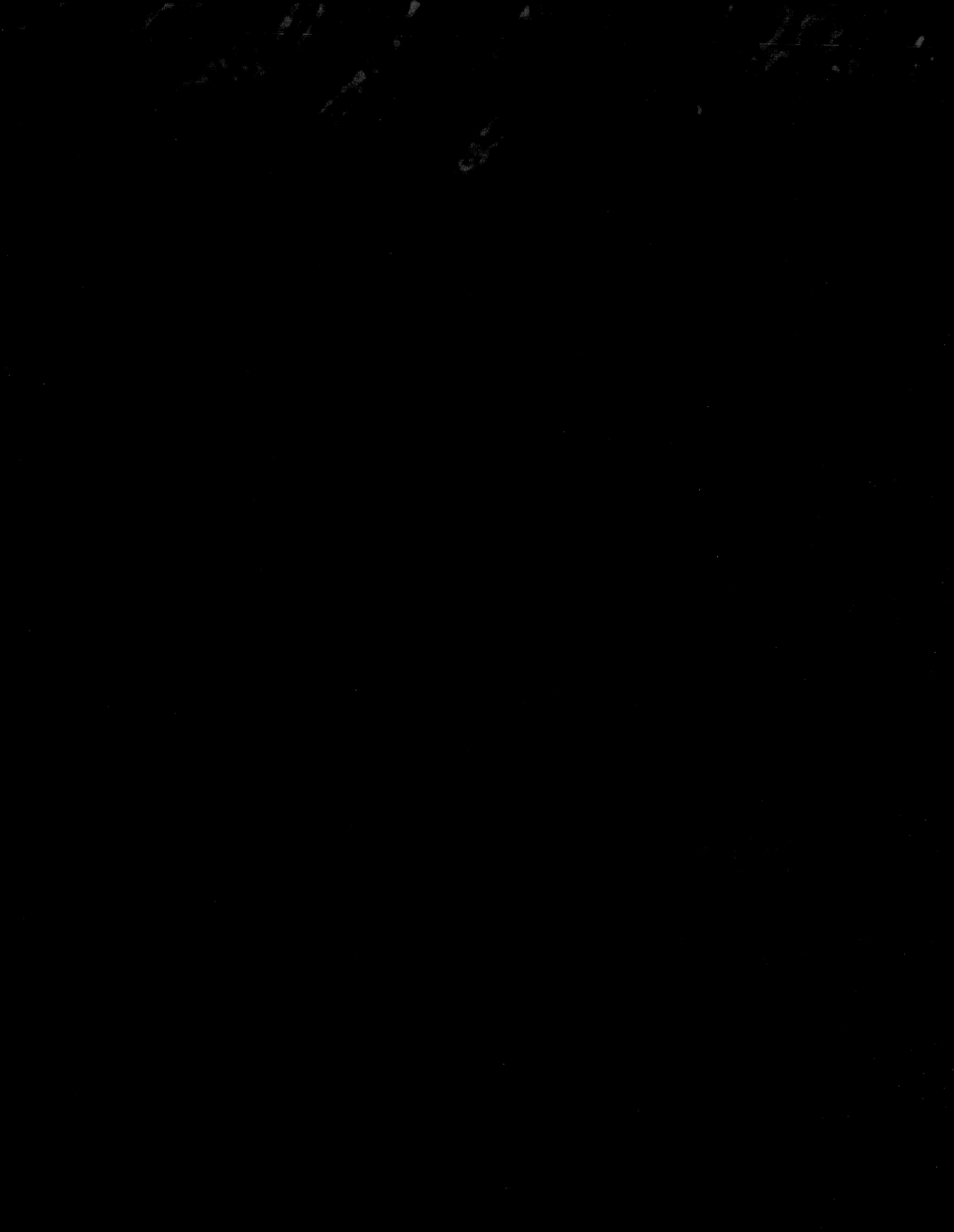

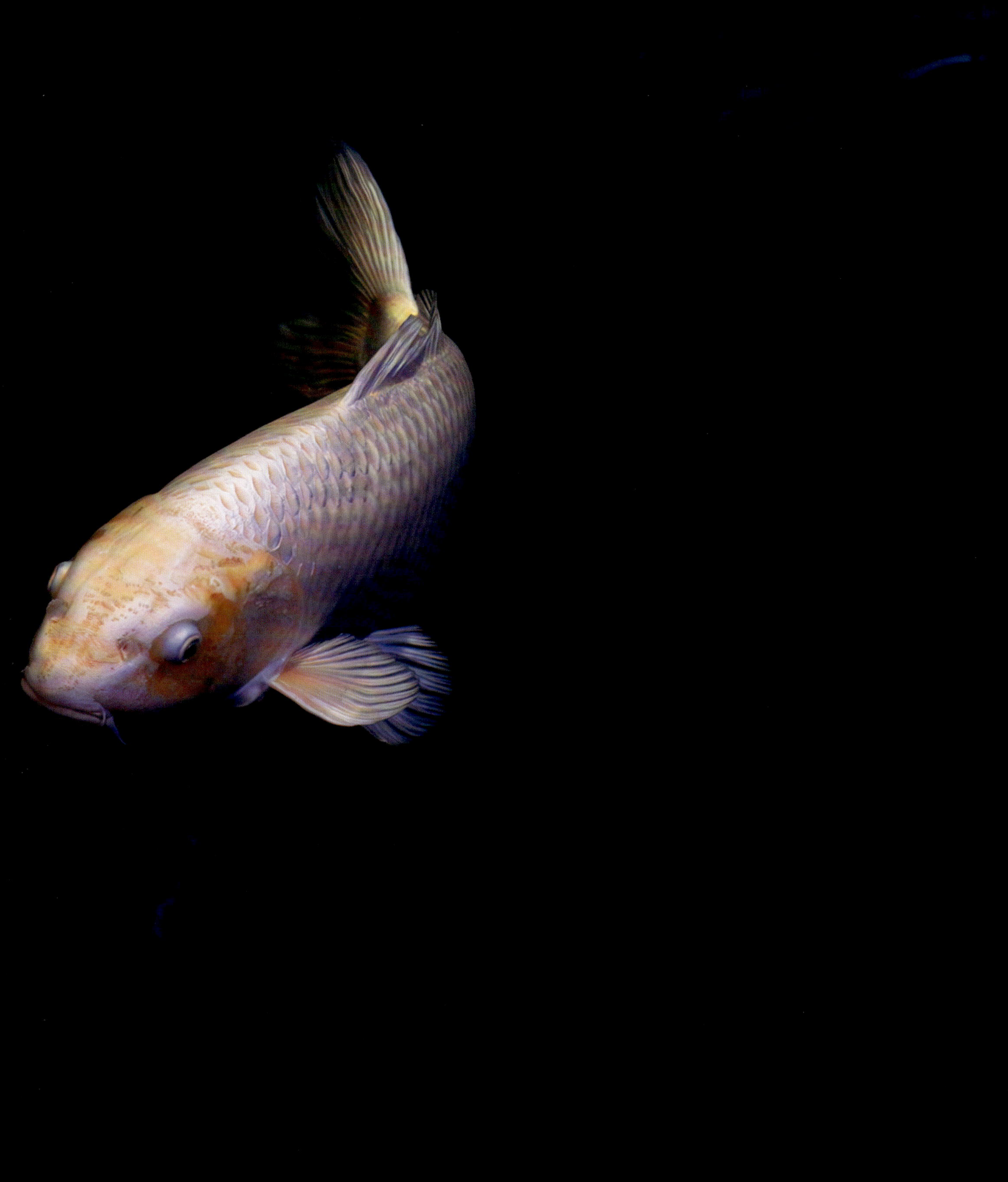

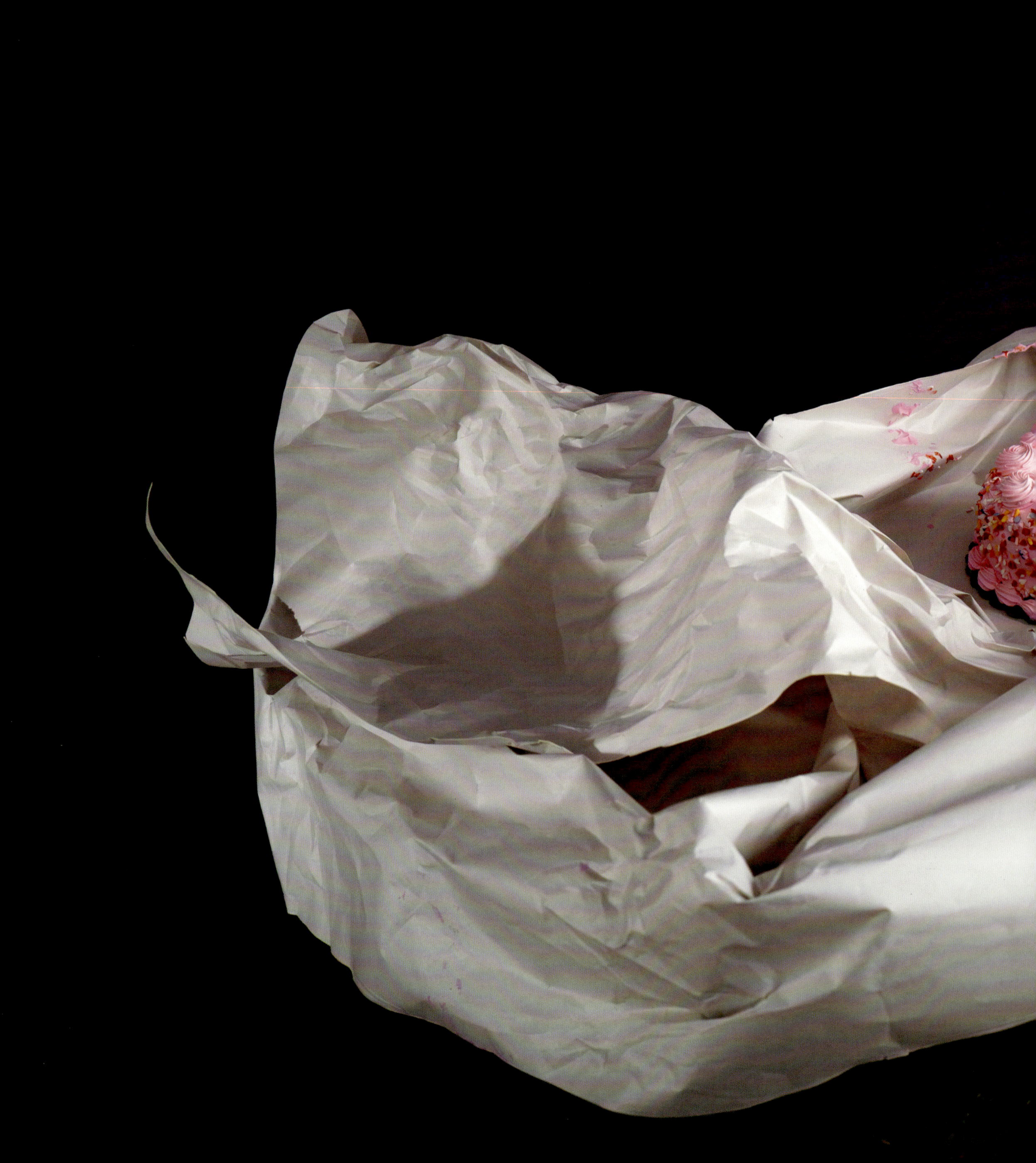

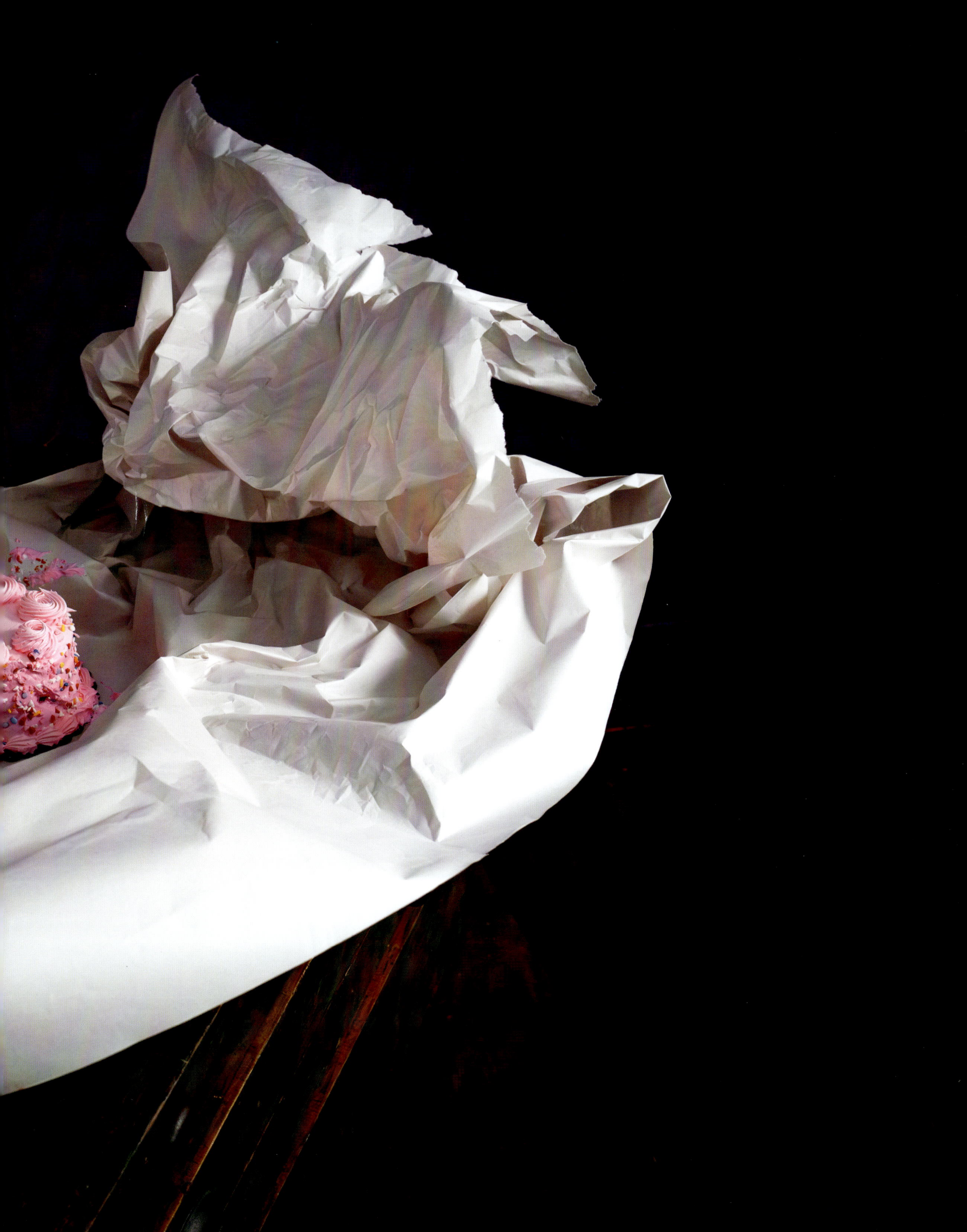

I've not been sleeping well recently, so I've started a ritual of painting my eyes a bright green to complement the dark purple circles underneath them and putting on an emerald silk nightgown to prepare for bed. Wearing green makes me feel powerful, witchlike. Doug asks me what I am doing. *I've got a forest inside of me*, I say.

The Egyptians knew the power of color and talismans. They adorned their bodies with thick gold chokers, red-eyed serpents eating themselves, midnight blue hawks, and the Eye of Horus to ward off evil spirits. They stacked their arms and legs with amulets, bracelets full of hieroglyphics, quartz, garnets, and iridescent scarab beetles. They crafted obsidian-jeweled head ornaments, amethyst chandelier earrings of birds with human heads, and fierce turquoise crocodiles to protect and nurture. Women mixed animal fat and black lead sulfide into a dense dark kohl paste to line their eyes. Using a thick brush, they painted their lower lids with a brilliant green malachite, covering the upper lids with crushed gold and a lapis lazuli blue paste.

I learn that one of the earliest symptoms of hormone imbalance in women in their thirties, forties, and fifties is anxiety out of nowhere. Overnight, a girlfriend developed a fear of driving other passengers; another chose to travel thousands of miles extra in a year to avoid bridges. My symptoms present as sleeplessness. I make a chart to tick off daily and weekly: cold plunges, hot yoga, a diet of cruciferous vegetables and seeds, vitamins, coconut oil pulling, meditation, apple cider vinegar, blood pressure checks, acupuncture, no devices in the bedroom. Nothing works. Each morning, my sheets huddle, tortured, twisted, and strangled.

Women muscle through each day with interrupted sleep and anxiety, maxed out on Tylenol PM and caffeine. Finally we seek help from our doctors, but instead we are often told *it is natural, lose some weight,* and are prescribed sleeping pills and antidepressants. The same doctors refer to a twenty-five-year-old, now debunked study, warning women about the dangers of hormone replacement therapy. Twenty-five years ago, we thought Teflon and Scotchgard were great and Lucky Charms, diet soda, and margarine healthy. So I write myself my own prescription of emerald green silk, amethyst stones, and a pea-sized dollop of over-the-counter progesterone cream made from warm yellow wild Mexican yam to rub on my tummy at night. It is so simple, cheap, and effective that I am simultaneously elated and furious.

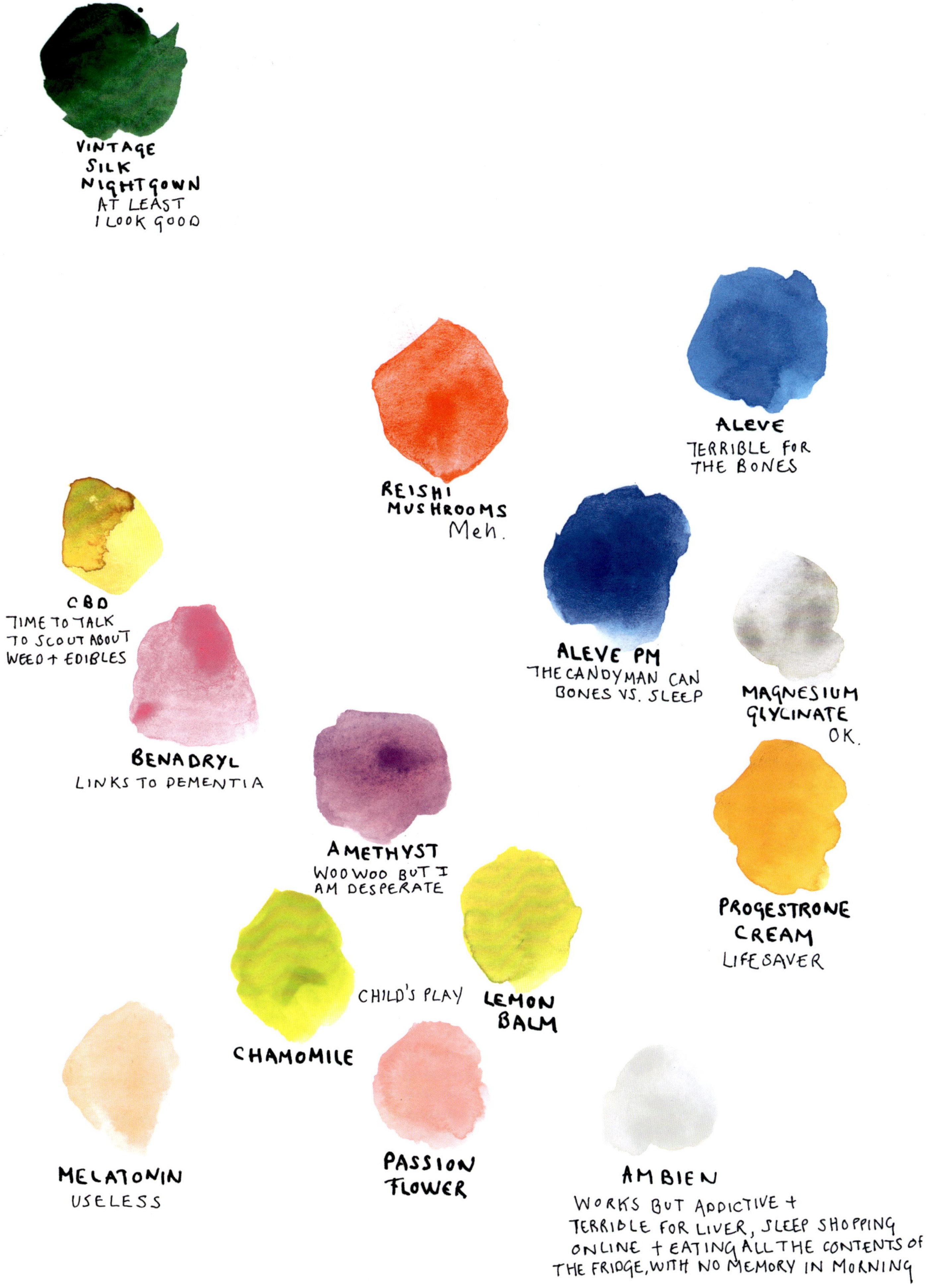

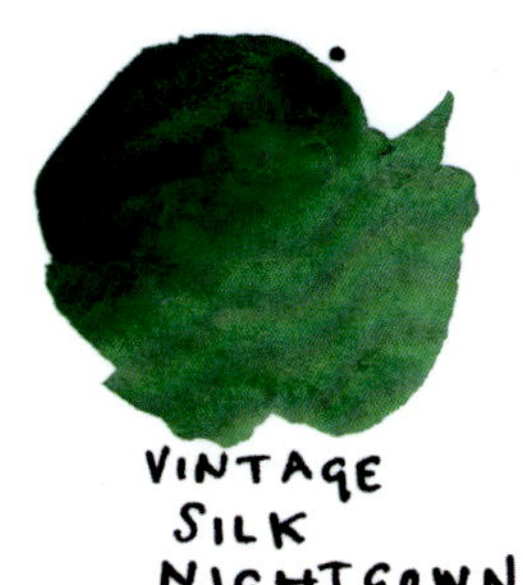

**VINTAGE SILK NIGHTGOWN**
AT LEAST I LOOK GOOD

**ALEVE**
TERRIBLE FOR THE BONES

**REISHI MUSHROOMS**
Meh.

**CBD**
TIME TO TALK TO SCOUT ABOUT WEED + EDIBLES

**ALEVE PM**
THE CANDYMAN CAN
BONES VS. SLEEP

**MAGNESIUM GLYCINATE**
OK.

**BENADRYL**
LINKS TO DEMENTIA

**AMETHYST**
WOOWOO BUT I AM DESPERATE

**PROGESTRONE CREAM**
LIFESAVER

CHILD'S PLAY

**LEMON BALM**

**CHAMOMILE**

**MELATONIN**
USELESS

**PASSION FLOWER**

**AMBIEN**
WORKS BUT ADDICTIVE + TERRIBLE FOR LIVER, SLEEP SHOPPING ONLINE + EATING ALL THE CONTENTS OF THE FRIDGE, WITH NO MEMORY IN MORNING

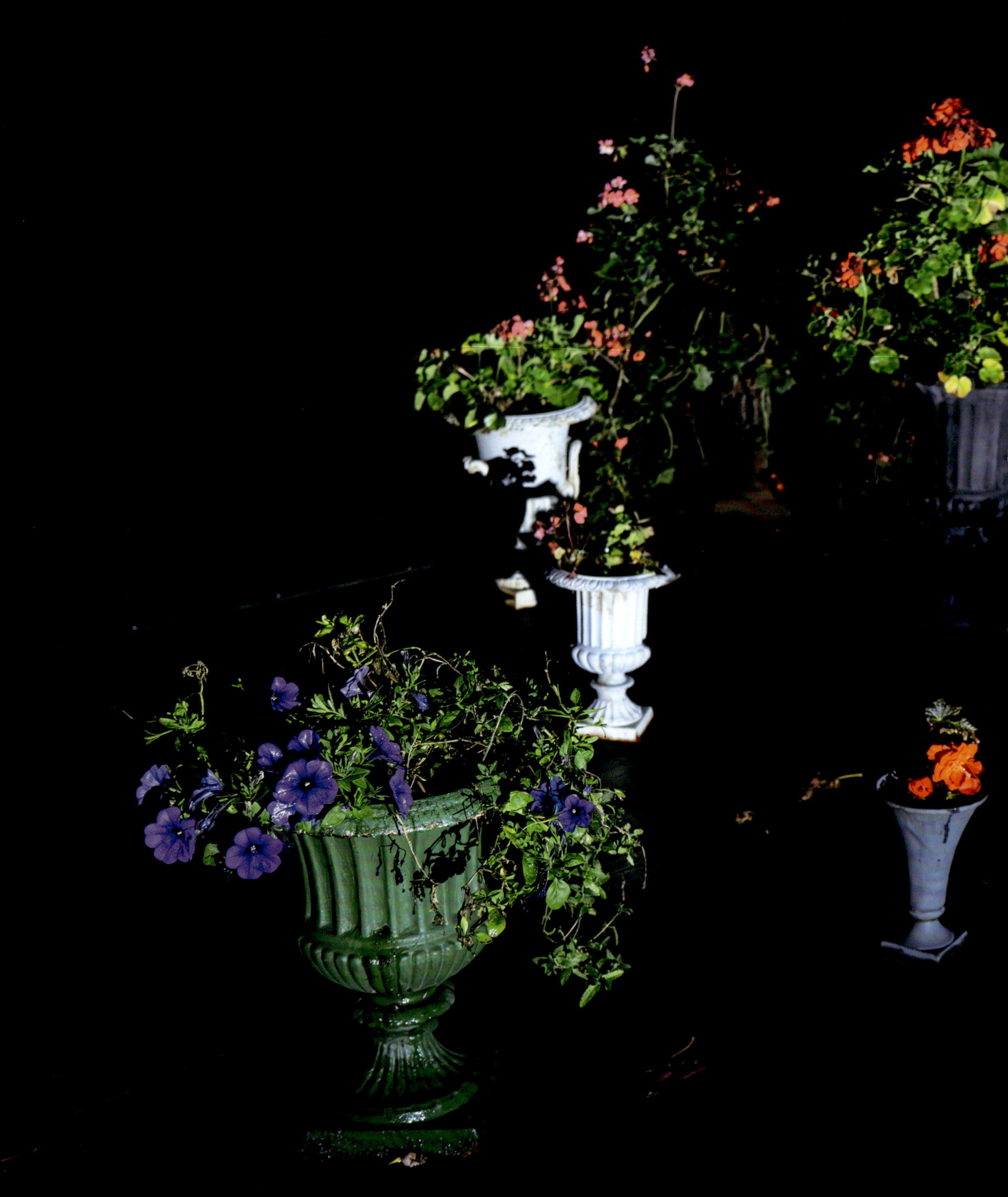

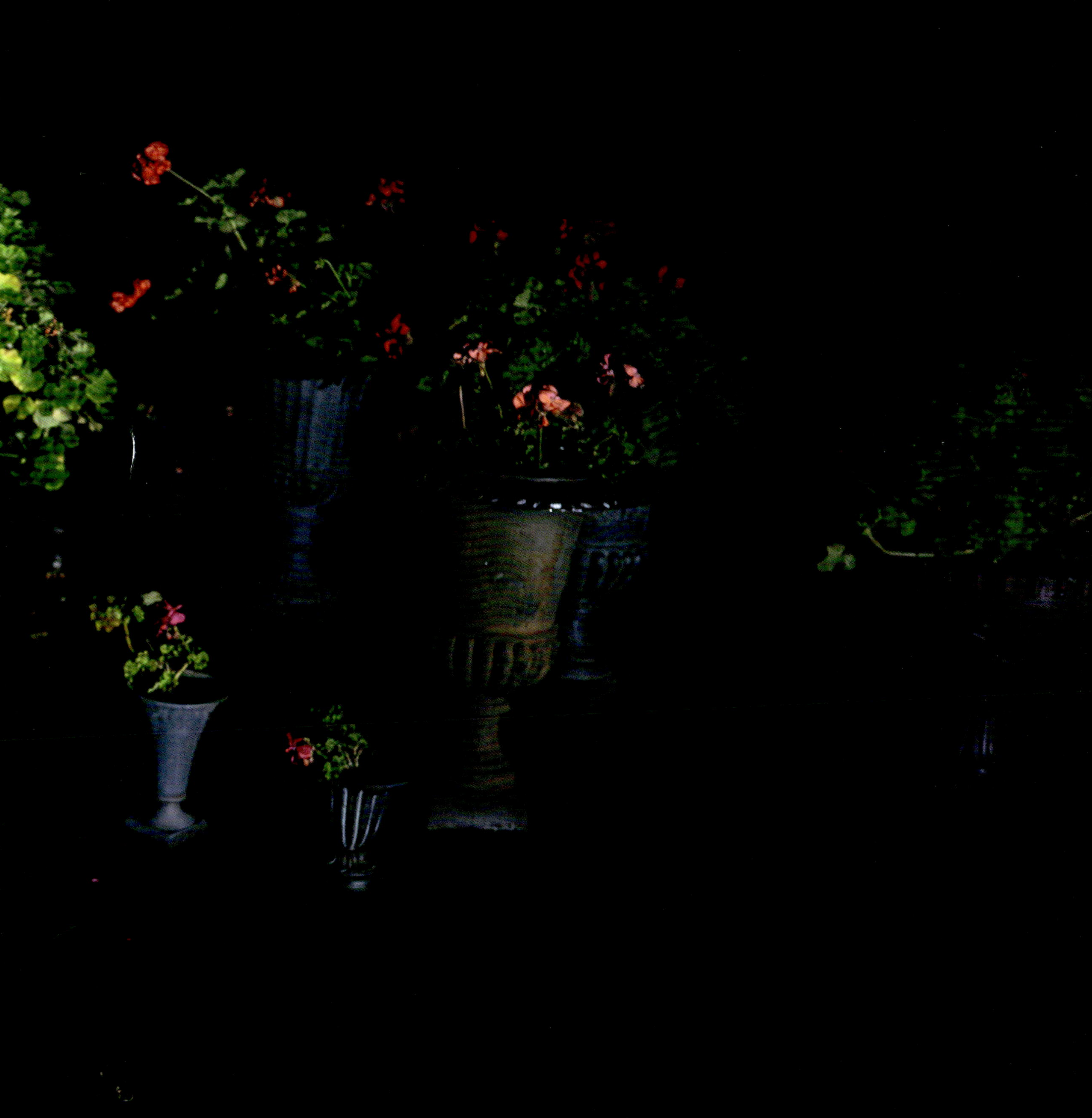

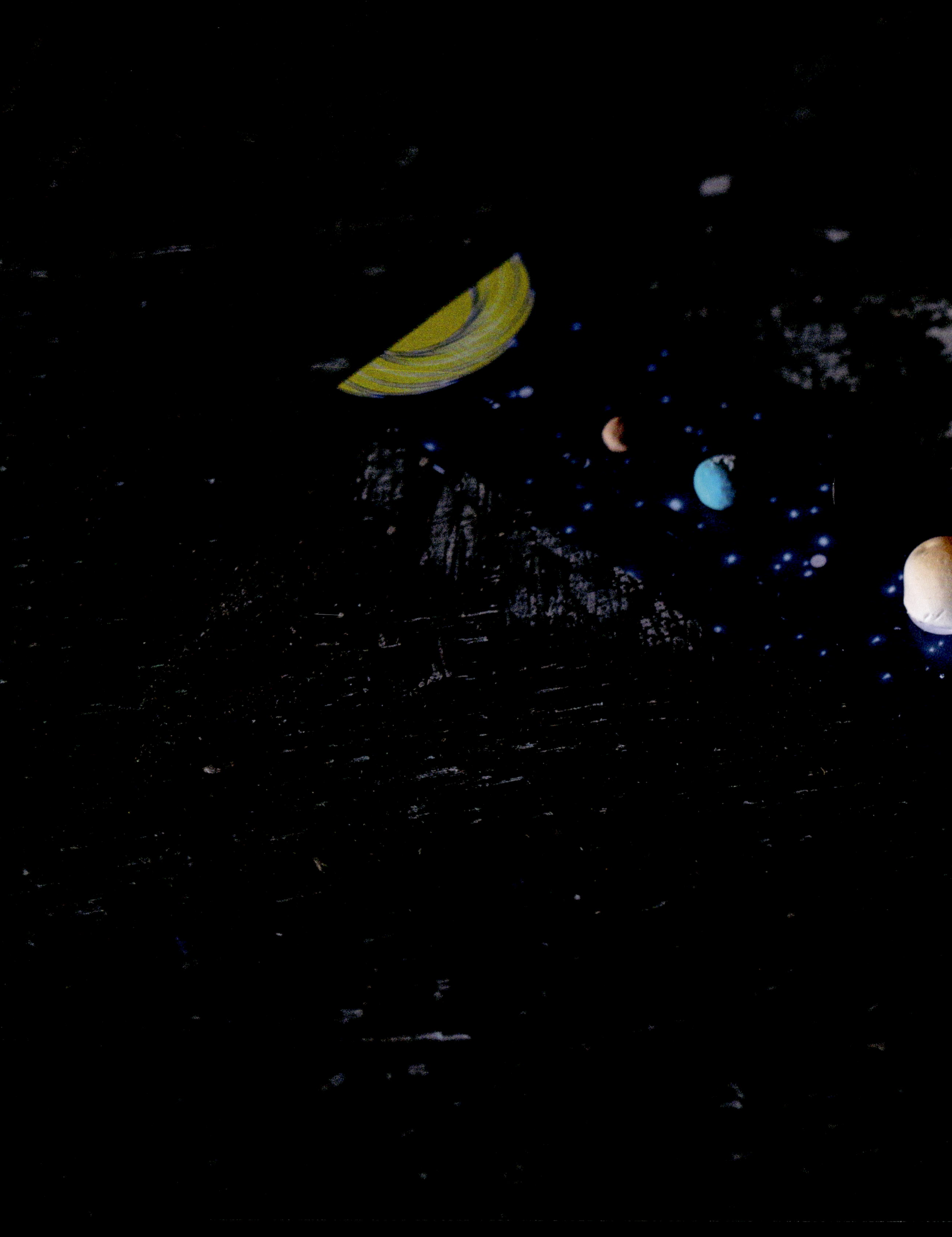

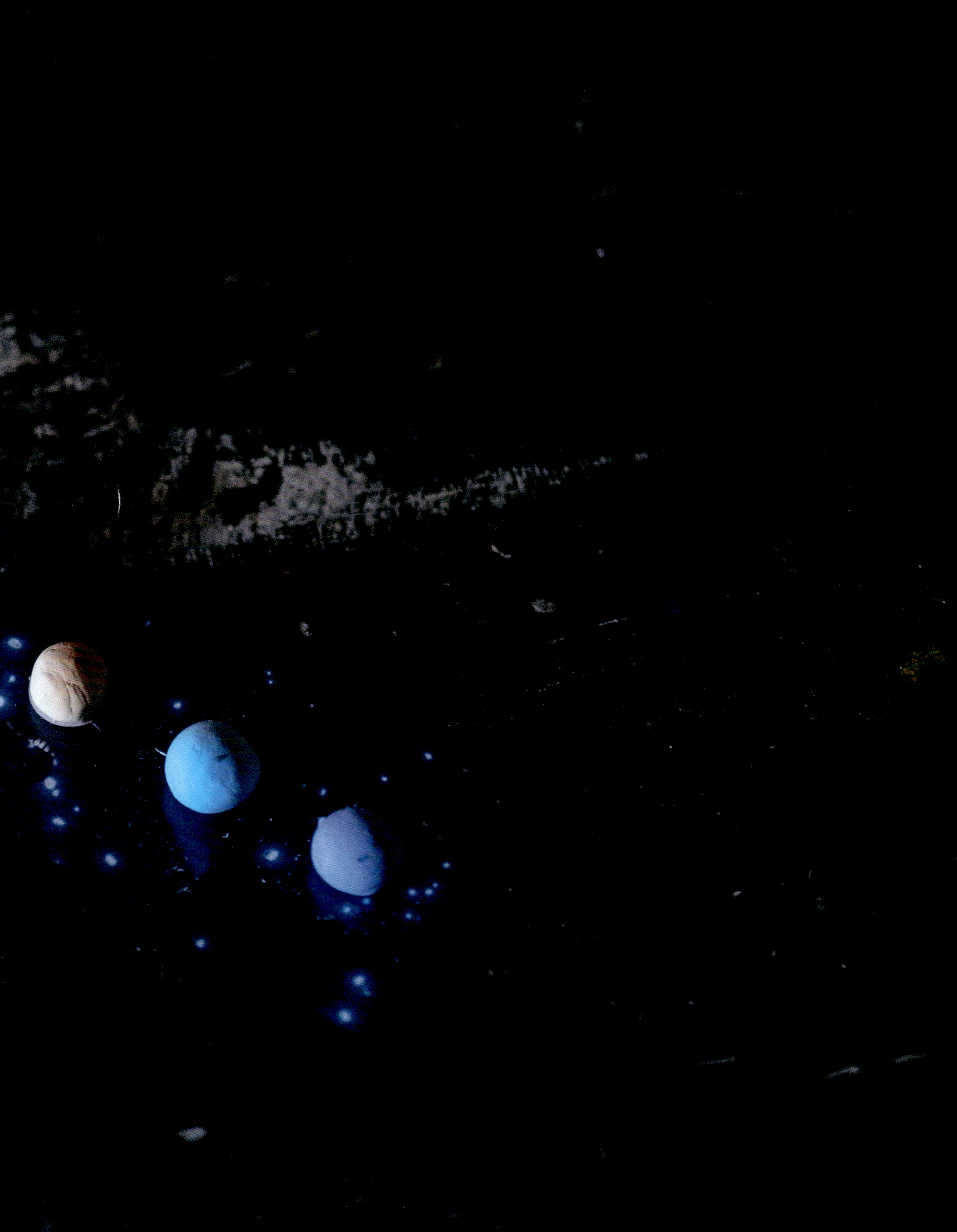

How to Make
a Silver Print

1 Put on your cloak and enter through the magician's circular door.

2 Let your eyes adjust to the red. It is light enough to see, but the edges are now smoothed out. It's safe here.

3 Find your enlarger. Turn on your music, something that lets your mind wander. A day in the darkroom is a day standing in your own head.

4 Place the negative, upside down and back to front, in the carrier. Open up the aperture of the enlarger lens and bring the image, a slice of your life, into focus on a piece of photographic paper on the easel.

5 Stop down the aperture at least two stops and adjust the contrast to suit the negative.

6 Prepare the test strips and expose the paper shiny-side-up in increments of 4 seconds, swatches of ever-darkening stripes. On the back, note the time and your mood in pencil.

7 Place the strips in the developer and gently rock the tray back and forth, back and forth, like a lullaby. Soon, as if by magic, you will see the latent image start to appear.

8

After 2 minutes, drain and move to the stop for 30 seconds. Enough picture already. Stop bath smells of preserved memories.

9

Move to the fix for 1 minute to set the image in stone. Then, immerse the strips in the wash. In the half-light, select the overall time that feels the closest to your vision of the scene and expose a full sheet of paper on the easel.

10

Repeat the steps in the trays above, but this time rock a little more vigorously in the developer. With each tiny wave, watch the Dmax deepen, the highlights shift to a hair off paper-base white, and the midtones fill in with questions and thoughts. *What shall I have for dinner? Should I be plant-based? I should have sex tonight.*

11

In a carrying tray, take your print outside to the lit-up whiteboard to judge your next steps. *How is the overall exposure? Do you need to adjust the contrast? How is my art/life balance? Where does it need dodging* (taking away time) *or burning* (adding time)—actions that require hand shadow-puppet maneuvers and a series of cardboard cutout circles taped on sticks.

12

Wash the print in the overflowing gurgling bath (it's like listening to somebody's tummy all day) for 20 minutes, and then pin it by a corner to the clothesline above the sink. You started the day with raw materials and some thoughts. But soon a day's work, pieces of paper, moving like skirts lifting up in the wind, are evidence you lived. You saw this. Here it is in a black-and-white print, a manifestation of what you are concerned with—how you feel inside.

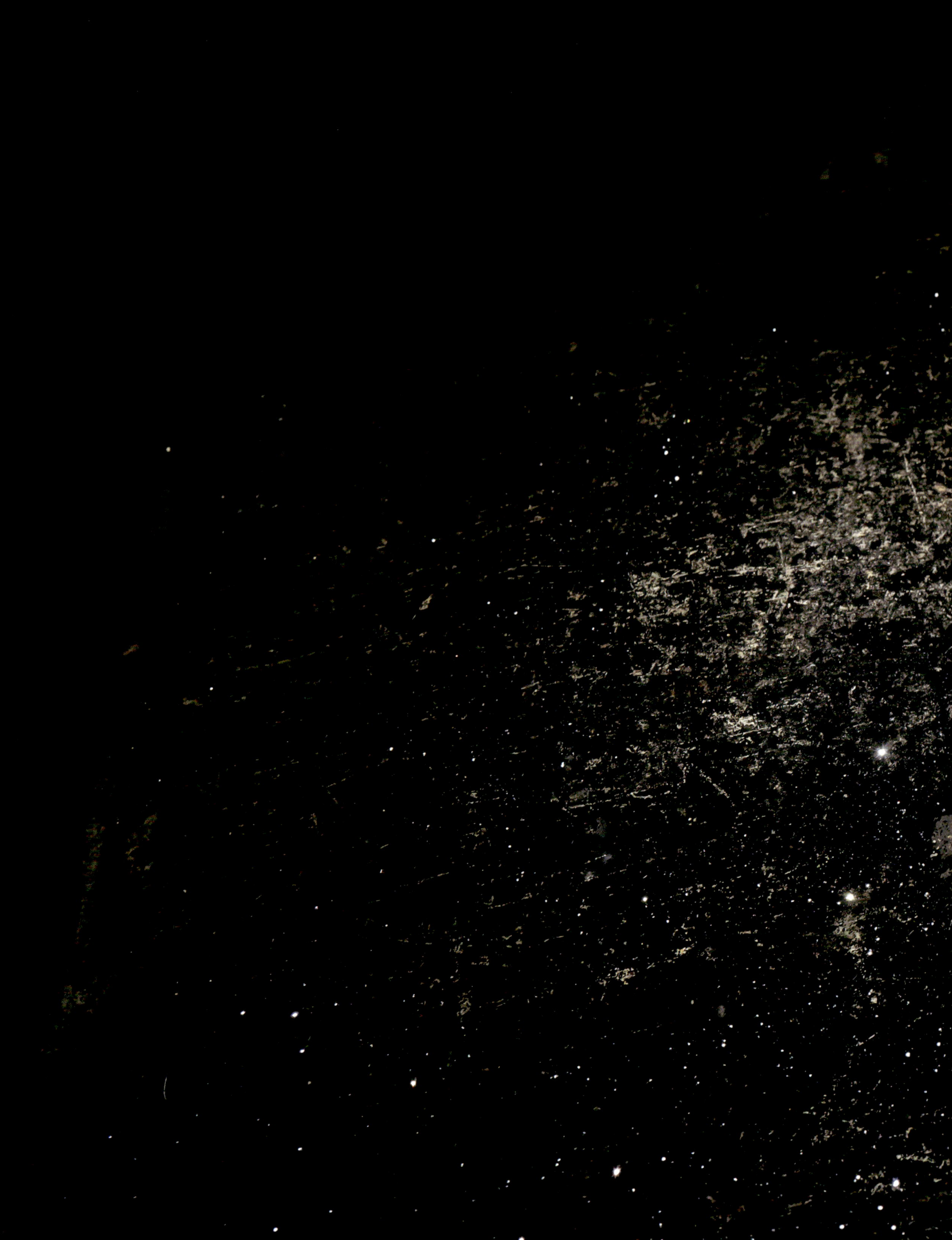

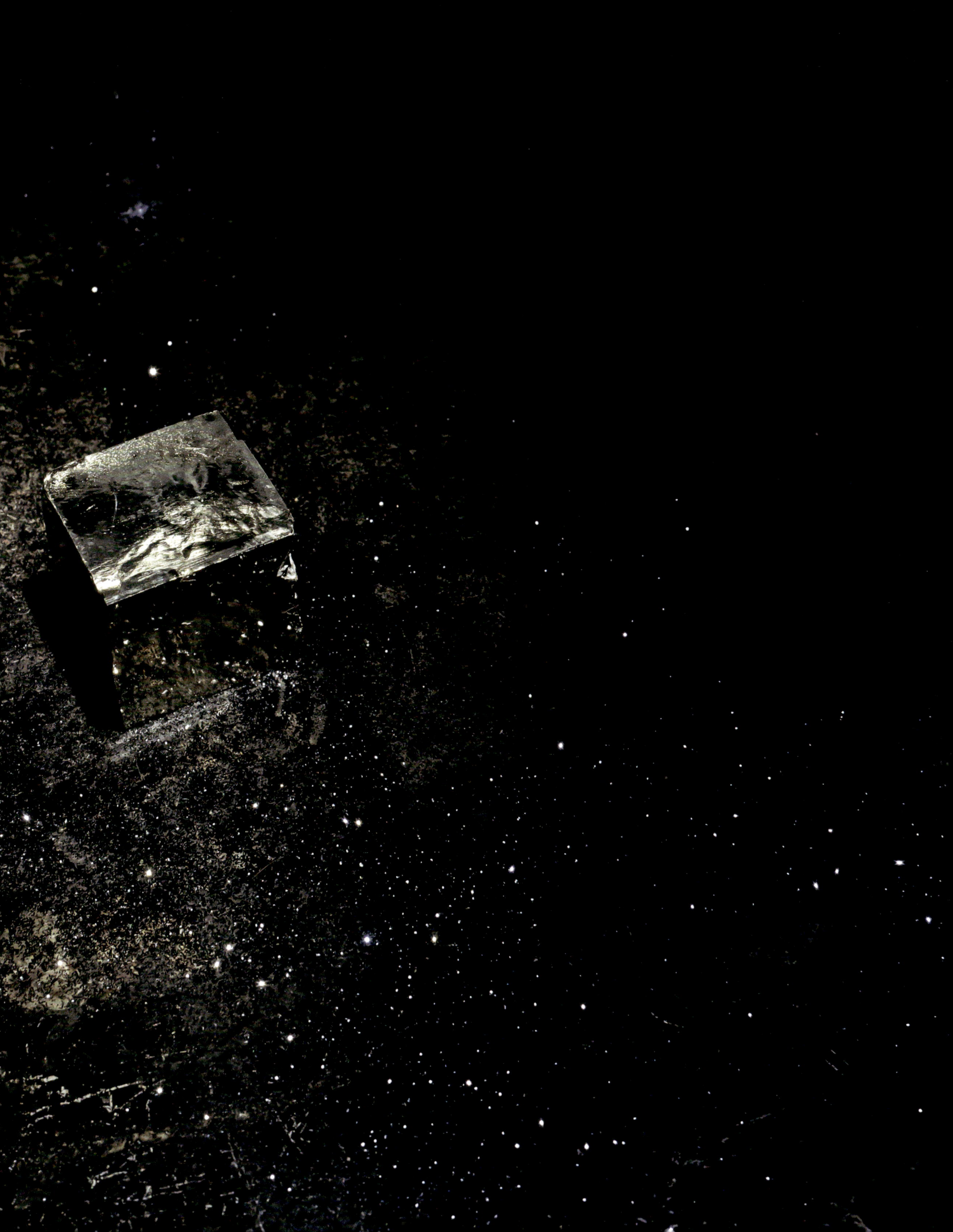

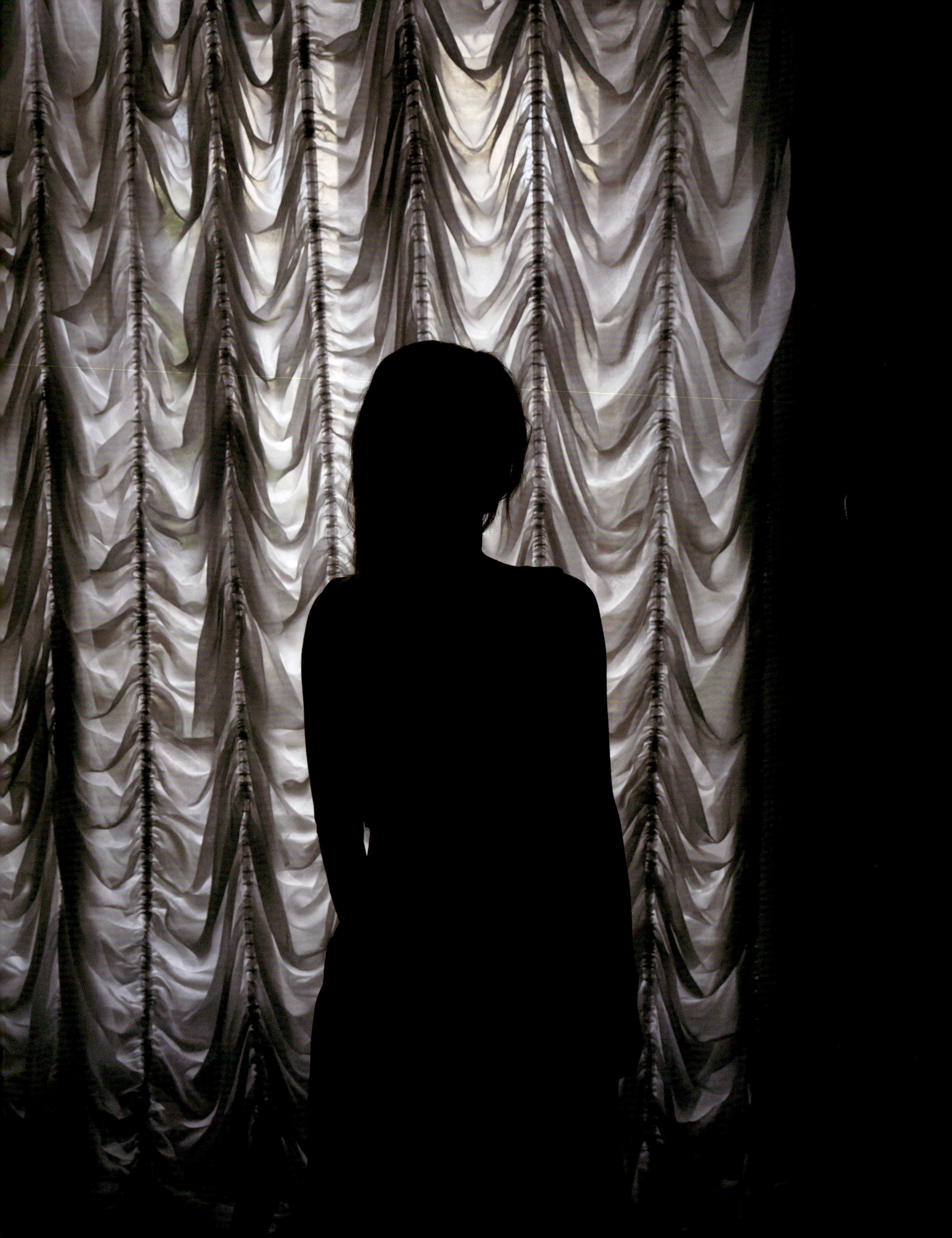

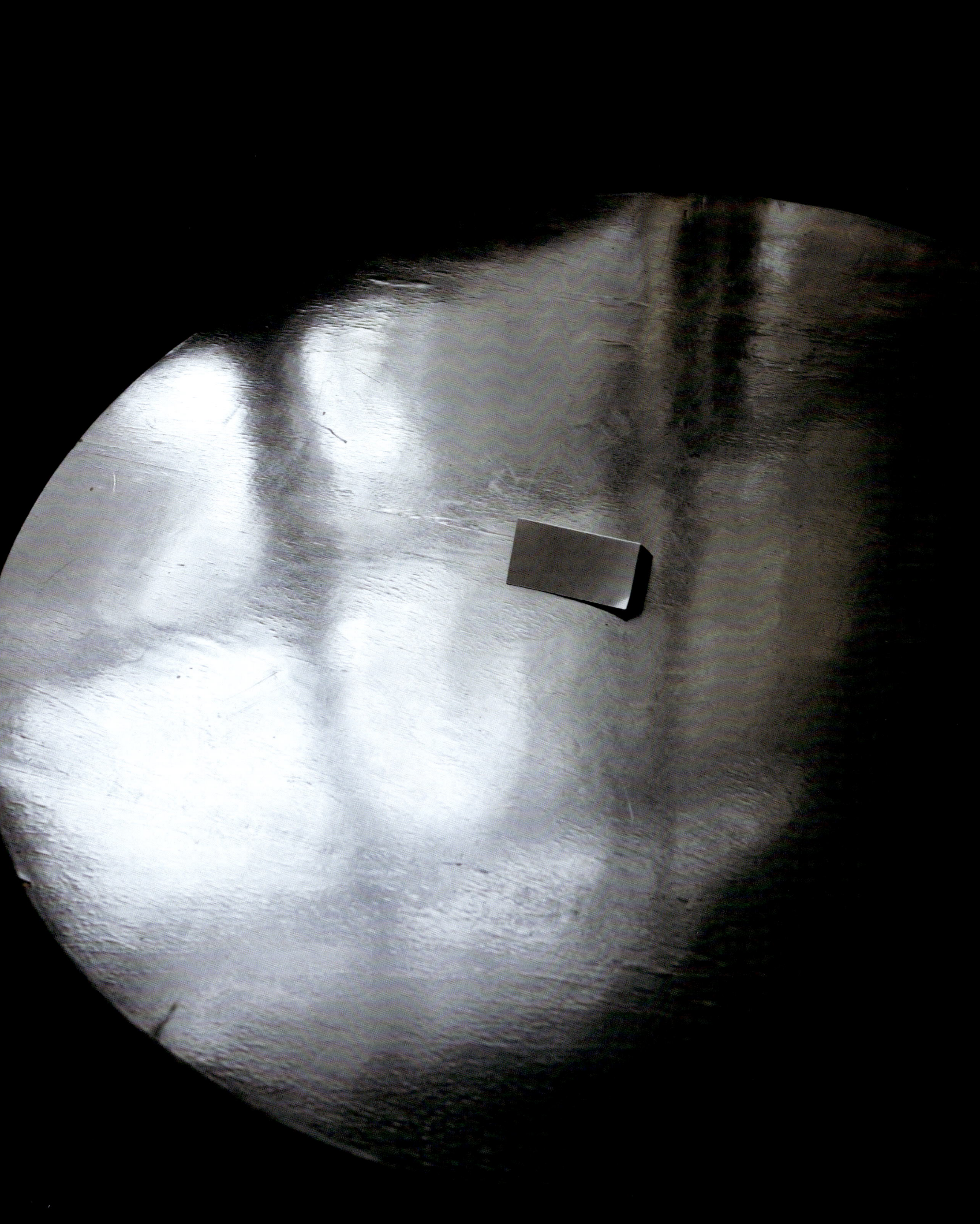

Some people say if you really love color, then white must be your favorite because it's all the colors combined. Mixing different colored light always makes white. I'm a maximalist, but white is not my favorite. That said, I do like to think of all the colors touching each other.

But mixing different colored paint pigments together, no matter in what order, the opposite happens: a compost of devastating blackish green. I learned this when I was seven years old. The garden was my laboratory, and I made perfume to sell from the rosebushes that my mother planted around the patio border. Petals of every color billowed in my bowl, and I scissored them into dust and added warm water. I wanted my perfume to be jewel-toned, but no matter how hard I mixed or added another dollop of yellow or a few more lighter rose petals, I ended up with the same murky paste.

I love earth tones. Milk chocolate is my favorite food group, and warm brown, my favorite color to wear. But add yellow and green and you're left with the boundaryless Pantone 448C, officially the world's ugliest color. It used to be known as Opaque Couché, French for misunderstood. It was a sad day when once again science pushed the arts aside and Pantone changed the names of their colors to numbers.

Ending up with that color is a formative moment in every child's life—perhaps the first of many times when you realize that what you hope for is not necessarily what you're going to get.

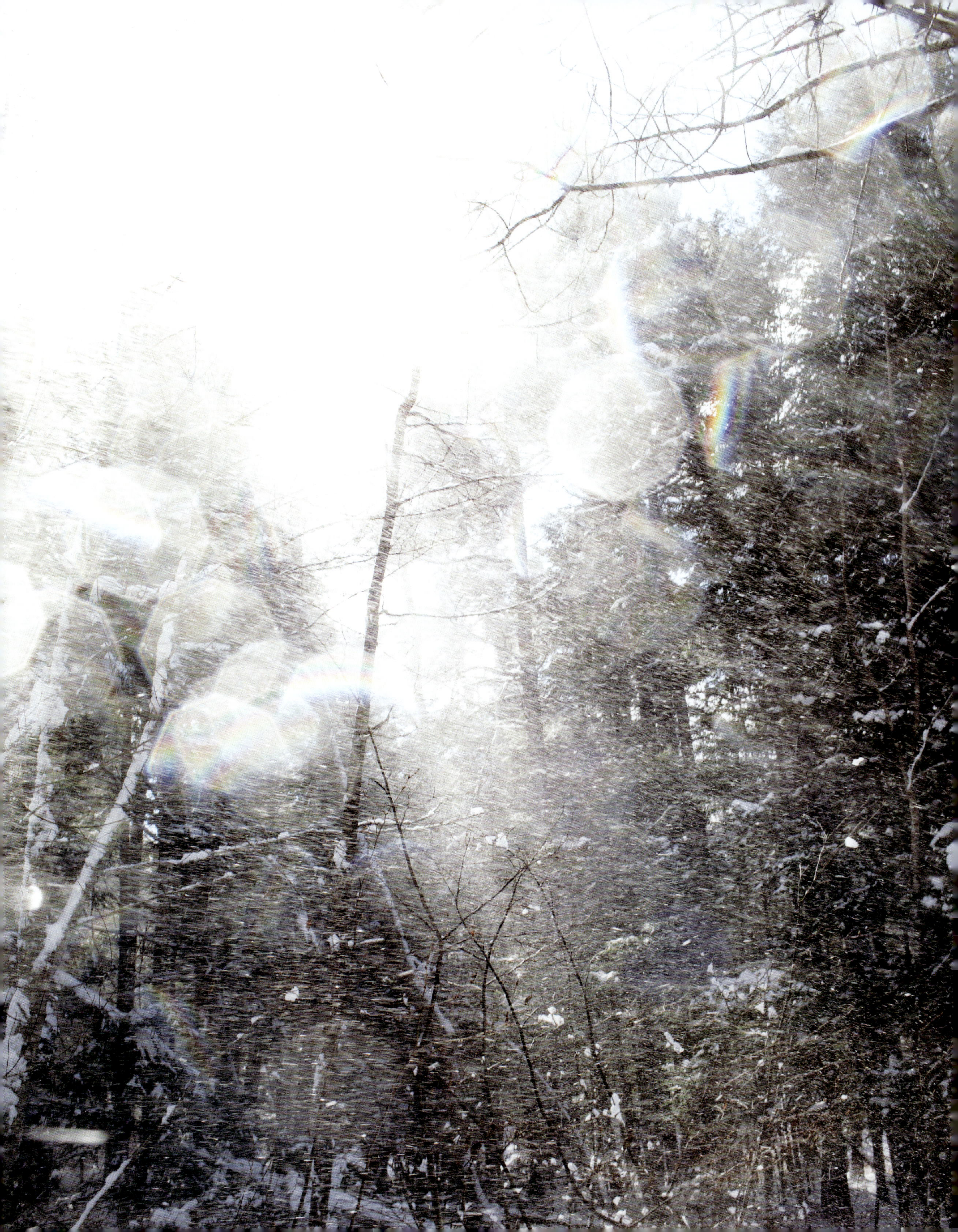

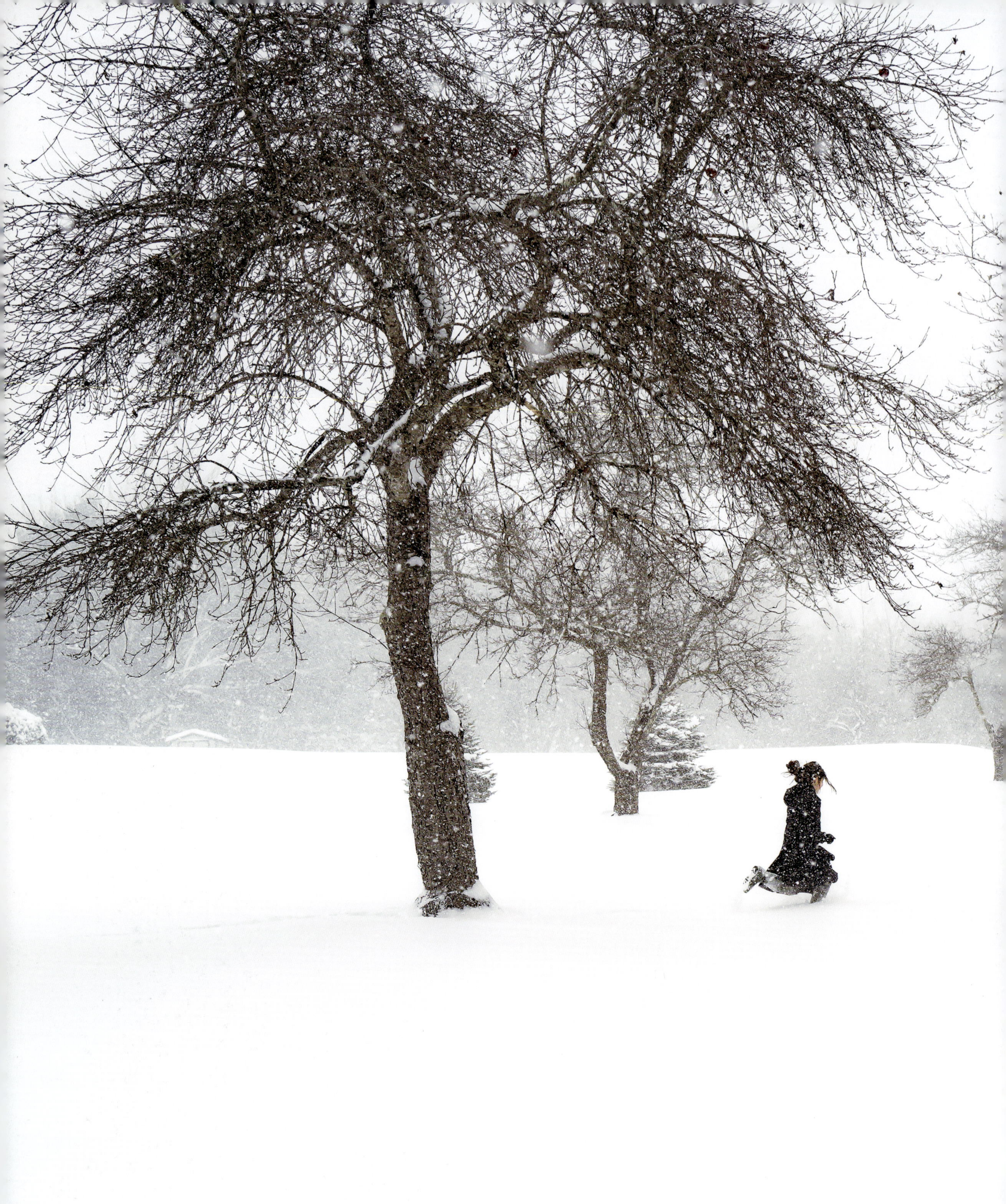

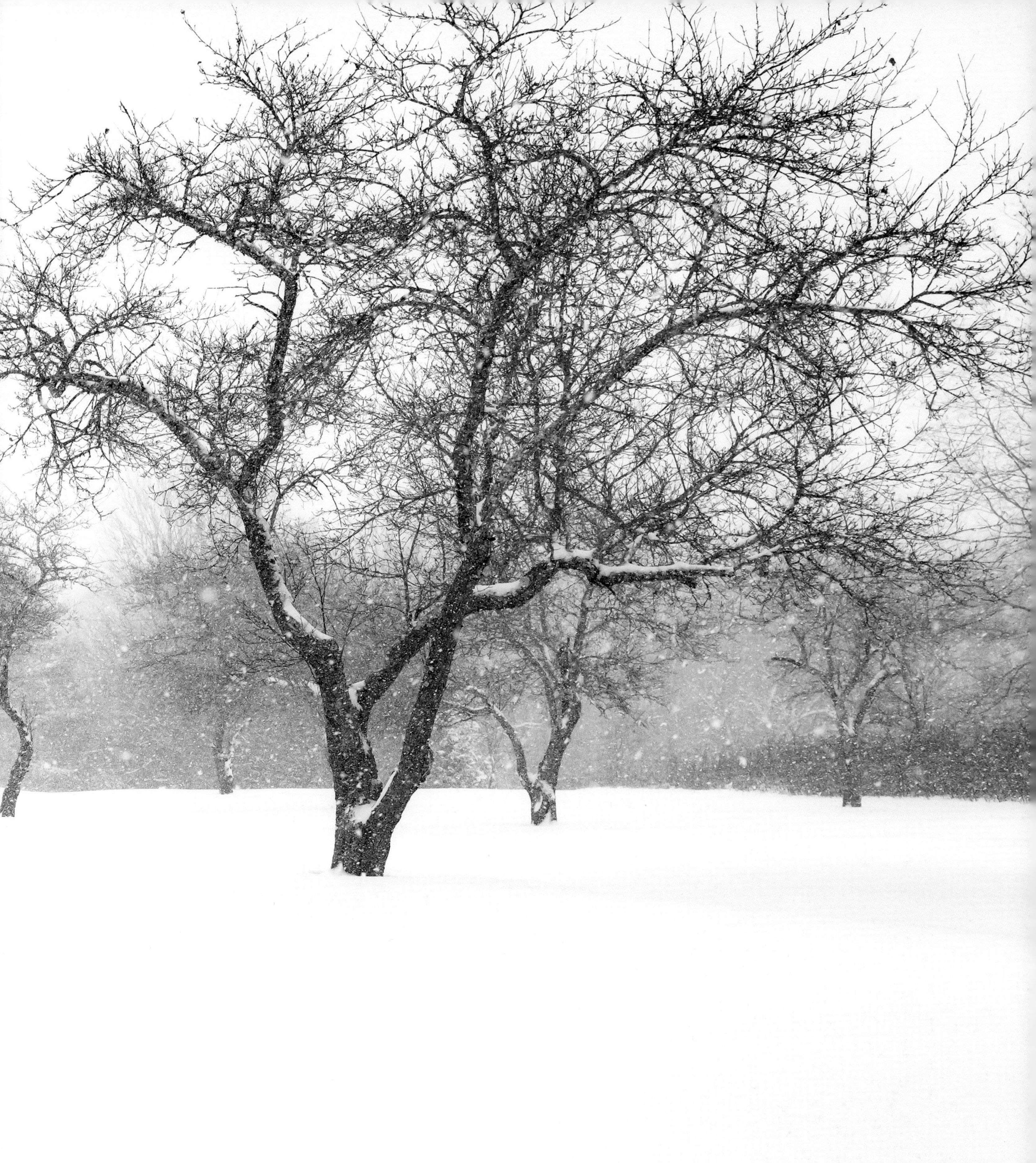

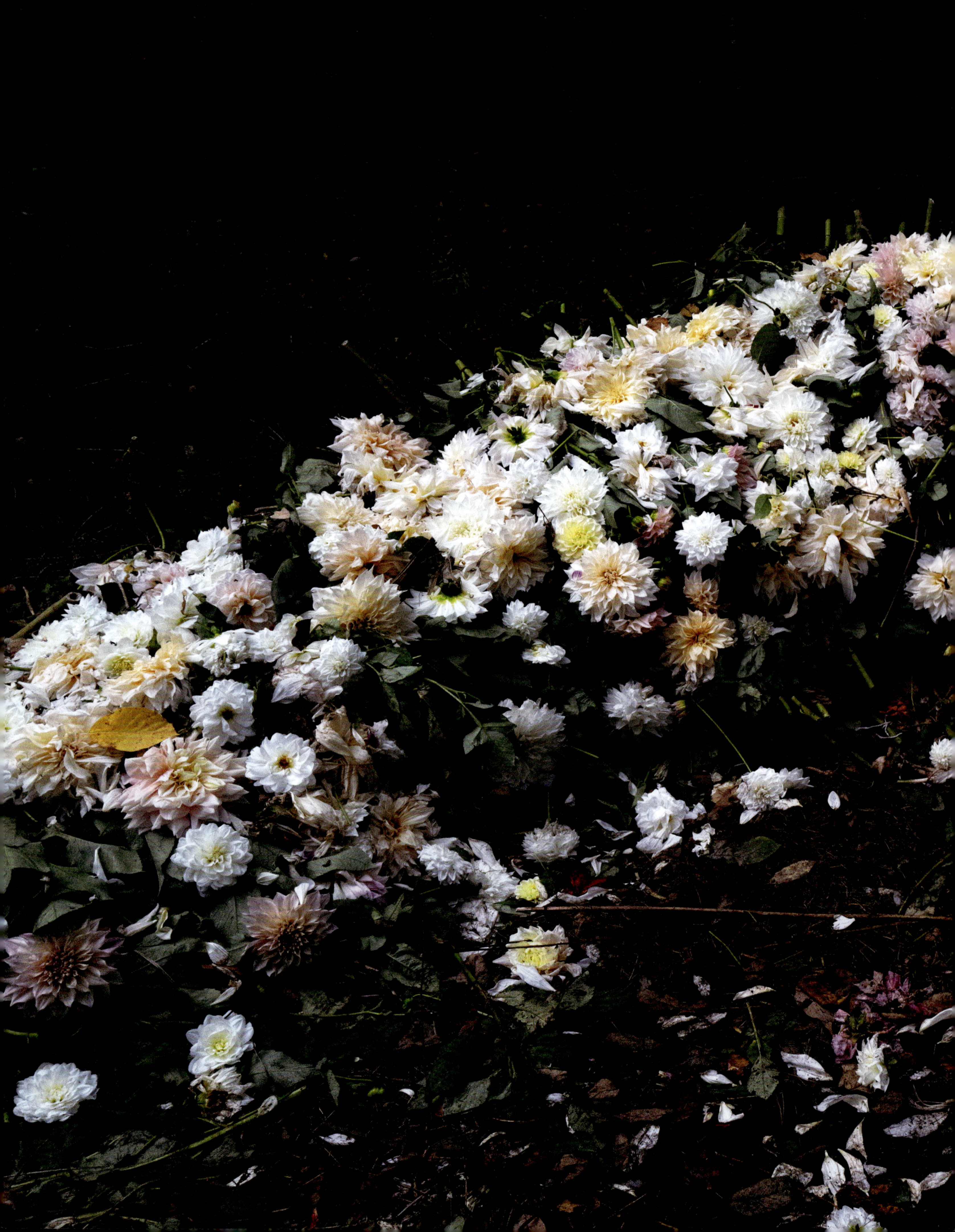

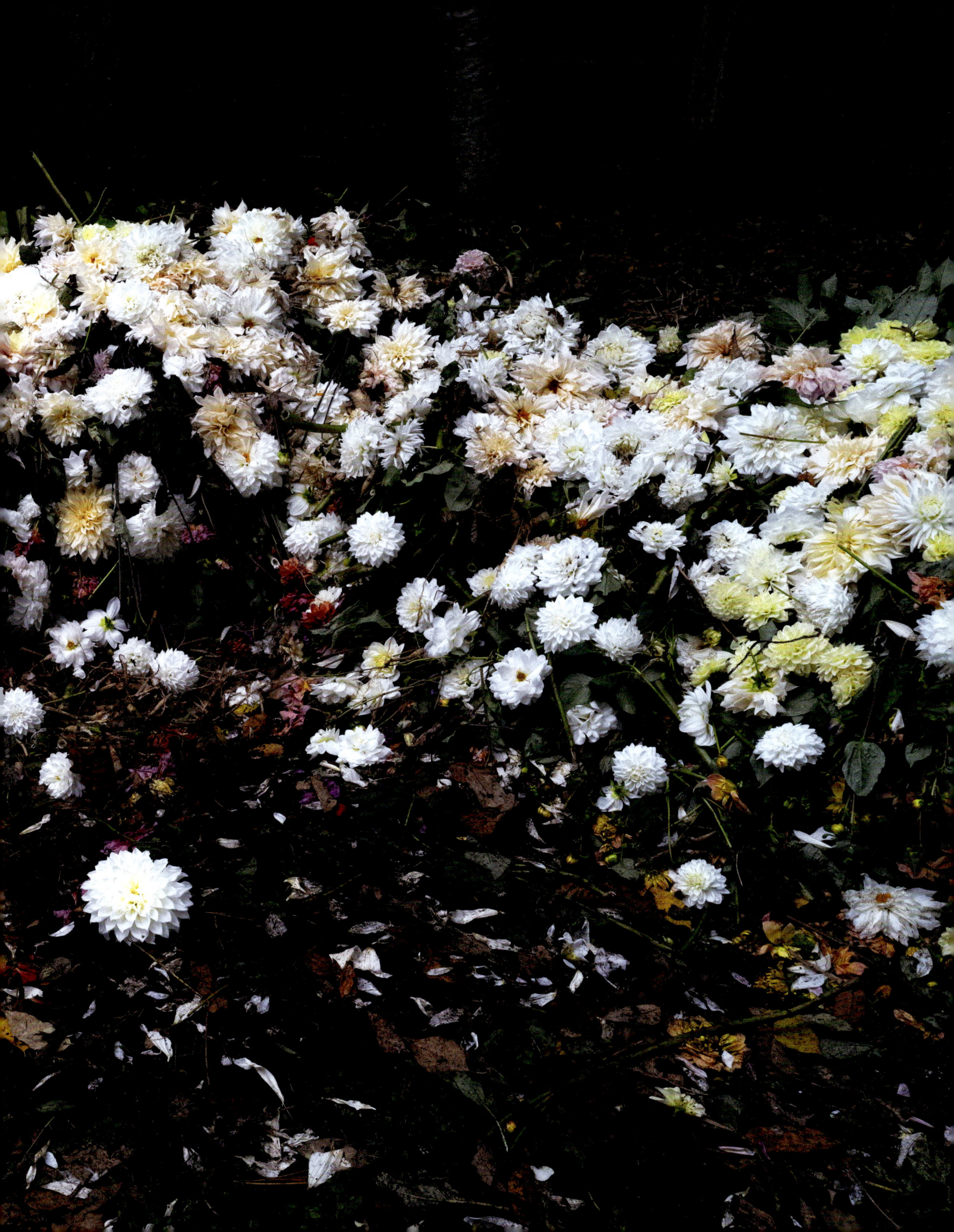

In 1985, the U.S. Supreme Court decided that it was possible to own a color. Vantablack™ was invented in 2014, the name derived from the acronym for Vertically Aligned NanoTube Array Black. Black is the absence of color in light. Vantablack™ is a superblack—so thirsty that its nanostructure absorbs all of the color, releasing no visual particles to scattering. Gazing at Vantablack™ is like being in a sensory deprivation tank—you can perceive nothing and are left with only your thoughts and past actions.

Some people wear black every day, either by choice (fashion or mourning) or as part of a uniform (judges, police, and priests). Queen Victoria was a melanophile, someone obsessed with the color black. She was publicly mourning, and grumpy by nature, so she wore black, with hot pink frilly panties underneath, every day for forty years.

In some cultures, black is a color associated with authority and sophistication, but also linked to death, fear, and depression. Black is considered unlucky in India. Color is complicated.

Wearing black can be a very elegant solution. I wear it from head to toe when I am overwhelmed and need to simplify. But mostly I prefer a complex life. Each morning, I put on colors that represent how I feel or what I want to accomplish or how I want to be seen for the task of the day: a warm magenta velvet tuxedo to present work on cakes or flowers, a deep chestnut cashmere cardigan to tap into truth when I am writing.

The Thirstiest
Black

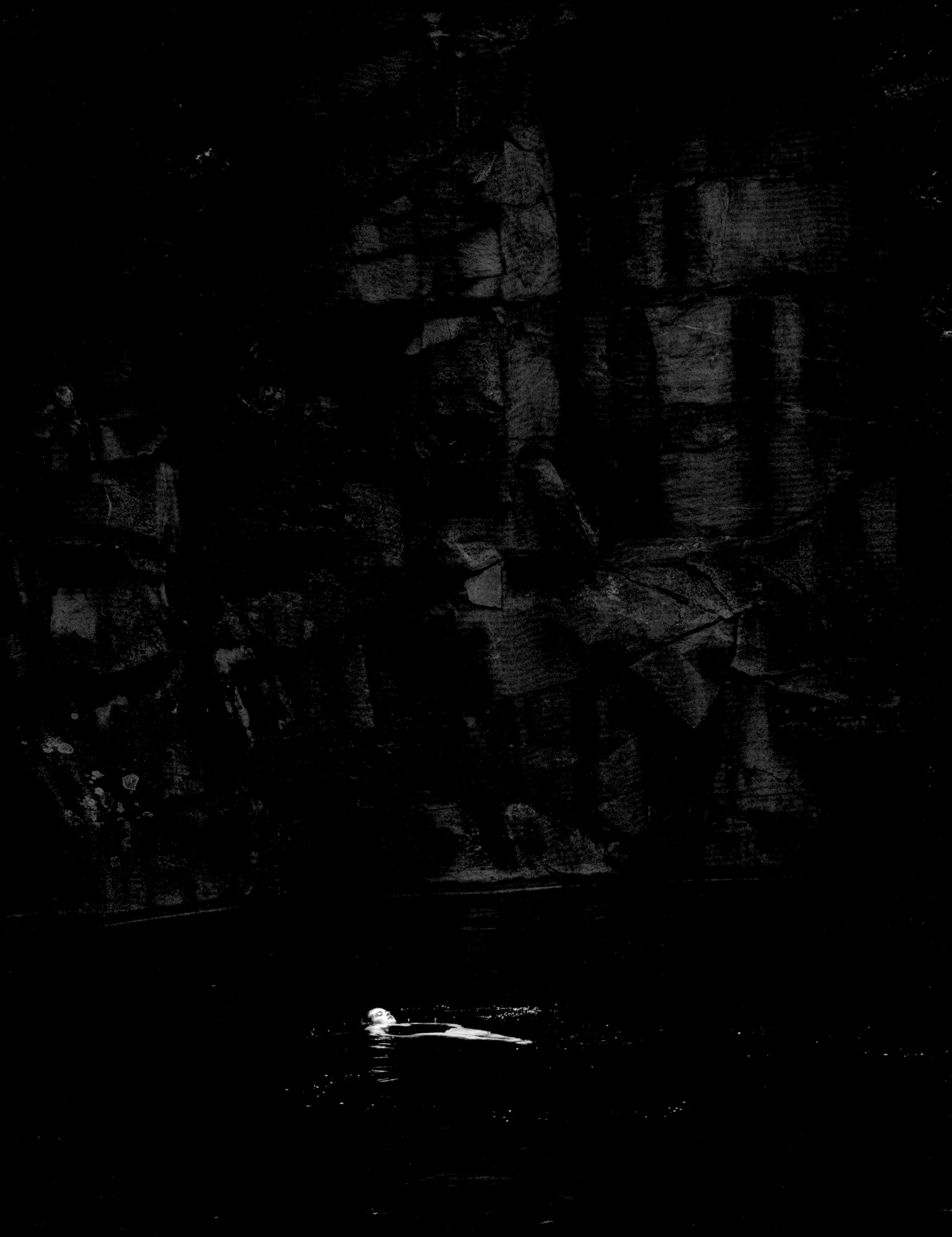

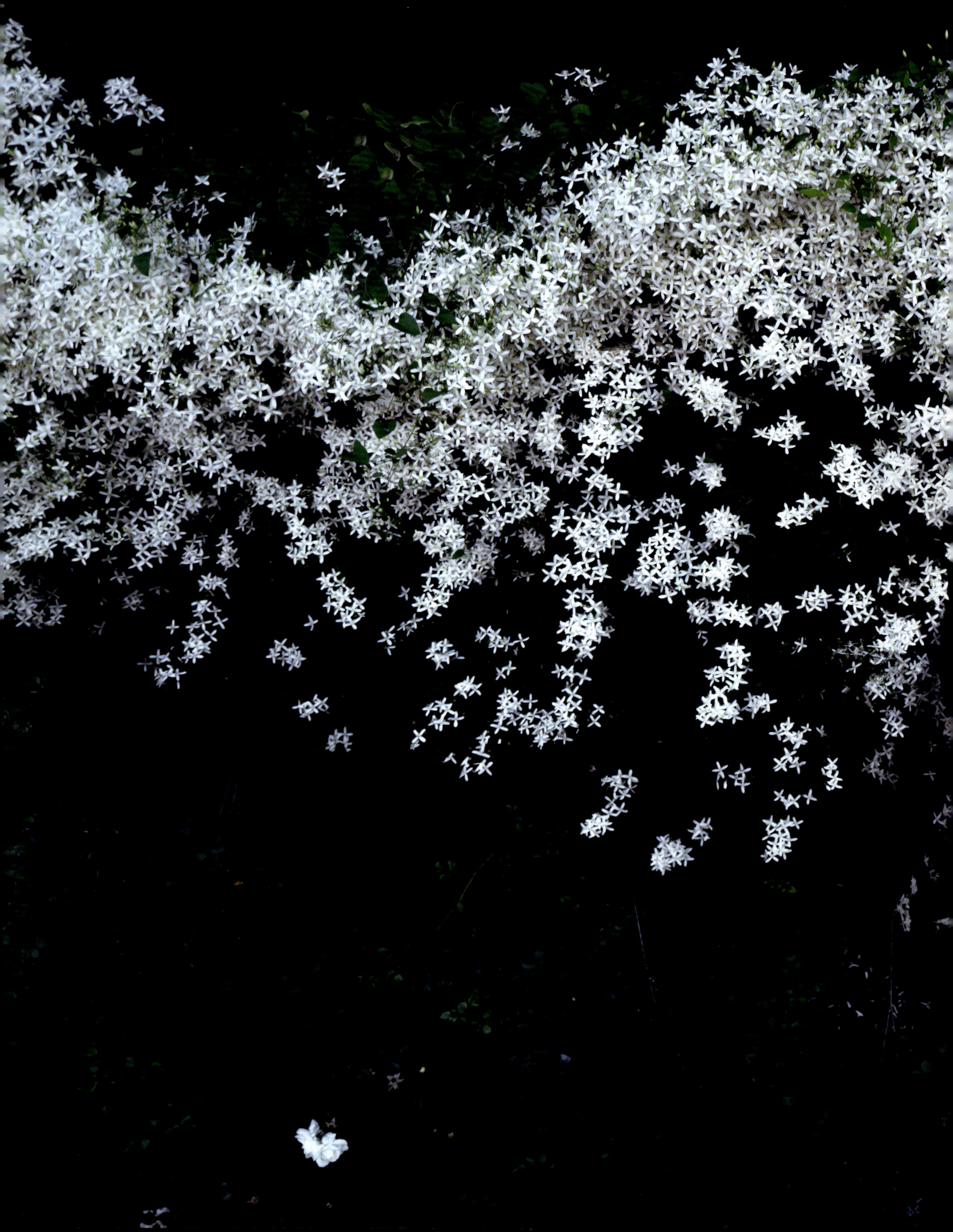

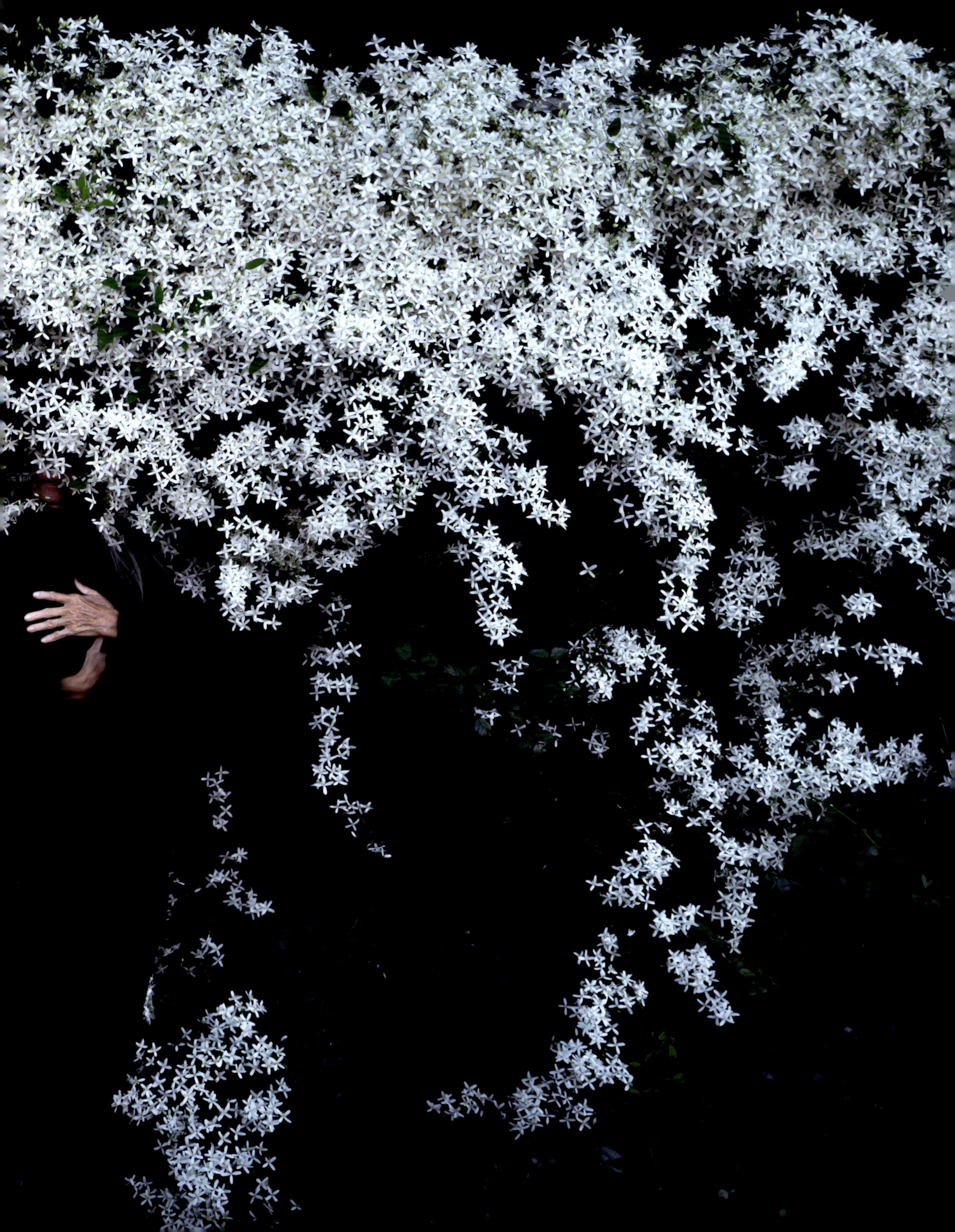

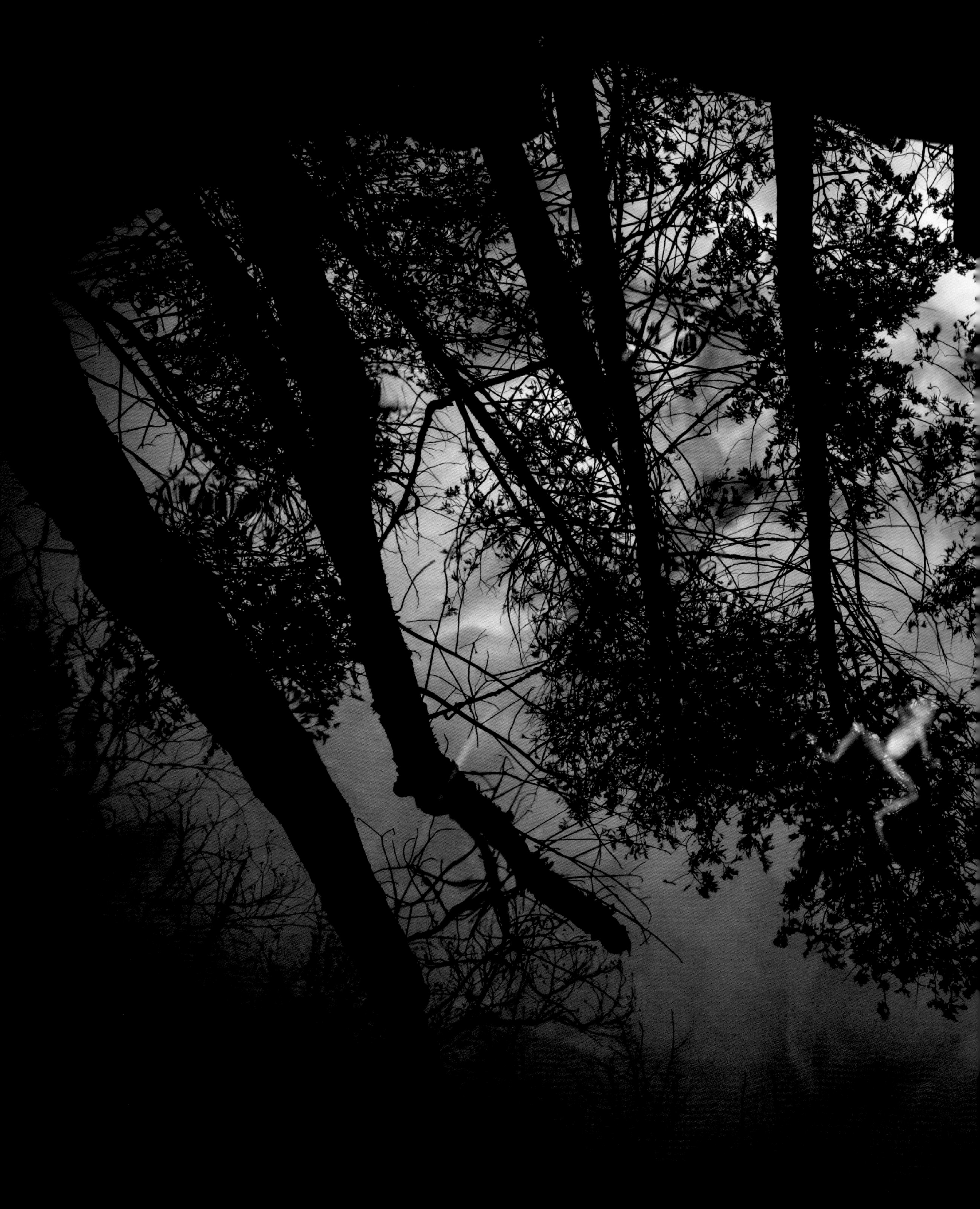

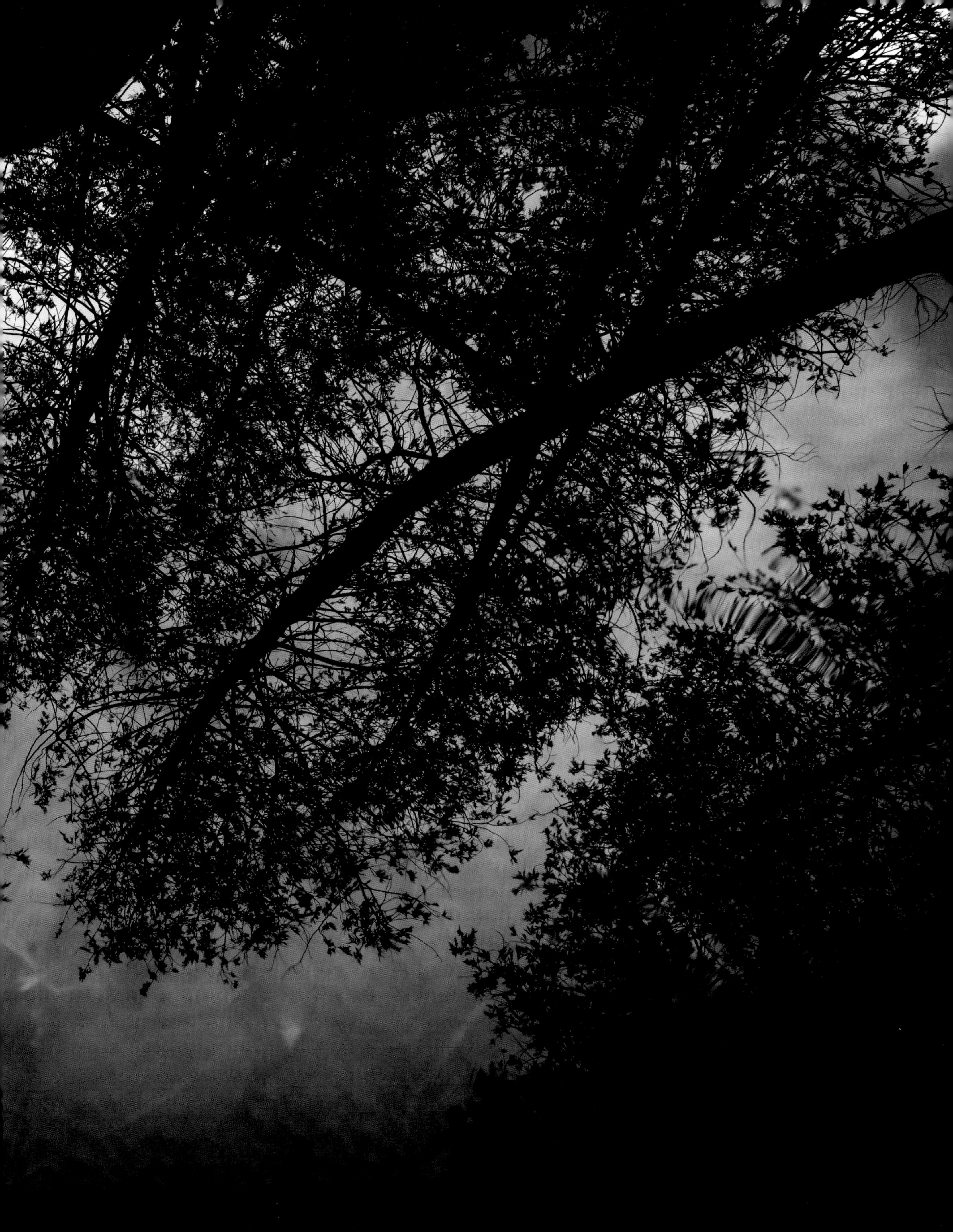

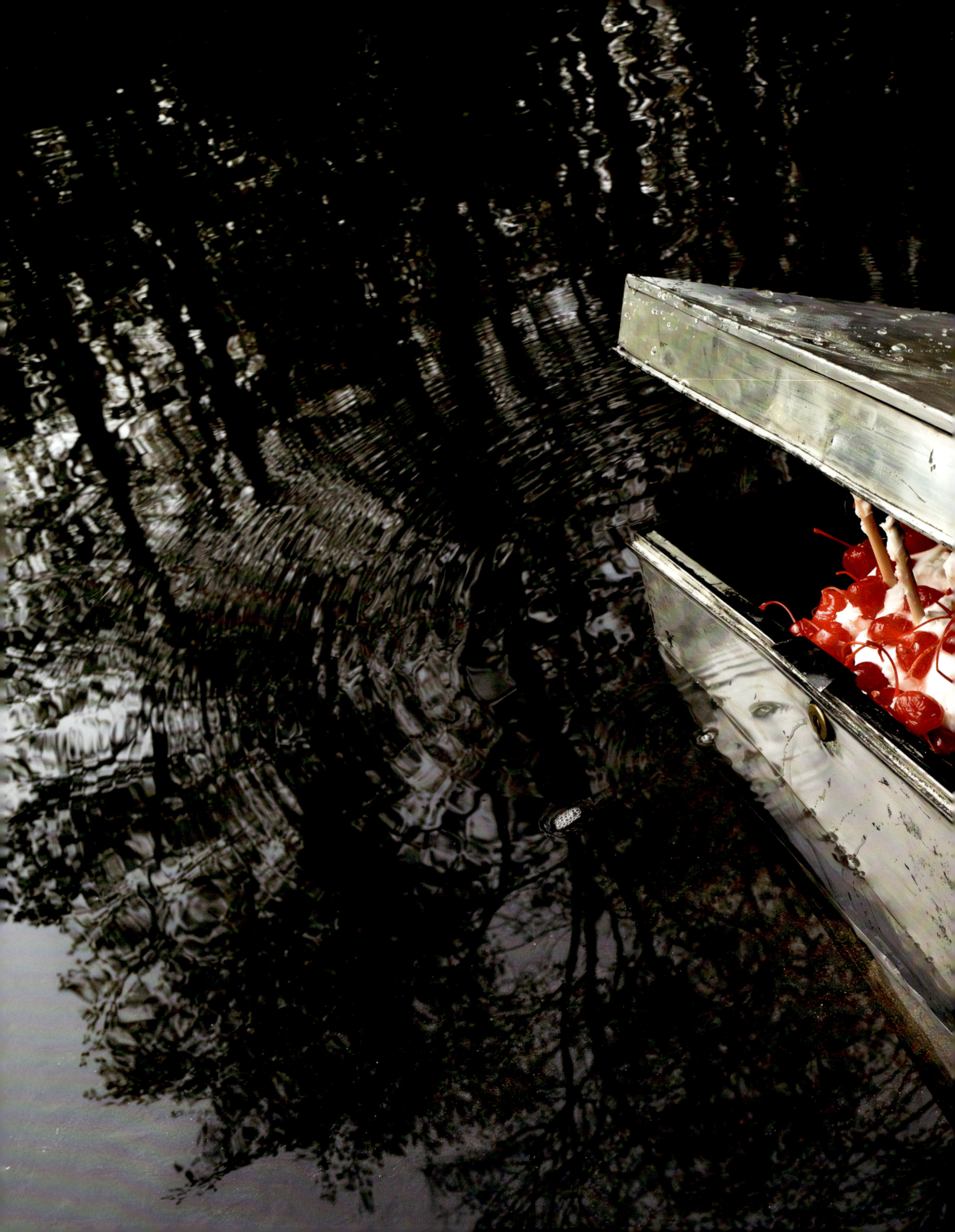

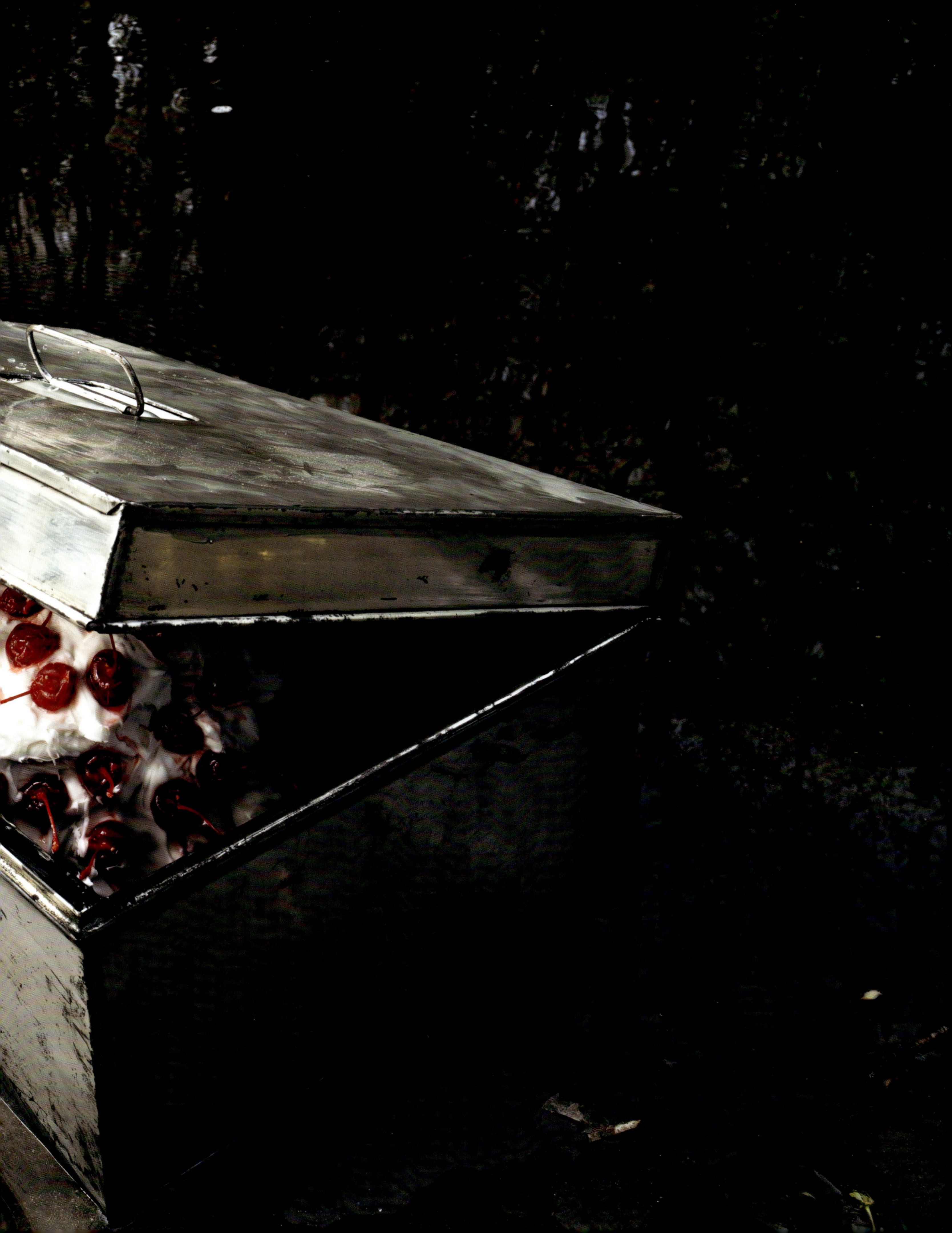

# A Red that Bites

Red is the oldest color.

Red is the first color we see as babies. For nine months, we live in rose-tinted worlds as we grow our bones, organs, and minds in the red planets of our mothers' wombs. For some of us, this goes on to mean the color red, the color of blood, symbolizes fertility; for others, war.

The first organic red paints, inks, and dyes came from animals, plants, and minerals: ocher from the ground, scarlet from the dragon's blood tree, crimson from kermes insects, and the dark rust of iron ore from space.

The Aztecs and Incas ran to catch meteorites, *the red that fell from the sky*. The Incas forged stonecutting tools out of these cosmic rocks to build Machu Picchu, a city to reach the heavens.

Maine is the place in the continental United States where the light hits first each and every morning. I live on the land of the Wabanaki, the People of the Dawn. The Wabanaki are thought to be the descendants of the Red Paint People, a five-thousand-year-old maritime tribe who thrived on the coast of Maine. They mixed seal oil and ocher to paint their dead red before covering the bodies in crushed red hematite, a mineral not found in Maine.

The Greeks stained themselves red to go into battle—iron rust was believed to heal wounds. Red is an antibiotic.

Madder is a green plant with black berries, yellow flowers, and brown roots. Early chemists used to crush it to make red pigment. Madder stains the bones, beaks, and feet of animals and birds. It's also poisonous to humans, turning saliva, tears, sweat, urine, and breast milk a radiant red.

Walking through the woods this morning, I hear the red berries screaming in the fog. Squeezing them in my fists, I make a winter soup that drips onto the cold, bare ground. I smear it over my coat in a desperate ombré and think about what would happen if I ate this meal of fire to warm my veins.

Red is both witness and evidence.

Five thousand years ago, the first red lipsticks were made from crushed rubies, and other ancient red cosmetics came from insects, pregnant beetles, and crocodiles. Animals imprisoned and specimened, laboring and dying to give us the color red.

Just yesterday, I saw a cardinal perfectly preserved midflight lying dead in the middle of the road. *Stop the clocks*, I thought, that beautiful crimson on the gray asphalt, the space normally reserved for the muted tones of raccoons, squirrels, and chipmunks.

Aniline red, an early synthetic dye made from coal, was known as *the red from darkness*. Cinnabar and vermilion, a beautiful but toxic red mineral, mined from the heart of volcanoes. One spring, I started my own eruption by planting one hundred scarlet runner beans in the front yard and came back three months later to the house on fire.

Red has the longest wavelengths in the color spectrum. It is the color we can see from farthest away, which is why it is used for warnings. Red has the loudest voice. Seeing red can alter our mood and raise our blood pressure. And yet red light doesn't disturb sleep; it soothes circadian rhythms and heals the body at a cellular level. In my twenties, I spent hours, days, and years mending my heart under the red safe light in the darkroom. In deep winter, I spread raspberry jam on my toast to interrupt the morning monotony. Doug knows if I cover our evening meal in pomegranate seeds, then beware: a creative storm is brewing inside of me.

I once released a massive red prayer balloon into a gunmetal sky, and as it rose, I was panicked by the audacity of its redness, imagining people driving into one another on the highway, mesmerized by the beauty of the red, hypnotic against the gray.

I use red in my pictures to make you stop. To make you stare. To make you lose your underwear. Red is a jolt. Red is a glare. I even like how the sound of the word *red* feels in the space between the top of my mouth and my tongue: round and long and breathy. From the beginning of time, red has been a seductress. She's a smoke ring blown into the air, a perfect circle, whole and complete.

But history has taught us that you must use red sparingly and not abuse its power. Search for a red with not too much blue weighing it down, with more yellow to lift it up—a red that bites.

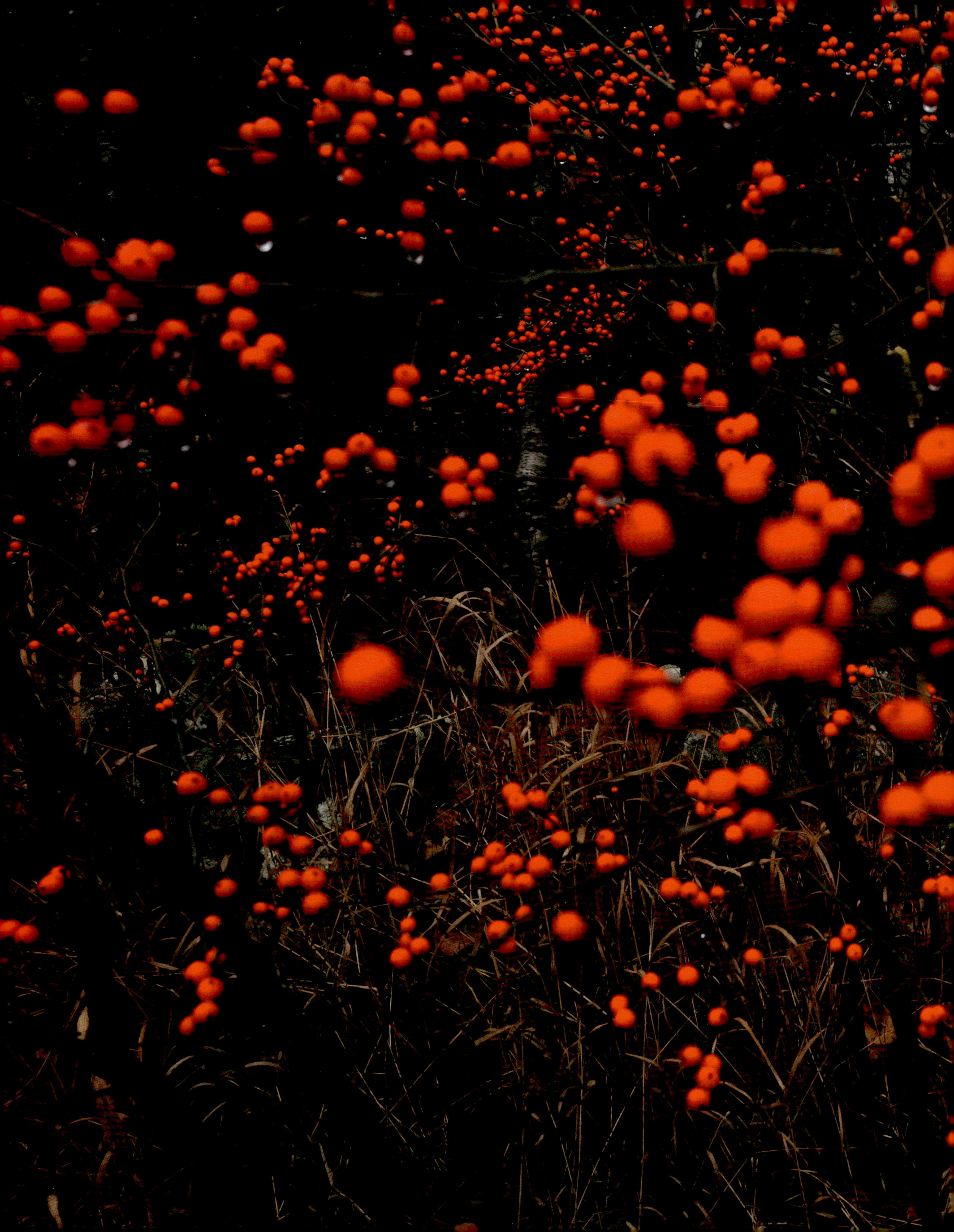

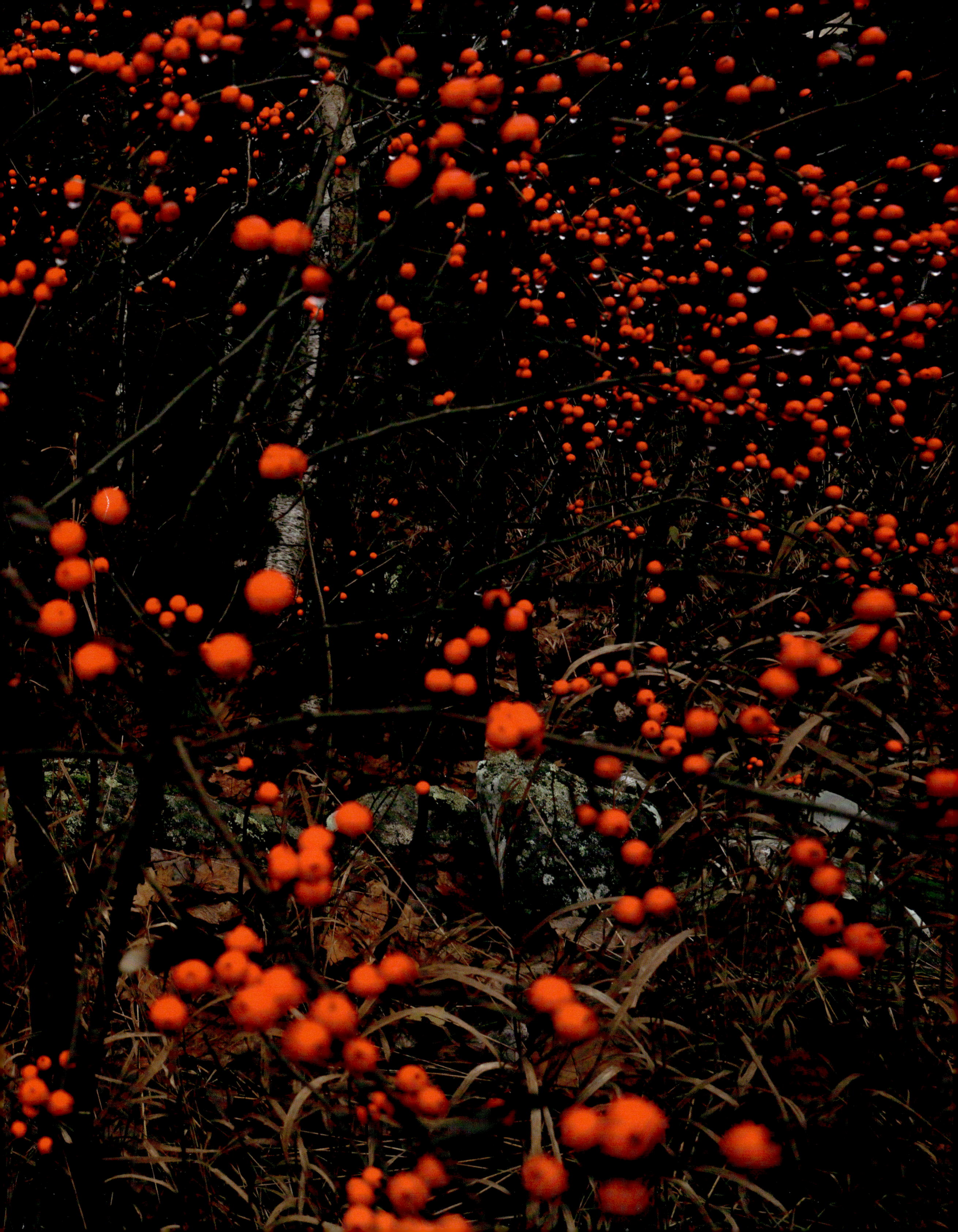

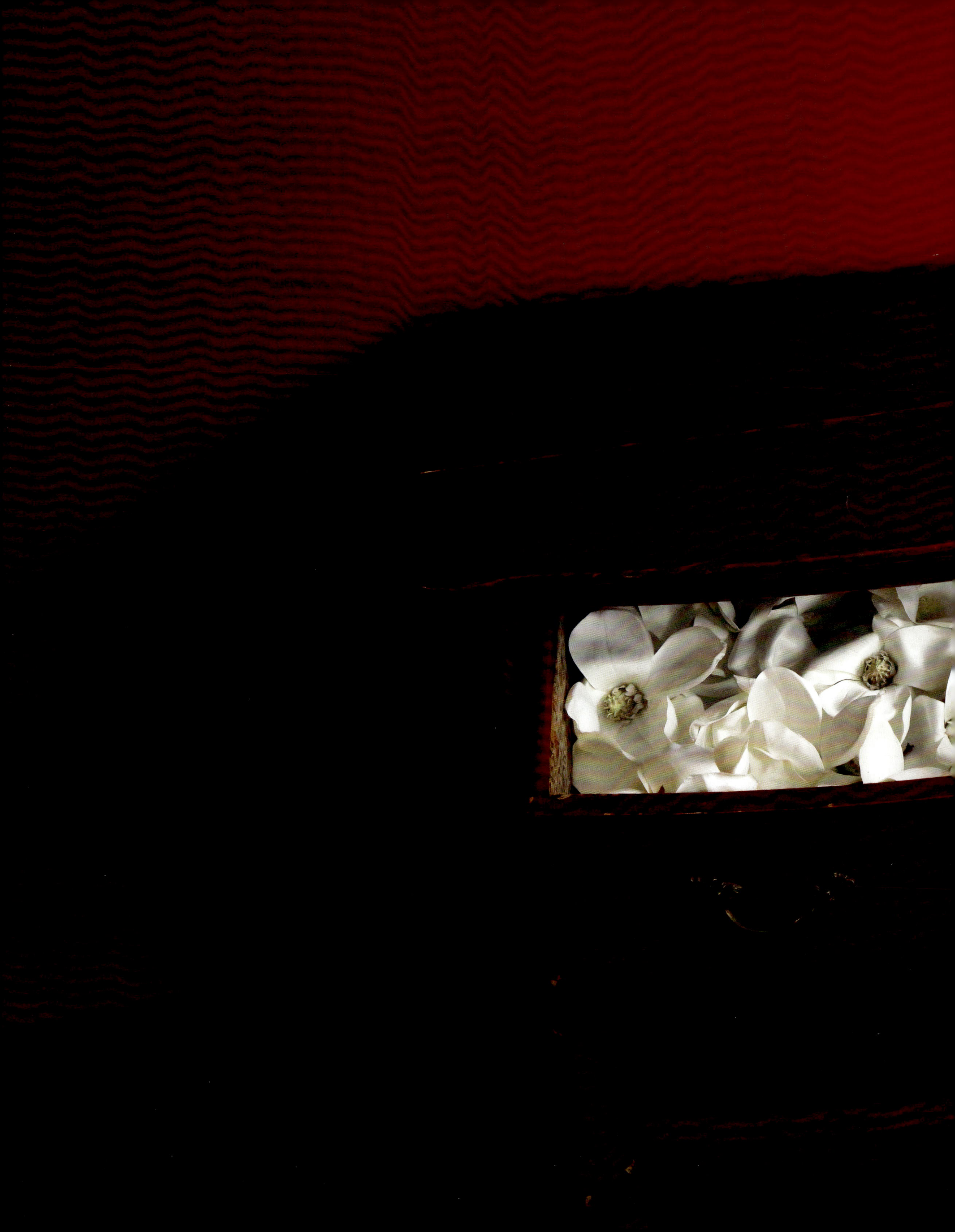

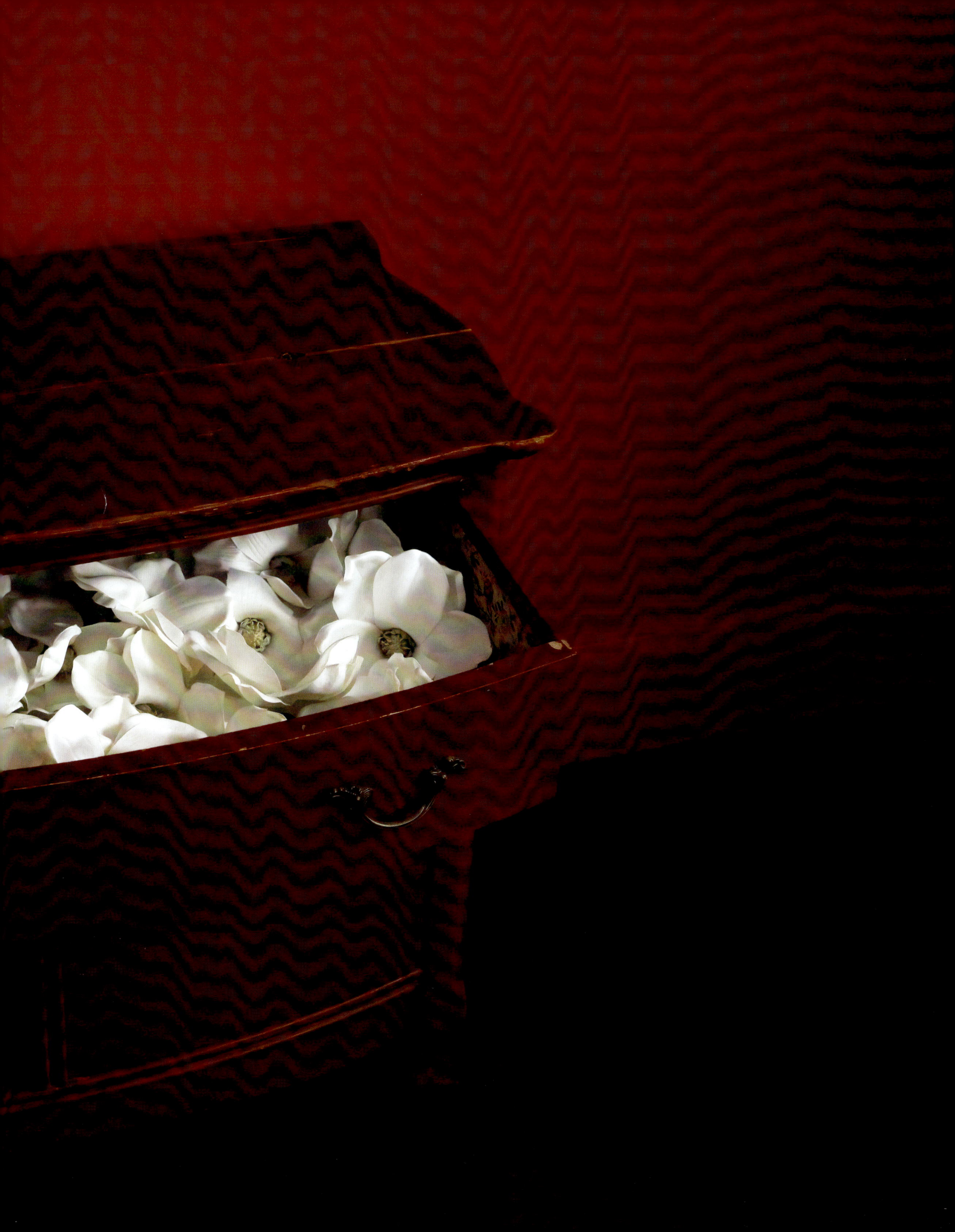

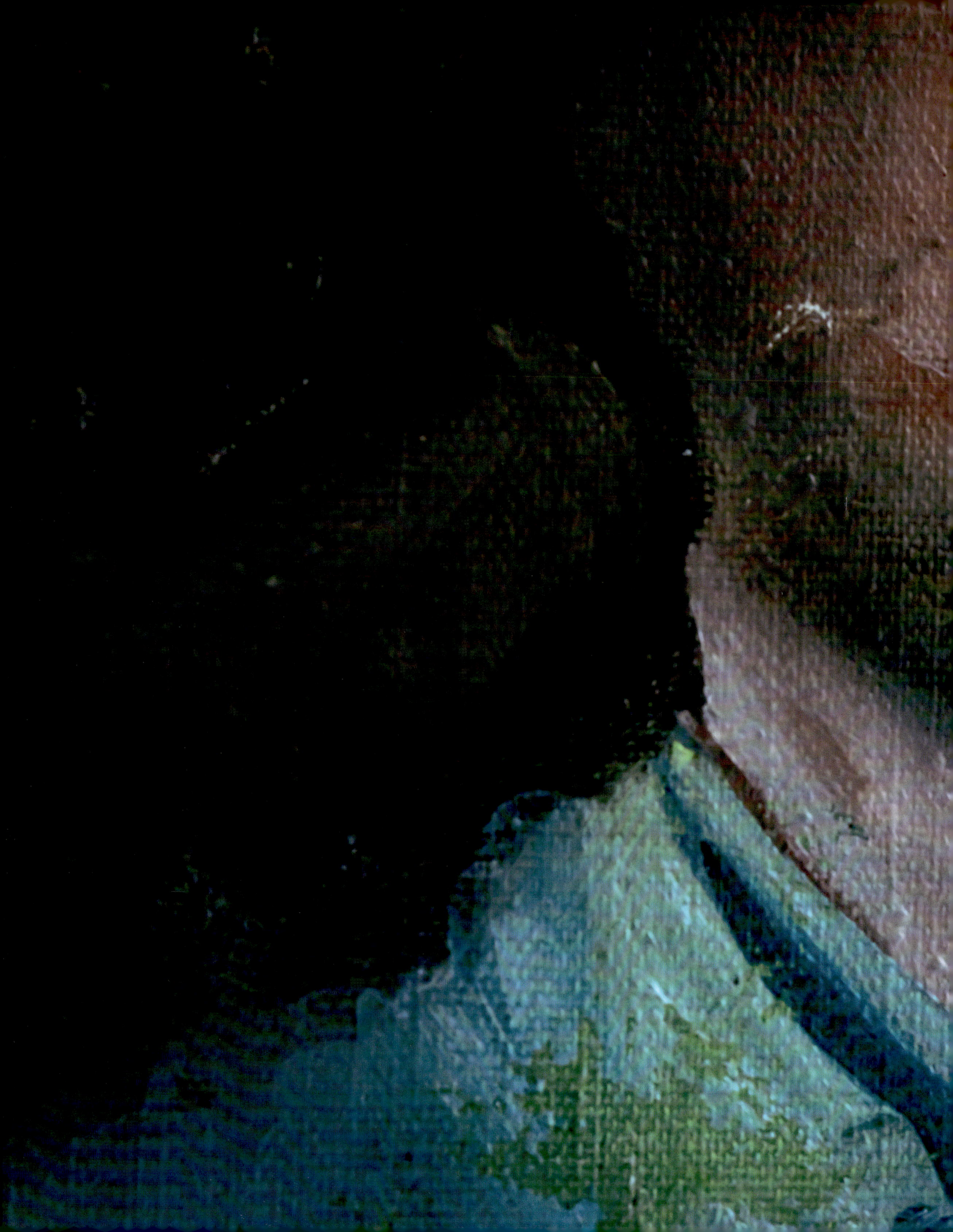

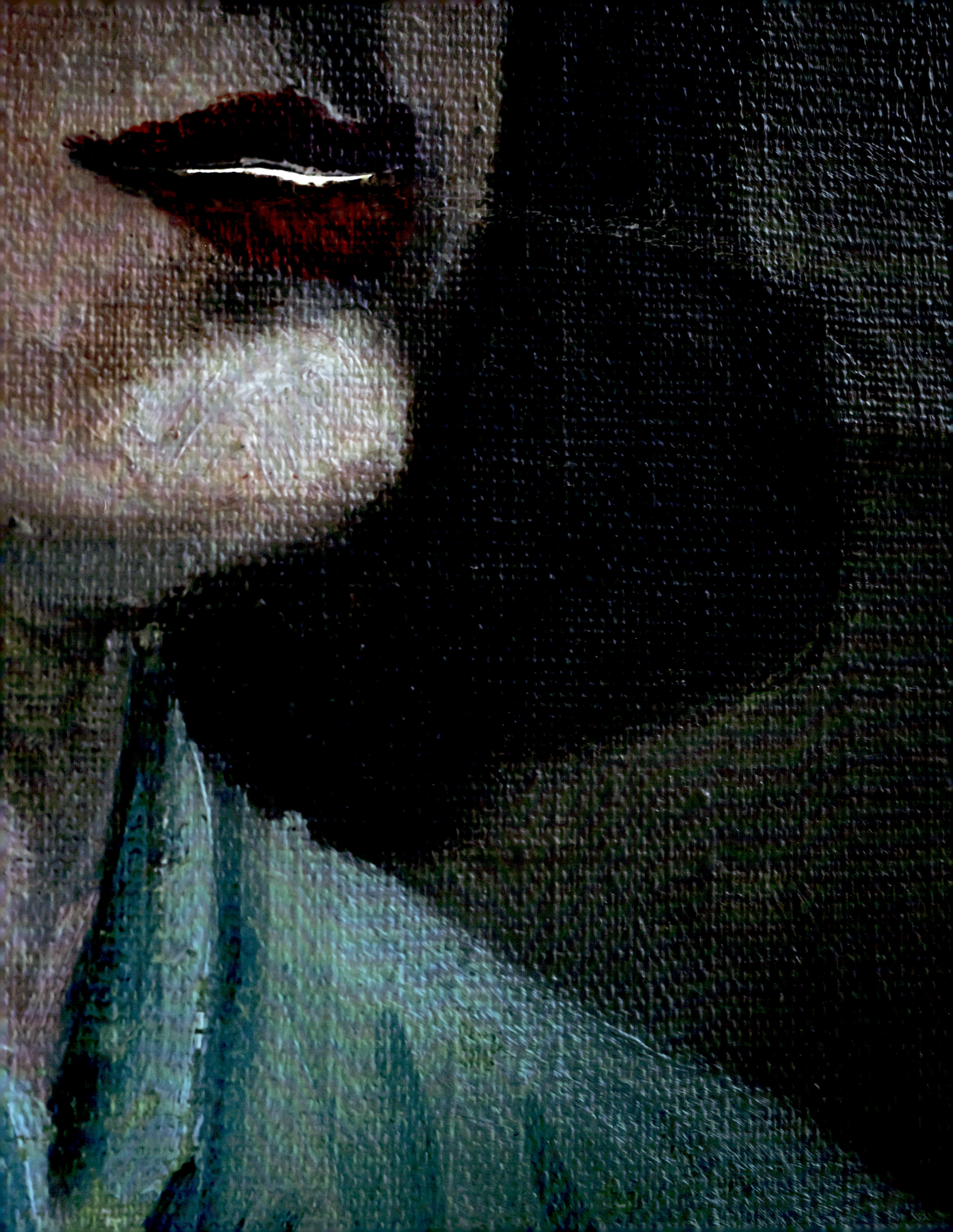

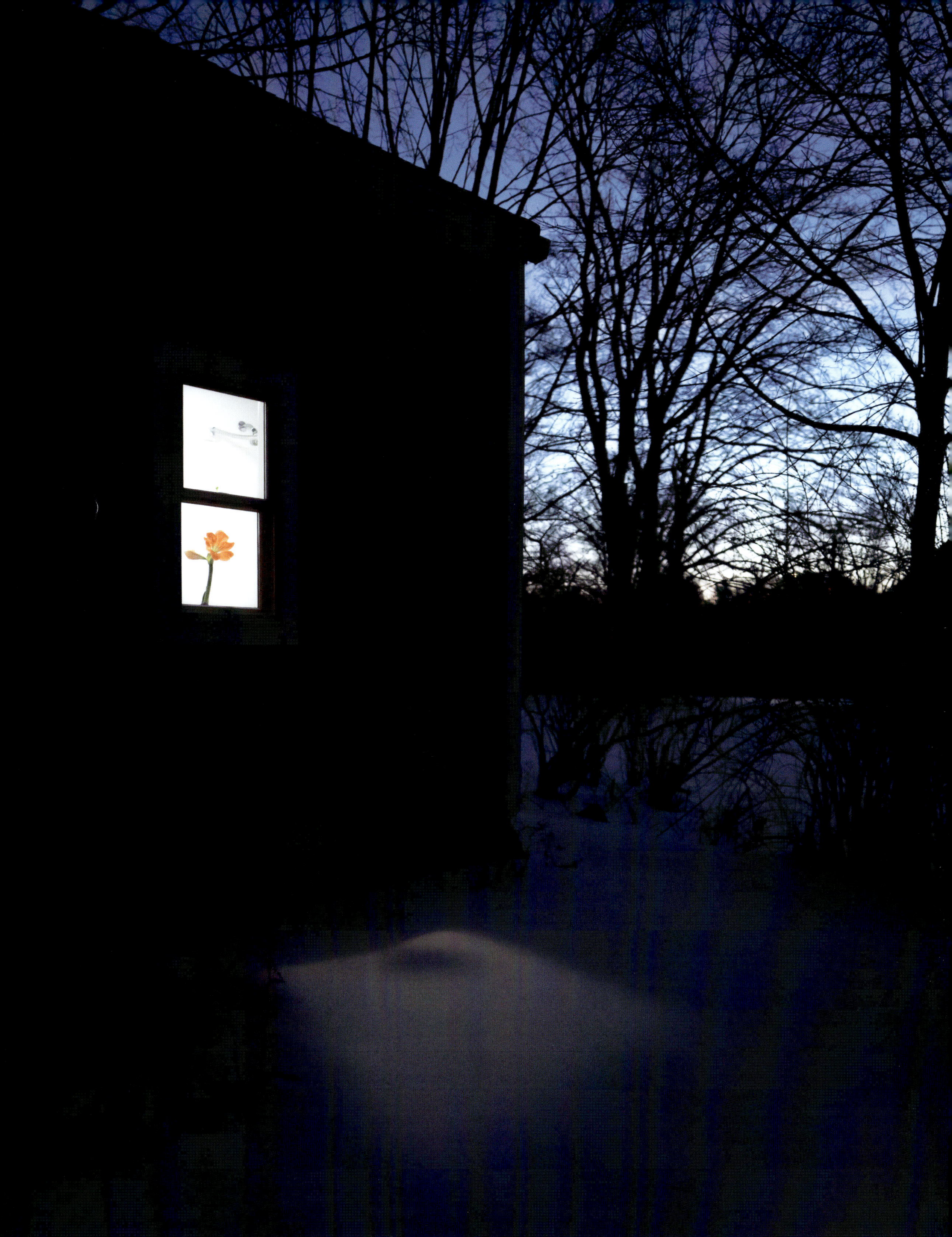

For my birthday, Doug builds a trellis around our front door and I plant my favorite flowers—honeysuckle, roses, and clematis—to climb all over it. By the following July, the entranceway is so alive with bees that Scout and I have to run through it to avoid getting stung. By late summer, it's like walking through the wide-open mouth of a rainbow to enter the chaos of the mudroom.

In Maine, the mudroom is the altar of the home. Among the multicolored offerings of keys, shoes, pens, sunglasses, coins, wallets, hats, scarves, bags, and business cards, are the piles of *Things* that Scout has outgrown, *Things* that need to be mended, and *Things* that need to be returned. The divine is in the everyday objects that make a beautiful life: a camera, a pink hairbrush, a black schoolbag thrown on the floor spewing out crumpled notes, a half-eaten jam sandwich, and Scarlet's orange lead on top of Doug's indigo felt slippers, threadbare, from when he rubs his feet together talking on the phone.

Years ago, over a cafeteria lasagna, I asked an astronaut what was the most beautiful sight he had ever seen. He thought for a moment and then said, *my wife Vicki's blue eyes*.

In times of trauma and crisis, all you wish for is an ordinary Tuesday where nothing really happens. Beauty is in the commonplace. Be here now.

Look
at *this.*
Experience
*this.*
Feel
*this.*

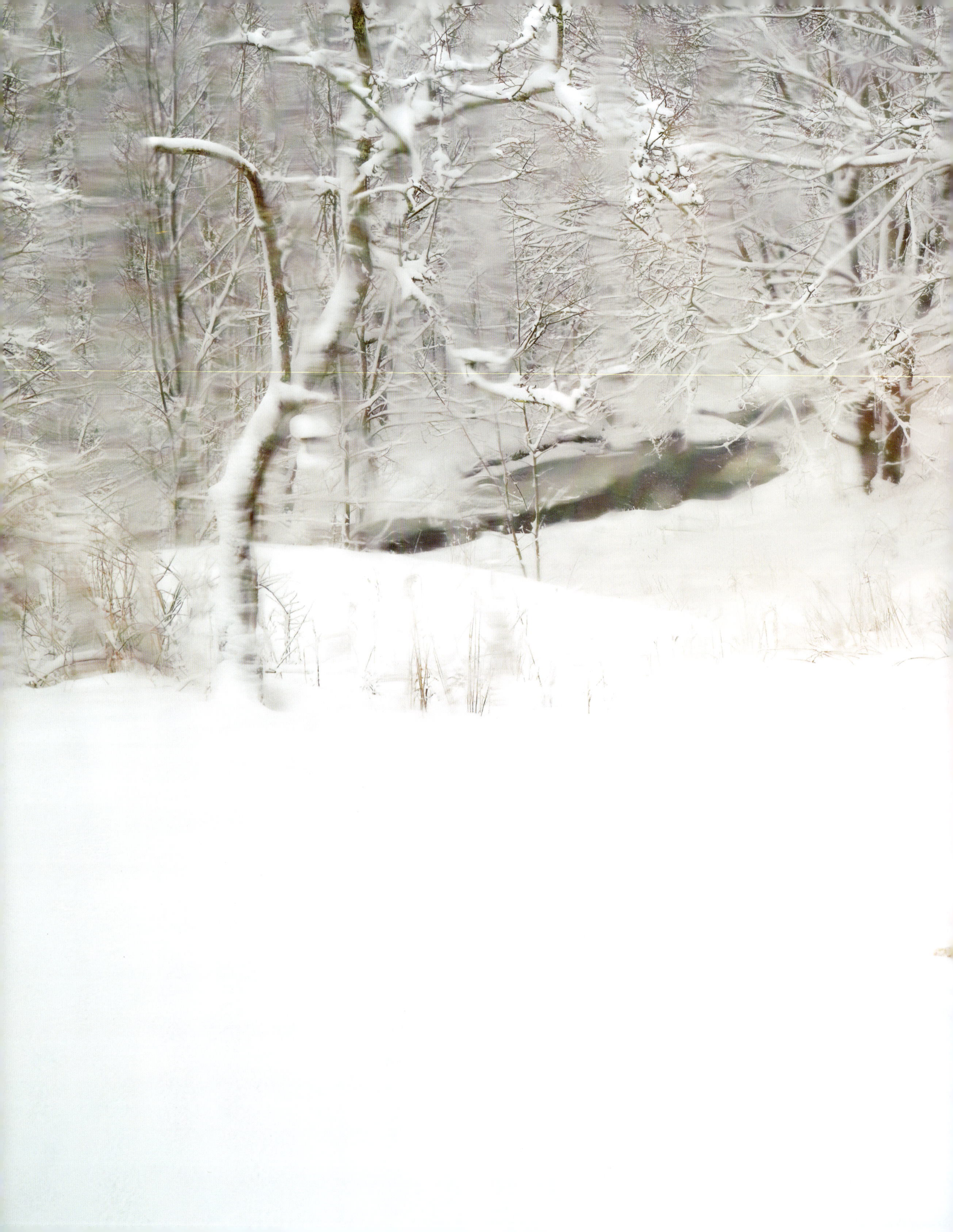

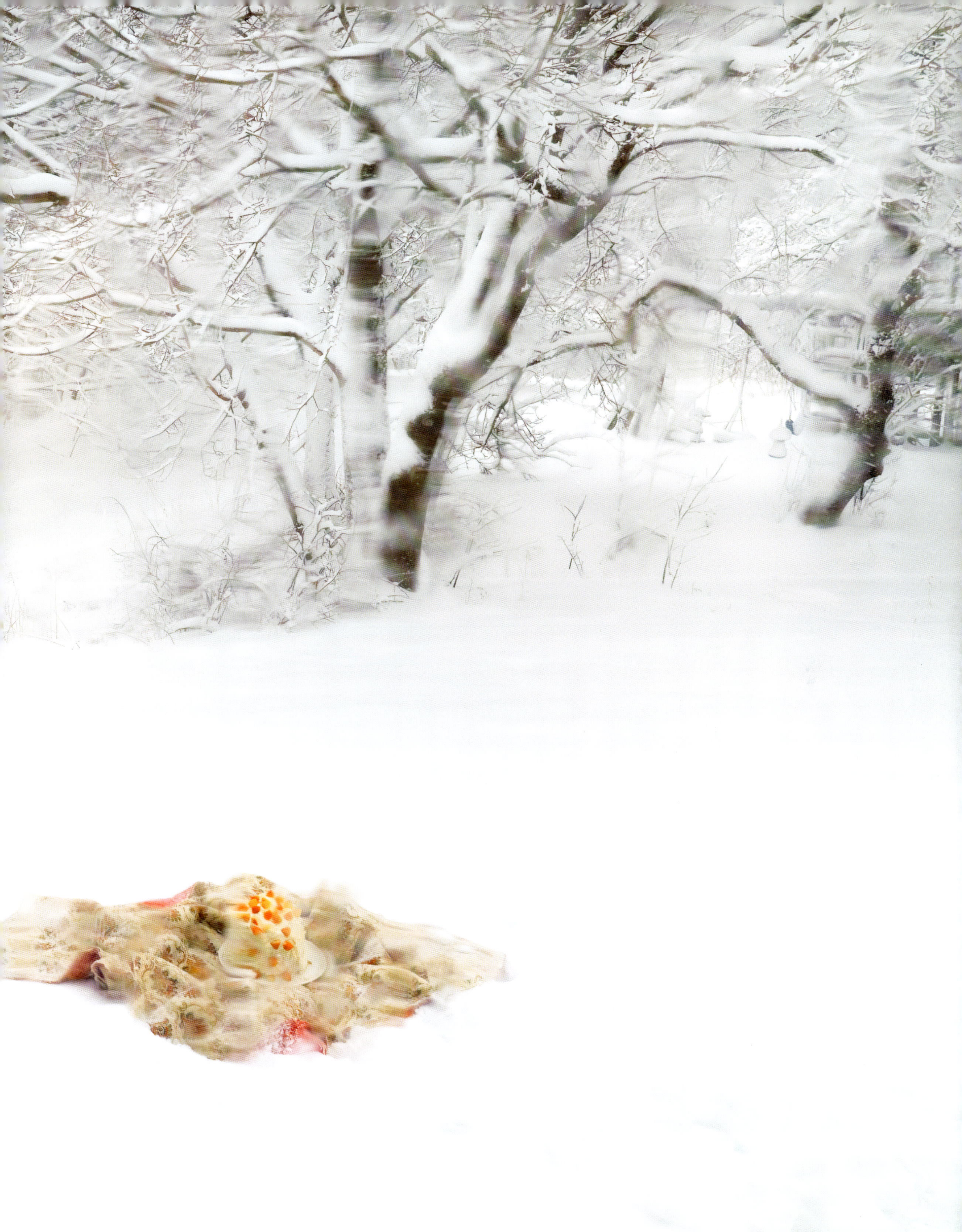

How to
Make a Cake

By Scout Harvey Stradley

| | |
|---|---|
| 1 | Preheat the oven to 350 degrees. |
| 2 | Open five boxes of Betty Crocker Super Moist Red Velvet cake mix and empty them into a big mixing bowl. The package says it will bring a weeknight wow to your dinner table. |
| 3 | Add 5 cups of water and 2½ cups of vegetable oil. |
| 4 | Crack in 15 eggs. |
| 5 | Mix everything vigorously for two minutes. |
| 6 | Pour the mixture into your mouth and the excess into four greased bundts and one greased round cake tin and bake for 40 mins. |
| 7 | Test to see if it is ready by poking it with a stick. If it pulls out clean, then the cake is done. |
| 8 | Let cool for 20 minutes *(if you can be bothered).* |

*In memory of Elizabeth [Boo] Ellison*

9 Open six small buckets of Betty Crocker cream cheese frosting. Don't be tempted to use a more organic or homemade variety; you will just be disappointed. *(Note: the word* cheese *doesn't belong on a cake.)*

10 Stack the hollow bundt cakes one on top of the other on top of the other, layering the icing between each cake as glue. Top with the round cake. *(The bundt cake gives more volume, and you can fill the middle with surprise ice cream and sauces.)*

11 At some point, the cake will start to lean this way and that. Don't worry about it. Just use BBQ skewers to hold it in place and keep adding. You must keep moving forward.

12 Decorate the cake with everything in the fridge and cupboards. Don't worry if it is not edible, it just has to look good. Use toothpicks to pierce the sides with berries, feathers, cherries, flowers, shells, postage stamps, jewels, a photograph.

13 If your cake falls apart, let the dog eat it, then go to supermarket and buy a cobalt blue Friendly's Celebration Ice Cream Cake.

# Be happy.

# Medicinal Estrangement: Cig Harvey's Semiotic Transformations

By Ocean Vuong

Before becoming a writer, I went to college to study international marketing, having succumbed, like many immigrant children, to the guilt-ridden obligation to "make a living" before pursuing my own vocations. I lasted all of three weeks before dropping out to couch surf and read poems in East Village bars, schlumping my way into a literary life, whatever that meant. But I was in the marketing program long enough to realize one thing: photography was advertising's central obsession, the form possessing both the potential to alter reality while also preserving the sense of the real, making whatever product appear, for the right price, tantalizingly obtainable, within reach. Marketing also co-opts photography's long-developed strategies: saturated, extravagant colors, taut compositions, macro-zoomed still lifes, at times even employing photographers themselves, exporting visions of personal projects into visionary corporate campaigns. In other words, beauty, for much of the twentieth century and beyond, has been a *method* of commercial coercion.

Against this cultural backdrop, Cig Harvey's work captures the less-understood—or even displaced—beauty. While others take photographs, Cig, I'm convinced, takes something else. This "something else" can be defined by her relationship to the beautiful—what it is, what it can do, and perhaps more pressing, how it becomes the vehicle for self-knowledge. "The clocks go back, giving an extra hour of sadness," Cig writes, revealing the vagus nerve in this new series, which, for all its exuberance and sensual decadence, is centered on loss. The baroque fullness of these images, in all their rich color and geometry, elicits a felt absence, the phantom limb of elegy made excruciatingly present through an unbridled desire for the world, the living; a book of grief articulated through immense, insatiable want. More than a project of knowing, this is a work of semiotic shifts. Cig's recurring motifs, or obsessions, are well-trodden ones, and not just in photography but in literature, too: flowers, children, food, nature, interiors. Using symbols often ascribed to women as denigrating and minute, effete and decorous (and thereby useless), Cig, like Sappho, Plath, Murasaki, and Woolf, like Maier, Mann, and Weems, leans into the "domestic" as inexhaustible subversion, taking the word's original Latin root, *domus*, meaning "of animals," and thereby the filth of birthing, rutting, and feeding—associations deemed beneath the offices of men—and centering them as potent and dignified nodes of imagination.

But any familiarity with these typologies is sent to rout by the images themselves. Cig makes the conventional so strange, so oblique and otherworldly, they become unfixed from the cultural wallpaper they've been trapped in. Russian Formalist writer Viktor Shklovsky argues that it's the writer's obligation not to shun the contrived trope but to rescue it from cultural death via what he calls *estrangement*. The familiar remains so only if allowed to fester in stagnant waters, but once ejected from its expected context, it comes alive, as in one of Cig's photos, wherein a decadent, gemlike cake, one fitting the banquet table of emperors, gains surprising personhood when shown stuffed into an iron box set by a rural riverbank, its whipped frosting coyly peering over the rusted lip. What strikes me in Cig's work is not just the compositions but how they reveal her way of seeing, considering, and believing in the world, and how it might be remade. That no subject is dead simply because others have replicated it. Her work, then, is the work of resuscitation via bewitchment. Regardless of the medium, such conviction toward reinvention is difficult, perhaps impossible, to teach. It requires duration and endurance, a stubborn courage even. Much easier, surely, to turn away from familiarity (the untouchable clichés), as many artists have fruitfully done, but much harder to make the familiar so new it feels *discovered*.

Though her work elides reductive categories like "pastoral" or "still life," these images fashion a dreamlike, alternative vison of the bucolic that answers the perennial anxiety of photographers, seasoned or novice: what's there to photograph in the middle of "nowhere"? But it's from this misconception of "nowhere's" inherent emptiness that Cig's work achieves its formal rigor: the call for the photograph, a medium of surfaces, to reach the subconscious. This Shklovskian displacement is achieved foremost by her daring manipulation of light, or at times the lack thereof, shooting not just in the gold or blue hours, but even in the pitch, her fast lens wide open, the frames at once sparked with speckled light and vignetted by obliterating darkness, flipping known locales—orchards, spring-fed heathers, the side of a house—into awestruck nether realms.

Mostly taken around her home in Maine's Midcoast, Cig charges images of rurality with vexed mythologies. The result is photographs that feel both deliberately made but also inevitably found. Her subjects—a spray of highlighter-yellow pollen on a country road, a cluster of flowers nearly crushed into the ghostly fog of a car window, the occasional family member or neighbor, even a gnomic dusk-drenched apple tree—appear thoroughly *encountered*, as if captured upon stepping through a clearing, revealing themselves seconds before the shutter clicks. But herein lies the fantasy of photography: what's sublimely serendipitous is often carefully constructed, placed, seen and reseen. The white-clad table strewn with flowers and elegant cakes set out for days, is meticulously built, its decay assisted by time, weather, the weak yet pervasive light of a full moon. In every sense of the word, these photos are *made*—but they are made in collaboration. Cig's frames portray a convergence of human and natural action, not to synthesize or balance the two, but to show the possibilities when vision and composition amplify the magic of the natural world through memory.

Cig tirelessly returns to flowers, children, nature and its decay, and the rhythmic scenes of dailiness through her robust and eclectic career, but this work marks a grander, bolder departure, and comes together in perhaps my favorite of her books thus far, if for no other reason than how it positions the photobook as an ambitiously layered, multifaceted medium, asking it to be more than the armature of images or the hardbound replication of an exhibit. Instead, it's a work of epistemology punctuated by essays that weave between lyrical, profound, diaristic, and edifying treatises on color and perception, retroactively changing how the images stain the mind as the pages turn, making the book's "bookness" indispensable to how the images are perceived.

There's also a gravitational, sensorial pull to this work. The pictures stop your breath with their use of bold color schemes, but here, too, the seduction is complex, circuitous: the shades across her landscapes appear thrown, lucent koi fish float in ethereal, near complete darkness, as though in outer space, the berry-jeweled cake robed in lustered, chiaroscuro light. Like adverts, these images also coerce, but the product they're selling is life itself, Cig's frames provoking us not to spend money but *time*, returning us deeper into the world, an experience both plentiful and increasingly difficult to afford.

Despite its ethos of charged mourning, *Emerald Drifters* is a rallying cry to exist in our bodies, where all the senses encounter the world. Viewing these images brings to mind an anecdote I think of often in relation to art: French colonizers, upon arriving in Vietnam in the nineteenth century, were aghast to see gold-clad Buddhas and stupas, porcelain and jade vases and statues, left in the open air, for anyone, even beggars, to touch. How can a people's finest enaction of craft be left so unguarded? they wondered. Quickly, the conquerors dislodged these treasures and locked them in vaults to be sent back to the empire's capital and displayed in museums as "relics." What does it mean to be so frightened by beauty's power that it must then be plundered and removed, caged? Recent psychological studies suggest that, for some communities in Asia, the touching of religious artifacts has medicinal results that rival the effects psychotropic drugs. In other words, it reaffirms what artists have known for centuries, and what Cig so deftly reveals to us here: that beauty, despite being degraded by commerce, or shunned as merely decorous, feminine fussing, heals. It raises the stakes of being so that death, the familiar, eternal trope that it is, becomes so new, so terribly *there*, we cannot forget its presence in our living days, and are better for it, drifters that we are.—OV

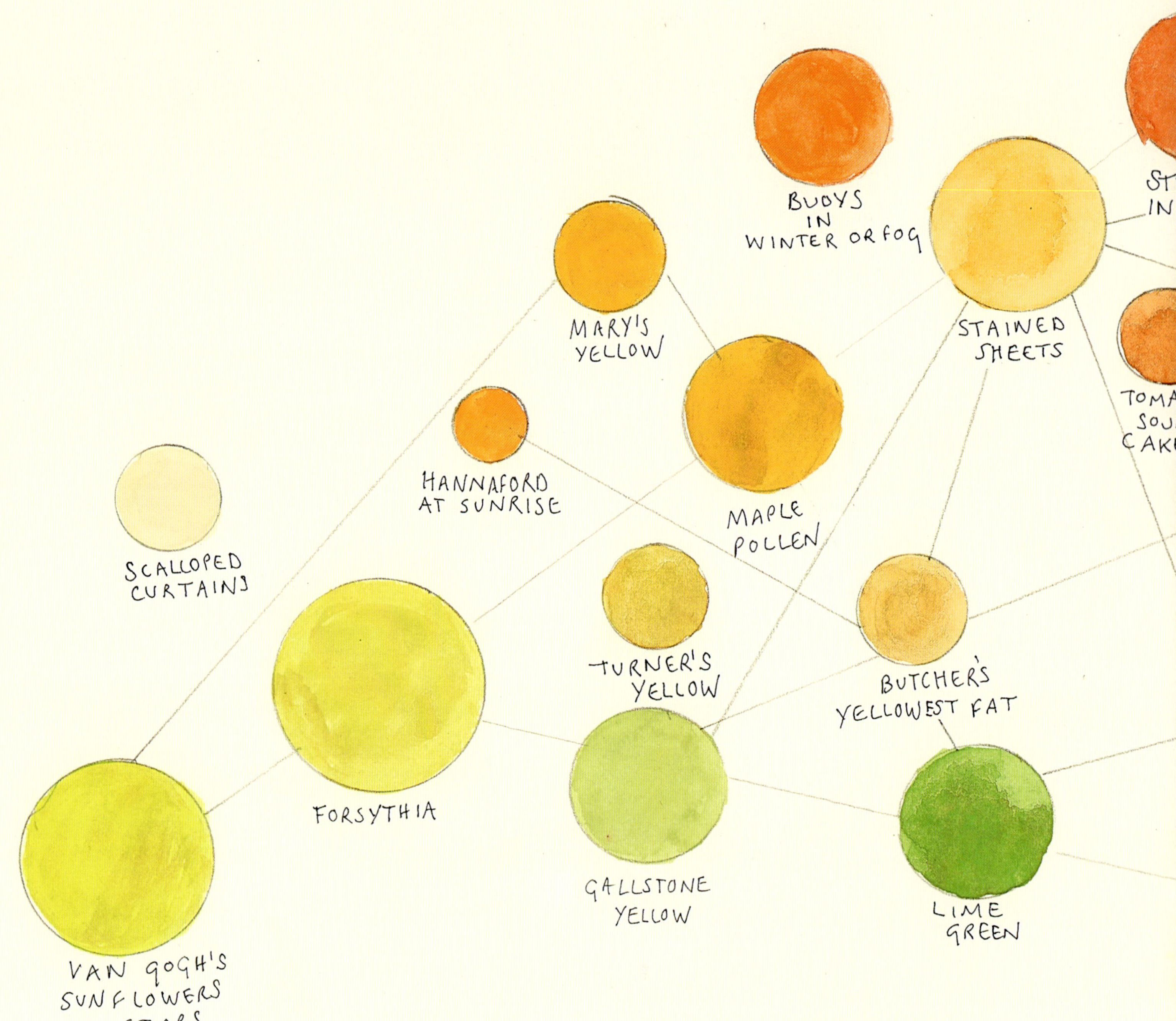
BUOYS IN WINTER OR FOG
STAINED SHEETS
MARY'S YELLOW
HANNAFORD AT SUNRISE
MAPLE POLLEN
SCALLOPED CURTAINS
TURNER'S YELLOW
BUTCHER'S YELLOWEST FAT
FORSYTHIA
GALLSTONE YELLOW
LIME GREEN
VAN GOGH'S SUNFLOWERS AND STARS

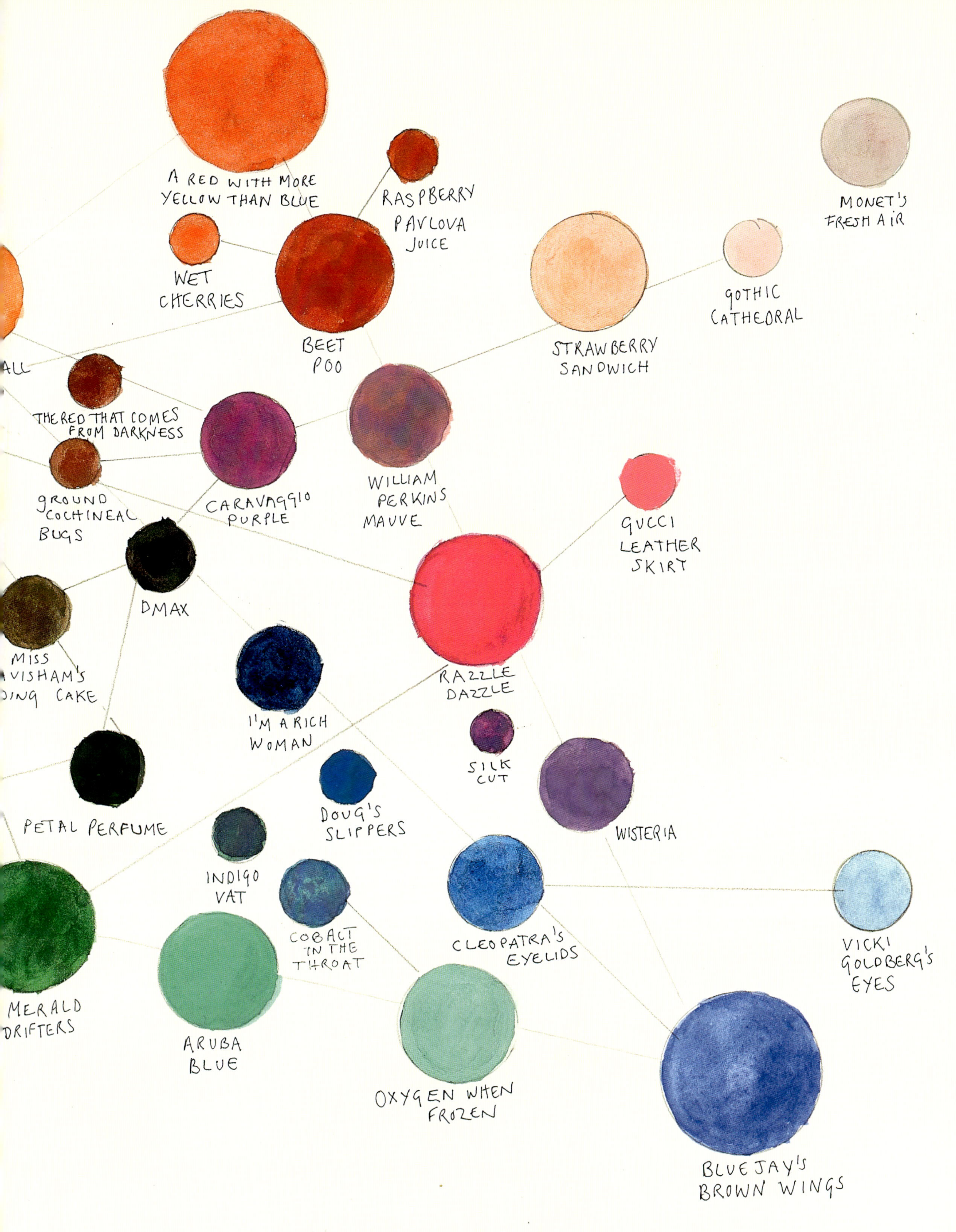
A RED WITH MORE YELLOW THAN BLUE
RASPBERRY PAVLOVA JUICE
MONET'S FRESH AIR
WET CHERRIES
BEET POO
STRAWBERRY SANDWICH
GOTHIC CATHEDRAL
ALL
THE RED THAT COMES FROM DARKNESS
GROUND COCHINEAL BUGS
CARAVAGGIO PURPLE
WILLIAM PERKINS MAUVE
GUCCI LEATHER SKIRT
DMAX
MISS
VISHAM'S
DING CAKE
RAZZLE DAZZLE
I'M A RICH WOMAN
SILK CUT
PETAL PERFUME
DOUG'S SLIPPERS
WISTERIA
INDIGO VAT
COBALT IN THE THROAT
CLEOPATRA'S EYELIDS
VICKI GOLDBERG'S EYES
MERALD DRIFTERS
ARUBA BLUE
OXYGEN WHEN FROZEN
BLUE JAY'S BROWN WINGS

## Resources

ON EARTH WE'RE
BRIEFLY GORGEOU
OCEAN VUONG

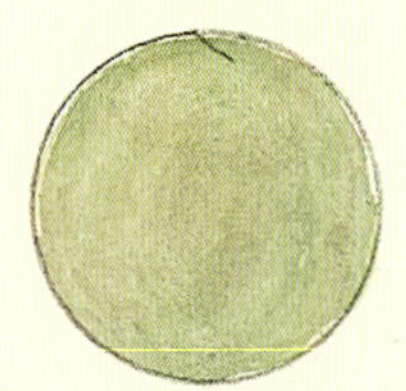

HOW TO WELCOME
THE UNWANTED
AUTHOR UNKNOWN
(IT SEEMS I MADE THIS
BOOK UP)

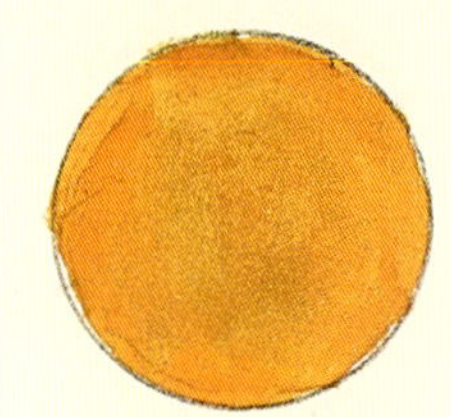

THE BRILLIANT
HISTORY
OF COLOR IN ART
VICTORIA FINLAY

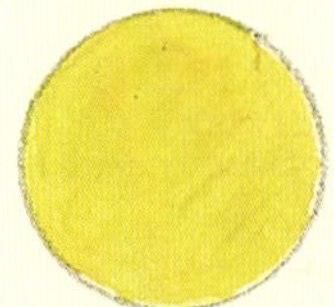

THE SECRET
LIVES OF COLOR
KASSIA ST CLAIR

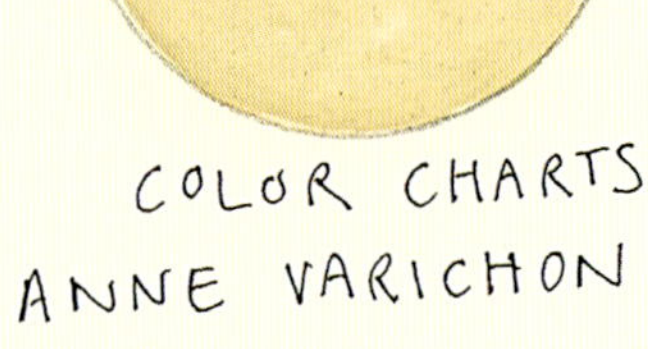

COLOR CHARTS
ANNE VARICHON

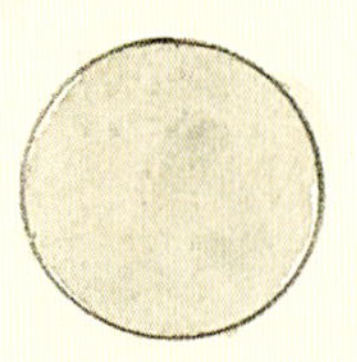

ILLUMINATIONS
ARTHUR RIMBAUD

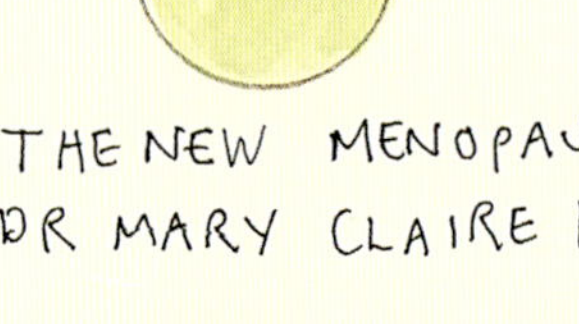

THE NEW MENOPAUSE
DR MARY CLAIRE HAVER

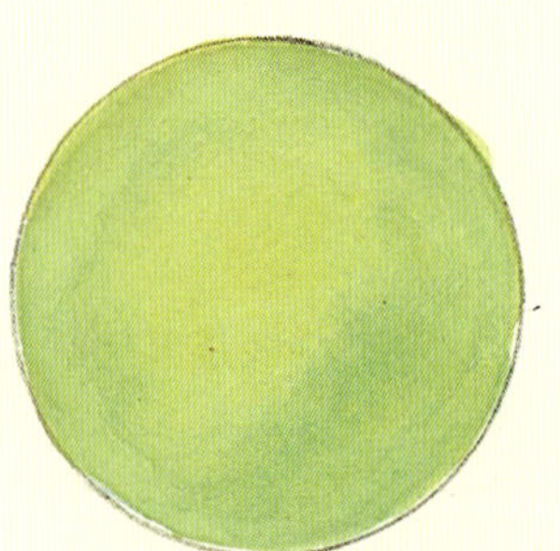

GREEN ISLANDS
GREEN SEA
PHILIP W. CONKLING

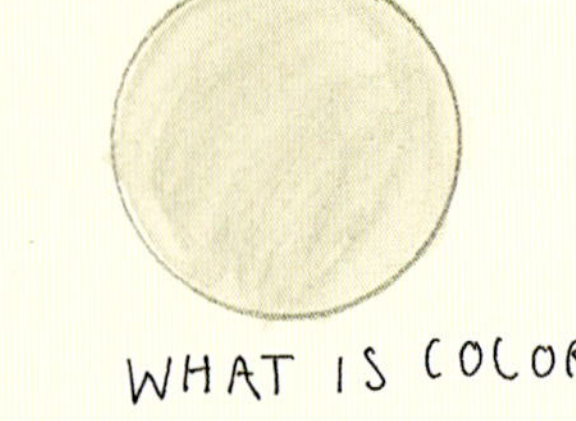

WHAT IS COLOR?
ARIELLE ECKSTUT
JOANN ECKSTUT

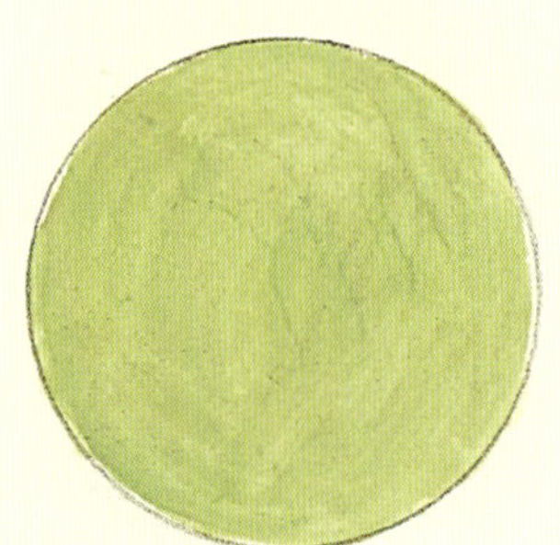

ON BEAUTY AND
BEING JUST
ELAINE SCARRY

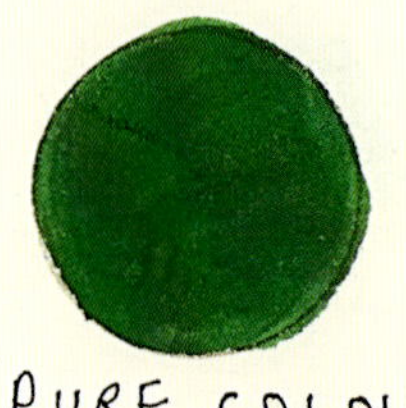

PURE COLOUR
SHEILA HETI

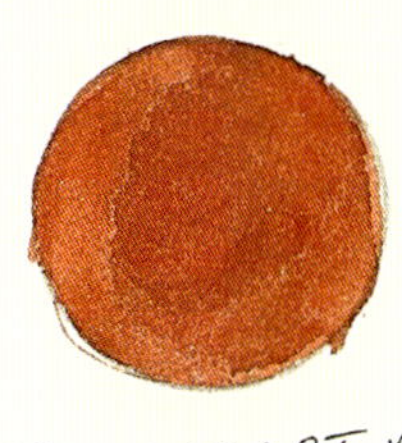

RED - THE ART AND
SCIENCE OF A COLOUR
SPIKE BUCKLOW

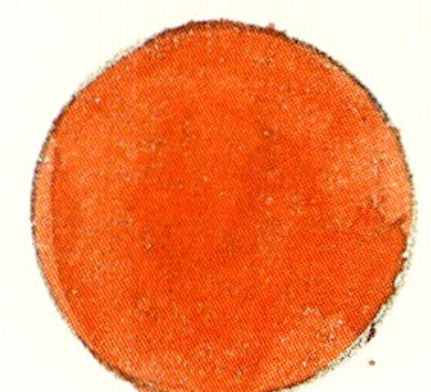

CAKE
ALYSA LEVENE

THE INTERACTION
OF COLOR
JOSEF ALBERS

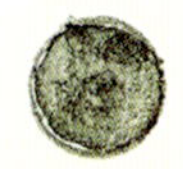

CHROMAPHILIA
STELLA PAUL

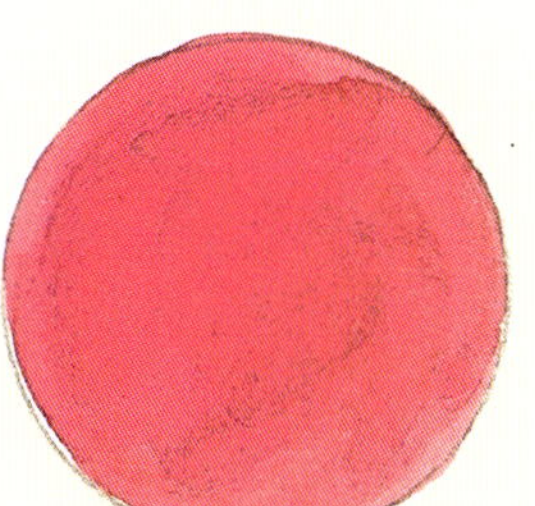

CHROMOPHOBIA
DAVID BATCHELOR

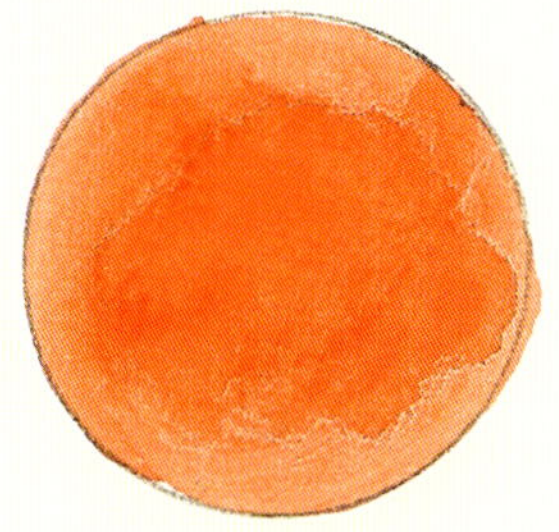

IN PURSUIT
OF COLOR
LAUREN MACDONALD

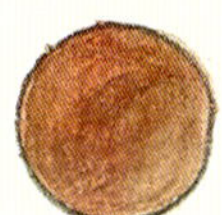

COLOR
A NATURAL HISTORY
OF THE PALETTE
VICTORIA FINLAY

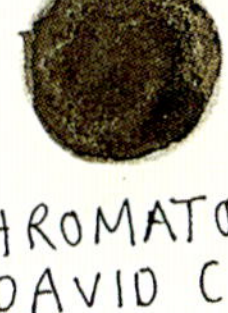

CHROMATOPIA
DAVID COLES

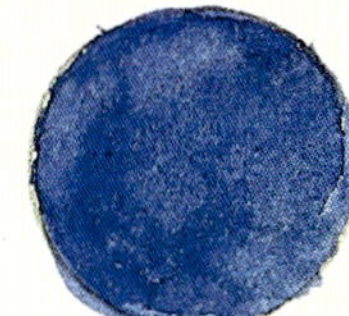

ANGELICA DASS
THE COLORS WE SHARE

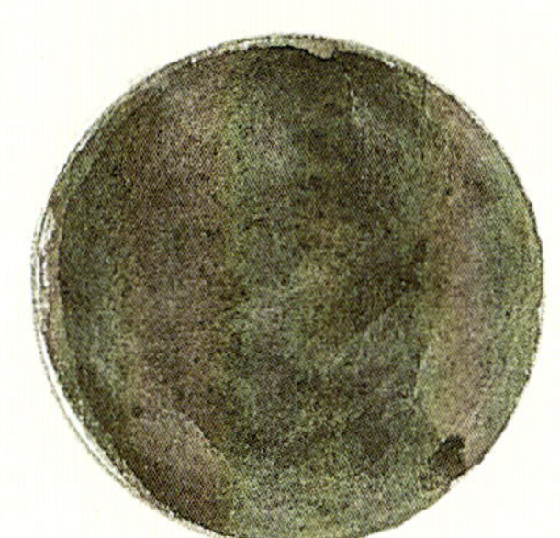

CHROMA
DEREK JARMAN

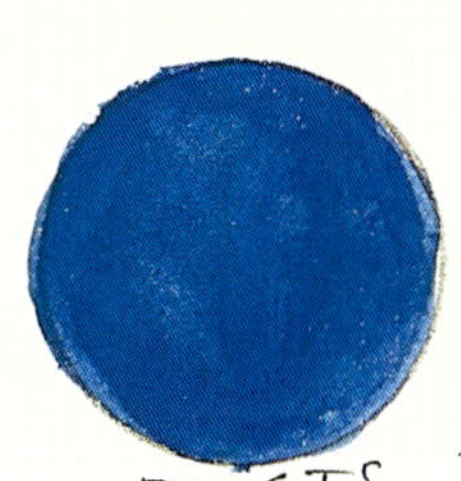

BLUETS
MAGGIE NELSON

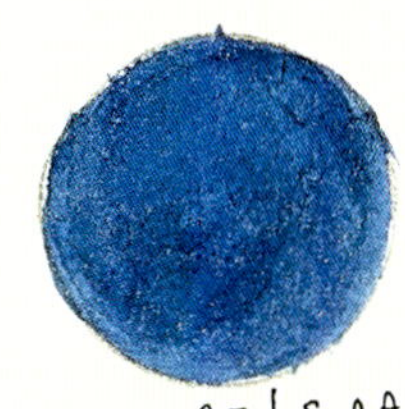

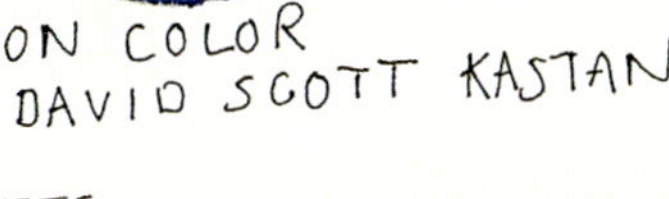

ON COLOR
DAVID SCOTT KASTAN

SEEING THE LIGHT
DAVID FALK
DIETER BRILL
DAVID STORK

NATURE'S PALETTE
PATRICK BATY

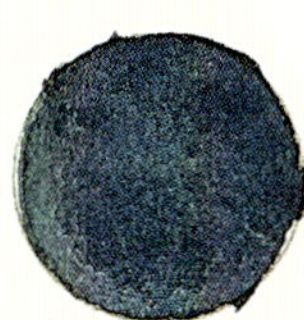

AN ATLAS OF
RARE + FAMILIAR
COLOUR
THE HARVARD ART MUSEUMS'
FORBES PIGMENT COLLECTION

WERNER'S
NOMENCLATURE OF COLOURS
P. SYME

## Acknowledgments

This book is dedicated to the loves of my life: my daughter Scout and my husband Doug. Thank you, Scout, for your wild cakes. Working with you has been the best collaboration of my career. Thank you, Doug, for your endless love and support. I still feel like a newlywed.

Deep gratitude to my friends and family who appear in the pictures in this book: Devin Fletcher, Donna McNeal, Elizabeth Noble, Madeleine Morlet, and Scout Stradley. Extra special thanks to Emily Seymour. Making pictures with you makes me appreciate the world in a new way each time. Thank you for letting me tell my stories through you.

Thank you to Tripp Harrington for always making my images sparkle. We have worked together for fifteen years, and I am very grateful. Love and thanks to Ghislain Pascal for your guidance, honesty, and friendship.

Thank you to my incredible first readers, all treasured friends, for their insights and feedback: Beth Storey, Daniel Stephens, Donna McNeal, Katia Dermott, Lucinda Ziesing, Maggie Meiners, Matthias Mann, Michael Mansfield, Nathan Perkins, Suzanne Kahn.

Deep love and gratitude to River Finlay for spending three years of her life making the documentary *Eat Flowers*. Your vision for this film was a bright star, just like you. You made a movie that touches the heart.

I am lucky enough to be represented by the following galleries, and I wish to thank them for their incredible support over the years: Bildhalle, Dowling Walsh Gallery, Jackson Fine Art, Peter Fetterman Gallery, Robert Klein Gallery, Robert Mann Gallery.

Thanks to my family and friends for their continued support: Alissa Hesler, Anjuli Lebowitz, Anna LaBenz, Anneli Skaar, Annemarie Ahearn, Ann Jastrab, Arduina Caponigro, Ariel Birke, Ariel Hall, Ashley Elliot, Brandei Estes, Bryan McCalister, Caroline Wall, Carol Walker, Catherine Couturier, Cheryle St. Onge, David Harvey, Donna Pinckley, Elizabeth Krist, Elizabeth Noble, Eliza Collins, Erin French, Gianluca Macheda, Jacoba Urist, Jake Dowling, Janet Stradley, Jesse Ellison, Jessica Jarl, Joe and Judy Barker, Johan Vikner, Jonathan Singer, Justin Stailey, Katrin Seitz, Ken Shure, Kirsten Surbey, Linden Frederick, Liv Rockefeller, Lizzie Fischbein, Mackenzie Lyman, Michael Frey, Polly Saltonstall, Richard Reitz Smith, Rufus Williams, Sam Adler, Sashka Rothchild, Sylvia de Leon, Tamara Beckwith, Tig Harvey, Valerie Duncan, Valkyries, Vicki Goldberg, Virginia Walck, and W.M. Hunt. Extra special thanks to Abby Kermode, for always having her bags packed and ready to travel. To Brenton Hamilton for over twenty years of mentoring and friendship. To Judi Shepard Macomber for growing the most marvelous wisteria all over her house. To Skip and Judy Klein for their long and steadfast support of my career. Thank you.

I want to thank the following institutions for supporting and collecting my work: Bainbridge Island Museum of Art, Boston Athenaeum, Bowdoin College, Colby College, Columbia University, Estée Lauder Companies, Farnsworth Art Museum, Fidelity Corporation, Fotografiska, Fujifilm, Houston Museum of Fine Arts, International Museum of Photography, George Eastman House, J.P. Morgan Chase, Library of Congress, Maine Media, Museum of Fine Arts Boston, *New York Times*, Ogunquit Museum of American Art, Philadelphia Museum of Art, Portland Museum of Art, Stanford University, Two Ponds Press, University of Delaware, University of Miami, University of San Francisco, University of Texas, University of Washington, Wellesley College, Wesleyan University, Yale University.

Deep gratitude for all at Phaidon / Monacelli Press: Keith Fox, Holly La Due, Michael Vagnetti, and proofreader Ashley Benning. And my wonderful friend and editor, Alan Rapp. Alan, I am forever indebted to you. Thank you for believing in me first with *Blue Violet* and, now, *Emerald Drifters*.

I want to thank Elaine Scarry for her seminal work, *On Beauty and Being Just*. This book gave voice to my internal struggle with beauty in art, and its influence shaped my vignette "The Sublime and the Beautiful."

The text in this book was nurtured and edited by my dear friend, Arielle Greenberg, all-around brilliant writer, teacher, and person. Working with you is always an inspiration.

Enormous love and thanks to Madeleine Morlet for her tireless editing and sequencing of the text and images. Books are your superpower, Madeleine. It is that wicked combination of instinct and knowledge. I loved working with you on this book, and I can't wait for yours. You are a light in the world, my dear friend.

Jeanette Abbink, you took my pictures and words and transformed them into the magical experience of this book. You bring my work to life. Working together on this, our second book collaboration, and talking with you about design, color, and beauty was one of the highlights of my career. You are a world-class designer and I am grateful for our friendship. Thank you.

Ocean Vuong, your books have changed the way I see. How you think about beauty and humanity makes this world a better place to live in. One word at a time, you help people feel seen. I love our friendship and am deeply honored that you contributed your words to *Emerald Drifters*. Thank you.

In memory of Mary Dowling (1982–2019). You are loved. You are missed.

**Cig Harvey** is a British-born artist and writer working in large-format color photography and poetry. She is the author of several monographs: *You Look At Me Like An Emergency* (Schilt Publishing, 2012), *Gardening At Night* (Schilt Publishing, 2015), *You An Orchestra You A Bomb* (Schilt Publishing, 2017), and *Blue Violet* (Monacelli, 2021), which was featured in *The New York Times Book Review*.

Her photographs have been featured in *The Times* and *Sunday Times*, *The Guardian*, *The Telegraph*, *Vogue*, *The Wall Street Journal*, *New York Magazine*, and *The Independent on Sunday*. She regularly contributes to *The New York Times*.

Cig's work is held in permanent and private collections across the world, including the Library of Congress; Museum of Fine Arts, Boston; Museum of Fine Arts, Houston; the Farnsworth Art Museum; the International Museum of Photography and Film at the George Eastman House; the Philadelphia Museum of Art; and the J.P.Morgan Chase Art Collection. Her first solo museum show was held at the Stenersen Museum in Oslo, Norway (2012), and a midcareer solo exhibition was at the Ogunquit Museum of American Art in Maine (2019).

In 2023, a documentary film about Cig by River Finlay, *Eat Flowers*, premiered at prestigious film festivals worldwide, winning numerous awards including the Audience Award at the Indy Shorts, and was shortlisted by the International Documentary Association for Best Short Documentary. She is the recipient of the Prix Virginia Laureate (2018), the Maine in America Award by the Farnsworth Art Museum (2021).

Cig lives in a farmhouse in Maine with her husband Doug and daughter Scout. The passing of time and the natural surroundings of her rural home have made her alert to the magic in the mundane.

**Ocean Vuong** is a writer, professor, and photographer. He is the author of *The New York Times* bestselling poetry collection *Time Is a Mother* and *The New York Times* bestselling novel *On Earth We're Briefly Gorgeous*, which won the American Book Award, the Mark Twain Award, the New England Book Award, and has been translated into dozens of languages. A recipient of a 2019 MacArthur "Genius" Grant, he is also the author of the critically acclaimed poetry collection *Night Sky with Exit Wounds*, a *New York Times* Top 10 Book of 2016, winner of the T.S. Eliot Prize, the Whiting Award, the Thom Gunn Award, and the Forward Prize for Best First Collection. A Ruth Lilly fellow from the Poetry Foundation, his honors include fellowships from the Lannan Foundation, the Civitella Ranieri Foundation, the Elizabeth George Foundation, the Academy of American Poets, and the Pushcart Prize.

Selected by *Foreign Policy* magazine as one of its 100 Leading Global Thinkers, Vuong's writings have been featured in *The Atlantic*, *Granta*, *Harpers*, *The Nation*, *New Republic*, *The New Yorker*, *The New York Times*, *The Paris Review*, *The Village Voice*, and *American Poetry Review*, which awarded him the Stanley Kunitz Prize for Younger Poets. He currently splits his time between Northampton, Massachusetts, and New York City, where he serves as a professor in modern poetry and poetics in the MFA Program at NYU.

**Jeanette Abbink** is the founder of Rational Beauty, a studio celebrated for creating magazines, books, and other print artifacts notable for their marriage of design rigor and visual poetry. In the course of her career, Jeanette has earned accolades and awards from a host of professional associations (AIGA, Type Directors Guild, D&AD, to name a few), and her work has been collected by the libraries of such august institutions as MoMA, the Metropolitan Museum of Art, the Courtauld Institute, and the Museum of Fine Arts, Boston. A prolific editorial designer, Jeanette was honored to create Cig Harvey's first book, *Blue Violet*, and to continue their collaboration with this sequel. Committed to helping guide the next generation, Jeanette is also a popular guest lecturer in the design department at the University of Texas at Austin. In all her endeavors, Jeanette embraces this observation by architect Louis Kahn: "Design is not making beauty, beauty emerges from selection, affinities, integration, love."

Library of Congress Control Number:
2024945748

ISBN 978-1-58093-687-3

10 9 8 7 6 5 4 3 2 1

Printed in China

Design by Jeanette Abbink
Rational Beauty

Monacelli
A Phaidon Company
111 Broadway
New York, New York 10006

www.monacellipress.com